AF505035

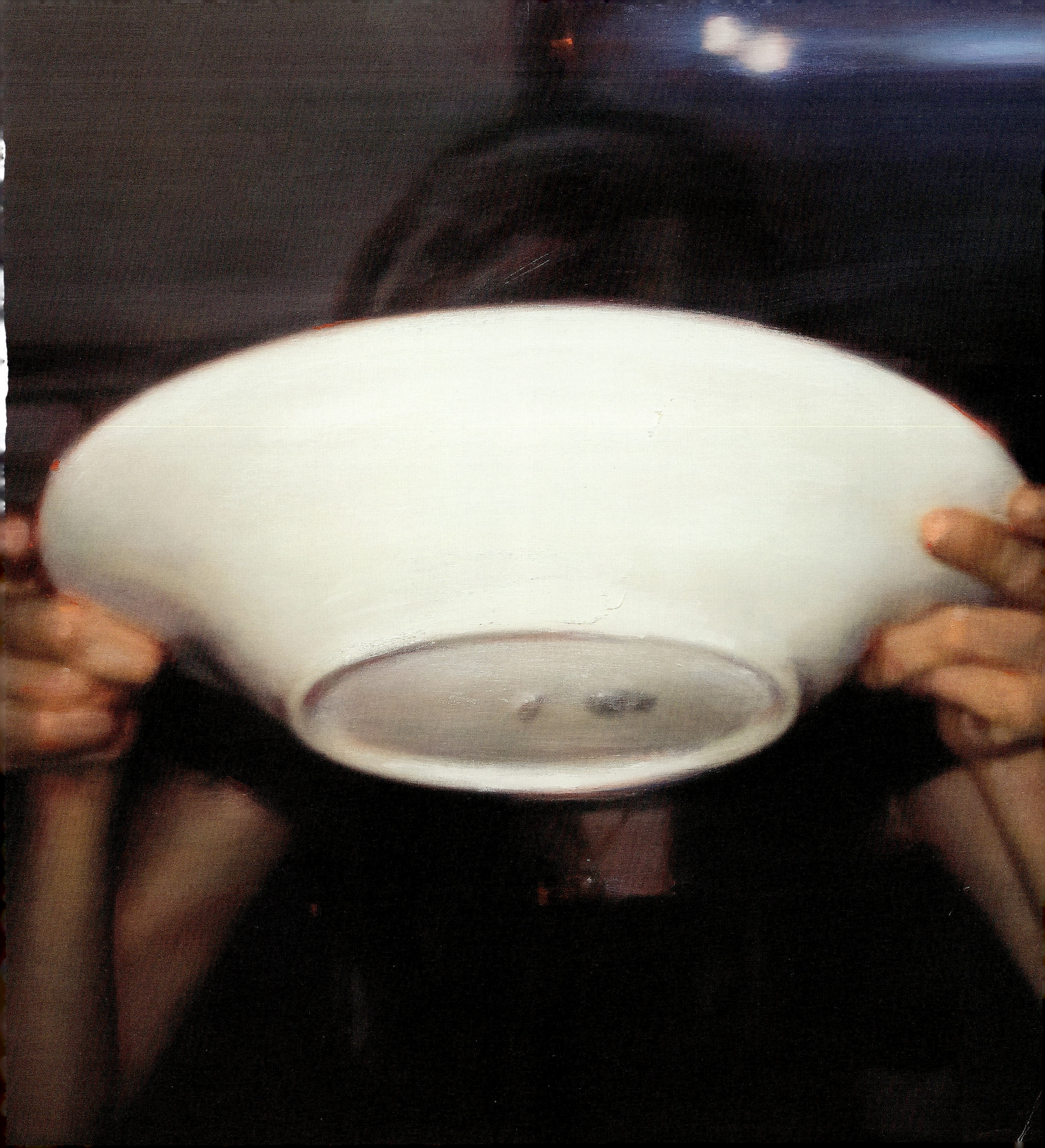

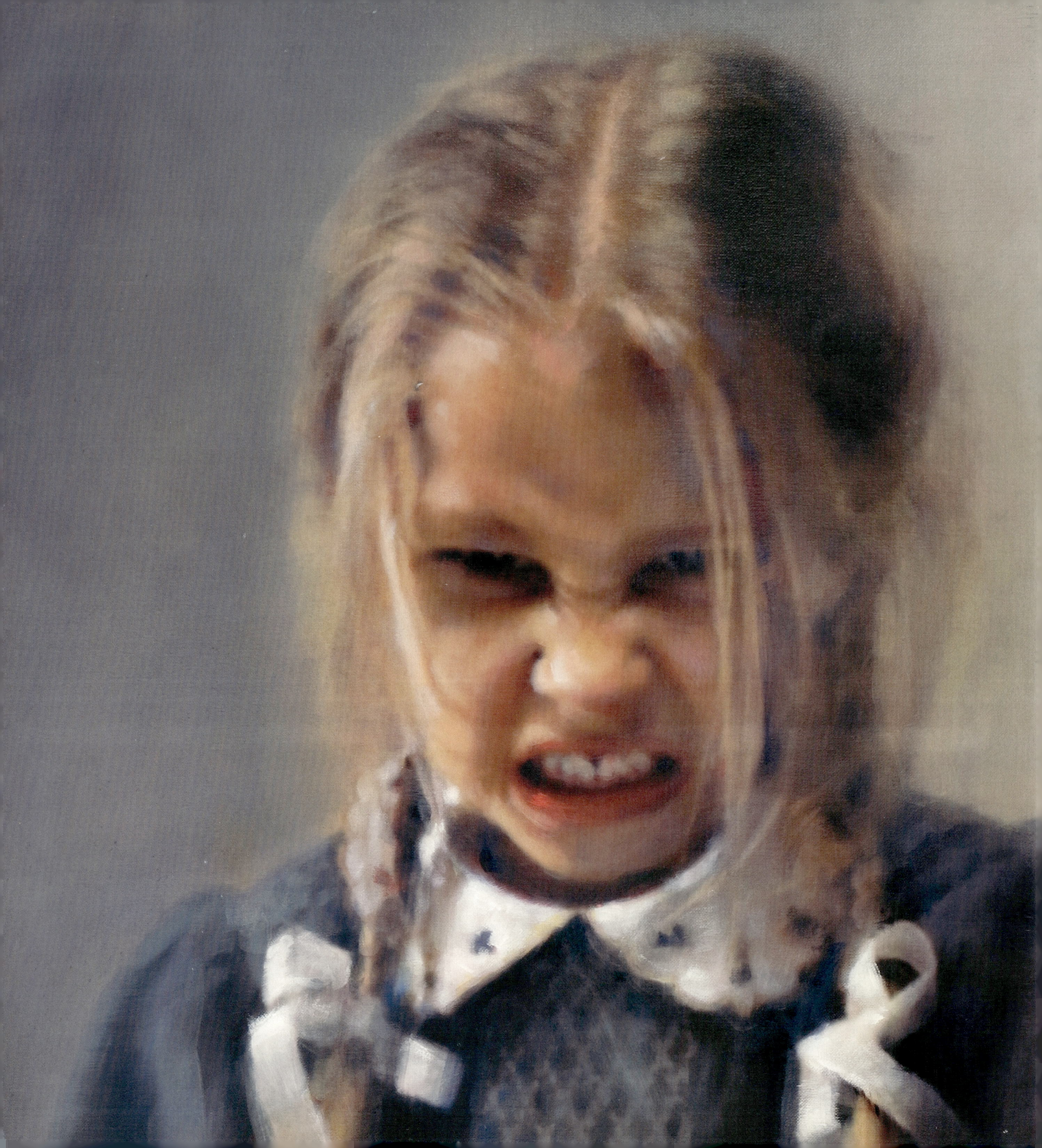

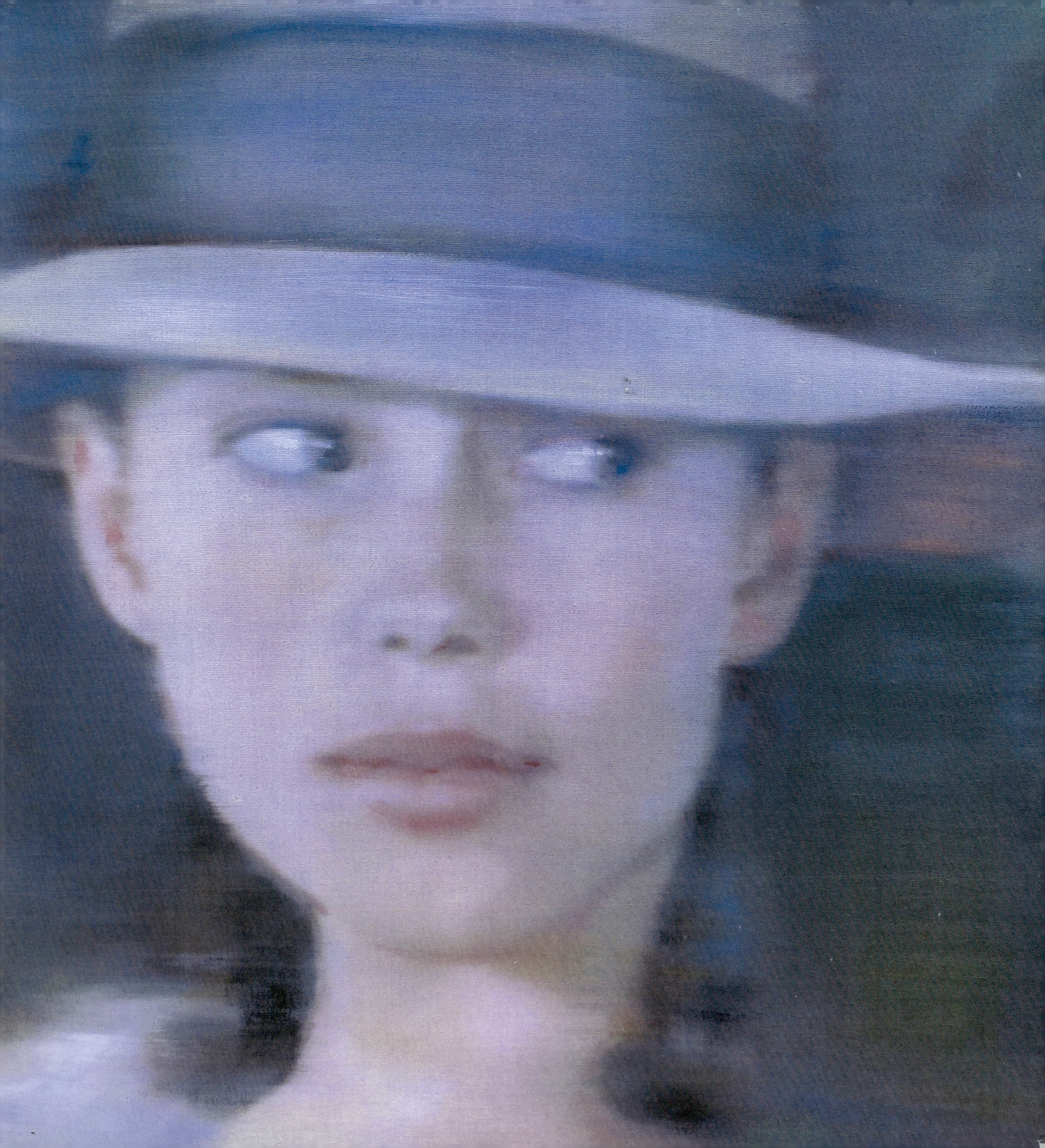

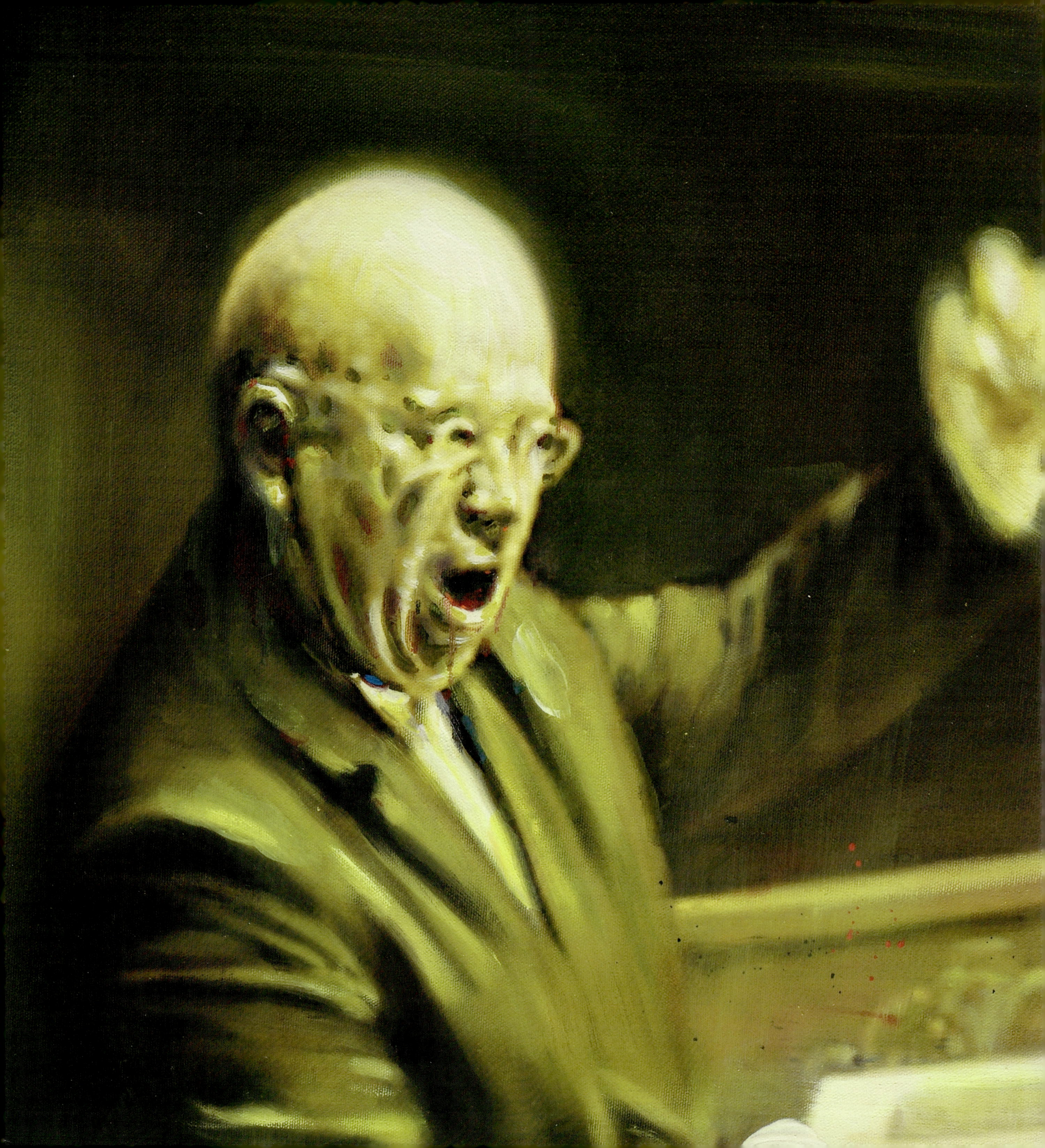

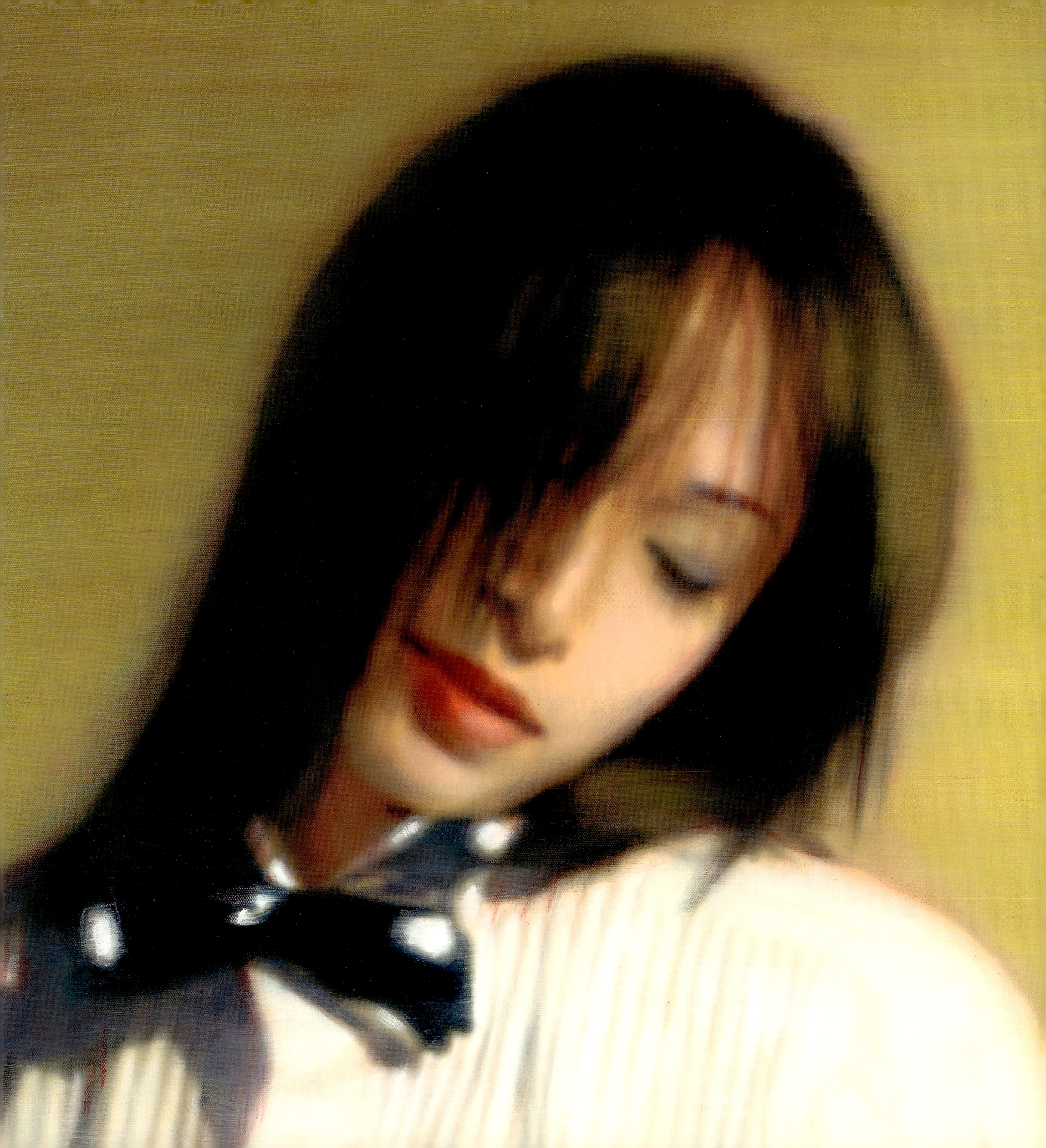

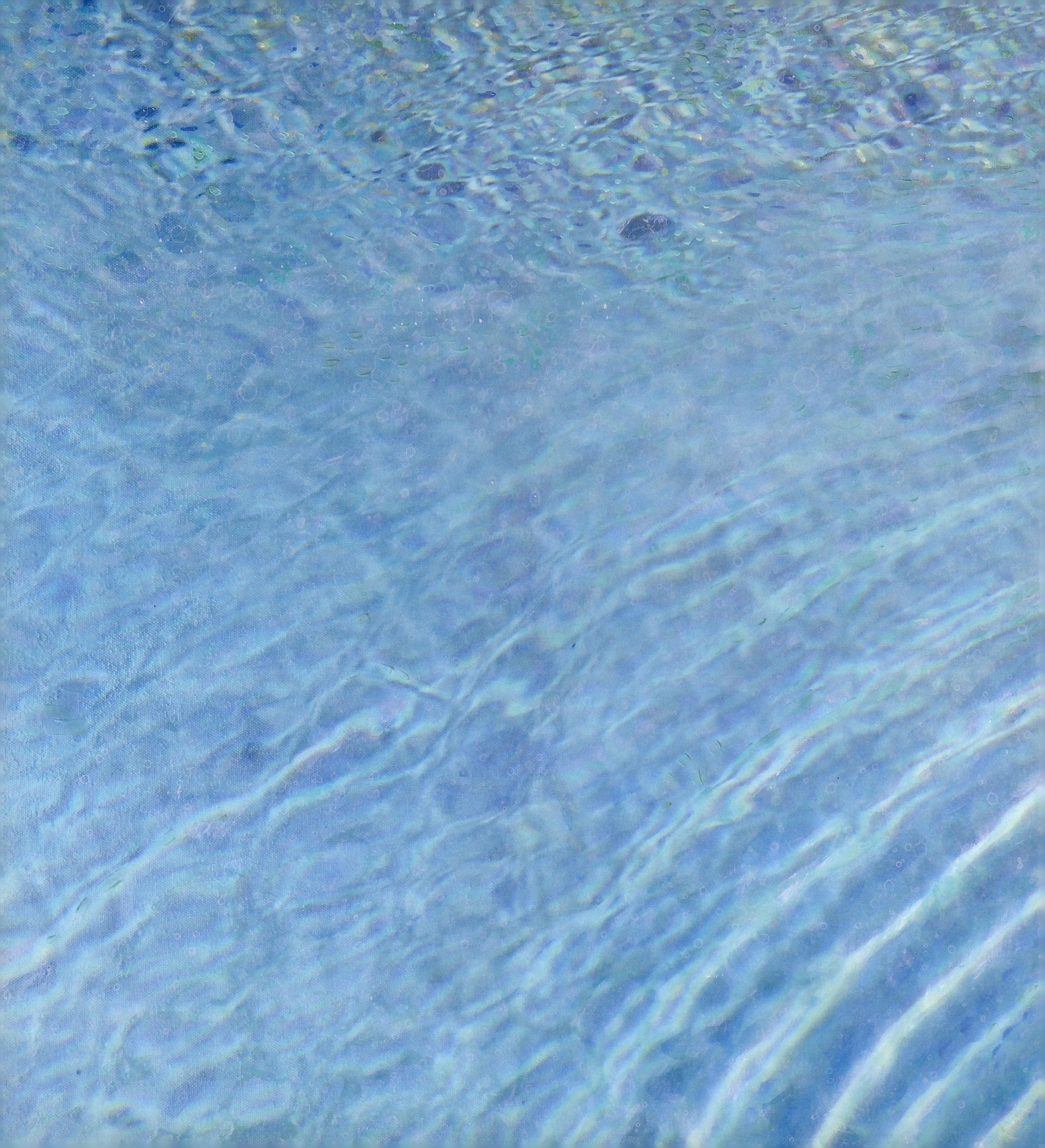

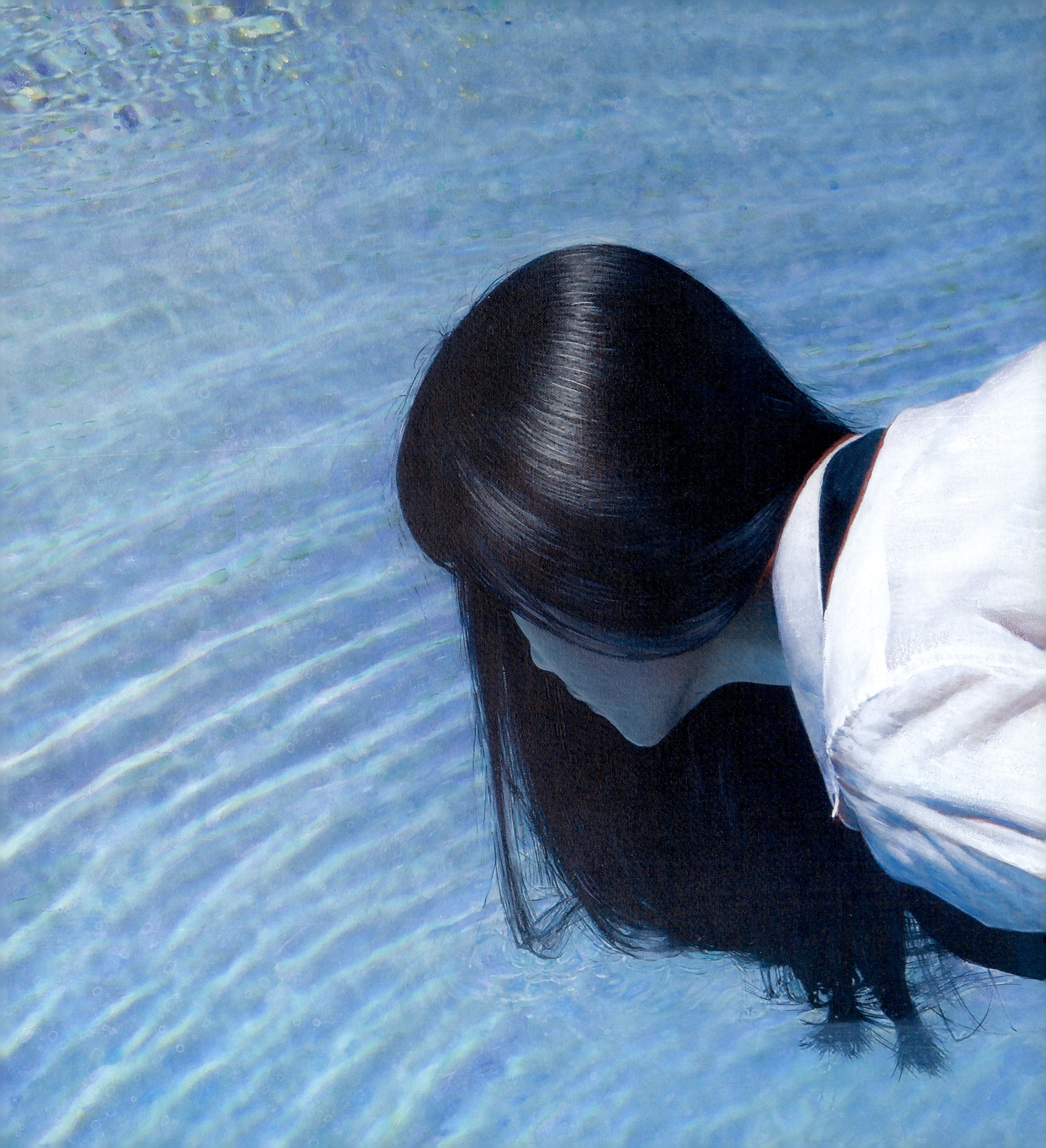

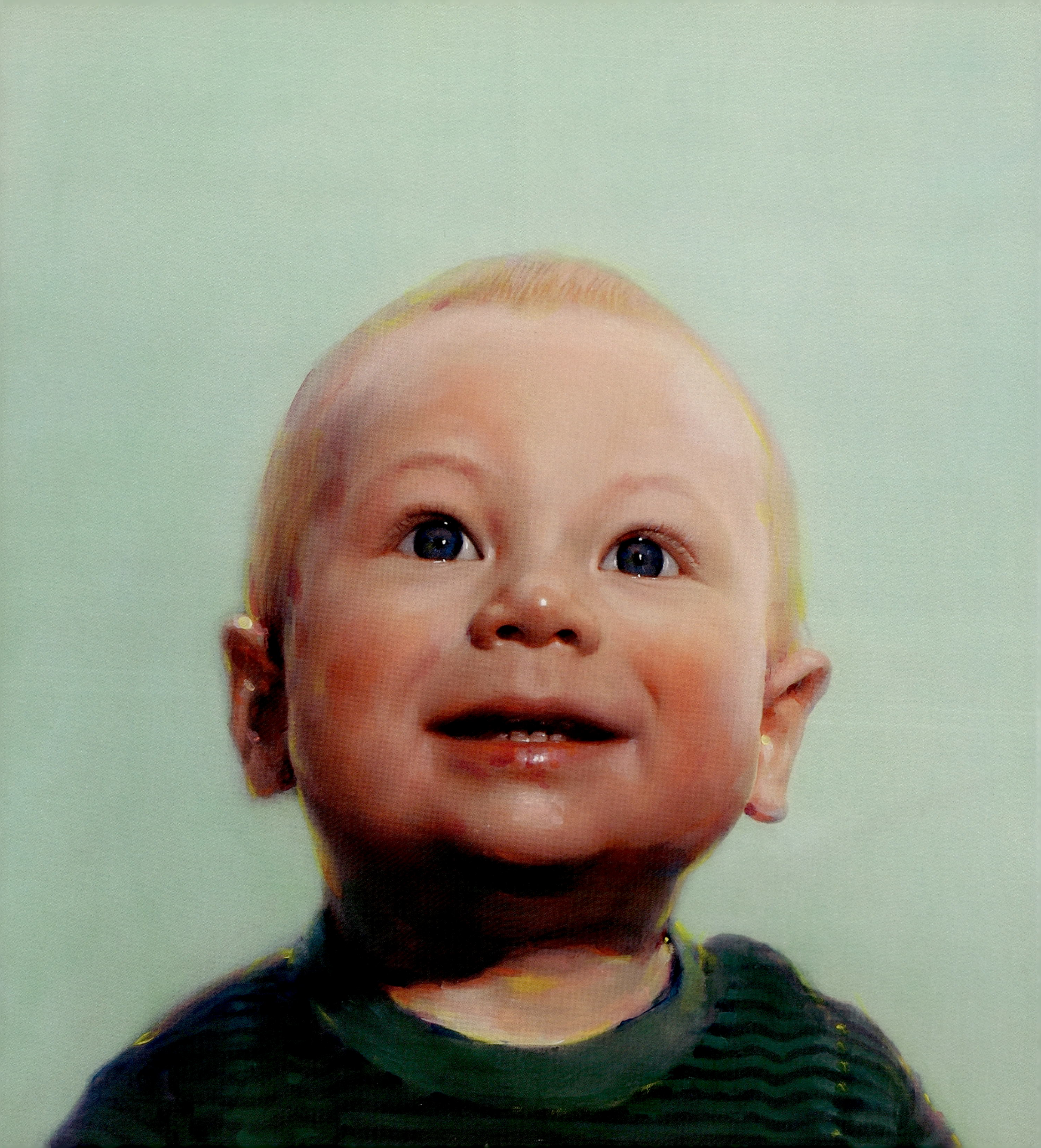

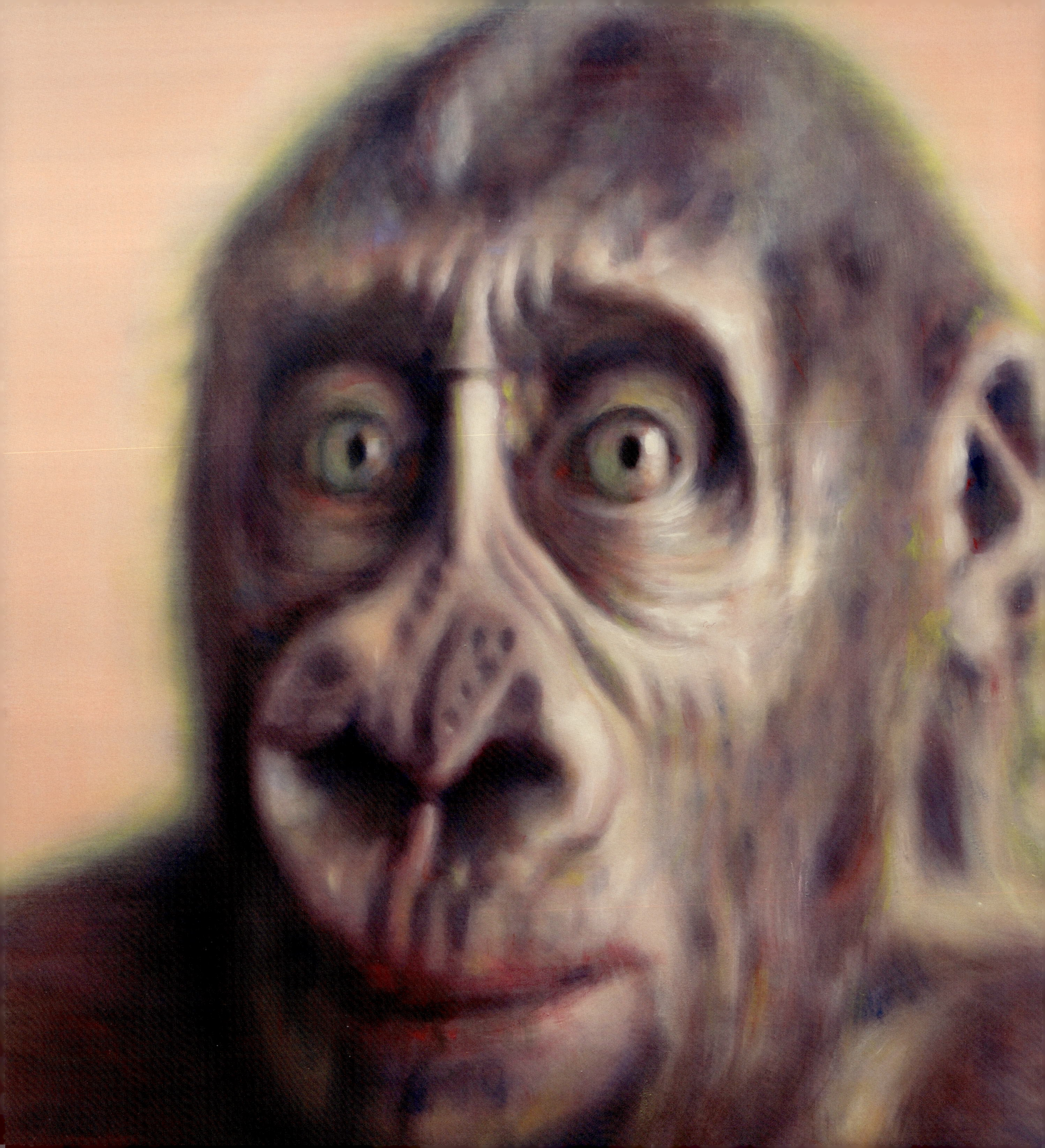

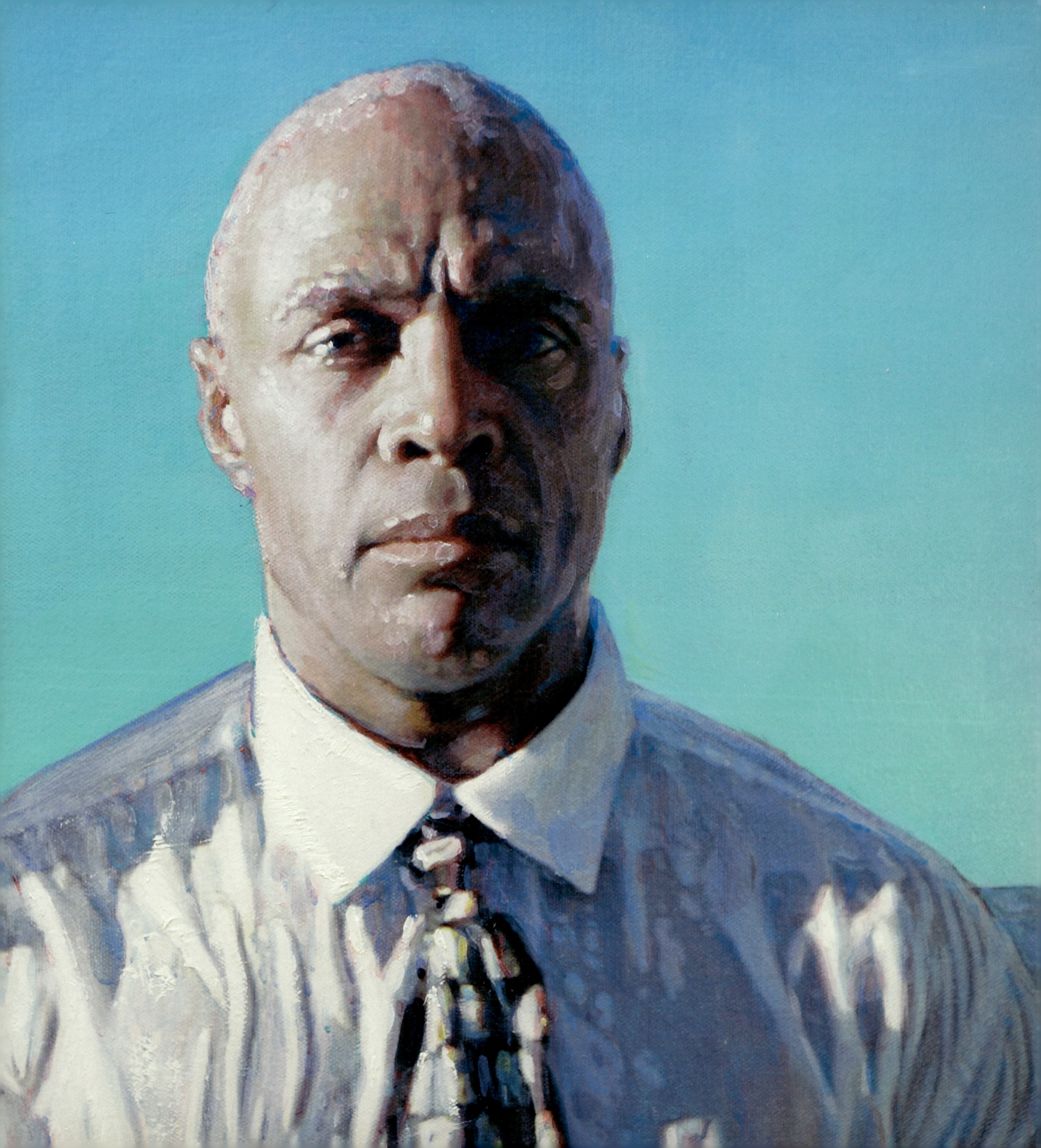

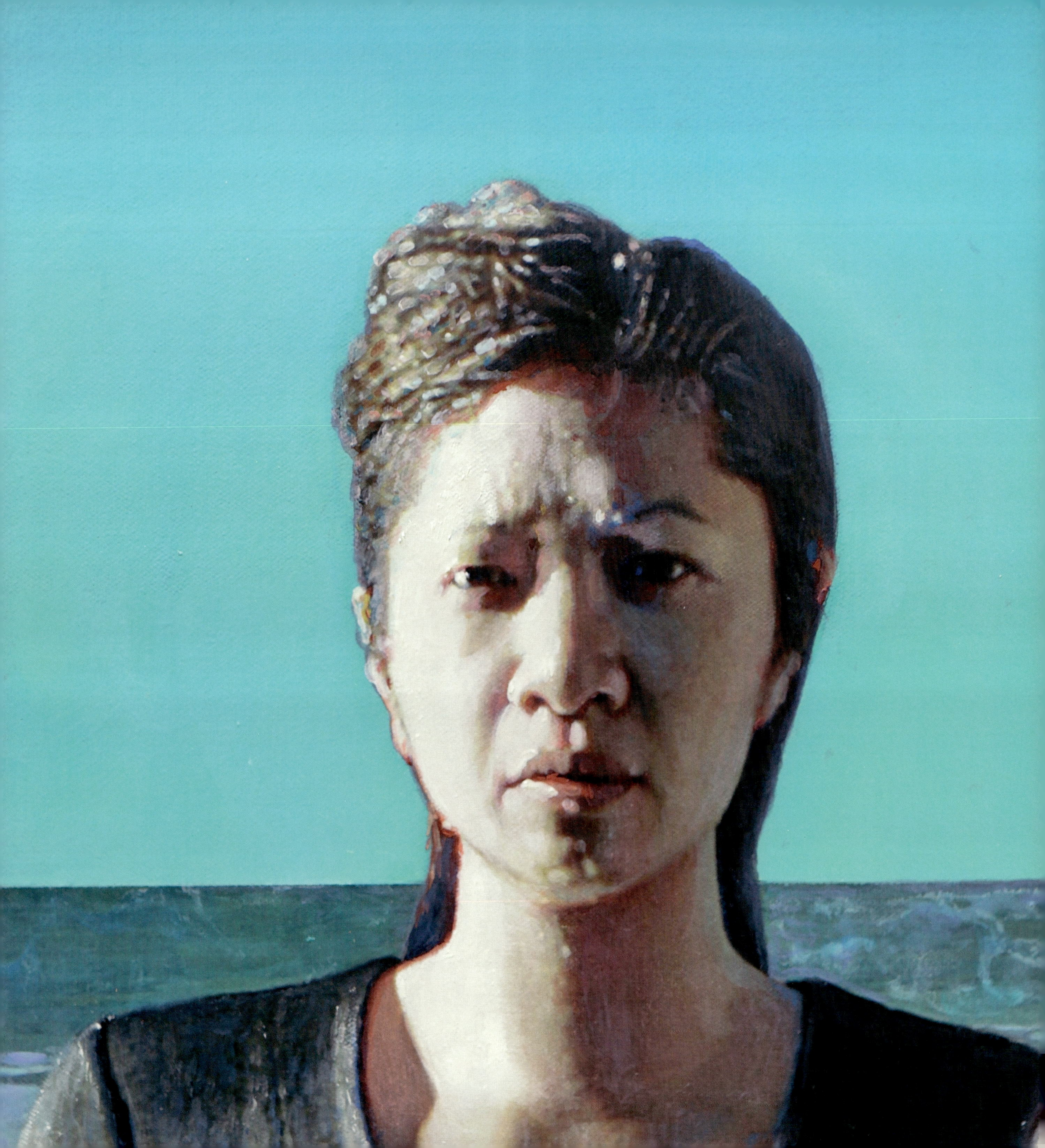

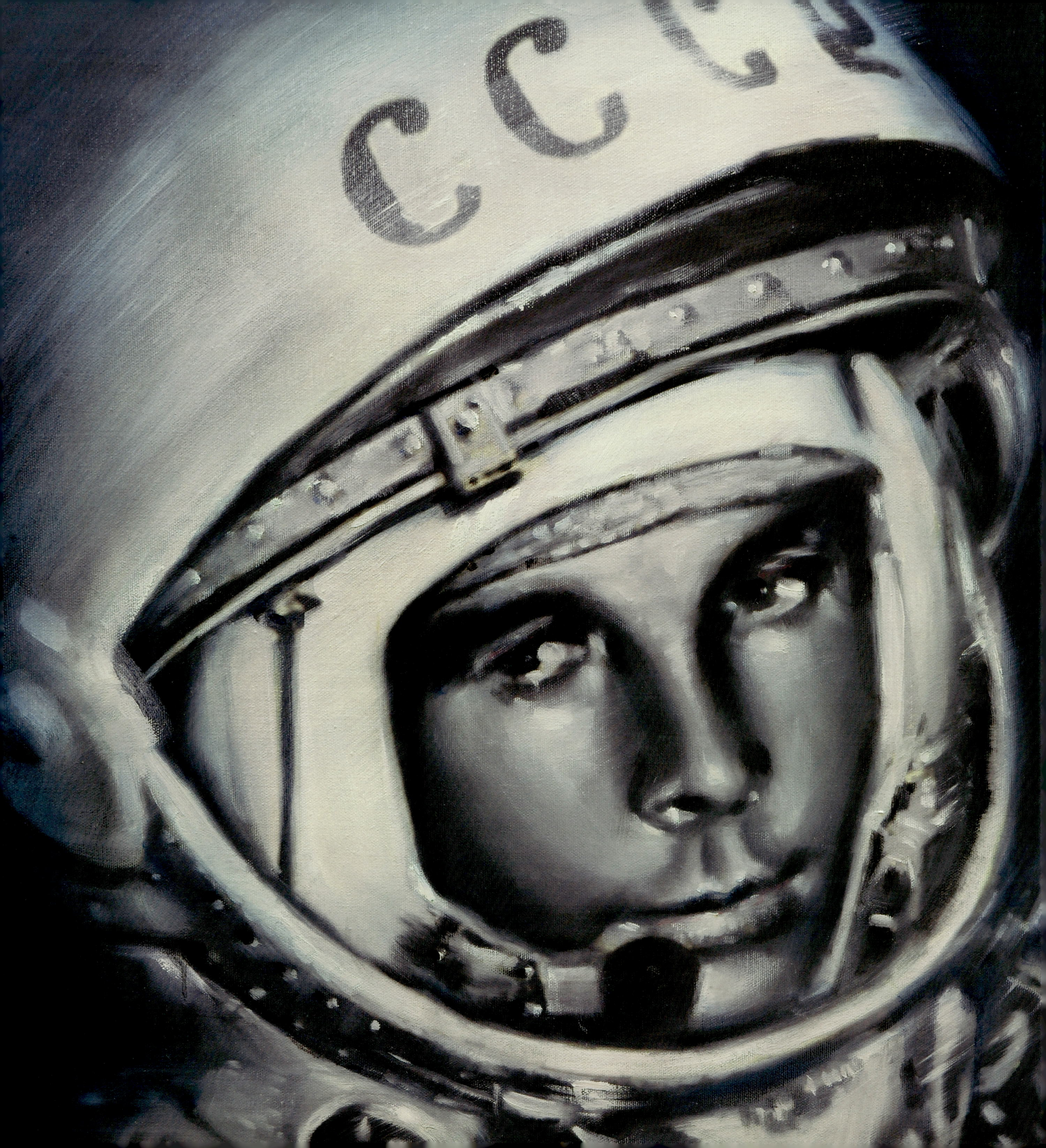
СССР

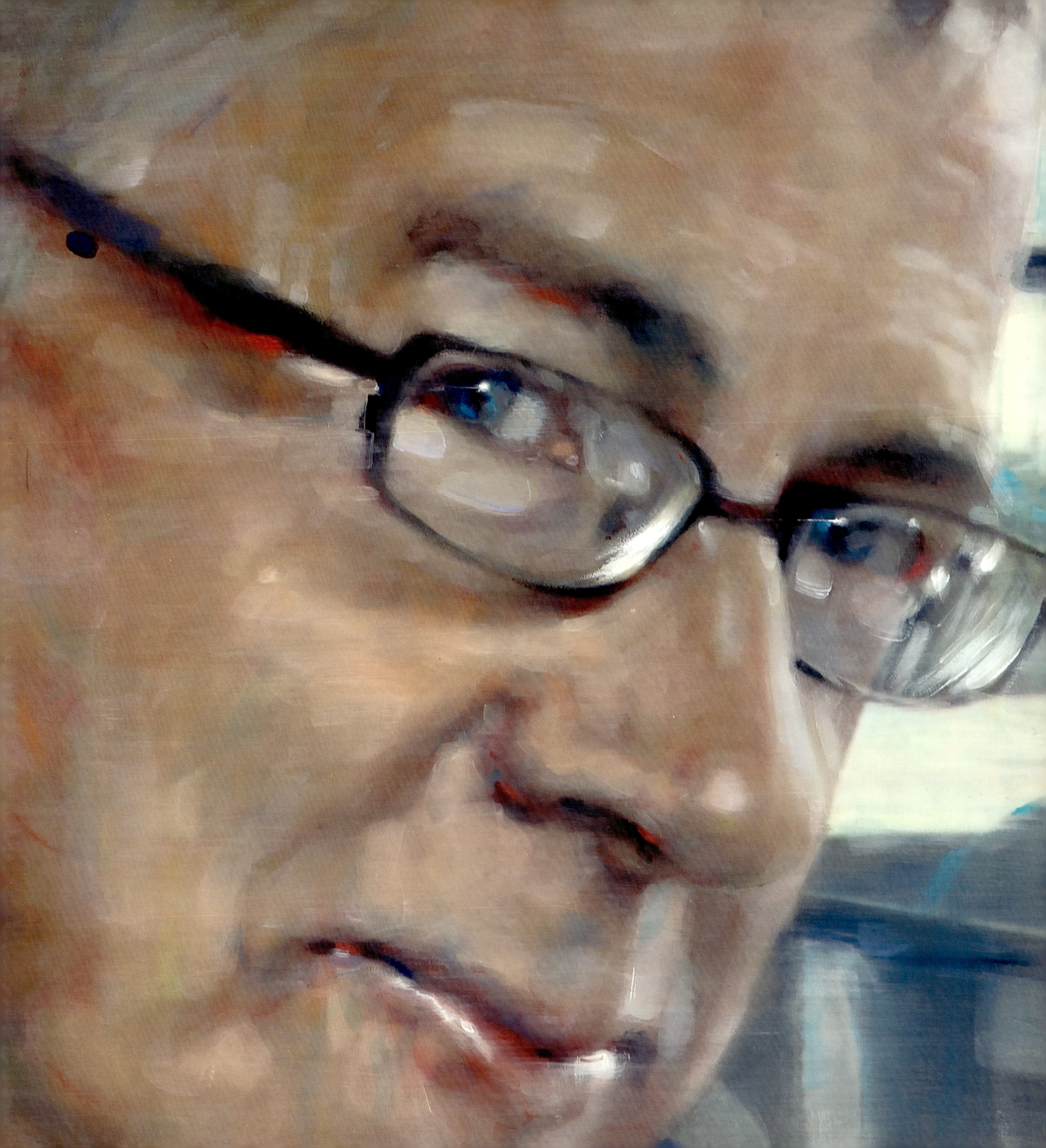

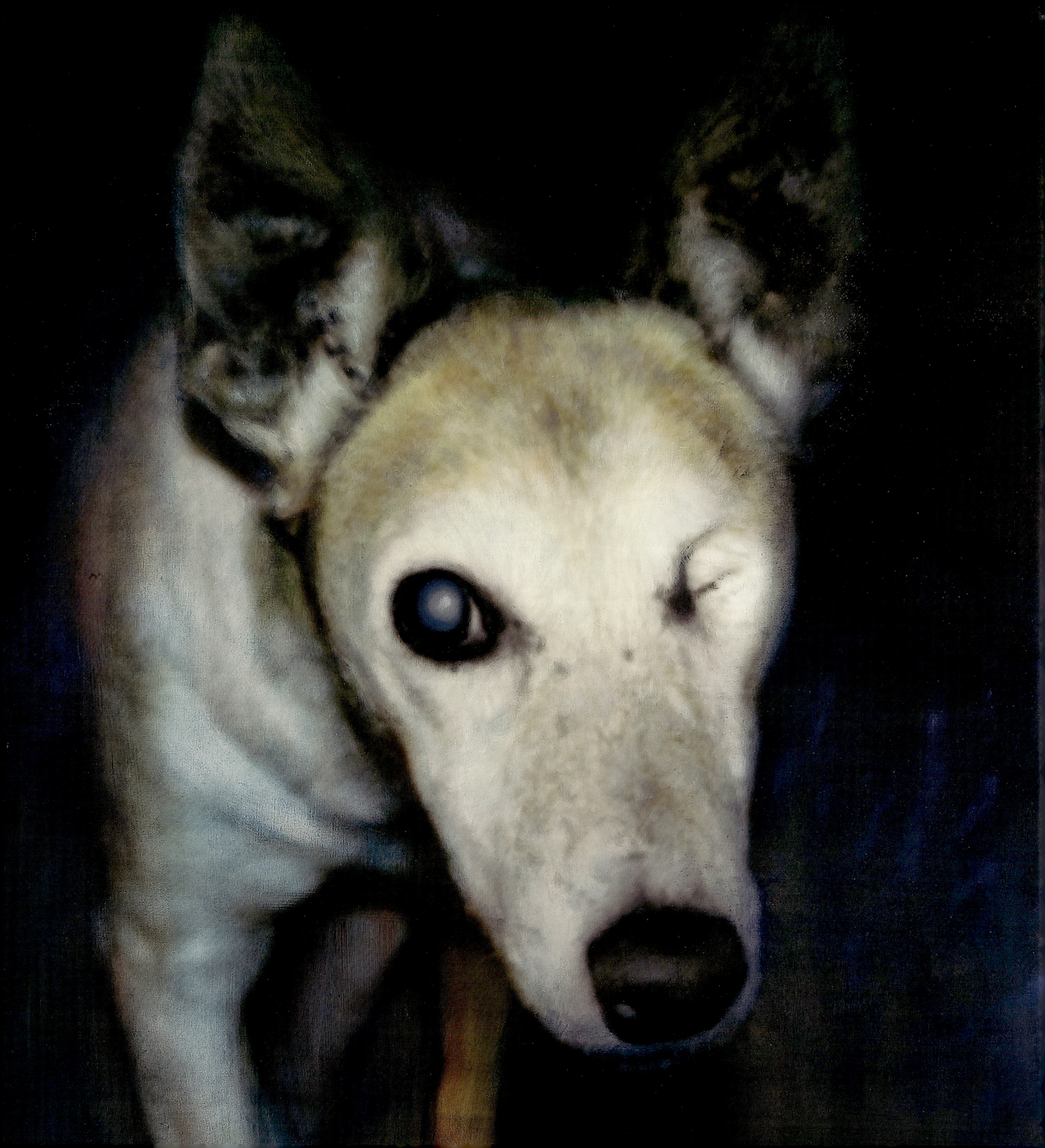

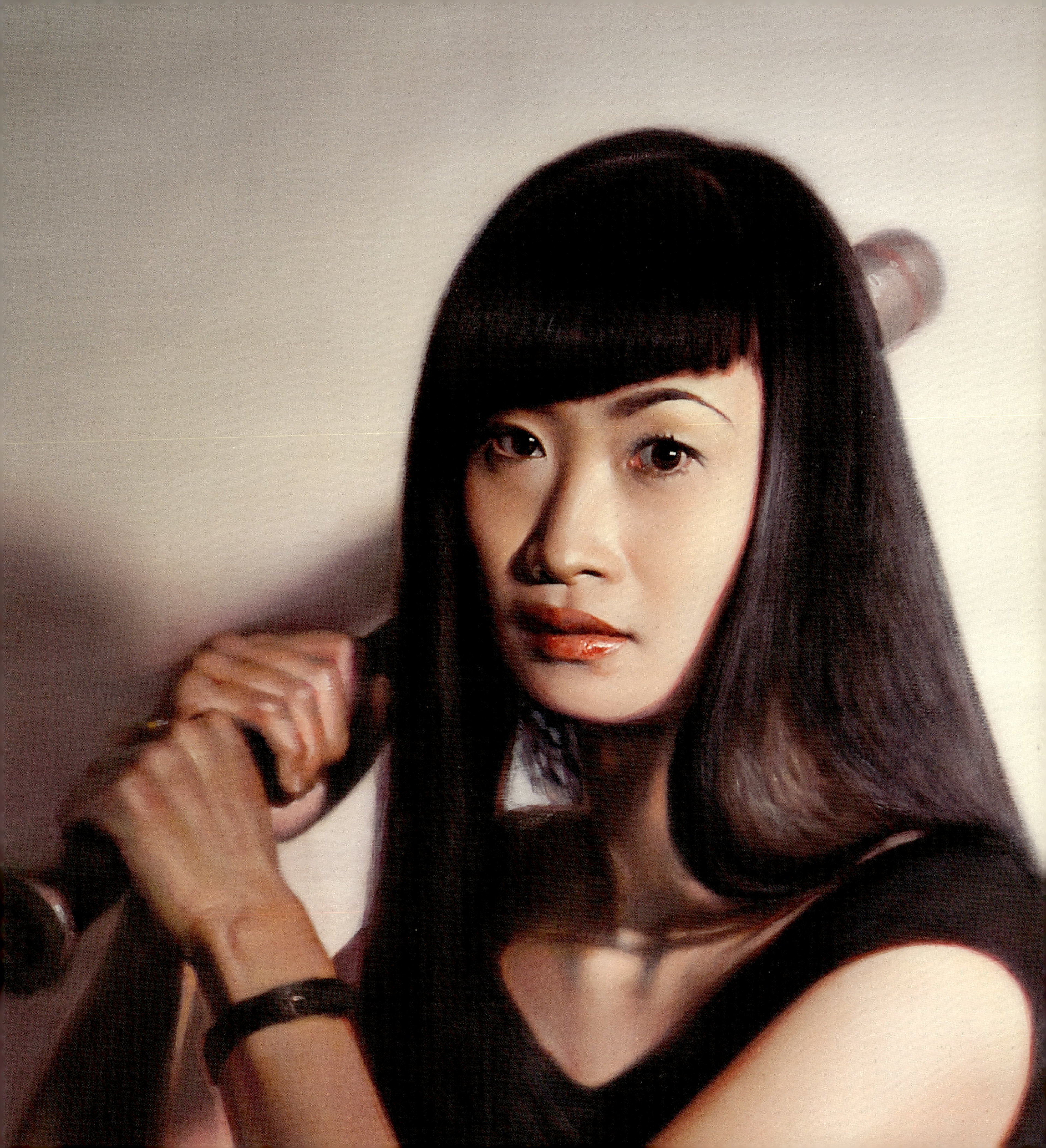

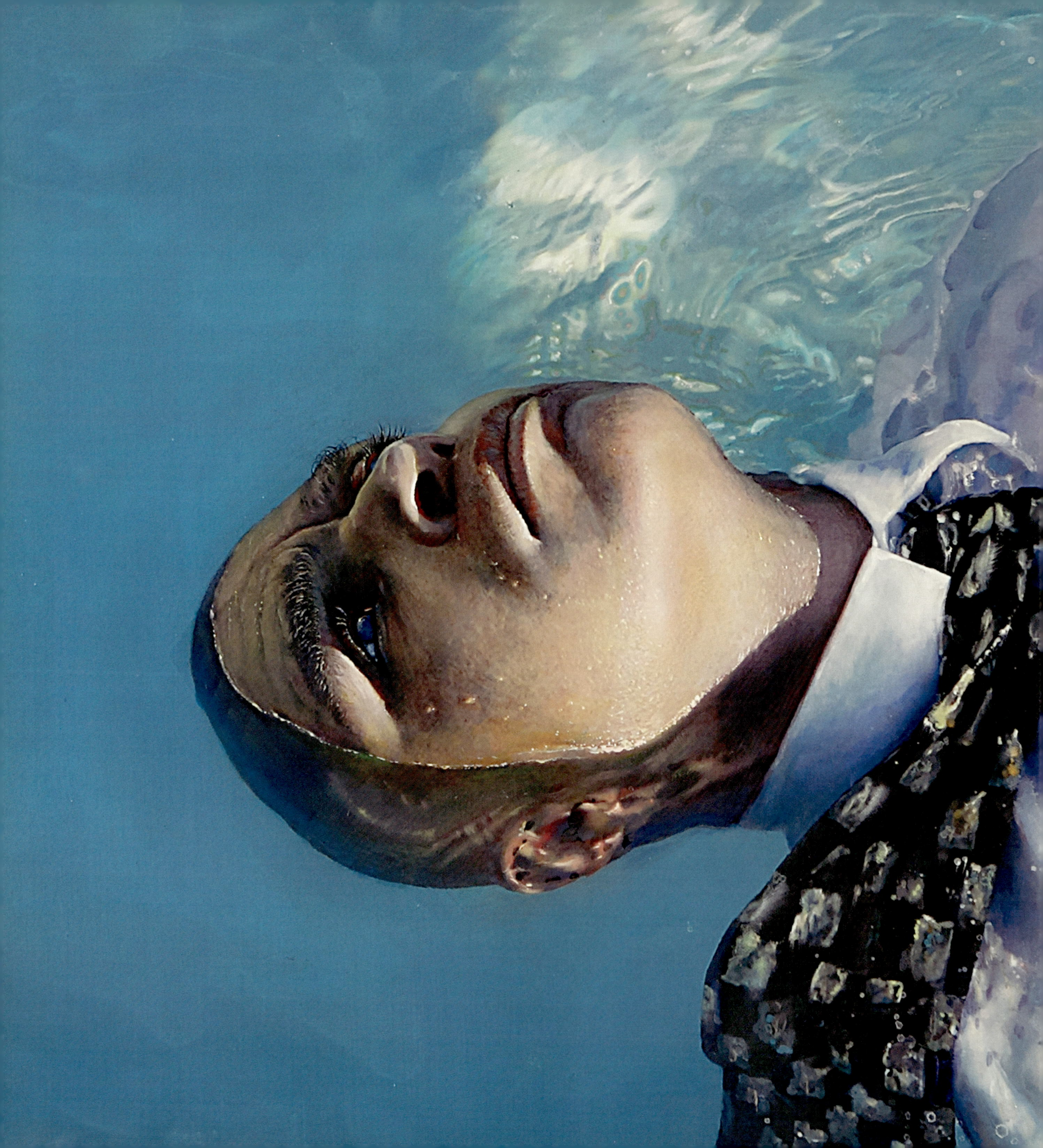

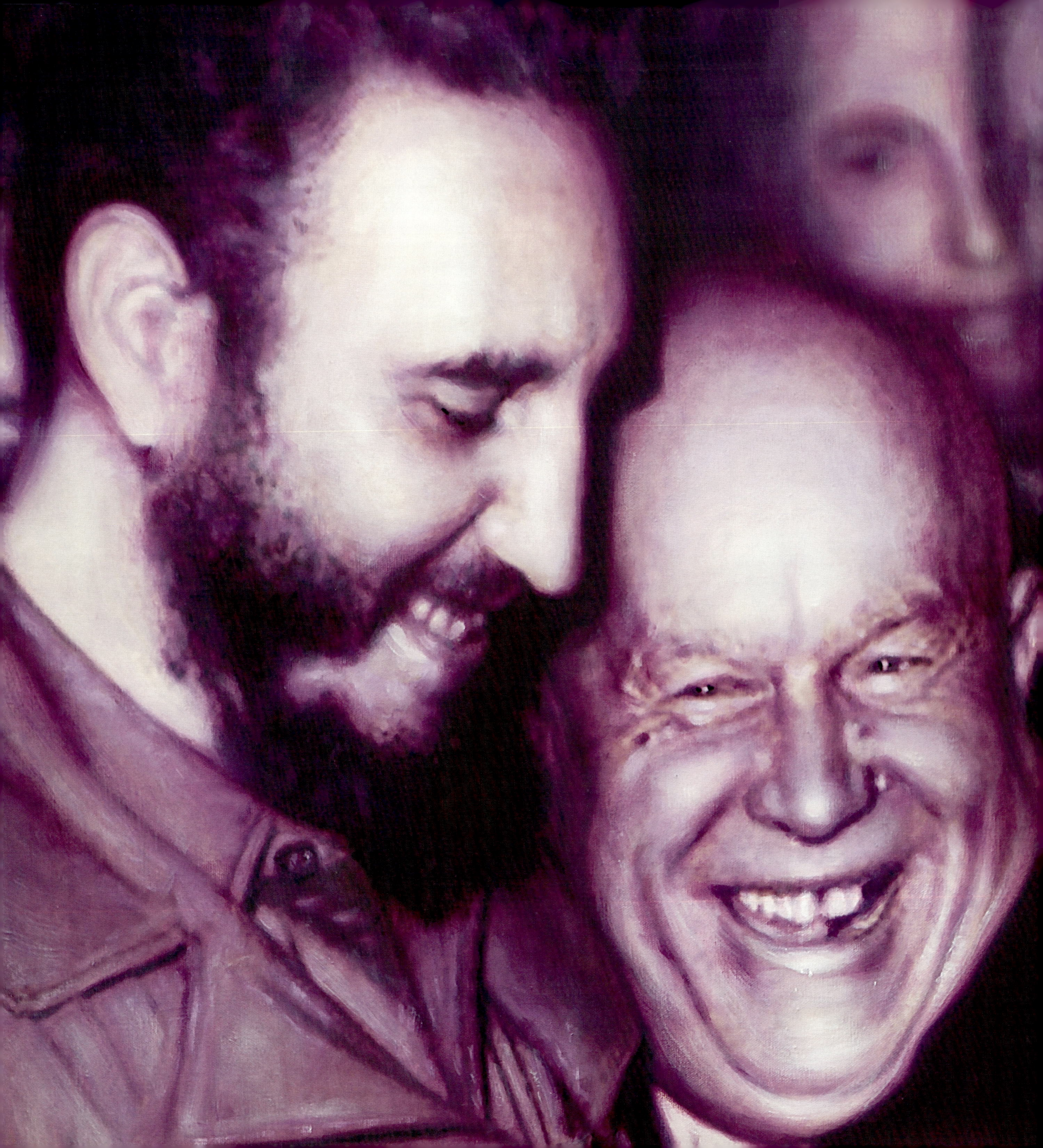

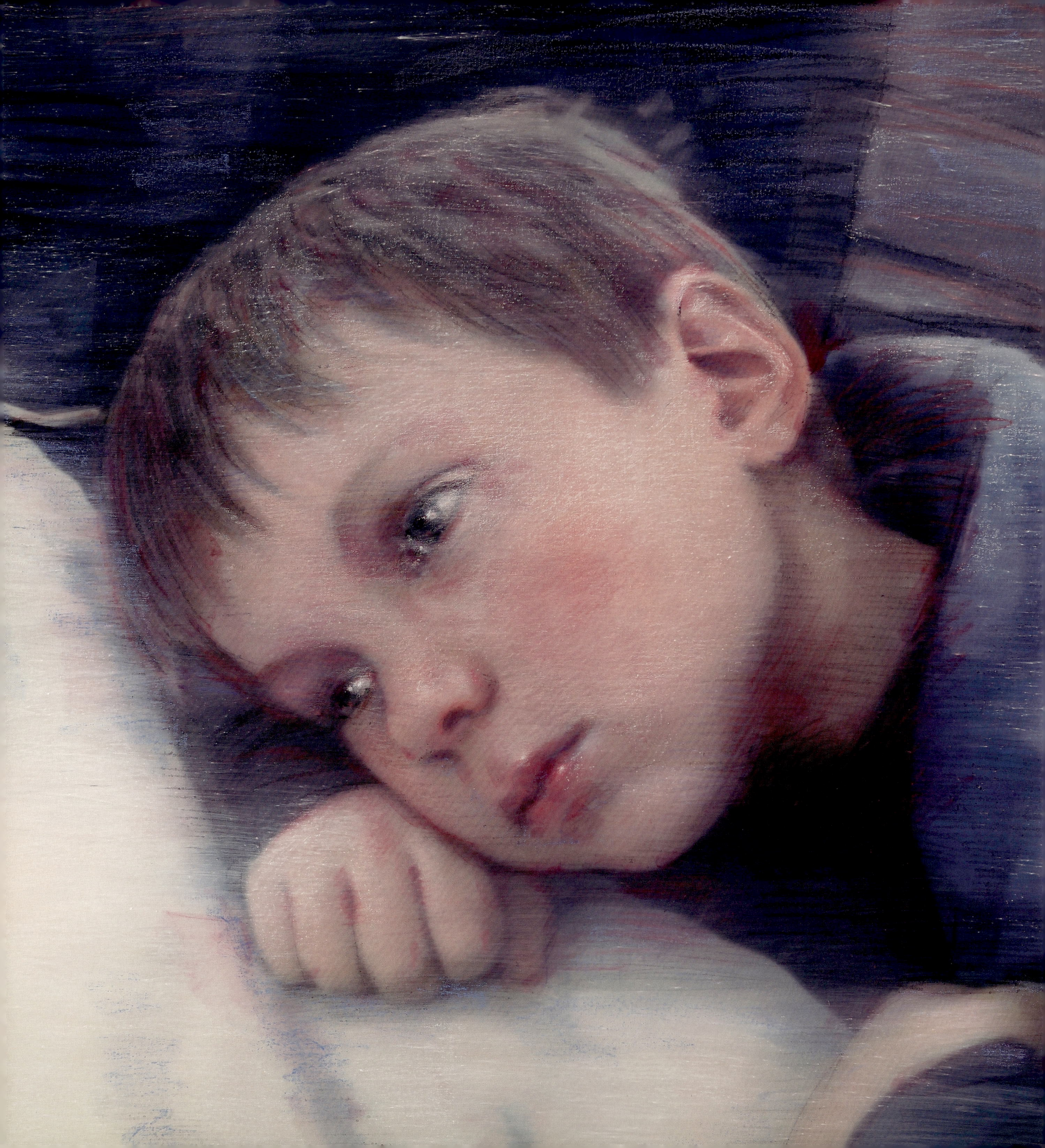

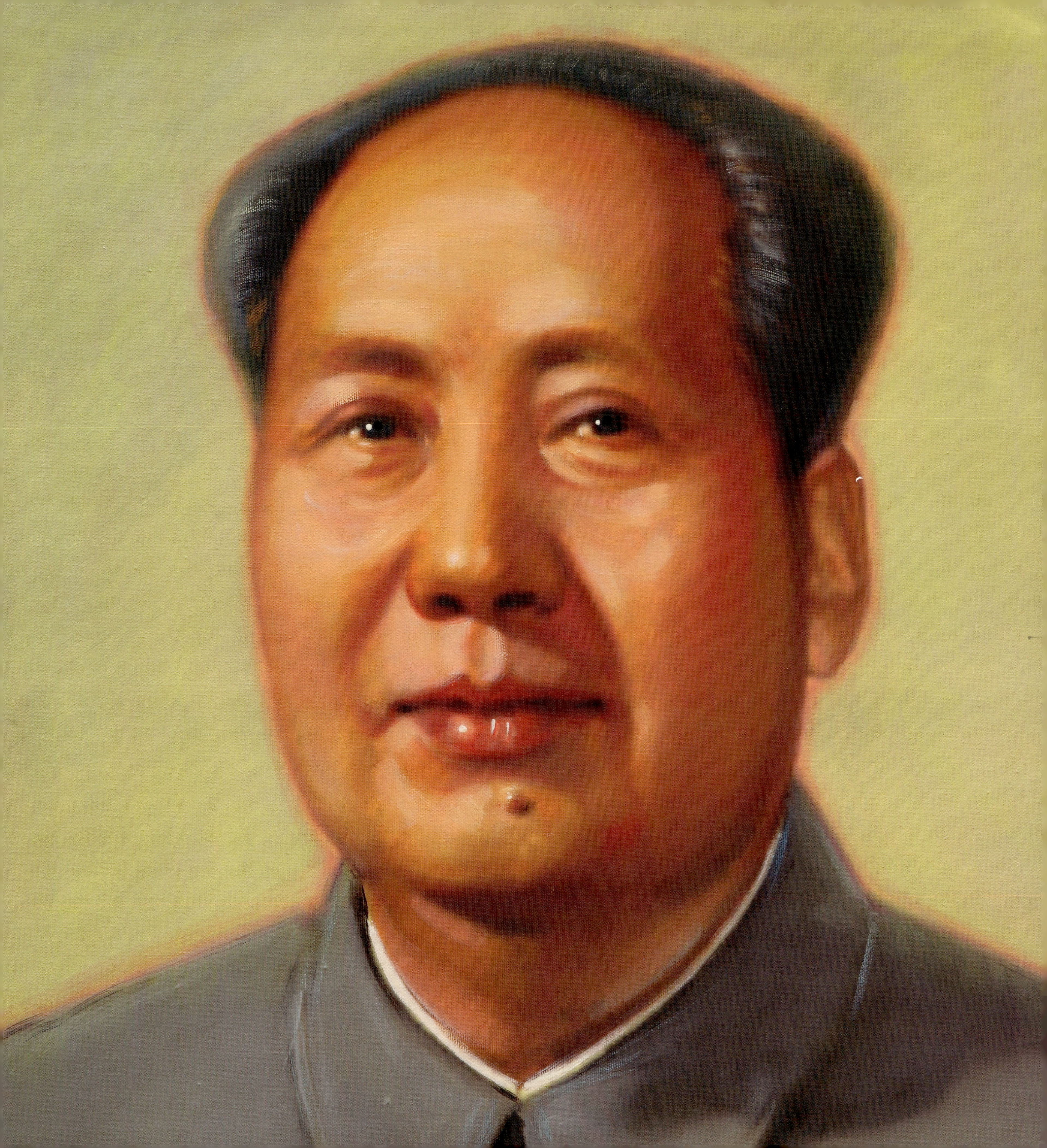

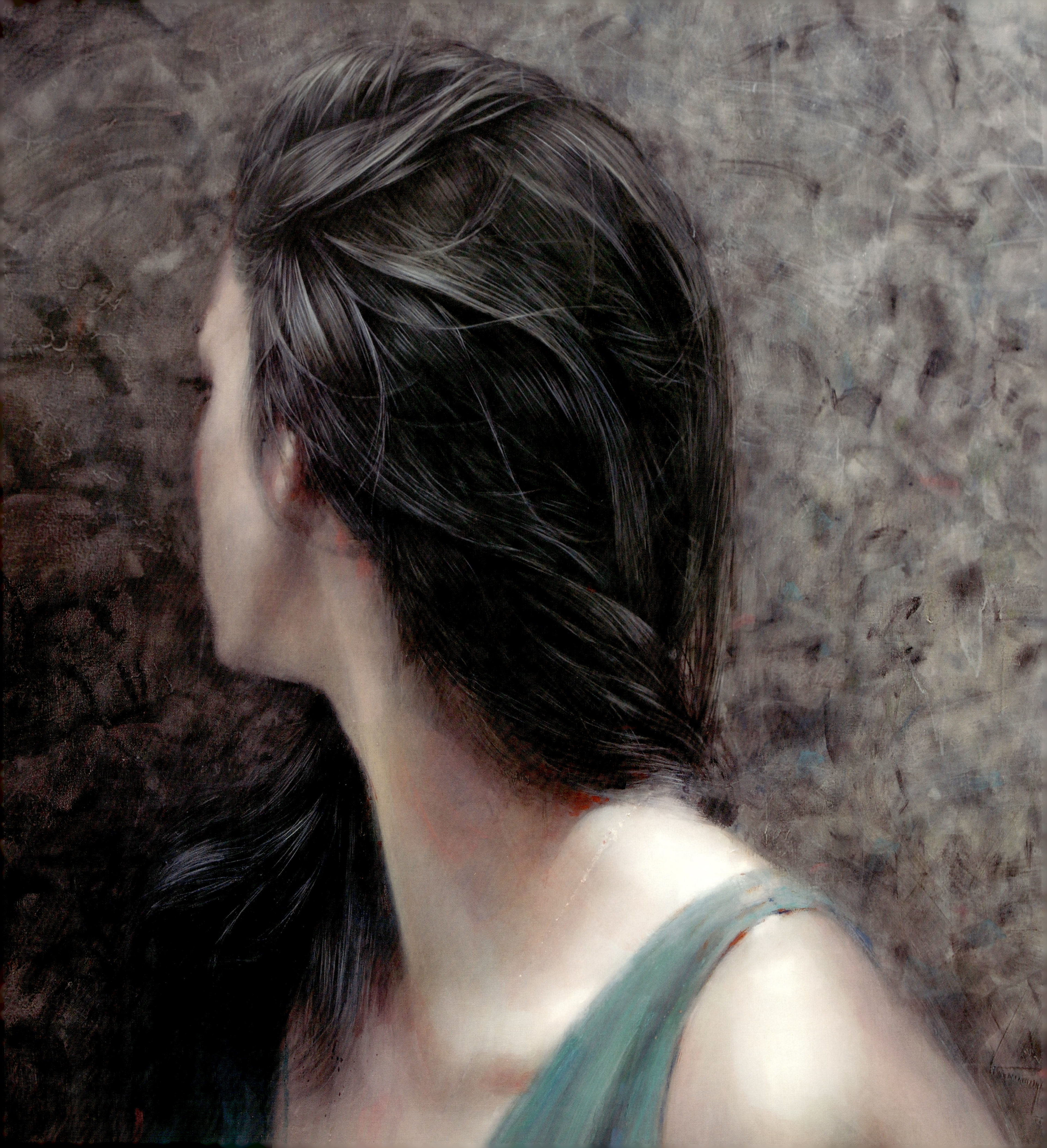

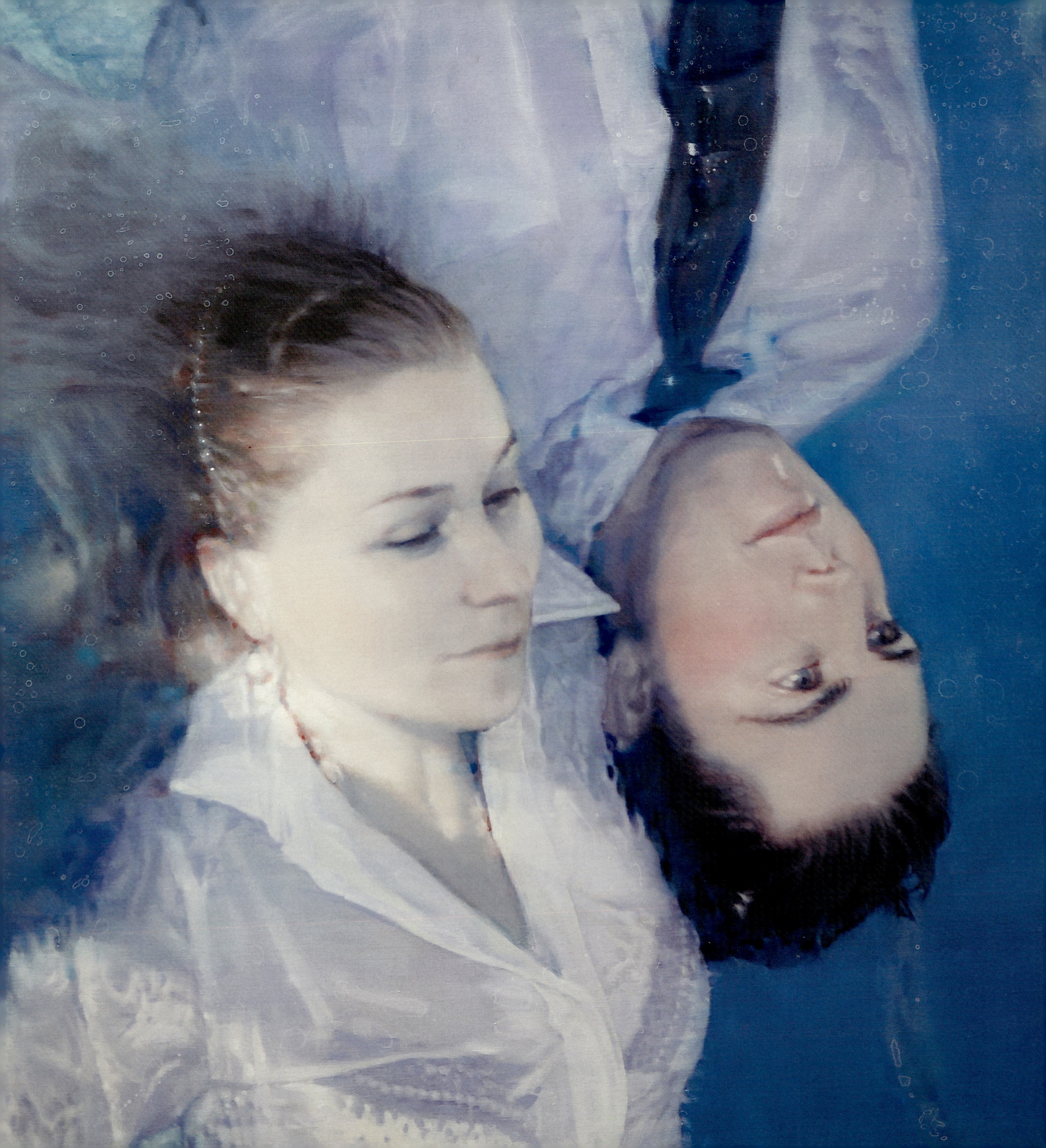

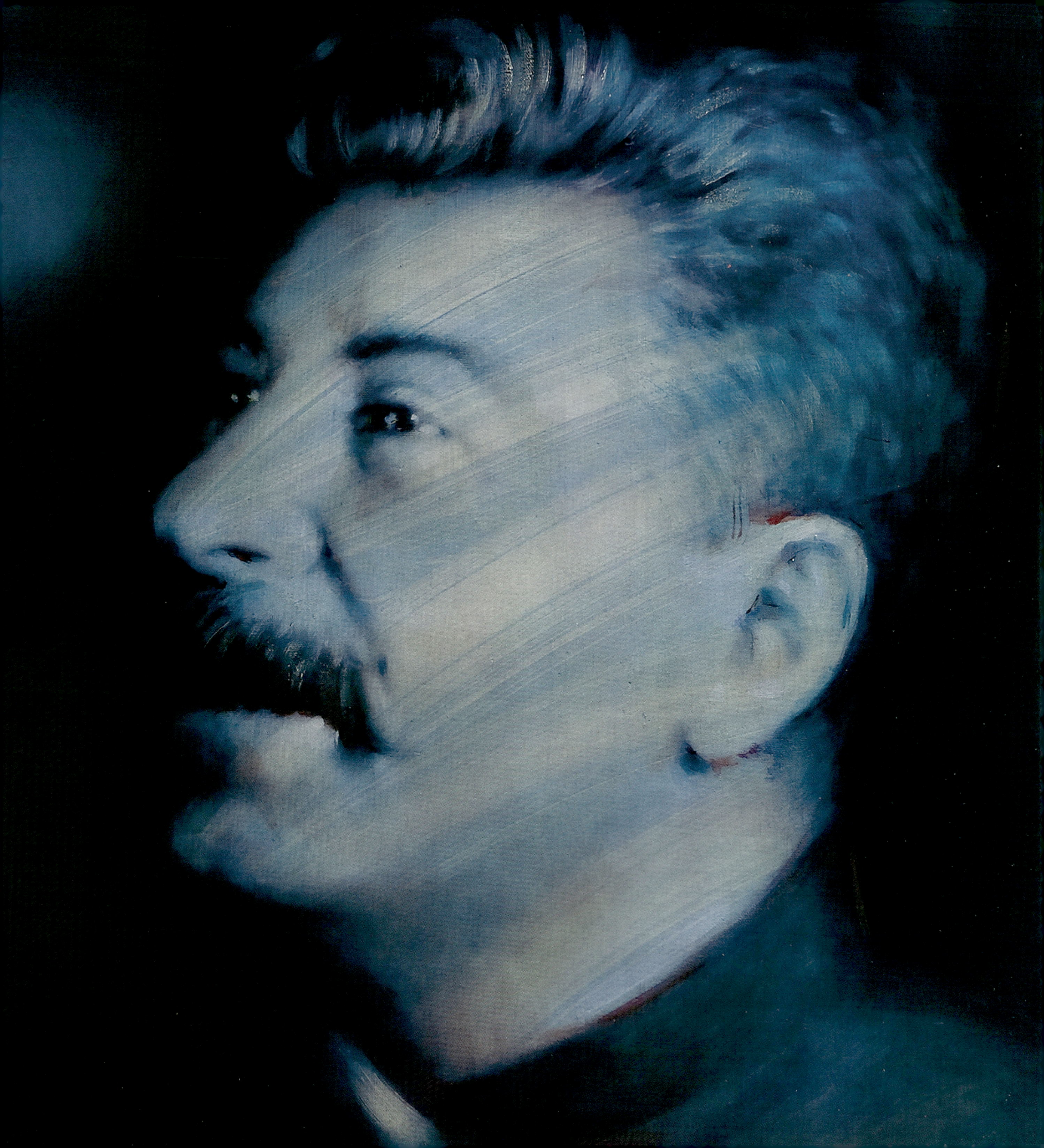

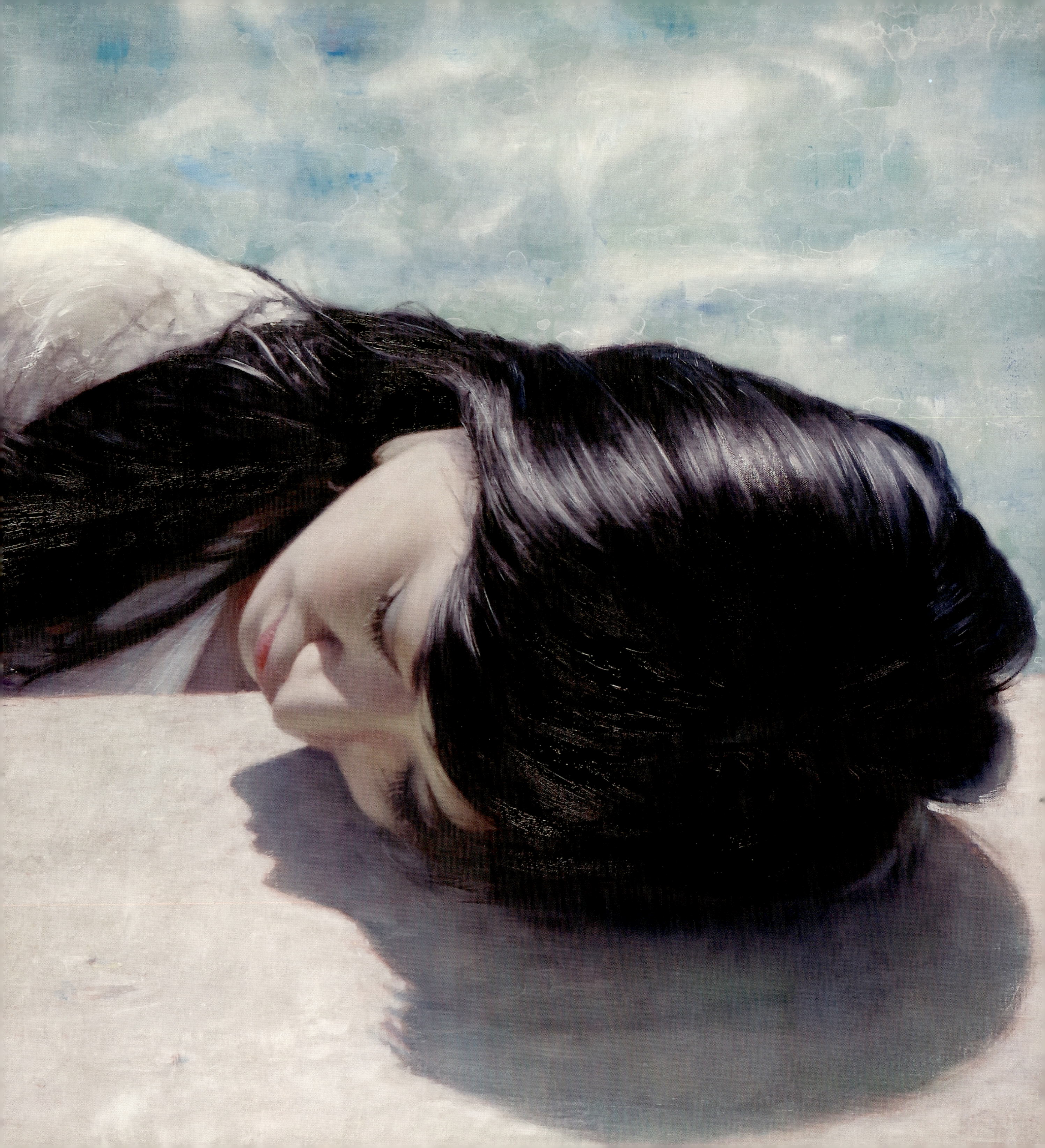

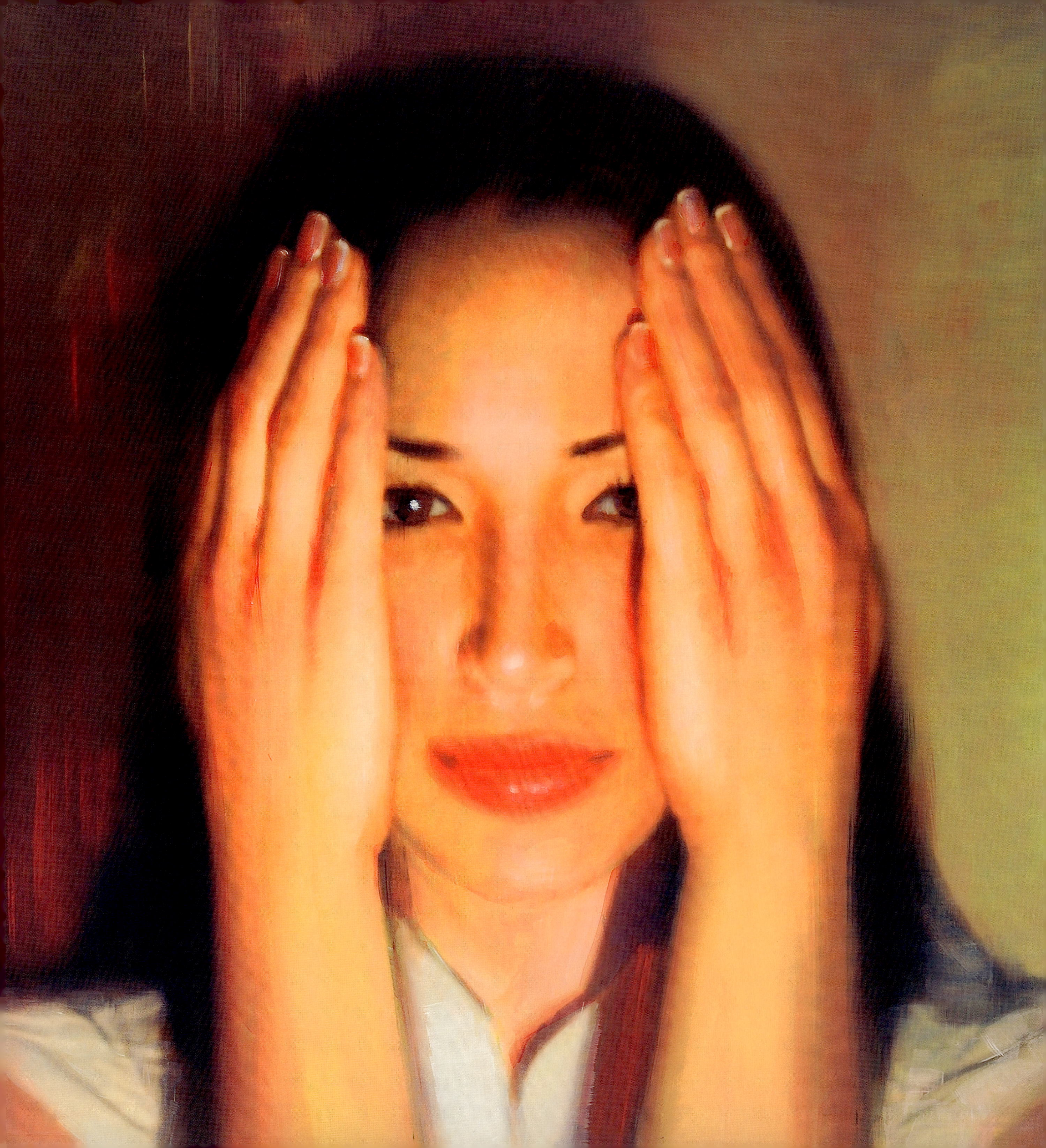

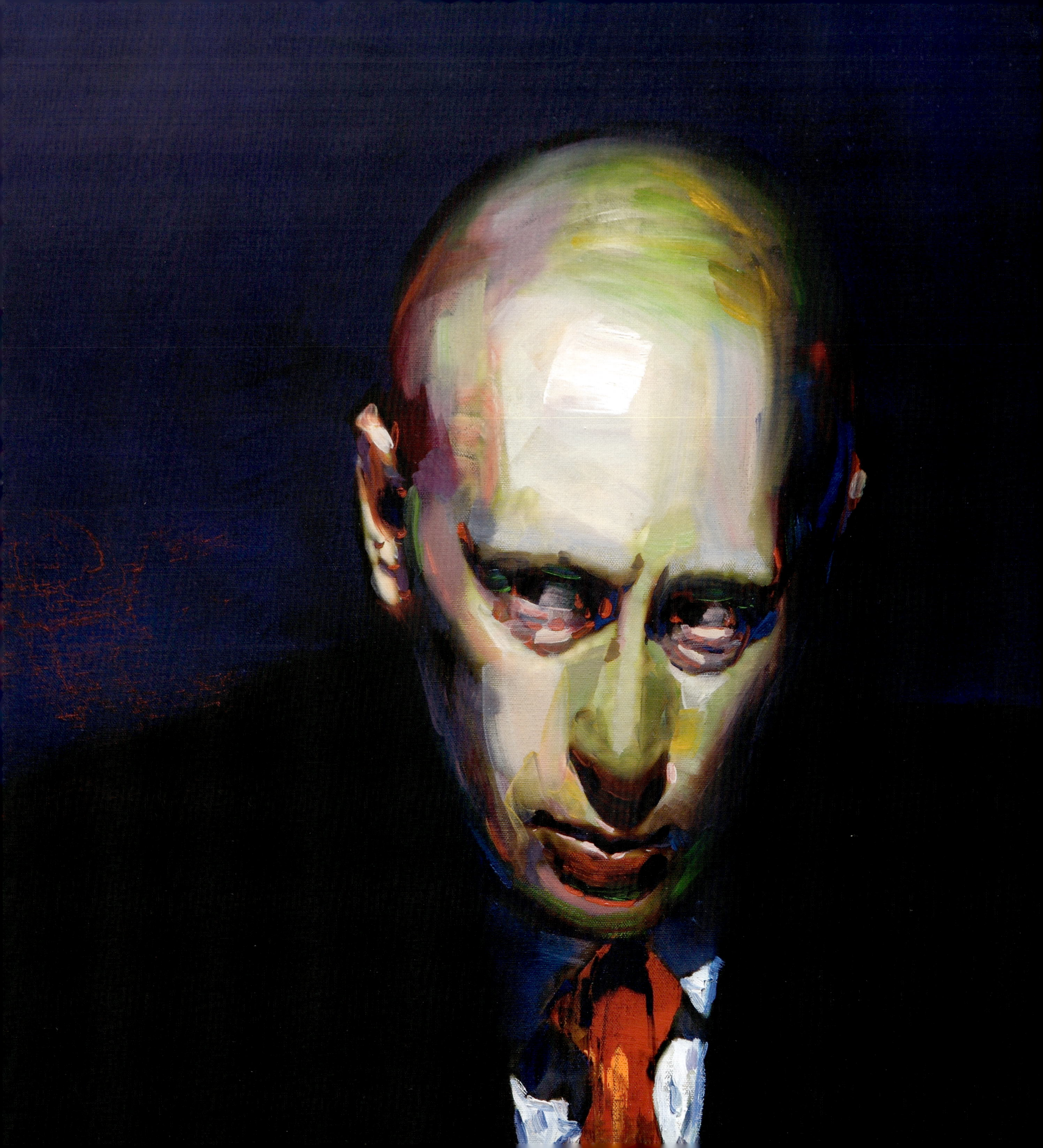

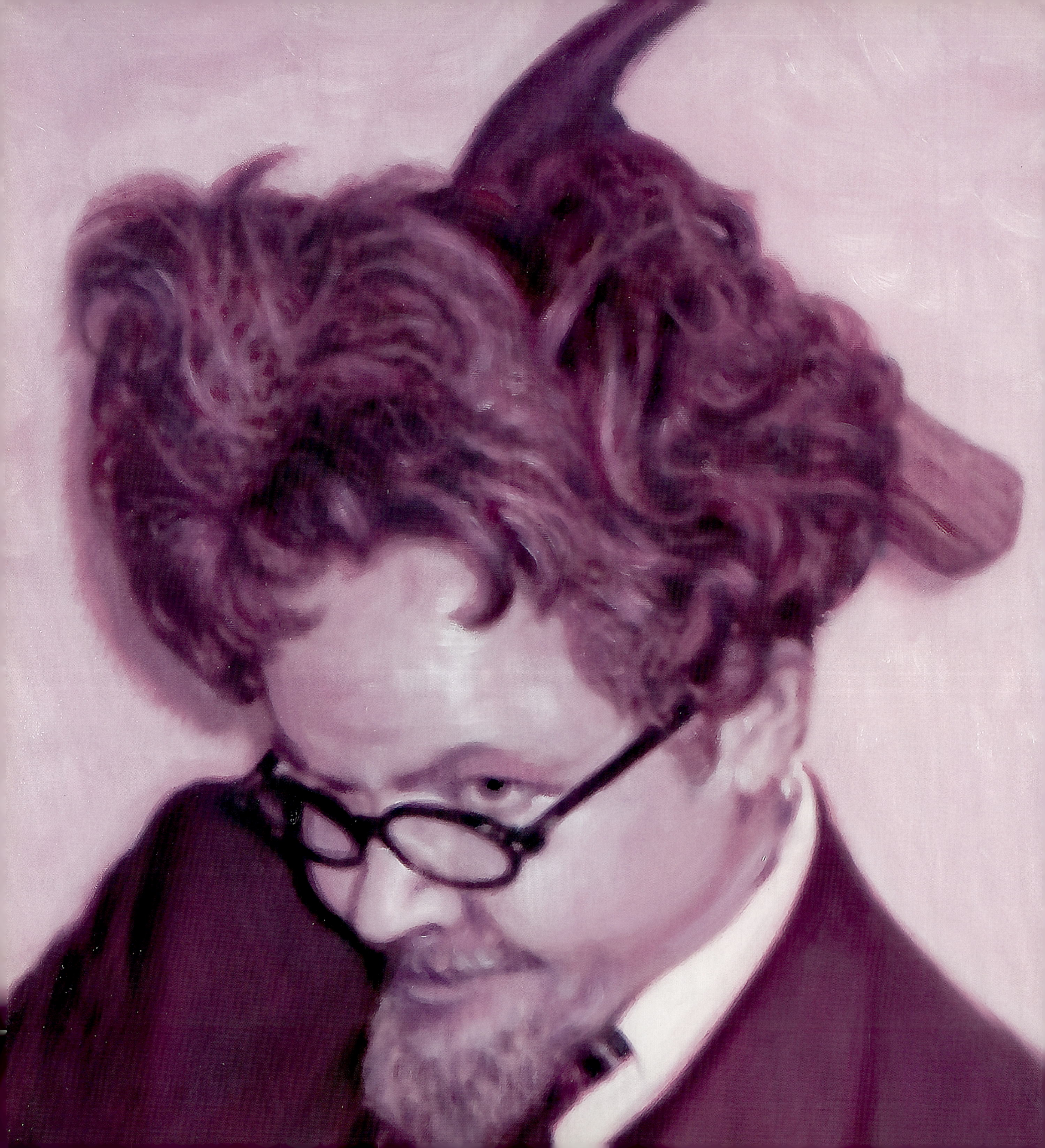

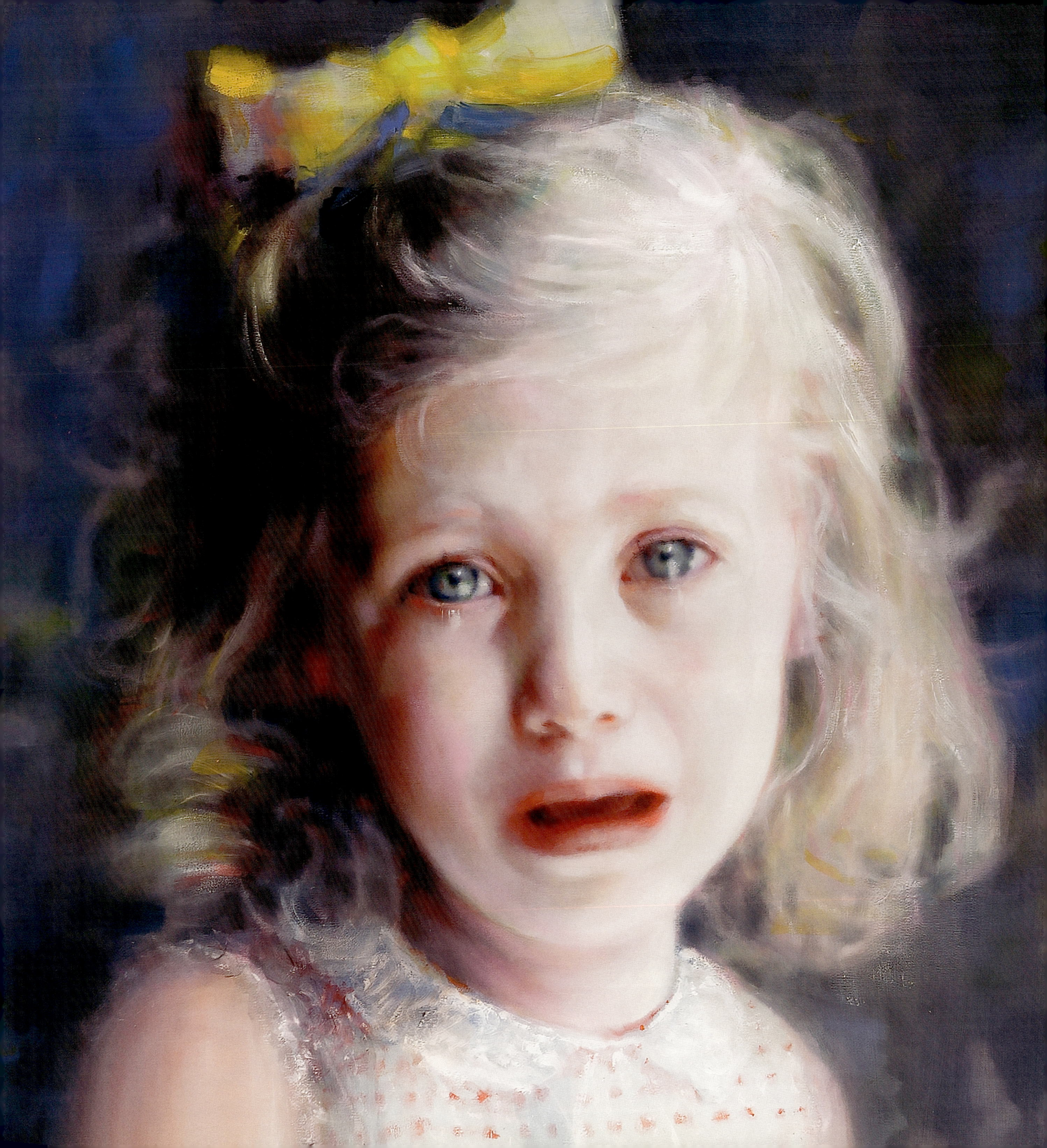

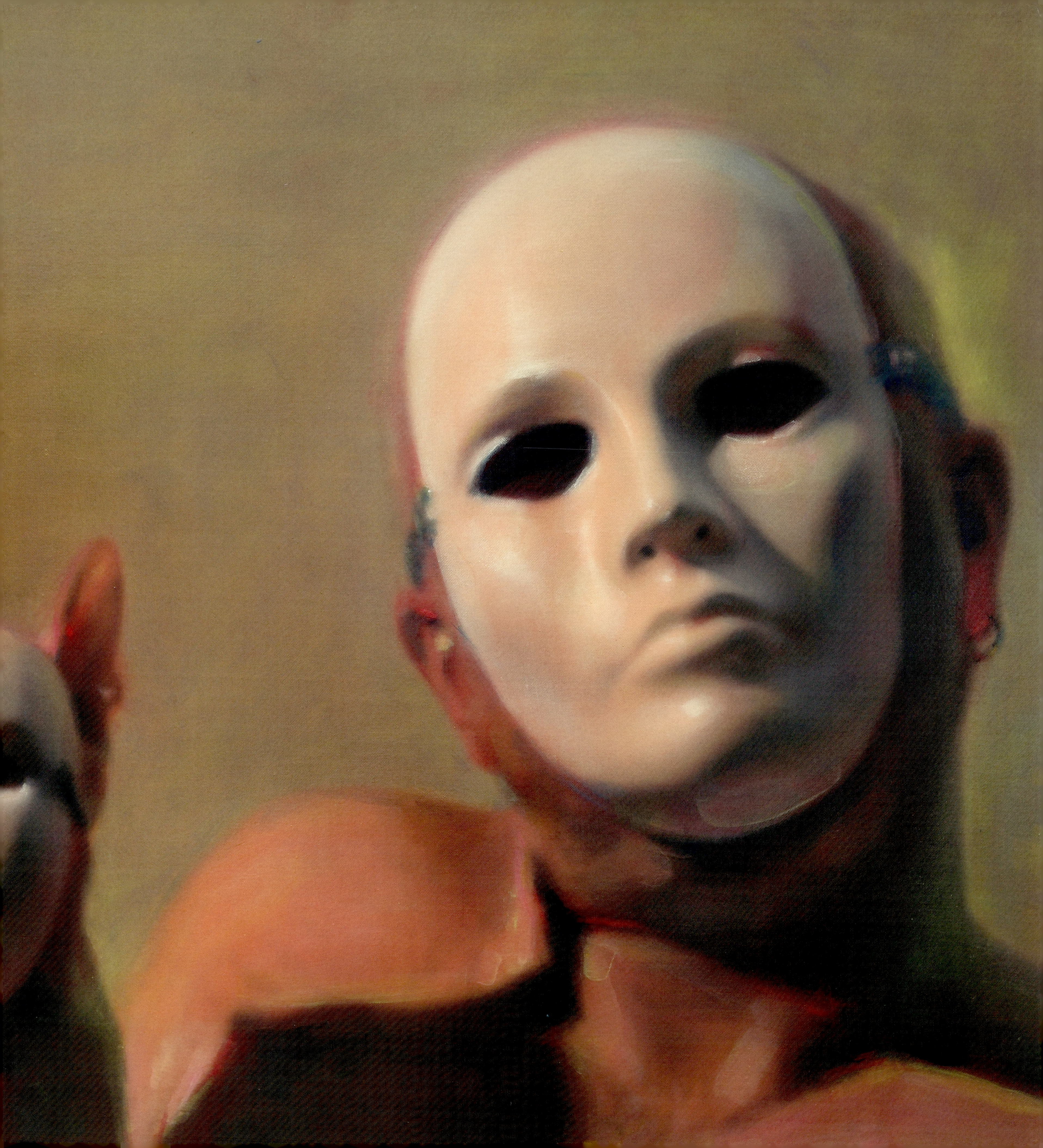

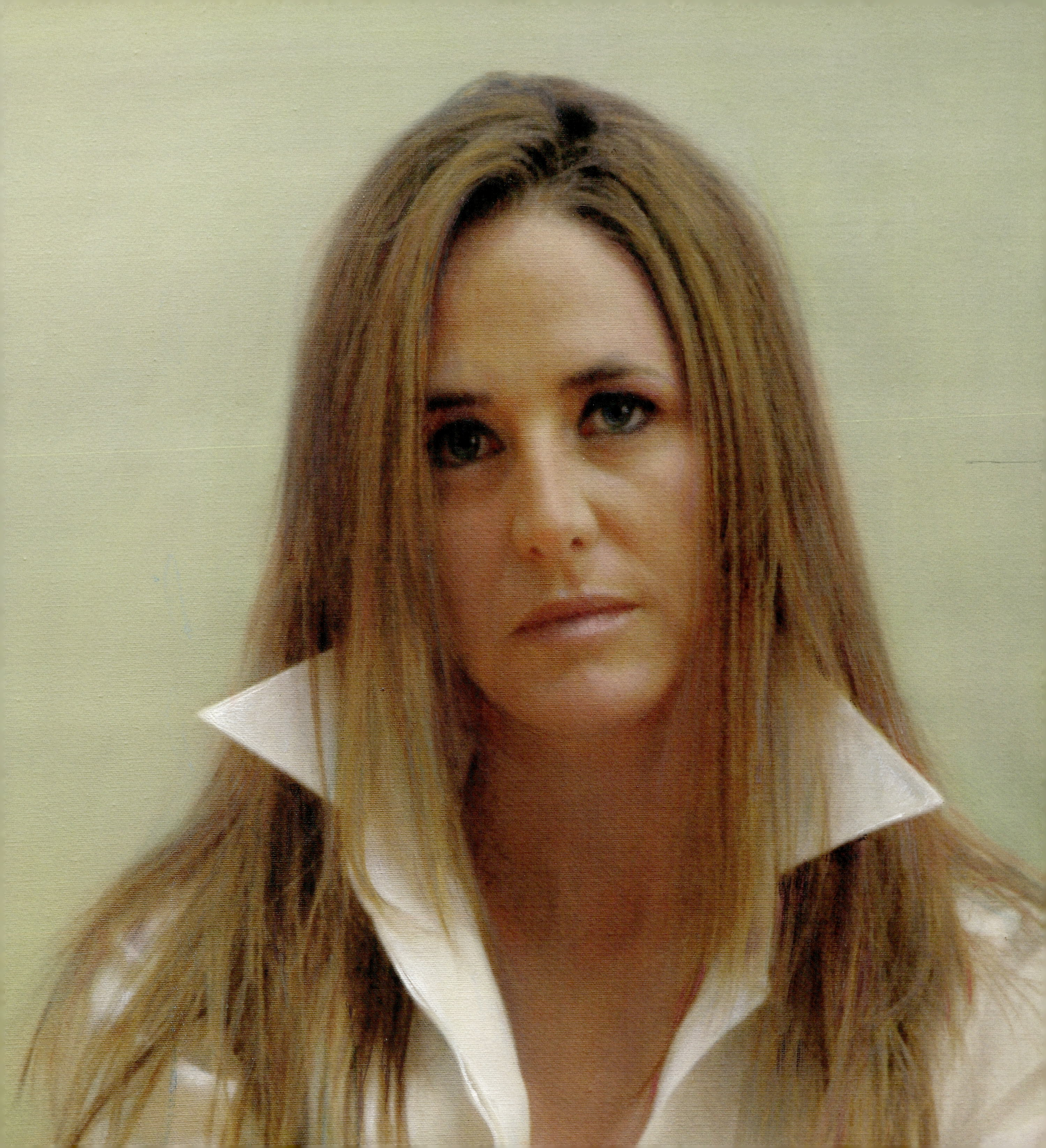

FACE

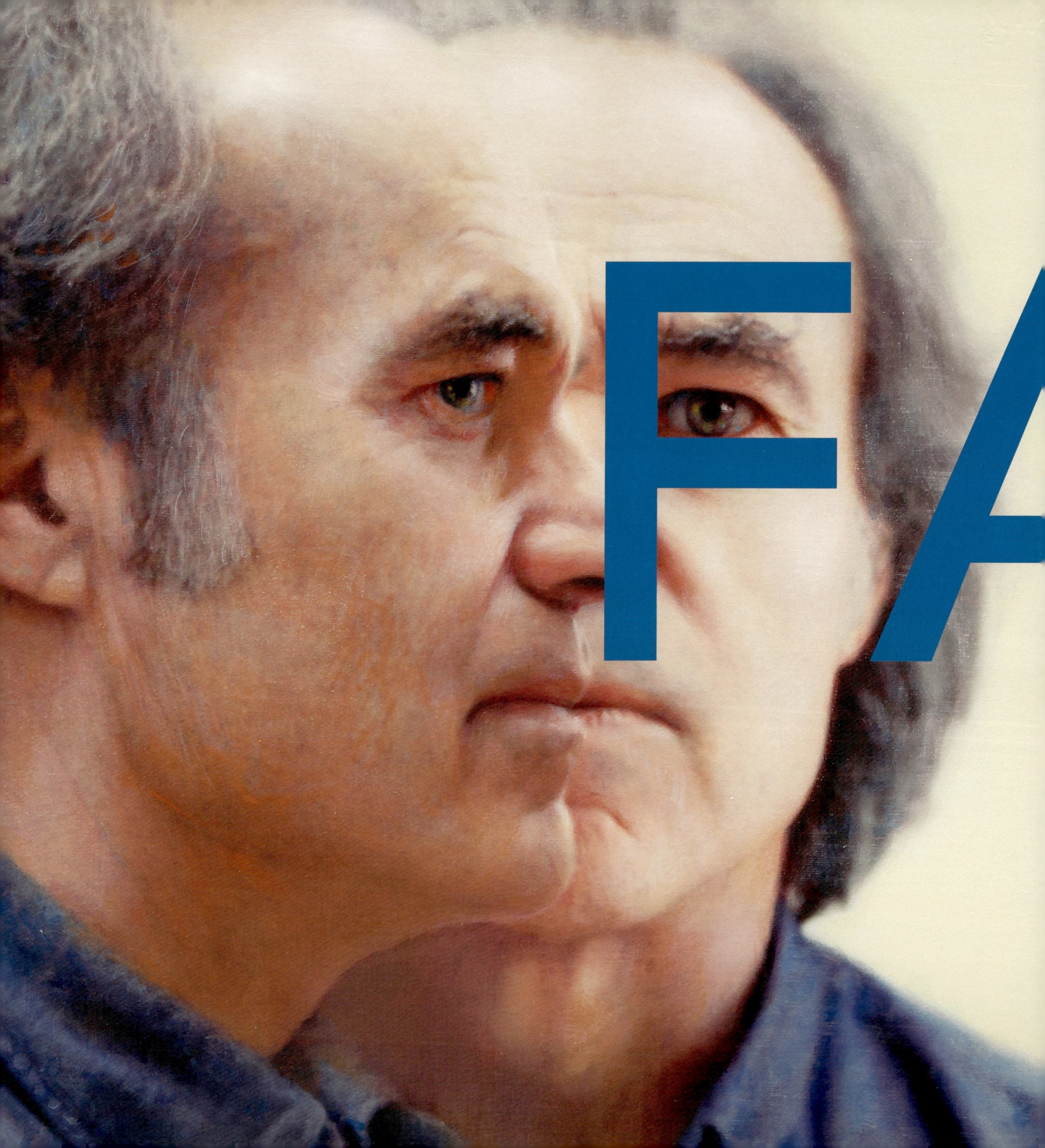
FA

Barnaby Conrad III · B. R. Gilbert · Andrei Ustinov · Lindsey W. Kouvaris

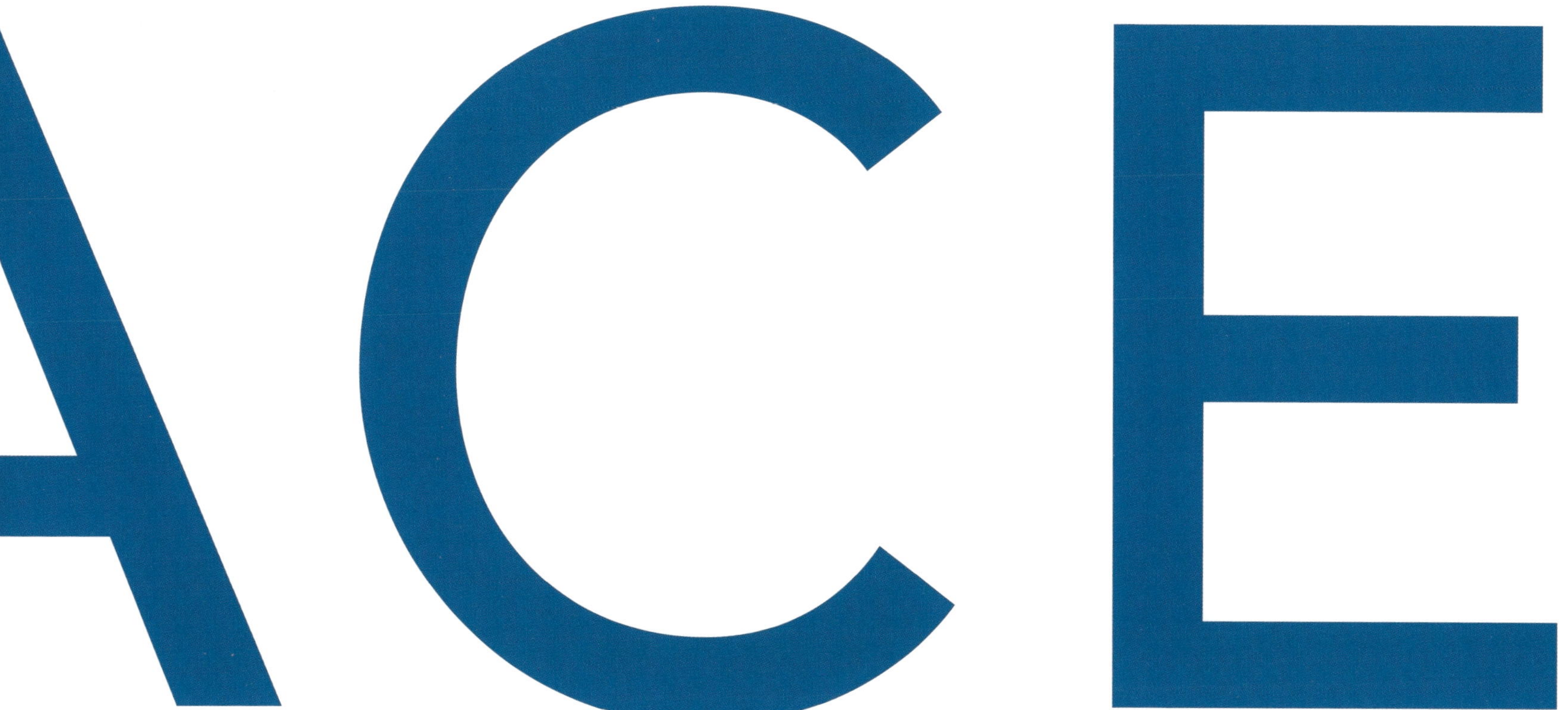

ACE

PORTRAITS BY **VALENTIN POPOV**

Conversation with **Peter Selz**

with a foreword by Rebecca M. Schapp

Soft Skull Press

Library of Congress Control Number: 2017933158
ISBN: 978-1-59376-651-1

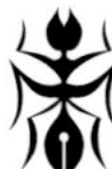

SOFT SKULL PRESS
1140 Broadway, Suite 704
New York, NY 10001
www.softskull.com

Printed in China

Distributed by Publishers Group West

10 9 8 7 6 5 4 3 2 1

This catalog has been published in conjunction with the exhibition
FACE: Portraits by Valentin Popov
organized by the de Saisset Museum, Santa Clara University
February 22–March 17, 2013, and April 12–June 30, 2013

de Saisset Museum Staff:
Rebecca M. Schapp, Director
Lauren Baines, Assistant Director
Stephanie Battle, Collections Manager
Chris Sicat, Exhibition Project Coordinator
Megan Watt, Senior Administrative Assistant
and de Saisset Museum student staff

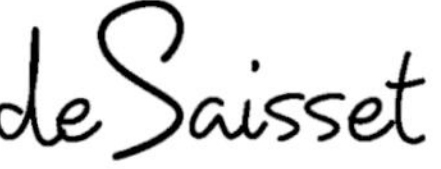

de Saisset Museum
Santa Clara University
500 El Camino Real
Santa Clara, CA 95053-0550
www.scu.edu/desaisset

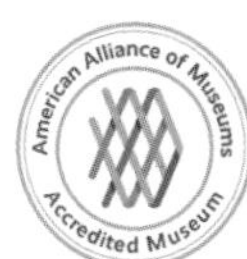

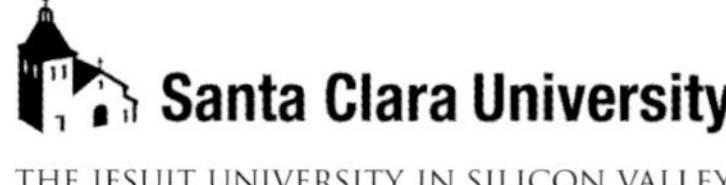

All photography is by Valentin Popov except p. 54 Moshic Mor,
p. 76 family, p. 130 Julie Soefer, p. 146 Victor Sydorenko,
and p. 180 Christina and Francisco Rodriguez.

Unless otherwise indicated, all paintings
are from private collections.

Front cover: *Caroline Talbert*, 2013 (detail, page 29)
Back cover: *Rob Nilsson*, 2013 (detail, page 7)
Frontispiece: *Charlie Winton*, 2016 (detail, page 103)
Facing: *From . . . to . . .* , 2009 (detail, page 217)

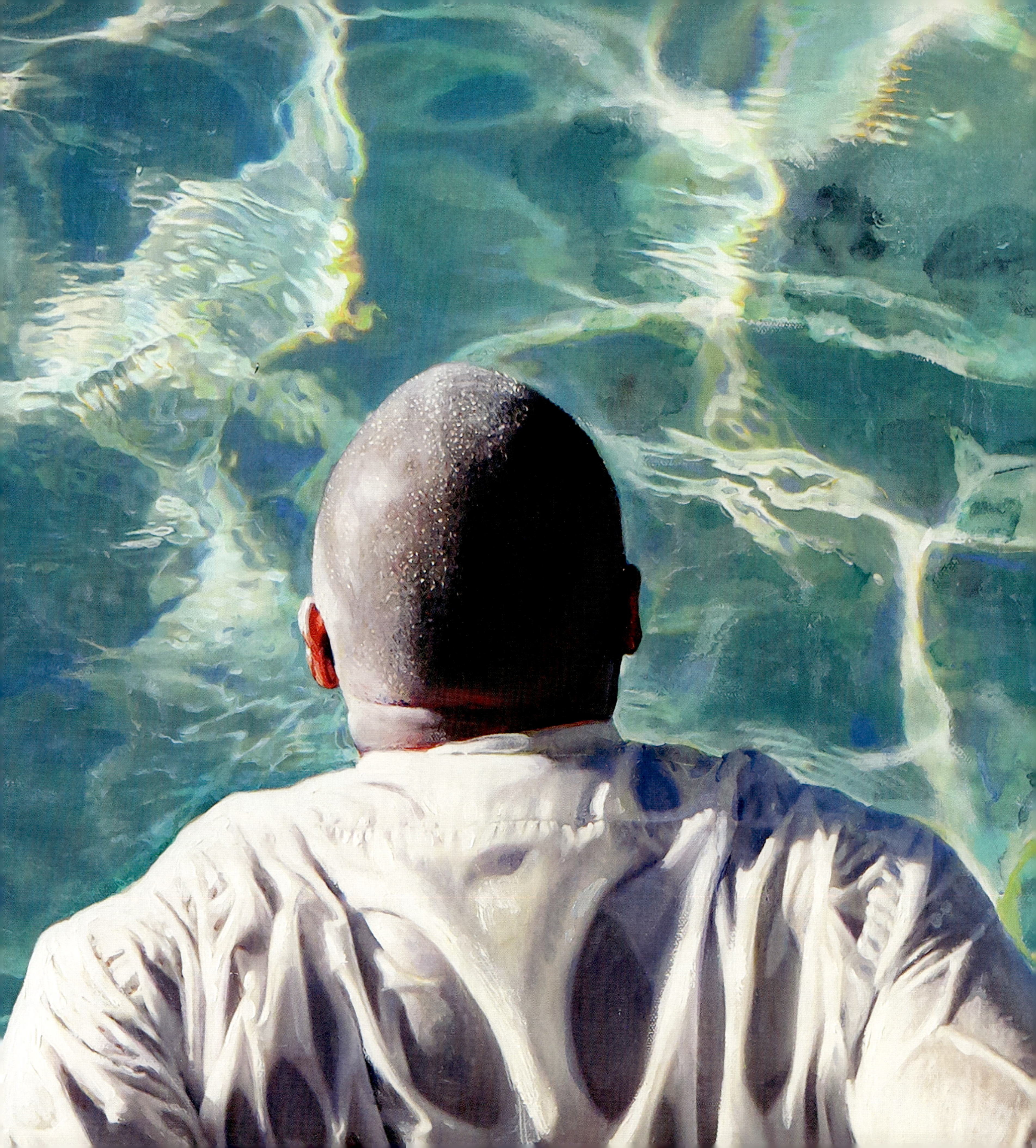

CONTENTS

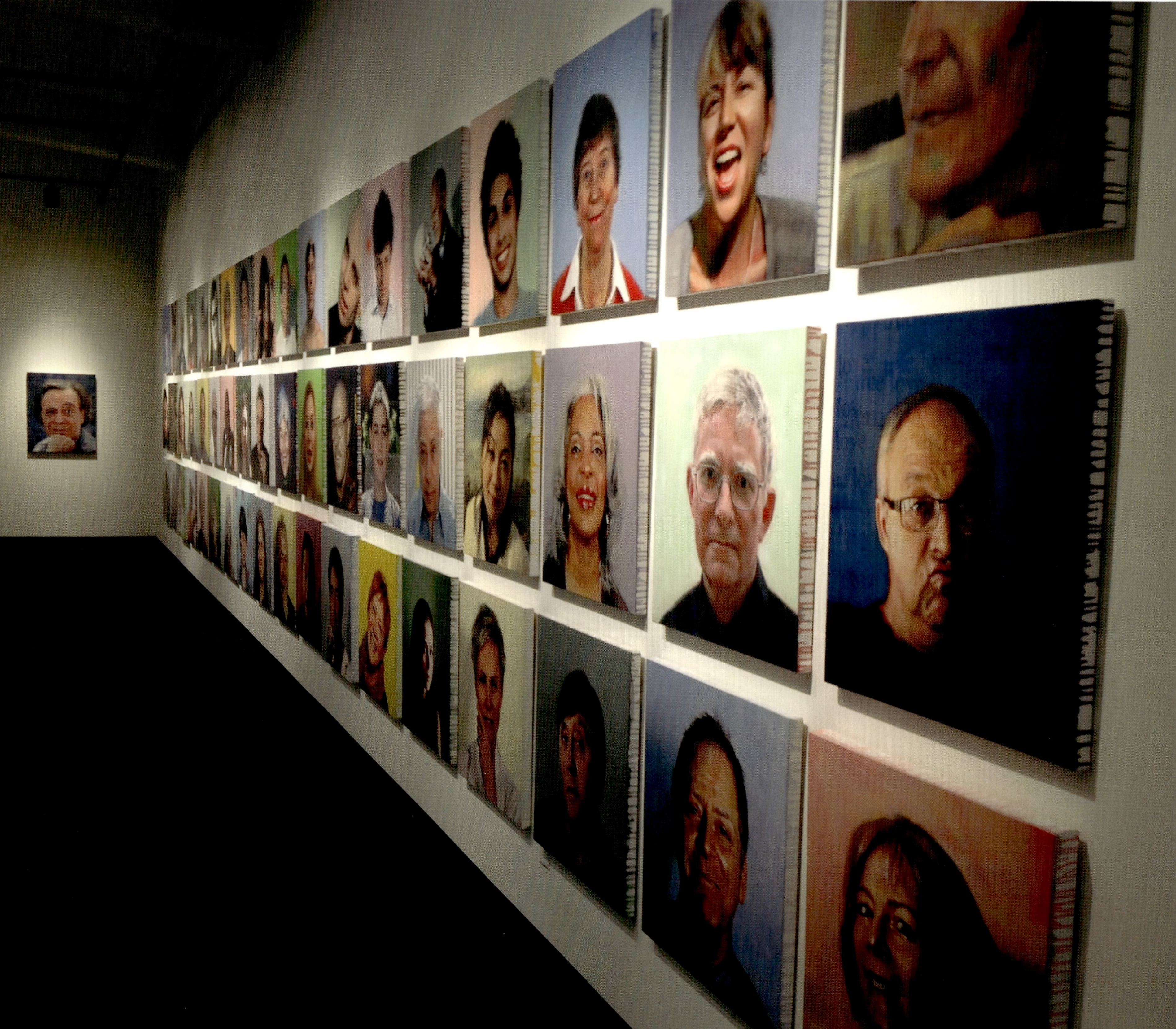

FOREWORD

Twenty-three years ago, I visited Valentin Popov's studio in Emeryville, California, for the first time. Since then, we have forged a relationship that has produced two one-person exhibitions, the second of which has inspired this much-anticipated book, *FACE*. Popov and I work through our collaborations by expressing our differences, battling our way through the issues, and always emerging focused on the *actual work*. That is what matters—the work itself.

In 1994 we presented our first collaboration, the exhibition *Romantic Cynicism*, which included Popov's *Saint Batman* series. The work incorporated Russian religious icons and classical art history iconography, which Popov altered and manipulated to create new meaning. It seemed as if Popov questioned whether or not our cultural icons had become Batman and if we, as a society, were desperately searching for a new hero, role model, and/or savior. Popov was born and raised in Kiev, Ukraine, where the romantic theory of giving and taking was soon dissolved, and he wondered if America might be lost, needy, and searching. His work spoke about the state of humanity and civilization within American pop culture. He forced us to think about our heroes: were they the right heroes? Are these topics relevant today? They certainly were then.

Our second exhibition, *FACE: Portraits by Valentin Popov*, was inspired by Andy Warhol, an artist known for popular images of mass-produced objects. Popov presented Warhol's idea to document the faces of friends and individuals who have influenced the artist's life in some way. The 2013 exhibition presented seventy-two out of one hundred proposed *FACE* portraits, created within a two-year time span; now, four years later, the remaining forty-six portraits have been completed. This publication celebrates the comprehensive one hundred works.

When viewing Popov's portraits, one immediately appreciates his exceptional technique and formal accuracy. His style can be loose and painterly, yet very precise and photorealistic. We are committed to his work, which displays skill that is both masterful and breathtaking.

We are excited about bringing Popov's art to our viewers, and many individuals have contributed to this project. We appreciate their support. Please enjoy these exceptional *FACE* portraits and the astonishingly unique personalities they depict.

Rebecca M. Schapp
Director
de Saisset Museum, Santa Clara University

The 2013 de Saisset Museum exhibition *FACE: Portraits by Valentin Popov*

SPONSORS

Roger Evans

Charles Winton

Monica Gerard-Sharp

Ali E. Wambold

Kevin and Rosemary McNeely

Paula Z. Kirkeby

de Saisset Museum,
Santa Clara University

Modernism Inc., San Francisco

The Baum Foundation

Zenko Foundation

Pierre-Yann Guidetti

Maureen Labro

hope & grace wines

Jon Witkin

Blair and Janice Savidge

Christina and Paco Rodriguez

Cecilia and Xavier Cervantes

Tancredi F. D'Amore

Katherine Smith Knudsen

Schumacher Family Trust

FACE

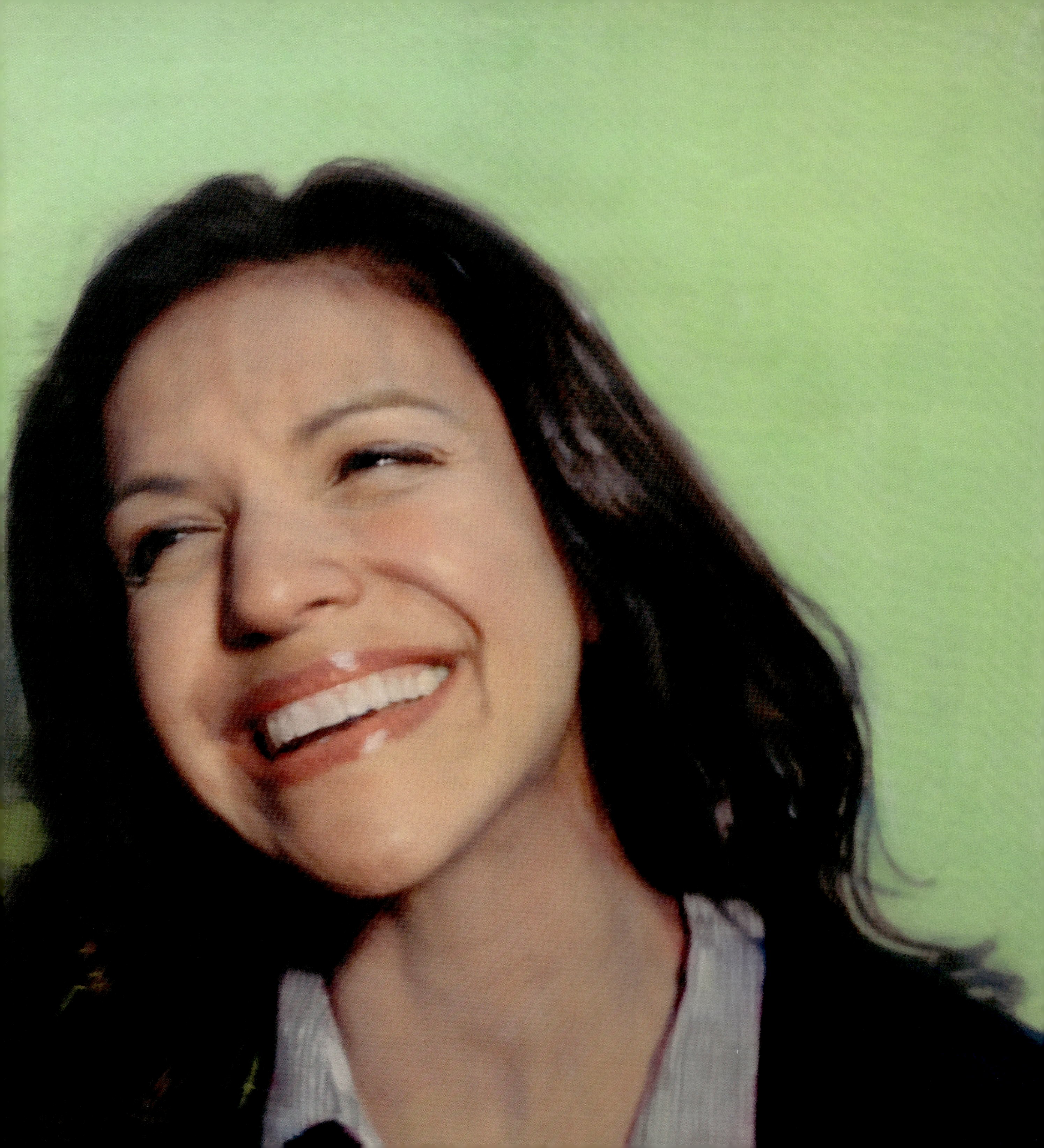

Lindsey W. Kouvaris

FACE PORTRAITS BY VALENTIN POPOV

The average person will meet thousands of people in a lifetime—classmates, teammates, colleagues, friends of friends, even seatmates on a plane, bus, or subway. They, in turn, will encounter hundreds, if not thousands, more—strangers passing in the airport, countless store clerks and restaurant waitstaff, and fellow attendees at a concert, performance, or museum exhibition. Each person carries with him or her distinguishing characteristics in facial features as defining as the uniqueness of an artist's brushstroke. When viewed in this context, Valentin Popov's latest series of portraits takes on added meaning. His pieces reveal more than strikingly convincing likenesses; they reflect true-life experience.

A visit to the gallery during the de Saisset Museum's 2013 showing of *FACE: Portraits by Valentin Popov* was nothing short of impressive. Standing in the midst of the museum's largest exhibition space, visitors were confronted by, perhaps even overwhelmed by, the presence of seventy-two faces. Roughly one-third of the paintings were created between 2005 and 2011. Rendered in various scales and dimensions, these pieces set the stage for a newer series of portraits. The majority of the works in the exhibition—fifty-four, to be exact—were completed within a two-year span between 2011 and 2013 (several arriving at the museum with paint still drying). Painted at a consistent size of 28 × 26 inches, the fifty-four portraits were installed in a floor-to-ceiling grid along the museum's longest wall. The installation was a landscape of Popov's life: friends, neighbors, collectors, artists, and curators. Though the portraits represented some of the significant players in the artist's life, they were perhaps unfamiliar faces to most museum visitors. Nonetheless, the inherent power of the viewing experience remained. The impact resulted from the cumulative effect of encountering a magnitude of painted portraits rather than from the satisfaction of being able to effortlessly identify all of the players.

This is not to devalue the individuality of Popov's sitters. Indeed, the artist pays close attention to the spirit of the individual, and his style of rendering— ranging from loose and painterly to precisely detailed

CATALINA CISNEROS, 2014
Oil on canvas, 28 × 26 in.

and almost photorealistic—reflects the personalities of the sitters as seen through his eyes. On a few occasions, the portraits include a personal object that hints at the sitter's profession or interests.

The *FACE* series and the museum's 2013 installation were inspired by an idea proposed by Andy Warhol. Perhaps best known for his popular images of mass-produced objects, such as Brillo boxes and Campbell's soup cans, Warhol also actively documented the faces of his friends and acquaintances through photographs and silk screen paintings, many of which were produced at a uniform scale of 40 × 40 inches. Warhol spoke of mounting an exhibition of portraits in which the walls would be filled from top to bottom with faces. Though Warhol was never able to realize his vision, Popov has used the idea as a jumping-off point.

Since the de Saisset Museum held the 2013 exhibition, Popov has continued to add new portraits and personalities to his cast of characters. The sizes of the painted images have begun to morph. No longer constraining himself to the almost square 28 × 26-inch canvases, Popov is working at a larger scale, bringing his sitters to life-size or beyond-life-size dimensions.

Though this publication has been produced well after the de Saisset Museum's exhibition, the book closely reflects the spirit of the show. To peruse these pages and encounter Popov's masterfully painted portraits is akin to the experience of viewing them in a gallery—at once breathtaking and overwhelming. The range of styles used to execute the works speaks of Popov's technical skills and formal abilities. In some instances the texture of the paint is tactile and beautiful in a way that makes you want to reach out and touch it. In other cases, you will swear you are looking at a photograph, such is the success of his photorealistic renderings.

The de Saisset Museum has enjoyed a long relationship with Valentin Popov. It began more than two decades ago with the planning of *Romantic Cynicism*, a solo exhibition mounted in 1994. Since that time, the museum has collected paintings, prints, and multimedia works by Popov and has continued to periodically exhibit his pieces in group exhibitions. *FACE* served as his second solo exhibition and most recent show at the de Saisset.

The museum's connection with Popov has been both purposeful and fruitful. Located at the heart of Santa Clara University's campus, the de Saisset Museum focuses strongly on education. Though the museum pursues a wide variety of educational initiatives, one of the main areas of emphasis is the enhancement of collegiate learning for the students on our campus. Through our programming we aim to open dialogue about important contemporary issues, encourage appreciation of the fine arts, and inspire critical thinking and creative problem solving. Popov's work touches on these goals in a variety of ways.

To know Valentin Popov is to know a man whose creative mind never shuts down. A new project is always on the horizon, and each series is executed with the same careful thought and skillful craftsmanship as the last. Popov is not an artist who often makes art for art's sake, though he is certainly capable of doing so. His works are grounded in observations of contemporary society, often laced with socio-political commentary, some of which is quite pointed and some of which is much more tacitly stated. His pieces speak to the lineage of art history, yet often vacillate between homage and parody. He regularly employs humor, irony, or Pop as a way to convey his messages. The use of these elements can create a more palatable entry into a difficult subject, but it can also reinforce a point, calling additional attention to an observation or commentary.

The paintings in Popov's *FACE* series are not loaded with commentary the way some of his other works may be, but they are not without art historical meaning and contemporary observation. The art of portraiture reaches back centuries, drawing on a long and varied lineage. The project itself, as referenced above, draws directly on the ideas of the legendary American Pop artist Andy Warhol. The concept of the series also touches upon the changing nature of human relationships in the face of modern technology. Smart phones, email, and the Internet make person-to-person contact less essential than it once was. In contrast to the sterility of modern communication, the proliferation of faces in this series—people with whom the artist comes into regular personal contact—calls attention to the importance of human relationships and the value of personal connections.

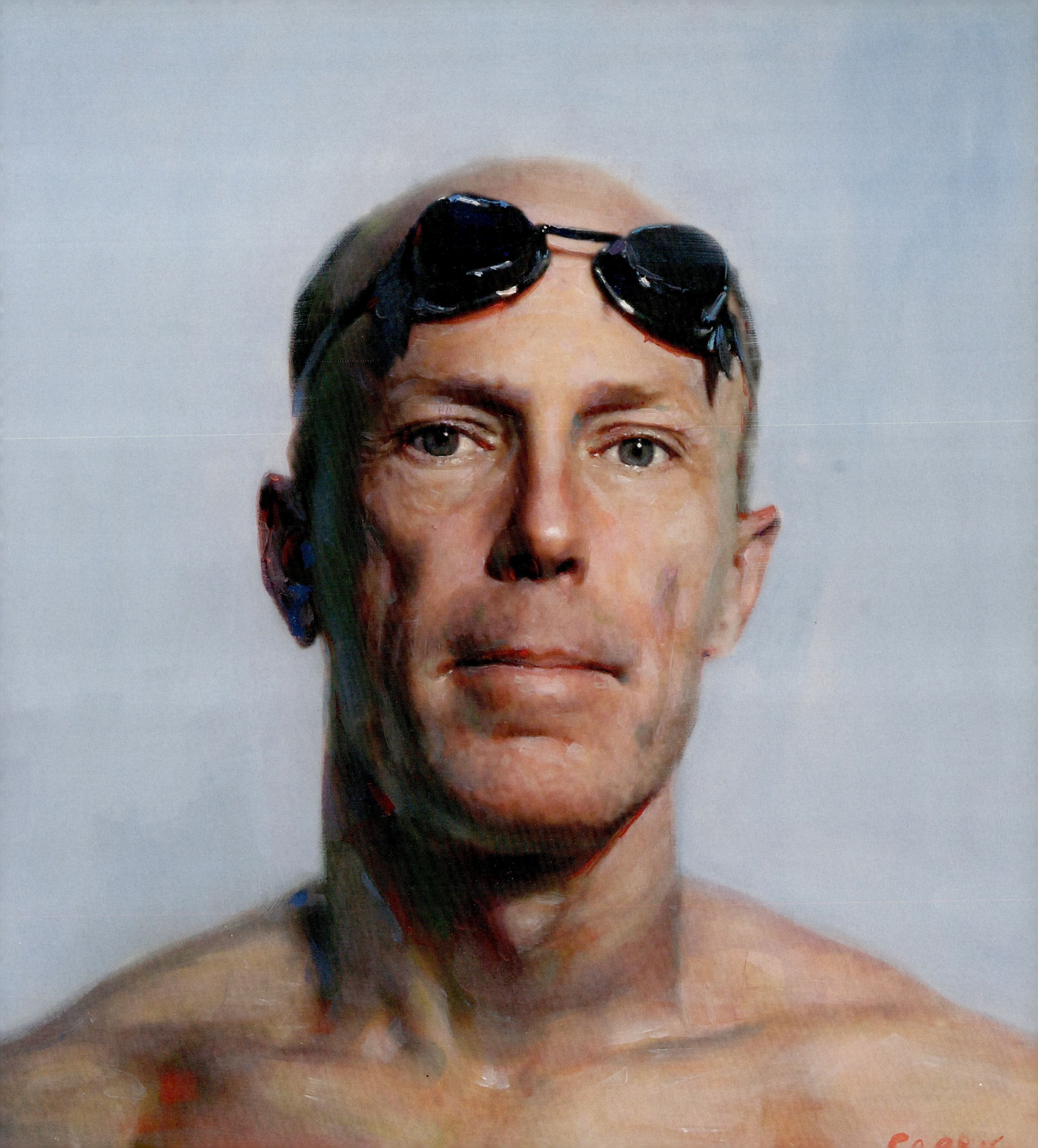

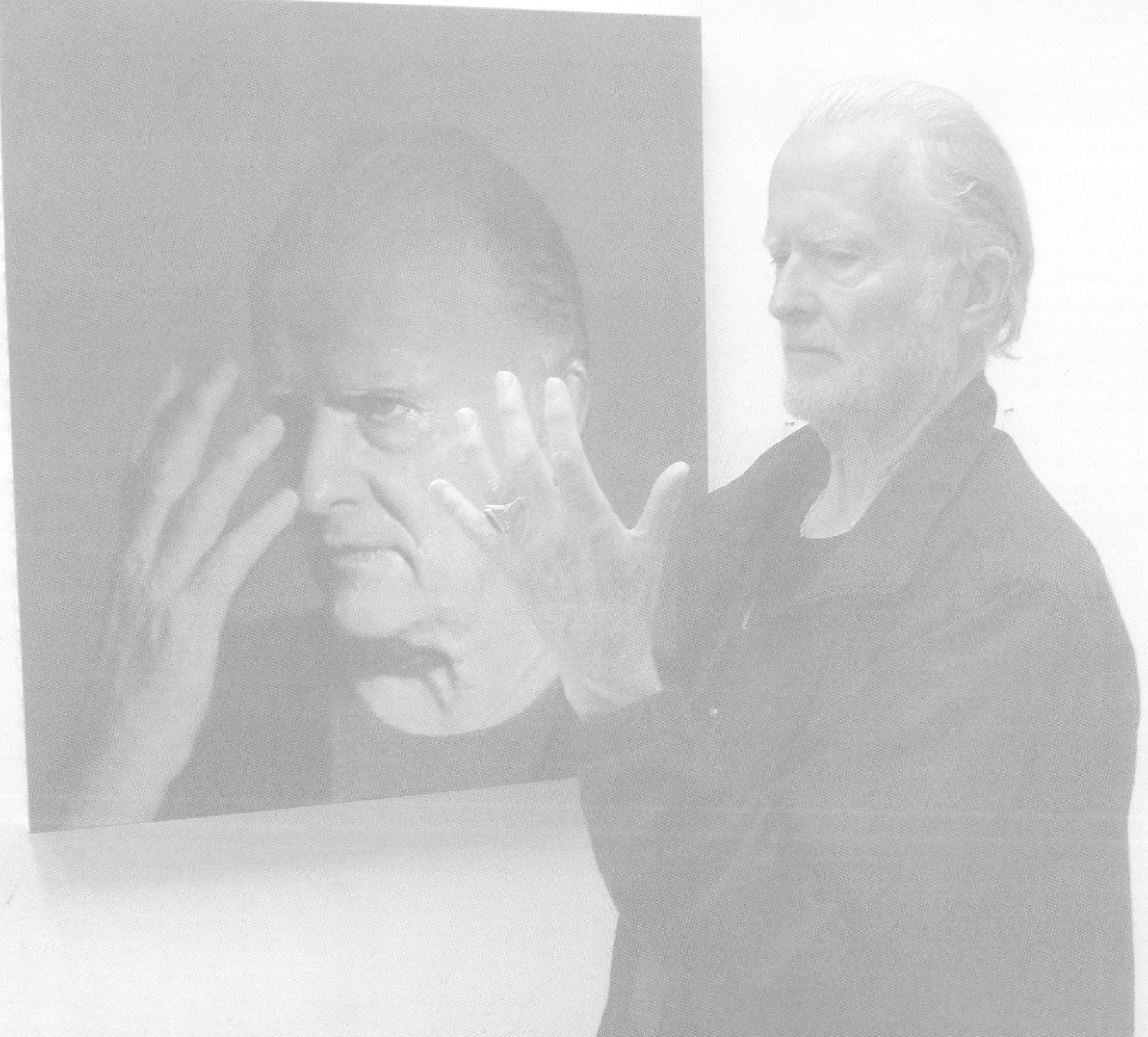

I was taken by the green background. It was neither dour nor cheerful; it gave the picture gravitas. And the painting made me uneasy, just as the source photo had done. But now I saw why. The hand in front of the face might be seen as a kind of proclaimer, a gesture of emphasis. But to me, it's the opposite. I see fear there. To me, the hand protects what the subject might not want to admit. There may be a slyness there, as well; not so flattering, but undeniable. I felt that I had been "found out" by the picture, and this was not comfortable.

ROB NILSSON

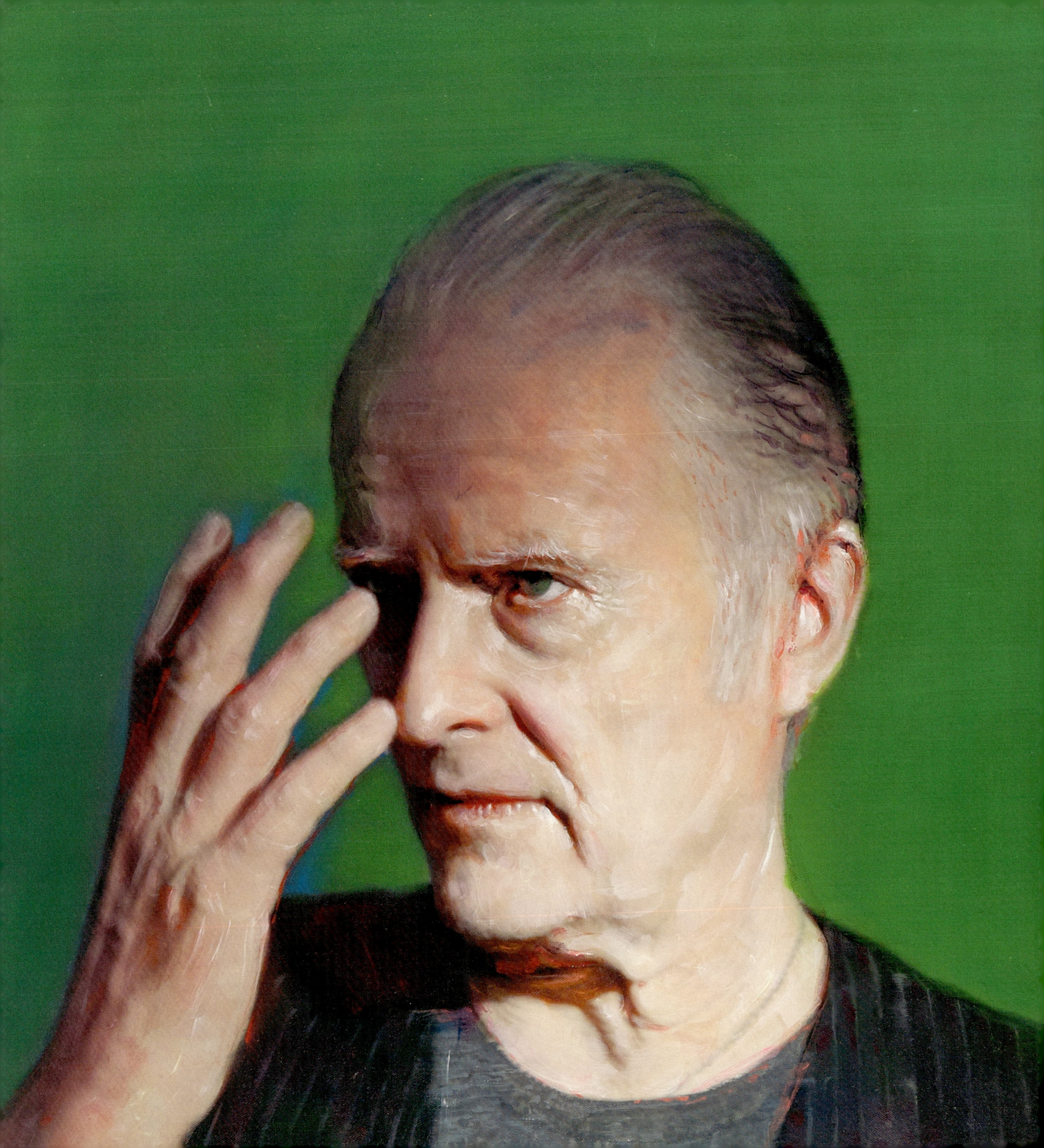

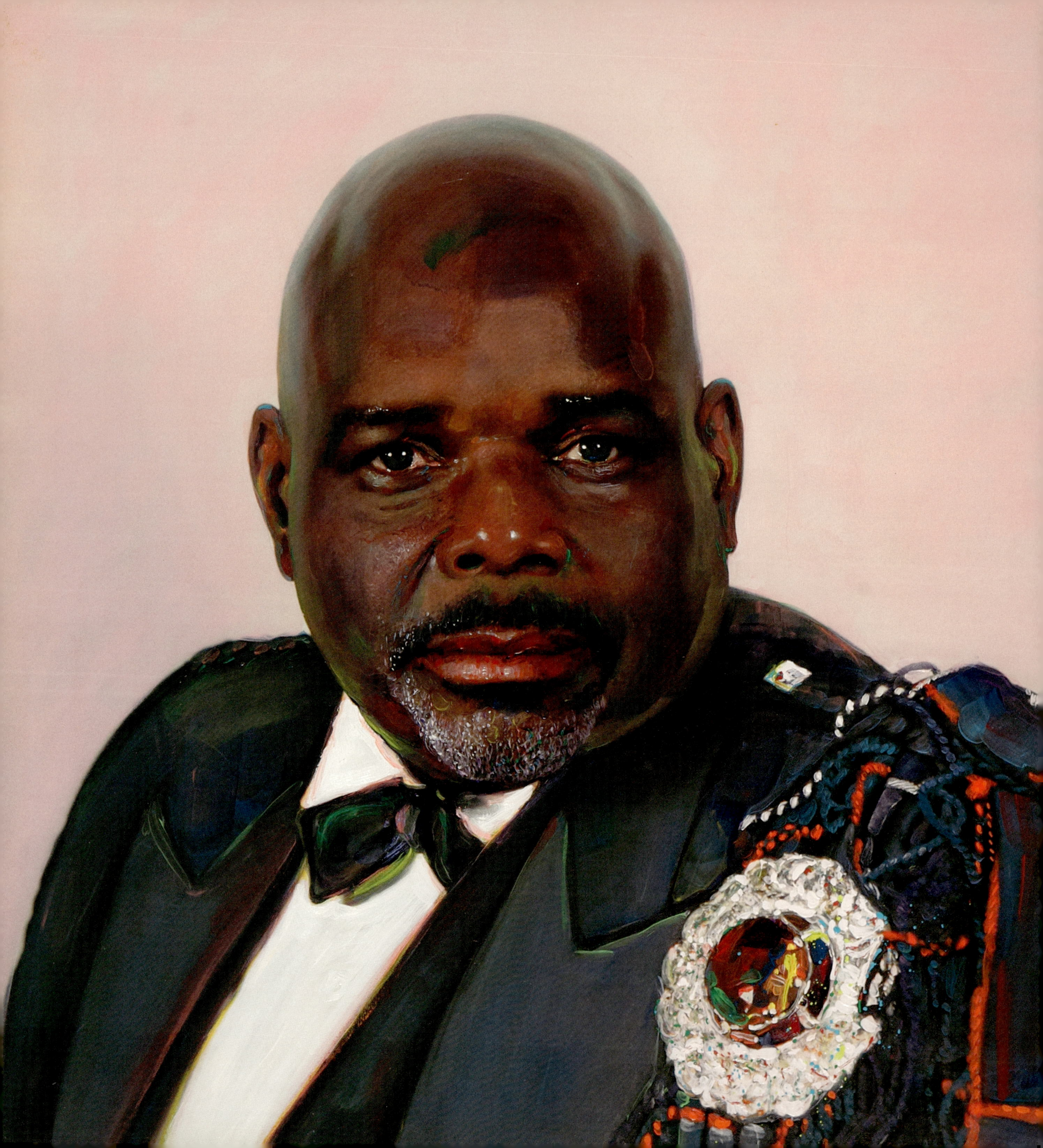

I was delighted to be graciously approached by Valentin Popov, who asked to paint my portrait. We decided to portray me as a modern gentleman dressed in traditional Scottish formal black tie, with jacket, kilt, and amethyst-and-silver brooch clasping a draped plaid off one shoulder.

I am pleased with its execution. I particularly appreciate his playful brushstrokes, which seem to dance across the canvas with masterful precision and whose flirtatious qualities are evident in the glint in my sharply focused eyes and the florid repoussé of the large silver brooch. Valentin's discriminate shade of pink coral for the background propels my image forward with grand exuberance, enhancing a distinctly dominant presence wherever the painting is hung.

OLIVER V. GLOVER

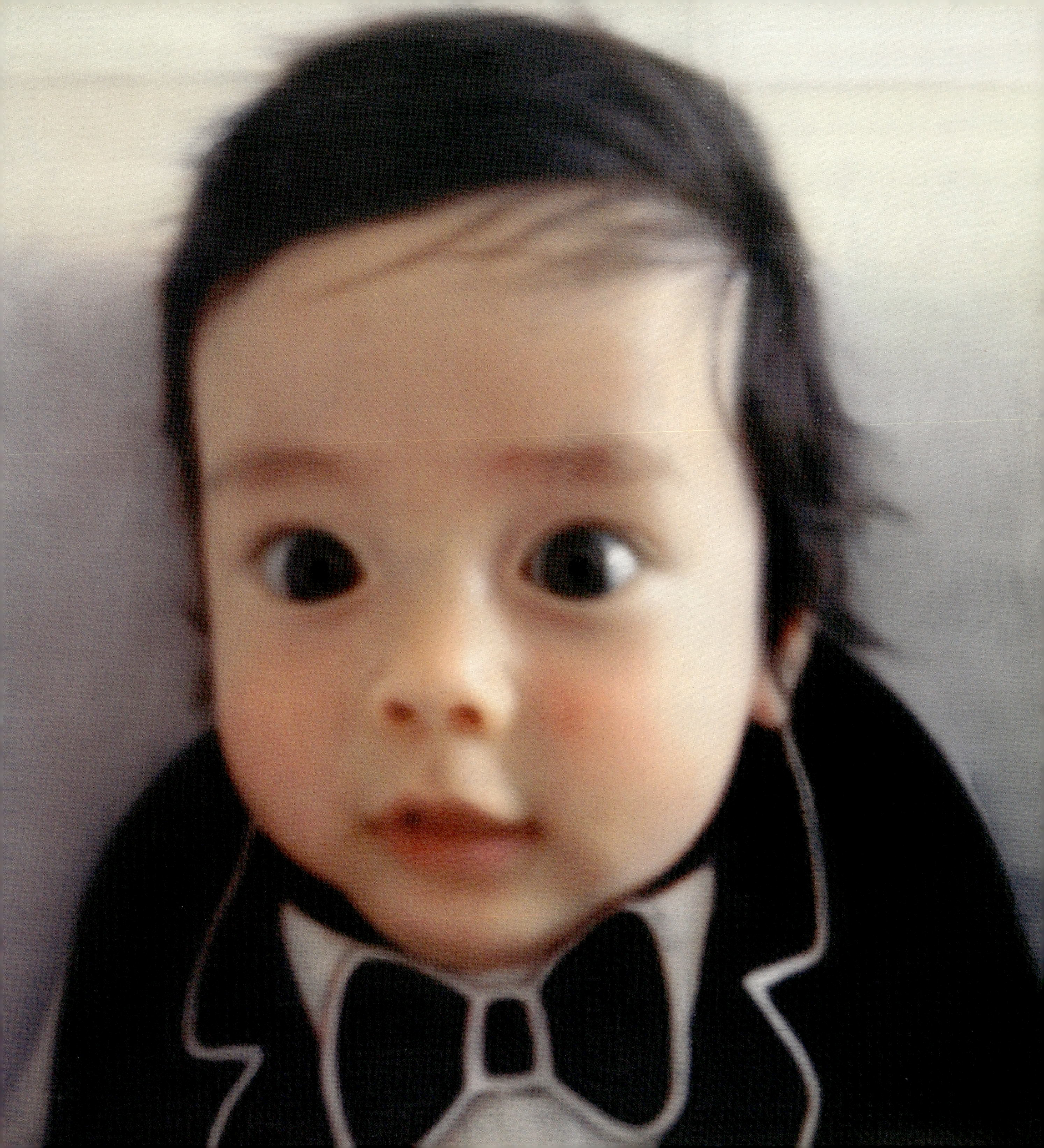

ROGER EVANS, 2015
Oil on canvas, 44 × 40 in.

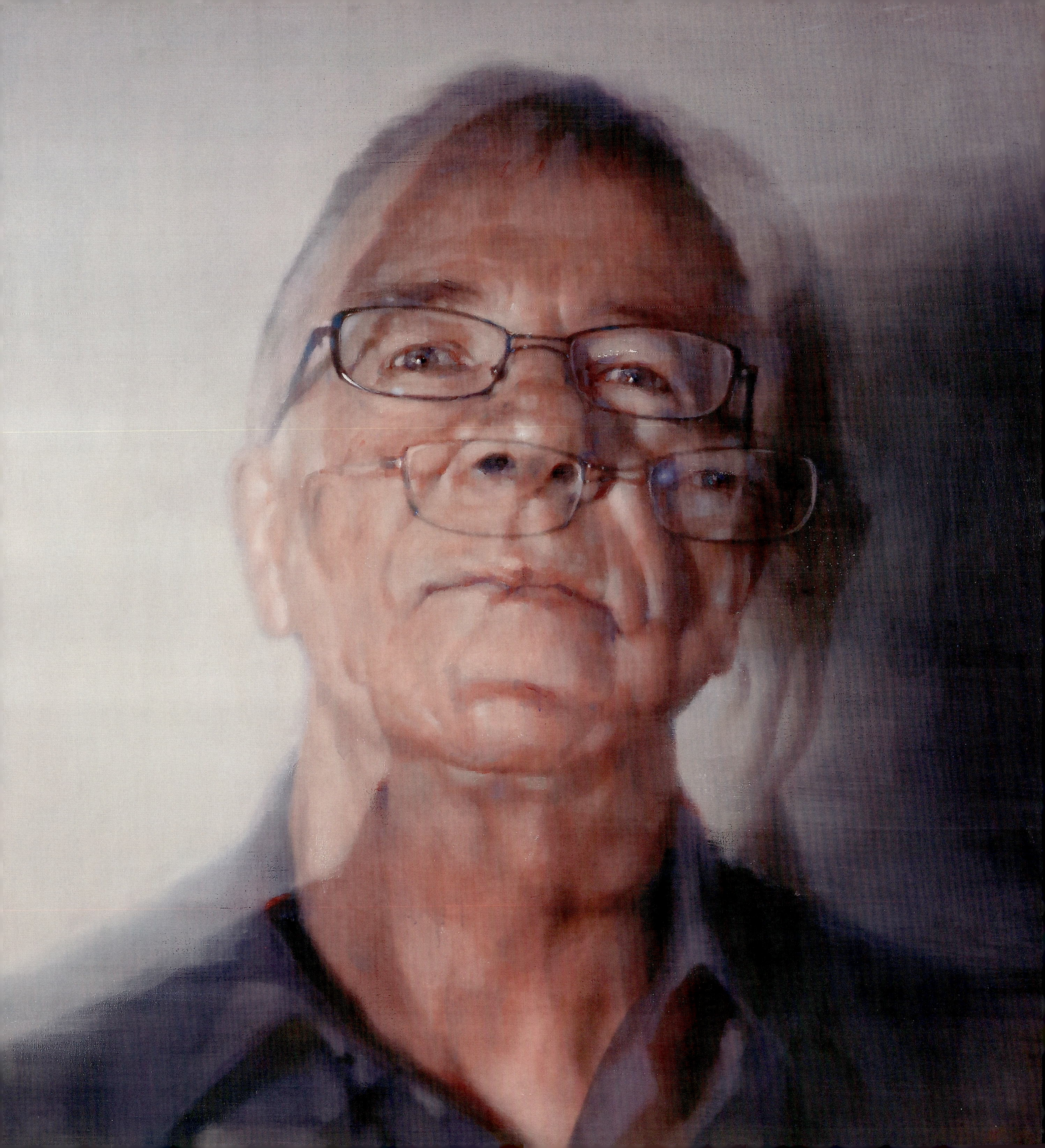

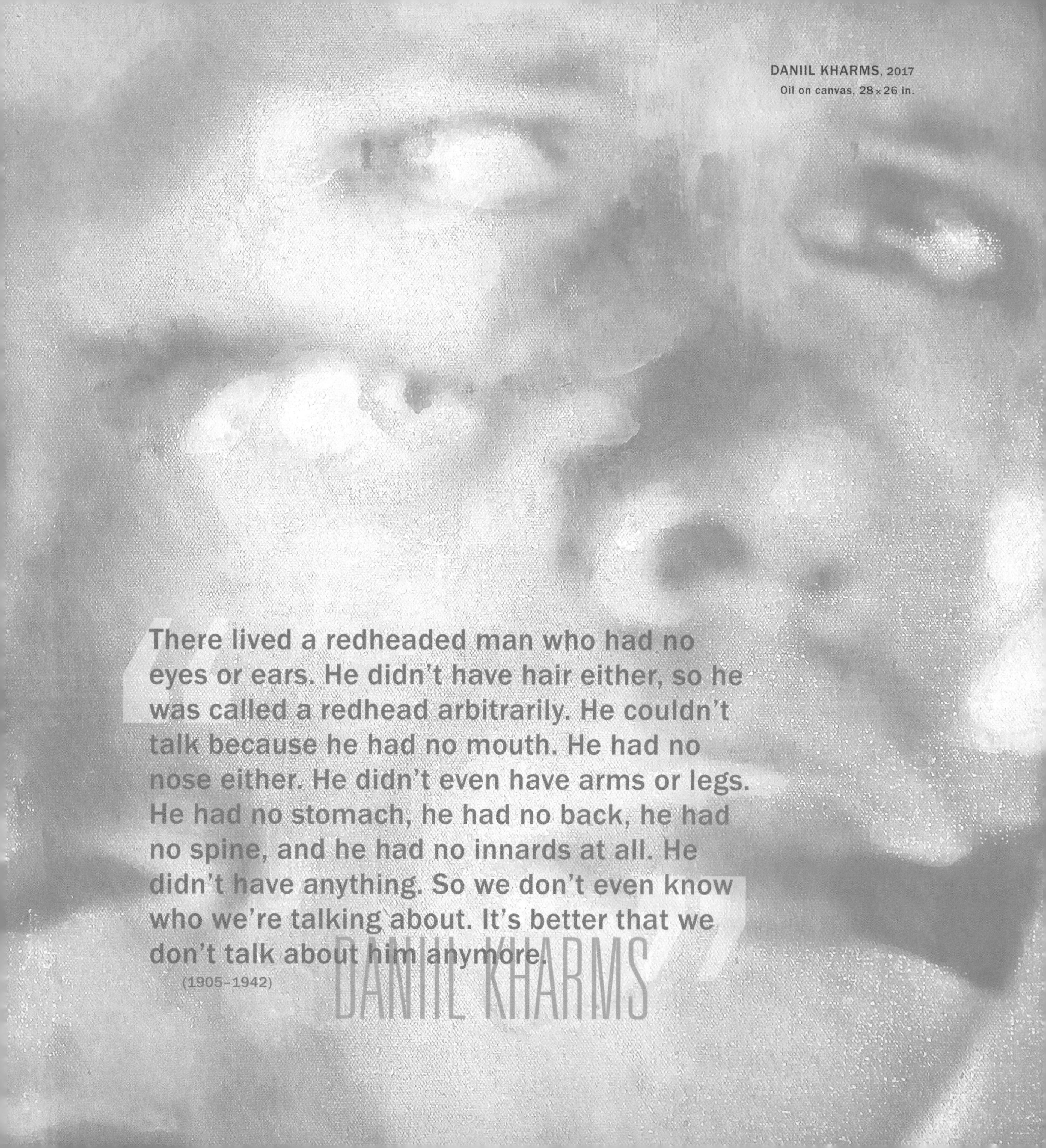

There lived a redheaded man who had no eyes or ears. He didn't have hair either, so he was called a redhead arbitrarily. He couldn't talk because he had no mouth. He had no nose either. He didn't even have arms or legs. He had no stomach, he had no back, he had no spine, and he had no innards at all. He didn't have anything. So we don't even know who we're talking about. It's better that we don't talk about him anymore.

(1905–1942)

DANIIL KHARMS

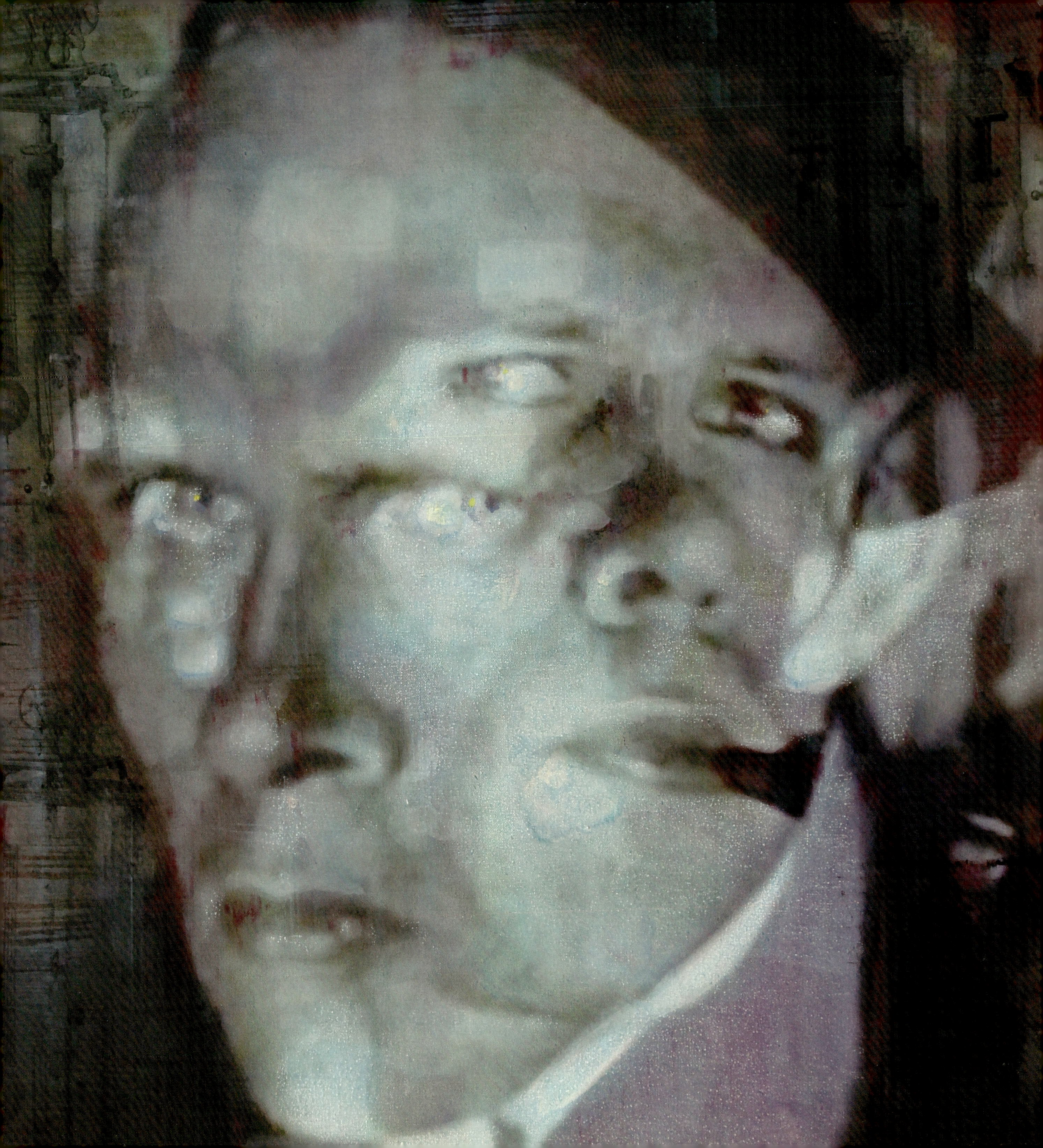

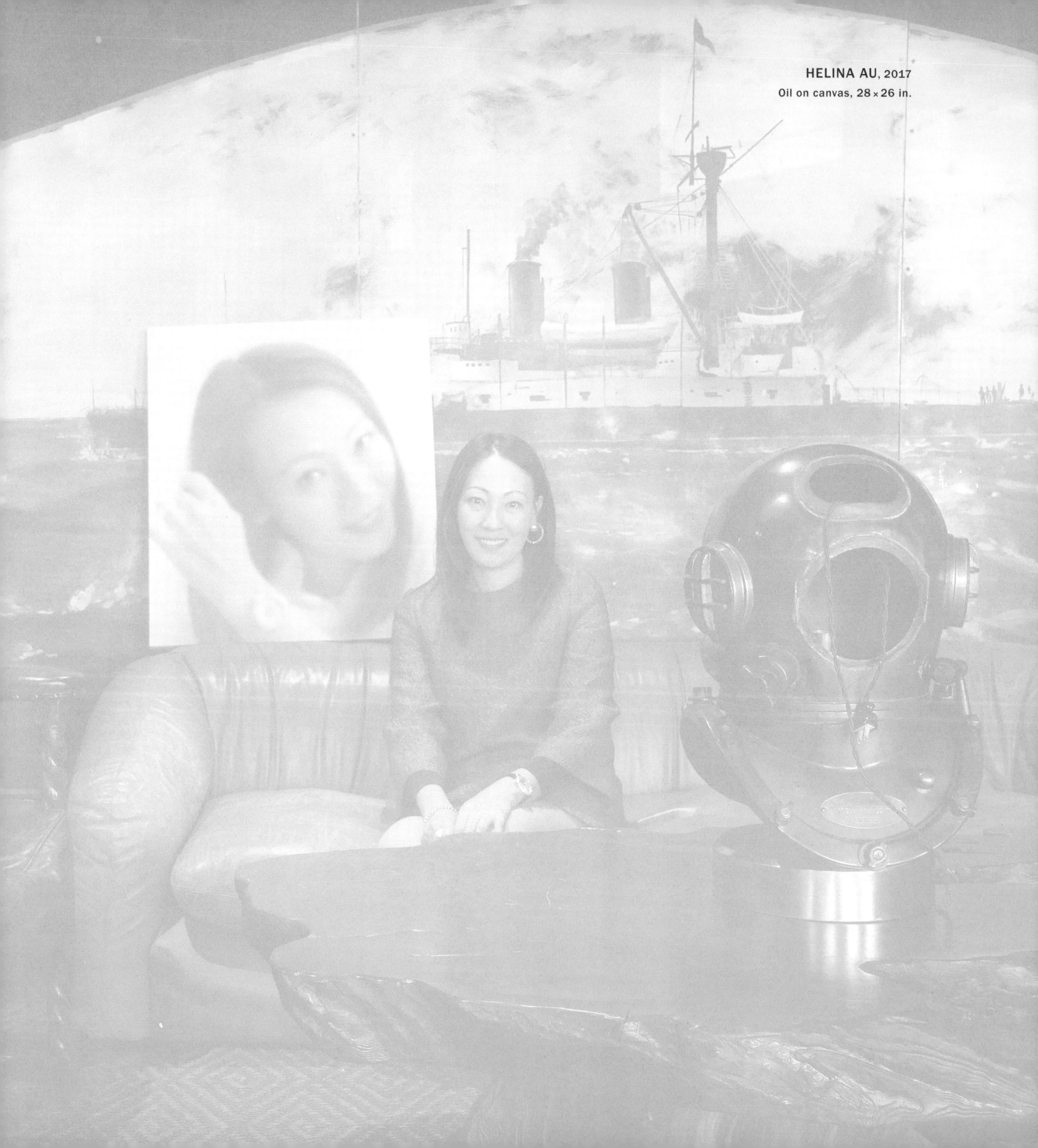

HELINA AU, 2017
Oil on canvas, 28 × 26 in.

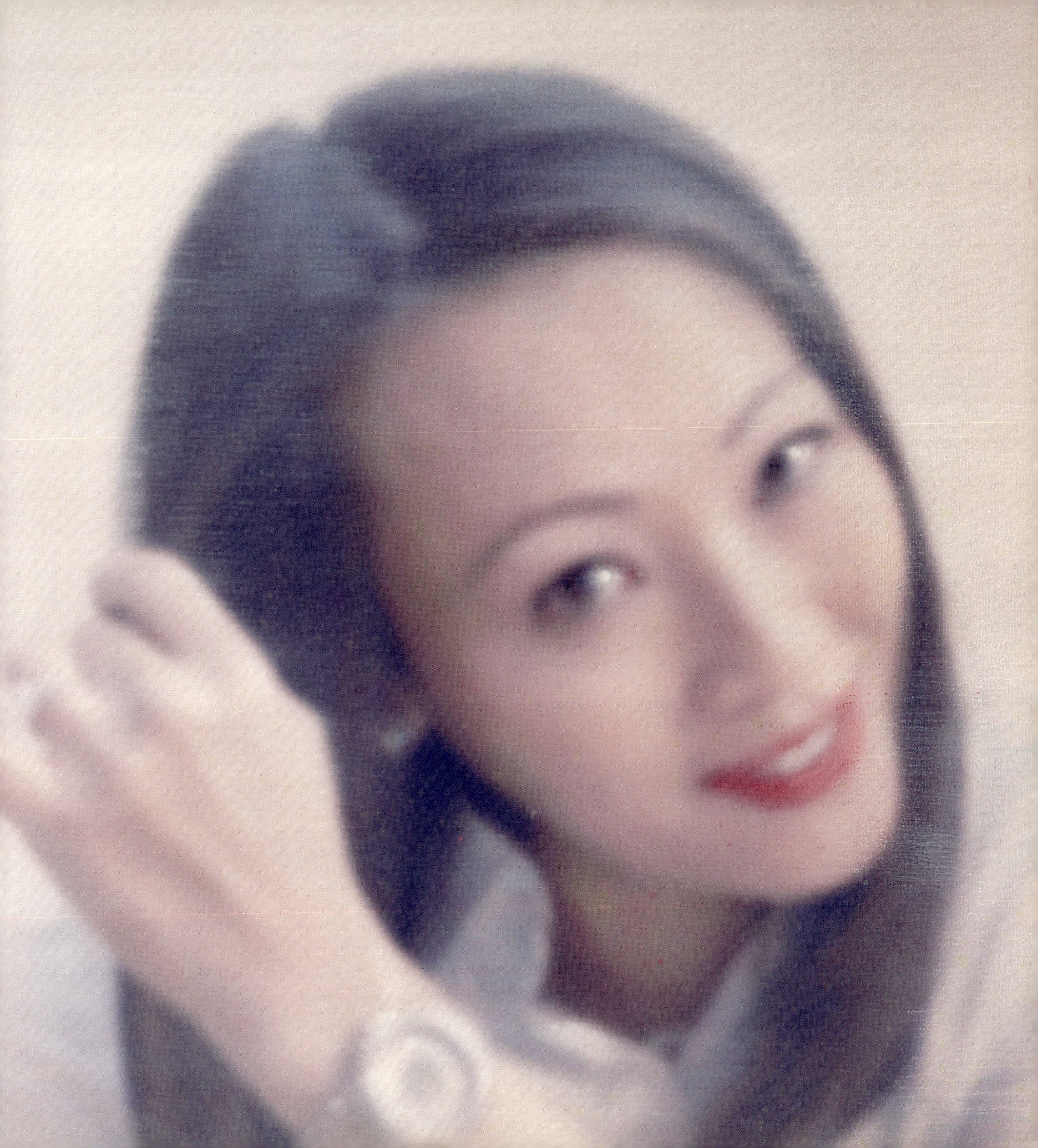

PETER SELZ VALENTIN POPOV

PETER SELZ Why are you drawn to practice portraiture?

VALENTIN POPOV In his novel *The Picture of Dorian Gray*, Oscar Wilde advances the concept that a portrait, on some level, captures the soul. This idea is shared by autochthonic cultures around the world. Accordingly, members of these cultures shun photography and all other forms of artificially engendered personal resemblance. In the final analysis, the impulse to produce portraiture can best be described as *soul-mapping* plotted with pigment and canvas.

PS History has witnessed a smorgasbord of portrait styles, from the candor of Frans Hals to the fragmentations of Georges Braque and the distortions of Otto Dix; from Greco-Roman formalism to the casual caricatures and sixty-second silhouettes of sidewalk sketchers. Are all these categories of portraiture legitimate subgenres or simply different stylistic departures?

VP As a postmodernist, I assimilate, quote, and appropriate from all of art history. My challenge is to absorb and apply this multifaceted discourse and distill from it an effective synthesis.

PS If we begin with the premise that portraiture generally employs one of two types of dimensional field—the face or the full-length figure—would it be fair to say that facial portraiture has its foundations in psychological study whereas full-length composition tends to bear witness to a sitter's social position or glamorous profession or, in the case of the nude, revolves around physical beauty, often sensual beauty, for its own sake?

VP Generally, this is true, except that portraiture's parameters are considerably more expansive than these two models would suggest. In the first place, the face is a landscape of a different order, with its own unique topography fraught with signposts. Full-length portraits, whether contrived or candid, frequently feature their own set of signposts— allegorical elements such as emblems of office, hereditary coats of arms, and occupational costume. Additionally, the subject of the portrait may be flanked by all manner of symbolic objects and ancillary personages—idealized visual indicators of personal interests, hobbies, or membership—the mythicized contents coaxed from each sitter's closet of secrets.

PS With regard to portrait painting, is the conventional nomenclature—*grotesque, elegant, fidelity, sublime*—still adequate for today's critical discourse, especially considering how many traditional approaches to painting have been reworked beyond recognition?

VP The old vocabulary is still in currency and is still useful. Recent decades have ushered in new terminology such as *ahistoric* and *social snapshot*. It's all valid. It all works.

PS Is it reasonable to think that any portrait can be reduced to absolute analysis?

VP Not really, because the creative process behind portraiture is complex and demands the exercise of the artist's interpretive faculties. The act of portrait making involves numerous levels of filtration and refinement, both technically and psychologically. Dissection of a work of art through critical analysis is itself highly interpretive. Certain objective standards and traditional aesthetic yardsticks can be used to measure a work of art in terms of brushwork and lighting and so on, but, ultimately, traits such as meaning, accuracy, effectiveness, "truth," and "beauty" are matters susceptible to a broad latitude of assessment.

PS In the classical paradigm, the purpose of portraiture was, for the most part, to ennoble, dignify, exalt. Modern portraiture emphasizes emotional depth and inner states. While the old approach relied on strictest realism, the advent of Modernism has seen the emergence of radical new methodology. Do you think that the guidelines governing traditional portraiture are irreconcilable with contemporary experiments in the genre?

VP From antiquity to the present day, portraiture has always enjoyed its quota of subtle novelty. More important is the dynamic stemming from the symbiotic relationship between artist and sitter and the dialectic between finished portrait and perceiver.

PS Some of the numbers in the present series might almost be described as "double-exposure" portraits since they juxtapose frontal and profile views or are structured in other unusual configurations. In quite a few cases, heads have haloes of ambient imagery, are enveloped by color washes, filmy textural skeins, and tissues of diaphanous graphics. Is this purely for decorative effect, or does it serve another purpose?

VP As with certain allegorical paintings of bygone eras, some of the portraits in the *FACE* series are surrounded by image fields which, while decorative, are more importantly concerned with establishing symbolic and emblematic references pertinent to the life of the sitter in a sort of visual subnarrative. The ones you call the double-exposure compositions represent experimentation intended to expand perspective and enlarge the vocabulary of portraiture.

PS You were born in Kiev, Ukraine, and spent your formative years there during the Soviet era. How did you end up in California?

VP The first time I came to the United States, I sent my work to the Museum of Modern Art in San Francisco, and I got a call from John Caldwell, who used to be the curator there. He said, "I like your work. Would you like to meet with me?" I went; I saw him. He suggested two galleries as prospective showplaces for my work. The first of them—Artists Alpert Gallery, which later became Olga Dollar Gallery—gave me a one-man show. I visited San Francisco again six months later and stayed for half a year. It was right after *Squeak*, during a difficult period for the economy. My art dealer brought me to Magnolia Press, and I showed them my work, and they were very impressed with my printing skills because I was an expert printmaker. I'm still a good printmaker. I know how to make plates, how to rinse the plates—and I was hired for two months. I was working as a printer at Magnolia Press, and one of the artists affiliated with the press was John Register, one of Martin Muller's artists. I became very good friends with John. John was a wonderful painter, but he had no experience with printmaking and didn't have the first idea about how to make etchings. At a certain point I asked him if I could help him do some engraving, and he said, "Yes, but make sure Martin doesn't know about it." Twenty years later, when Martin was at my place, long after John [was] deceased, I asked Martin, "Did you know that I was engraving some of John's images?" Martin said, "I know." So, after meeting and interacting with a lot of people over a number of years, Martin drew me aside as I was leaving one of his openings and declared, "I admire your work and would like to show it." So, the courtship took about fifteen years, at the end of which I formalized my relationship with Martin's Modernism gallery in San Francisco.

PS So, early on, you were primarily making prints rather than painting?

VP My father was an artist. He was a professor of art and was chief of an institutional print department. He was my teacher, and we were living in an apartment building surrounded by his fellow academicians. Lots of my friends from childhood were children of artists. After a lengthy, convoluted process, I became very engaged with art, and I enrolled in art school. Next, I advanced to the Academy of Fine Arts. The first two years there you pursue general education. You study painting, watercolor, drawing. In the third year, you decide exactly what you want to do. I was in the graphic department, and I chose to specialize in book illustration because it offered an easy escape from painting tractors, people digging potatoes in fields, heroic factory workers, and the rest of the standard iconography of Social Realism. Instead, I was creating illustrations to accompany Japanese poetry and a wide-ranging assortment of masterpieces of other world literature.

PS What kind of art did your father do?

VP He was a major figure in his field. He was a lithographer. He was one of the best draftsmen I've ever met. His forte was exquisite realistic art based on the French School done with simple graphite pencil. He and his fellow practitioners didn't use erasers. They used little pills rolled from lumps of soft bread. At my house, I have incredible drawings of his models when he was a student during the 1950s, before I was born. It was very realistic imagery. He was also doing some illustration. In the latter part of his career, he got very much involved with watercolors and also did lots of pastels. He was a great traveler. Because he was an art professor, he was able to travel in the era before perestroika. He visited France, India. He got around. He spent a lifetime traveling and drawing, drawing and traveling.

PS How familiar were you at that time with the great Russian abstract painters—Tatlin, Gabo, Rodchenko, Kandinsky, Malevich?

VP When I was growing up, they weren't promoted very much since Social Realism was the dominant aesthetic doctrine. Later, of course, things changed. Artists like Malevich and Tatlin came to attract attention again. I remember a book about 1920s Russian art that was going the rounds. Everyone was so proud of what was done in the twenties—a great time! All the same, the official focus remained Social Realism. Then again, because we were living in a country beset by harsh climate and subject to cold winters, we read a lot and went to see a lot of movies. You couldn't buy certain books, but otherwise inaccessible volumes were printed and distributed as Xerox. And these ad hoc publications were hardbound. There were many such "books," often by noted writers, which you couldn't buy in stores. So these materials were circulating hand to hand. Of course, being art students, we all were a little revolutionary. So we were digging up all the information we could about Western art. We discovered Jackson Pollock, for example, and devoured everything we could find about him. We cherished a very famous magazine called *Foreign Literature* that was all but impossible to obtain, but to which, because my father was a professor, he was able to subscribe. You needed to be a member of *the charmed circle* just to get it. In its pages you could read wonderful German literature and numerous American writers. This is how I was exposed to a broad roster of contemporary authors from around the world.

PS Things like Philip Roth and Salinger: were they translated into Russian?

VP Some of them, yes, but it was always difficult to find translations. There was an underground network of translators typing up Russian versions then "mass producing" limited editions, which were passed from hand to hand. This was how most of this information was moving at that particular point.

PS You were able to visit the United Kingdom and California several times and then return to Russia. Was that problematical?

VP That traveling phase took place during Gorbachev's "opening up," which is probably the only reason I was able to go to the United States; and during that time, I had the good fortune to meet a wonderful couple, Sheila Cohen and Richard Mazze, both professors of medicine from Stanford University. They invited me to visit them and sent me a fake invitation from Stanford offering me a show.

Consequently, I was able to prepare exit documents through the Association of Fine Art, and because I was invited in connection with a cultural enterprise, I was allowed to come to the States. This was practically my first trip out of the Soviet Union in my lifetime, and I was a grown man, thirty-three years old. This was the age at which Jesus was crucified. I jumped at the chance.

PS And then you made all these incredible paintings based on literature and all that?

VP My fantasy world.

PS Your fantasy world, as you say.

VP Well, if you're wondering about the origins of my fantasy world, I can tell you. My father had a splendid library, and I pored over his art books, savoring the wonderful pictures. When I was four years old, I came across a Dürer book, and one of the images blew my mind: the famous *Knight, Death, and the Devil.* Somehow, on my Russian child's imagination, it had an incredible impact. Five years ago, I found this print in an auction. And now I have it in my entry hall. Every day, when I walk into my house, I see this image—the scariest and most exciting image of my childhood. It's all a bit surreal. Because, you know, you live in a country saturated with fantasy and dreams. The reality was sour. But the lucky part was that when I was growing up, it was also quite a special time. We went to space. I remember staying up late and listening to the radio when Sputnik got going. We felt so proud to be Russians—that we, you know, were first into space. Then, later, because art was such a big part of the culture, I had what was probably the best education available. I have eighteen years of professional education, including scholarships and grants. After six years at the Academy of Fine Art, I spent an additional three years as a fellow of the Academy of Fine Artists of the USSR and was given a studio, money to live on, art supplies, an acid room where I could print; and as soon as this expired, I got a grant from another association. It was superb, actually.

PS You know, we are so misinformed in America. We did not know how terrible things were in the Soviet Union, and nobody could do anything. Even so, we were brainwashed against Russia. We didn't know about the positive things that were going on, either. You could freely go to school and study what you wanted to study.

VP And it was free. You had to be good. It was competitive.

PS And it was supported by the state.

VP Yeah! It was competitive, you needed to be good, but it was free. And it was very, very good education. It all collapsed when everything became capitalist. . . . Now it has become like a free market economy. I guess when I was growing up, we, to some extent, were under political pressure to produce great art. Of course, later it changed to economic pressure. When the old system collapsed, you needed to support yourself, so artists who were otherwise serious and high-minded found themselves turning commercial from a need to sell to tourists simply in order to survive.

PS Growing up in Russian Ukraine, were there any great difficulties between Ukraine and Russia?

VP Not really, because it was all the same country, although I always felt a little weird living in Ukraine since my family all the way around is Russian. And I spoke three dialects of Ukrainian. After independence, Ukrainians became much more nationalistic. On my third trip to the States, I decided to stay in the USA. When I lived in Ukraine, I always felt a little out of place, anyway. I was an artist, I was romantic, I was shy, I was Russian. Everyone was speaking English or Russian. Everybody. The official language was Russian. After six years in the States, after securing a green card, I went to Kiev and attended a reception, where I

bumped into a couple of childhood friends from Russian families, which was very . . .

PS When was this?

VP It was probably 1996.

PS Where was this?

VP In Kiev. When I came back to Kiev, I saw friends from my childhood, from Russian families, wearing Ukrainian shirts and conversing in Ukrainian, which they barely spoke when they lived there in the old days. For me it was slightly shocking, because it's become a totally nationalistic country.

PS Are the two languages similar?

VP Yes and no. I would compare them to languages that are similar but distinct, like Spanish and Italian. Ukrainian and Russian are both Slavic languages, but even Western Ukrainian, which has lots of Polish, Hungarian, and German words, sometimes can be barely understood by Eastern Ukrainians. So it's a pretty complicated situation. Lots of similar words, but Russians can scarcely understand Ukrainians.

PS Then you settled in California. What were the first works you did after you settled here?

VP One of the first things that happened to me in California was being selected to participate in the Djerassi Foundation artist-in-residence program in Woodside, and I spent a month holed up there painting. In my monograph there is actually a whole chapter titled "Early California" that touches on the transition I underwent from my early painting phase in Russia and the work I did based on memories of my trip to the Vatican to the explosion of colors I unleashed when I moved to California. Suddenly, my subject matter changed, and everything became colorful. Ukraine settled into a dimly remembered haze of black and white. When I started working at Magnolia, I learned about handmade paper, so I started doing collages. My work underwent a dramatic transformation. And I remember I was having an interview with some Russian newspaper in New York, and the interviewer asked me, "Are you becoming too Californian too fast?" And I joked that if Paul Gauguin were interviewed in Paris, they would probably ask him if he had become too Tahitian! We absorb our surroundings, so I guess my visual sensibilities were fascinated by all the wonderful museums, the glories of nature, the freedom to paint anything without ideological constraint and to explore new subject matter—lots of things changed.

PS The imagination that I see here is just truly, truly remarkable! The combination of great imagination and superb execution. All these wonderful images . . .

VP I still draw inspiration from my childhood. My favorite artists then are still my favorites now: Goya, Hieronymus Bosch, Dürer. With Dürer, you know, there's always been some kind of Nordic mystery. When I was a child, and for some time thereafter, I read lots of fairytales. Those by the Brothers Grimm had a strong influence on me. I could relate to fairytales and their allegorical messages because I lived with the contradiction of the romanticized and idealized theory of Communism and the day-to-day reality of a country built on the fake promise of a beautiful theory which never worked.

PS What about Saint Batman? How did you get to Saint Batman?

VP Shortly after I came to the States, my prints got bigger and bigger. Then, with the help of Paula Kirkeby, I moved to monotypes. Paula suggested a few projects. They proved highly productive, and I became sold on the new medium. Meanwhile, my black-and-white prints became larger all the time, and I started painting huge mounted and aluminum paintings. They looked like gigantic color etchings because I still was not able to depart from my printmaking. It was like I was unleashed in a field of paint.

Two things happened: I did my first big California show with the title *Romantic Cynicism*, a self-designated style. Saint Batman was part of this. I saw this startling duality from my childhood, where I grew up in a country framed by the most amazing romantic theory—Communism—a system under which everybody works as much as he can and takes as much as he needs—in theory, amazing; but in reality, beyond terrifying! Think of the Second World War and how many people were killed by Stalin. The country was enveloped in the most romantic theory and subjected to the most cynical execution of it. And I've always had this wandering, slightly ironic eye, about which I would probably say I am a romantic who refused to grow up, and still does. Then you see the cynical aspect. So I did a series of paintings tinged with a delicate, romantic, French sensibility of high beauty interposed with snatches of limericks— vintage American limericks. Then I stumbled on Batman.

What happened with Batman was that when I moved to the States, after growing up in a pretty much antireligious country, I remained at first deeply atheistic, but gradually new feelings began to stir. I still don't like organized religion, although I consider myself a spiritual person. There was a point of insight. I discovered religion and superheroes simultaneously. I never came across Batman in the Soviet Union. I'd never heard of this character. When I was thirty-three, I discovered Batman, Batman movies, and all the related memorabilia in the States. I found Batman fascinating because he is not an invisible, supernatural entity, but a human who tries to punish everybody. He is acting as a god; he is deciding who is right and who is wrong and punishing people. So I decided religion is so confusing, especially the multiplicity of contrasting religions, so why not believe in the religion of childhood? And Batman is a type of Jesus, a savior, so I created a number of icons featuring the baby Batman and Madonna. And this joke embodied some serious truths. In making the first icons, I incorporated wood carved in Ukraine by people who have been making icons for centuries, applied gesso and gold leaf, and scratched off the images and painted over them. I was covering real eighteenth- and nineteenth-century Russian icons with gold and silver leaf and painting, in place of the traditional holy personages, the figures of Superman, Wonder Woman, and Batman.

PS Then you did these wonderful cities, especially Venice and Berlin—lights, lights, lights.

VP Yeah, and, actually, during most of my early history in the States, I was doing collages. I was also doing gigantic paintings on aluminum. I was doing monotypes, and I never did oil paintings. I wasn't interested in oils until probably less than a decade ago. And the reason why I started doing them was because I discovered this idea of unfocused, fuzzy imagery, and by now, being officially American, I was able to travel everywhere, so, like a kid in a candy store, I explored Paris, Berlin, Italy, Venice. I exploded with painting. Then I got my first show with Martin. Finally I got myself into a style with which Martin could resonate, and we started working together. Then what happened was that my painting moved from being totally out of focus into sharper and sharper, amazingly focused, super-realistic work—and as I continue, my focus has once again disappeared into the fog. So I guess the creative surges carry my imagery in and out of focus wherever the muse may lead, as they say.

After my travel paintings, I started making portraits, and this was a very interesting development. I had never, ever before had the slightest interest in painting portraits. Not that I was all bad at it. . . . I was pleased with the first formal portrait I ever did, which was one of Carl Djerassi. It was one of his ideas. Carl's face is so unusual—simultaneously serious and funny. When I painted Carl, I painted two faces of the same guy on one canvas divided by a little line. Then I painted a portrait of Alexander Djerassi, Carl's grandson, my friend Dale Djerassi's son. Next I painted some portraits here and there, and, you know, it grows on you and becomes something which you think you really want to do, and you start formulating images in your head—so does the sitter—your fantasy of who you want to be. Painting portraits is something I learned, through experience, I'm actually very good with, but, oddly enough, I never was formerly interested in doing. Once I started, though, my resistance dropped, and I just went bananas with portraiture.

Then I was struck by this crazy idea, based on an unrealized concept of Andy Warhol, to paint portraits of uniform size and paint like hundreds of them and hang them so as to cover one enormous space or one huge wall—just to see all those faces— or one room full of them. I remember I painted maybe a dozen faces when I invited Rebecca Schapp, director of the de Saisset Museum, to come to my studio to see the work, and I shared with her the plan I had for a monster display of faces. She came right before Christmas with Lindsey Kouvaris, curator, and I showed them my work and said, "This is what I'm thinking." She liked it. She said, "Let us get back to you; let us think about it." She contacted me shortly and said, "We really like the idea. You have two choices: we can give you a show in four years, which is normally how far out we schedule exhibitions, or we can give you a show in a year. We could move something. We'll find you a good spot." I didn't want to wait four years, so I said, "Okay." My decision backfired on me a little bit, because I had committed myself to producing sixty paintings in a year's time, so it was kind of crazy, close to impossible. I felt totally overworked, but then I had a wonderful show, and I continue working on it.

I continue to collaborate with filmmaker Celik Kayalar, who has done a wonderful documentary about the show. I'm working with Christine Taylor on a book based on the project titled *FACE*. I'm looking for a new venue for the next installment of the show, and this time I'm planning to do a hundred portraits like those shown at de Saisset, plus now including some increased to a larger size. I want to paint at least three gigantic faces, each of them maybe like six feet high. The project covers a cross-section of people, from film directors to neighbors to artists and critics. Many of them I know very well, and, of course, with some galleries I get commissions. As with most things, you learn to like what you do, it doesn't matter what. It's a function of the profession. When you spend time with a person, sometimes years, you have a particular image of this person. And I reached a point where I felt compelled to capture these images. While I continue to expand this ongoing project, I'm still working on a new series of collages, I'm thinking about doing more monotypes, and I have something like fifteen paintings in progress. But most of my present effort is focused on the next big show of a hundred portraits.

PS In a way, you've always gone against the grain. When you were in Russia, realism was all-pervasive, and you made not realist paintings, but fantasy prints. And these days so much abstract art is being done, and you're going back and making very realistic portraits. Some would call these portraits postmodern. Do you think they are postmodern?

VP My mentality is postmodern. I consider myself definitely a postmodern artist. I reflect on lots of different art from all over the world and many different historical periods. When you're a little kid in Ukraine in the wintertime, and you're dreaming about a world which you might never see, and you're reading literature about the world which you might never know, and you see art from all over the world, you're basically living in your mind in an alternative consciousness. But then you have a really good technical, professional education. You have all the skills you need. You can paint, you can draw, so the issue is what do you really want to do, and then you find yourself playing, combining things, basically. You take a little bit of realism, add a little bit of abstraction, and combine this and that. Instead of creating a new beauty, I am just playing with already established versions of beauty, stirring them together, and serving them up as new cuisine. This is how my mind works. But in the midst of this sort of collage mentality, you have the strangest visions which sustain and stimulate you and keep you moving forward. I go from A to B without necessarily knowing where I'll ultimately arrive. I don't know how to explain it. I just do art and go where it takes me. I try to stay intellectually detached from the results. The focus is intense present action. This is my favorite place when I work.

PS Are you still in touch with any Ukrainian artists at this point?

VP Yes. Now, of course, with Facebook and all this stuff, you're easily kept in touch. Some of my artist friends and colleagues moved to Moscow. It's been a long time at this point—twenty-five years—a quarter of a century. I had a funny conversation with the consul of Ukraine. He asked am I Ukrainian or am I Russian, and I said, "I'm American." I kinda feel like I am Californian. I consider myself a Californian. The life of an artist is an interesting journey. It's a long journey.

PS Do you work every day—paint every day, most of the day?

VP Sometimes yes; sometimes no. Painting every day is my ideal, for sure. I discover that in the morning I am always engaged with something else. The best time for me to paint is afternoon. When I am lucky, I paint until the daylight fades. And slowly, while the light is disappearing, you can see special colors; you can see differently. It happens when you can barely see, but you see better tones. Recently, I put myself under a strict regimen: every day I'm painting about three, four hours. Actually, I feel incredible, it's a matter of consistency . . .

PS Concentration . . .

VP Concentration, plus I'm working on many paintings at a time. A number of them I've just left marinating for months and months and months, half-done, so when I get back to them, I don't need to spend time adding information, I just dive into finalizing the execution. Then there's the drying process. When you're working on many different paintings simultaneously, you can get really frustrated. It's like juggling with too many plates at the same time. But then you have to have the discipline to turn them face to the wall, most of them. And then to take them one at a time and bring them to the next level, and then again turn each of them towards the wall and try to ignore them while beginning work on another piece. One of the best stages is looking at the pieces with all their information in place, yet still very raw; they haven't found a destination yet. With a teensy-weensy brush, I work them in order to fix the tiniest details, and sometimes I build or subtract layers with a huge brush. This morning I looked over a painting and realized what was missing . . . that a reflection needed to be rendered in a cold color, that it should be blue while the shadow in the face needed to be more reddish. So suddenly I decided to flip a super-realistic painting into an exercise in Fauvism, and the decisive changes probably can be accomplished with a couple of brushstrokes. But

there are advantages to working this way, because as the painting is drying, you can be mixing liquid. I like to use liquid which sets up as a kind of gel. You apply a particular stroke, and if you don't like it, you can just wipe it off. You can try a different treatment, and then you can smear it. This technique almost feels like sculpting. Its strength is flexibility.

PS So while you're doing these portraits, you're still doing other things, like more fantasy prints or monotypes?

VP Yes, I'm planning to do new monotypes. I have a staggering amount of material ready for my next series of collages. It's been some time; it has been a few years, and I actually can't wait. At my home I have a guest house where I've set up everything pertinent to the collages. So I continue to do paintings in my studio while I have a whole other workspace reserved exclusively for collage. Recently, I spent some time in Venice, where I took about 2,000 photographs. Intentionally, I haven't looked at any of them yet, but I have two or three ideas percolating about how to use them. First and foremost, I feel a powerful craving to finish the portrait cycle, and at the same time, I want to lay out huge canvases and slather with thick layers of oil massive, outsized renderings of Venice rich in gradations of tone and color and texture. I have this crazy vision. But I need to be patient. I've found from experience that it's much better for the work when you don't immediately follow up on a great experience and jump in right away. You let time pass by. It is kind of like letting your memories and impressions age and ferment. So from the first stage, which is emotion, you move to the second stage, memory, then add fantasy and imagination to the mix, thereby insulating yourself from the impact of unfiltered reality.

PS And your new Venice-inspired pieces will be different from the Venice paintings you did before?

VP Yes. I feel I want to paint more impressionistically, with the oil running, because I did a couple of Venetian scenes, as part of a larger portfolio resulting from my Italian journey, that really triggered a sense of secret harmony. My first show at Modernism included one of these Venice nocturnes. I got totally fascinated with the reflection of lights there at night, and the resulting artwork was a blend of fuzzy and super-realistic. I'm really enjoying painting technique for its own sake. Maybe because I started painting when I was almost fifty years old, using oil colors. I'm like a starving man let loose at a lavish banquet. I love varnish; I love turpentine; I love the smell of it. Having deprived myself of these things most of my career, I now find them intoxicating. I'm not all work and no play, however. When I am working, I sometimes take substantial breaks, like months at a time I don't work at all, if possible. The longer I can afford to not work, the better, because then I feel famished, I feel hungry again, refreshed and renewed. Because, being a professional artist, I started making art at age thirteen, which makes forty-five years I've been at it . . .

PS How old are you now?

VP Fifty-eight. For forty-five years I've been doing art, and I'm still excited about what I am doing, and I think that when you lose this excitement, basically it's over. Because if you lose your excitement, your personal involvement, you have nothing to share except technique. That fascination and energy when you work, that's much more important. And it helps to change styles and technique: it helps you to not get rusty, stuffy, or stuck in one technique. I've noticed that when an artist works in one particular style and one particular medium, the work becomes ever more perfect, but less interesting. That's my experience. So some artists strive to get rid of glitches and imperfections, but glitches are most interesting. I love to see interplay and resistance. When something is done perfectly, it is, ironically, deficient.

PS There has to be more of a soul quality, not just technique. There is a lot of stuff going on now in the art world which has none of that spirit at all. You know, people experiment with whatever it may be, but they're still doing conceptual art and installations. They work a lot with computers. A lot of computer art. There is no reason why a computer couldn't make great art, but it hasn't happened yet. Maybe it never will. No personal touch.

VP I think the connection between spirit, brush, and canvas is much shorter than through the wireless Internet. I think it is more complicated to feel, to see the spirit. Sometimes when I am painting, when I am not happy with the results, I just smear with my hands, so basically it's a question of how you connect. You almost feel like you're sculpting.

PS I can see that in your work.

VP Texture is important. I love surfaces, I love . . .

PS . . . the art process?

VP Indeed.

From *Valentin Popov, FACE*, a documentary film by Celik Kayalar, 2013. Transcription by Hannah Baker.

One year later, this conversation was resumed in Valentin Popov's studio, with artist Mel Ramos sitting in. Soon afterward, the following exchange ensued.

PETER SELZ So, Mel, do you have a favorite portraitist?

MEL RAMOS Not really, no . . . not unless that may be you, Valentin.

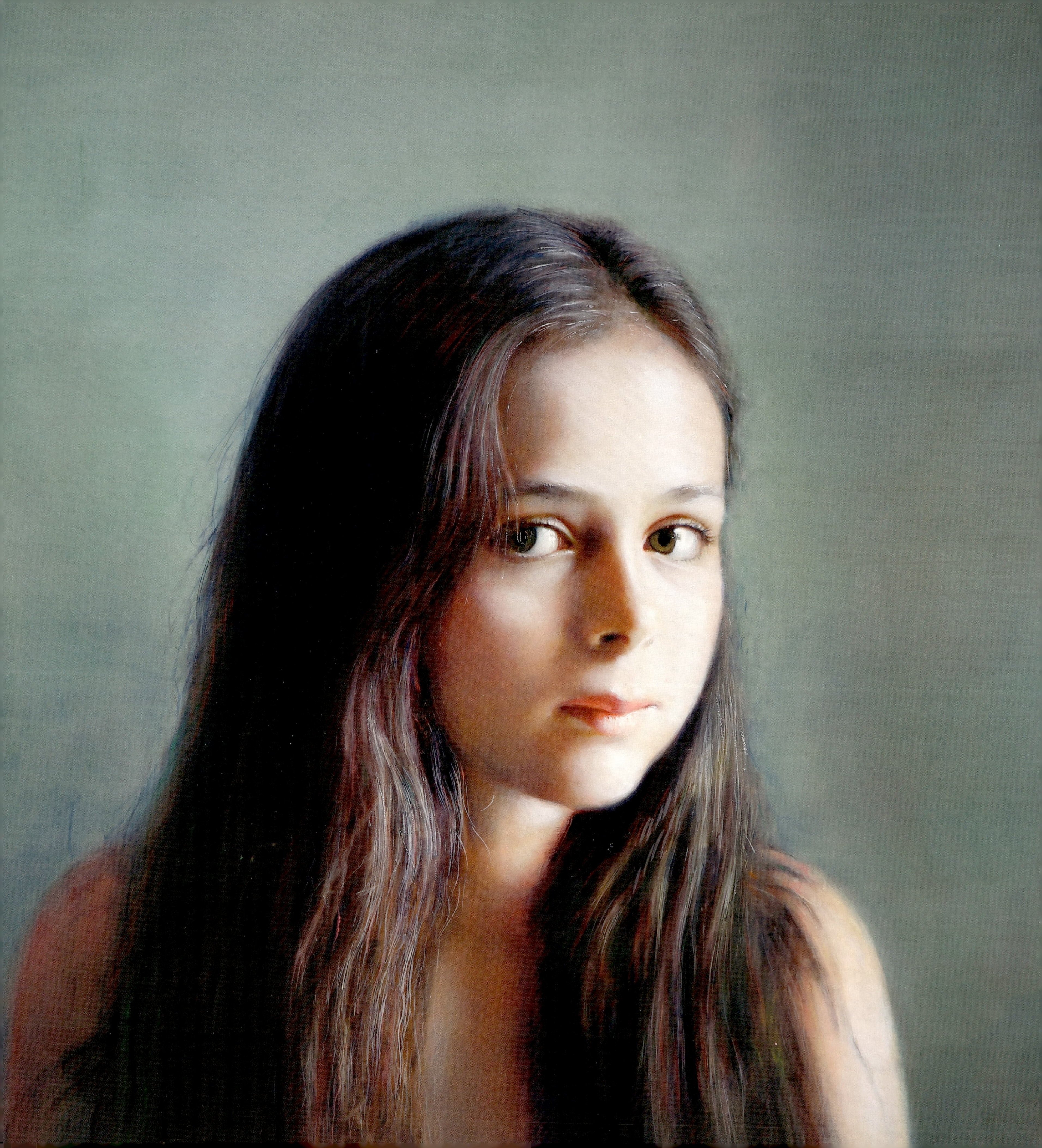

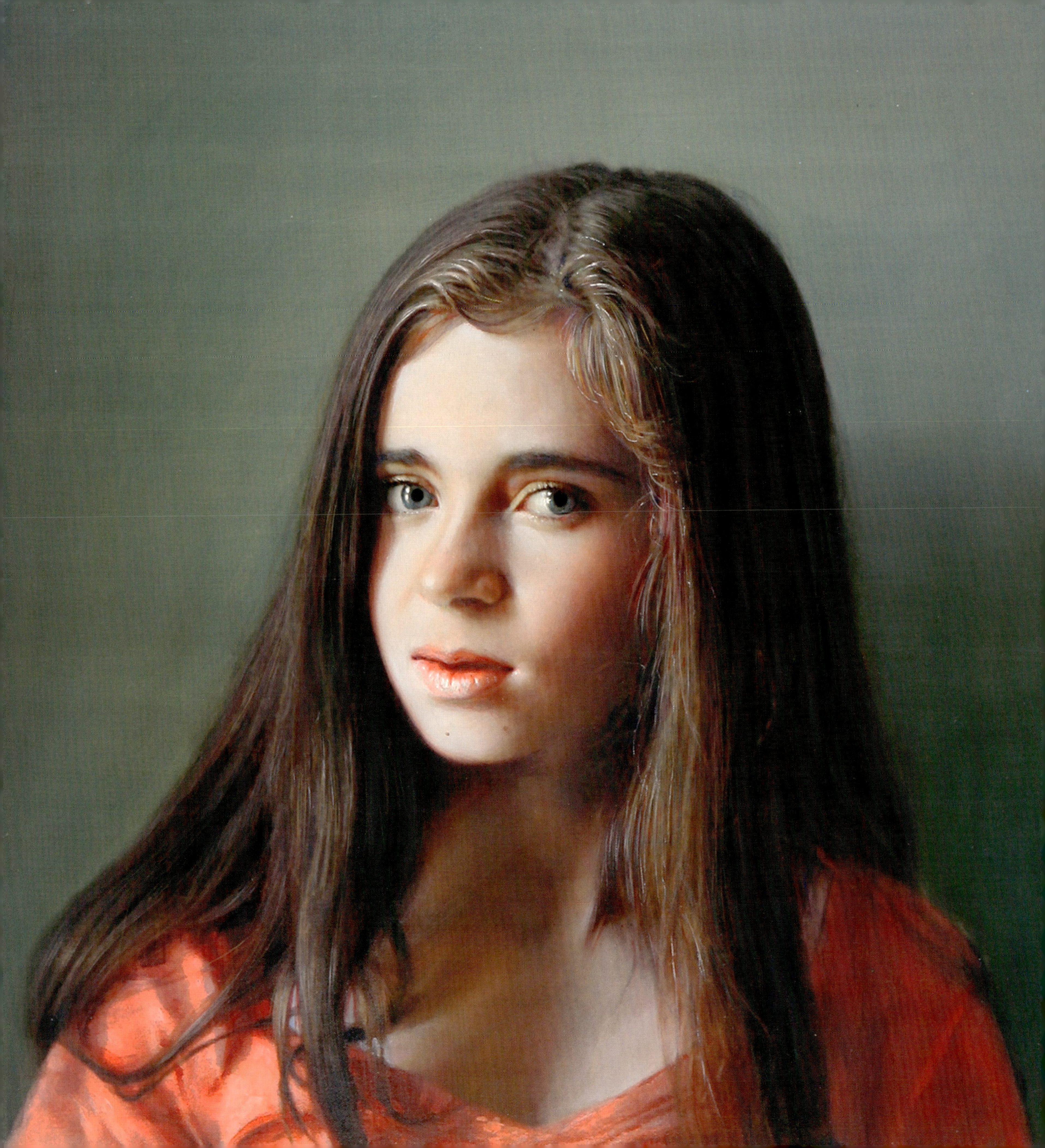

previous, left: **EMILY TALBERT**, 2014. Oil on canvas, 28 × 26 in.

right: **CAROLINE TALBERT**, 2013. Oil on canvas, 28 × 26 in.

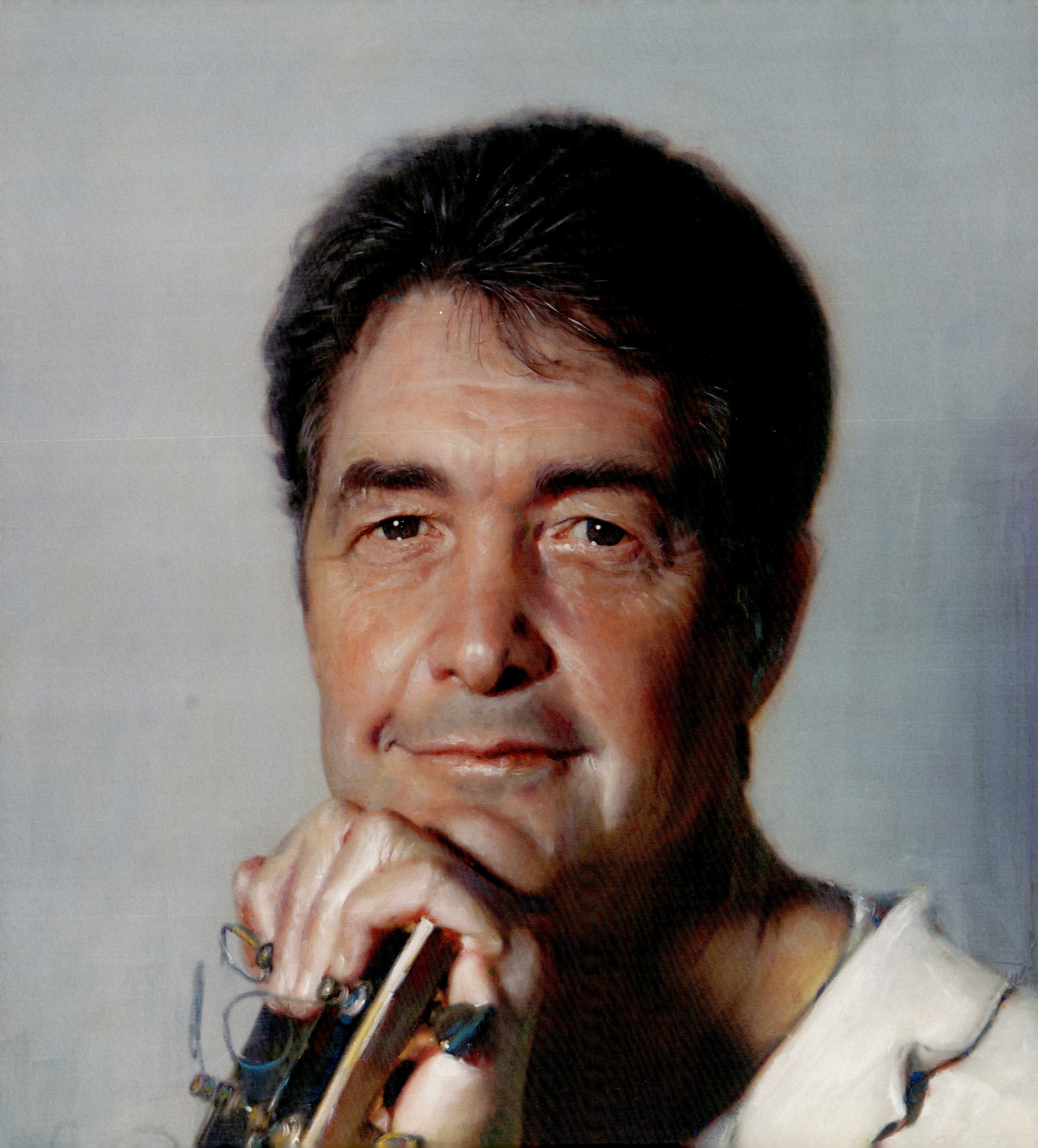

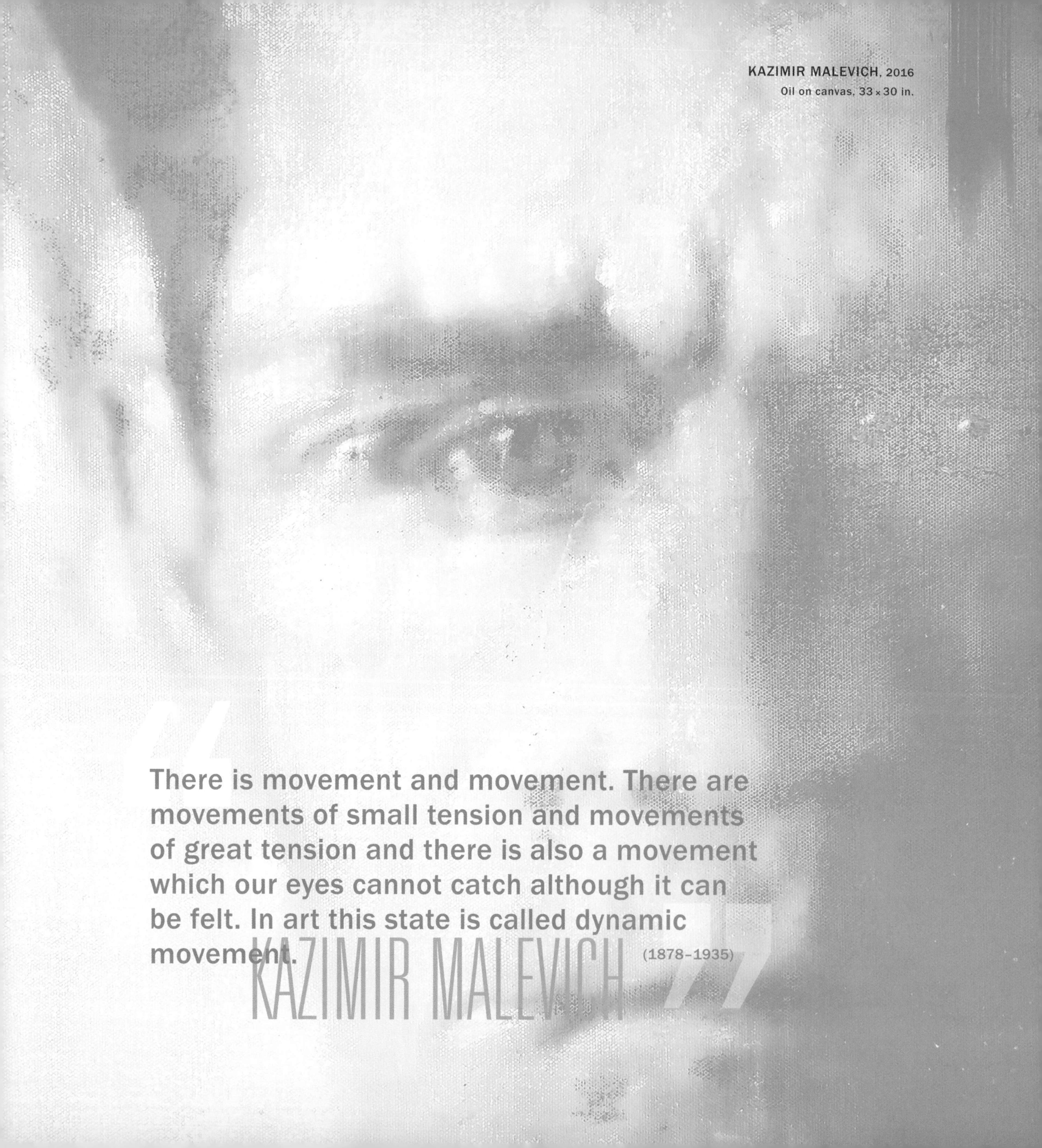

"There is movement and movement. There are movements of small tension and movements of great tension and there is also a movement which our eyes cannot catch although it can be felt. In art this state is called dynamic movement."

KAZIMIR MALEVICH (1878–1935)

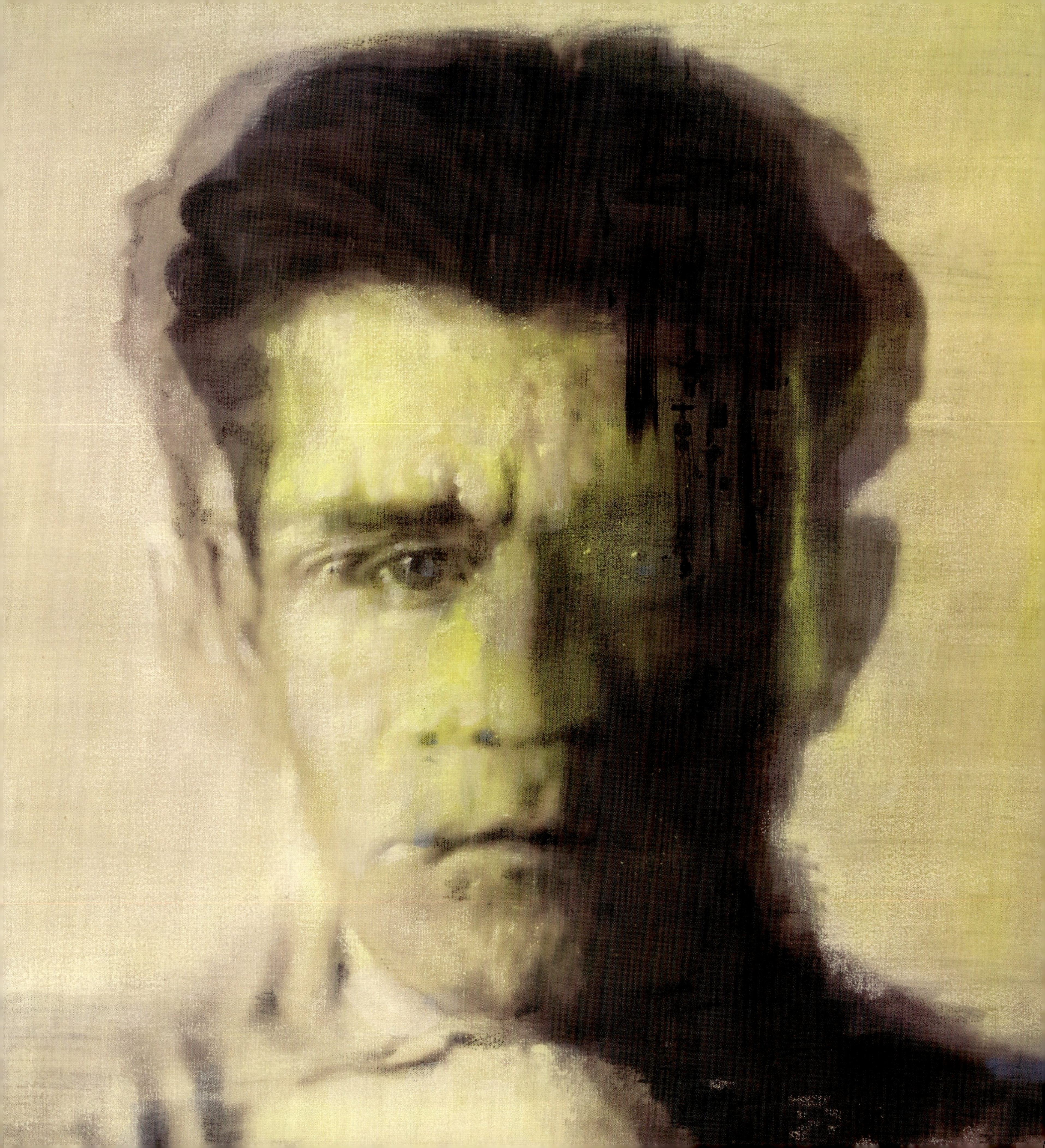

IVAN POPOV, 2016
Oil on canvas, 28 × 26 in.

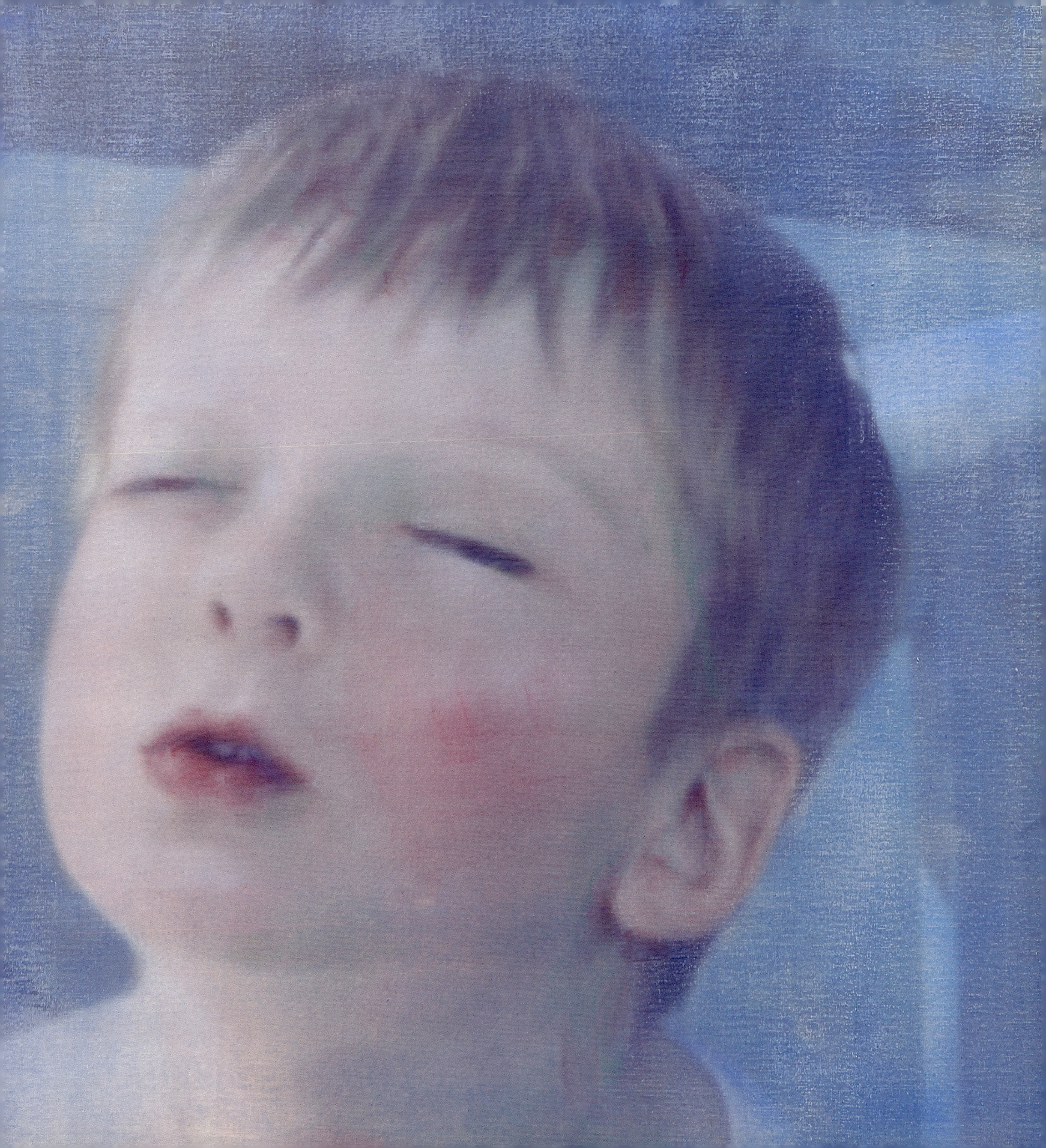

Valentin Popov, as a Ukrainian postmodern artist, has captured some of the current sensibilities of America in his paintings. His grasp of American consumerist obsessions, with a wink to "Pop Art," has resulted in works that mix, in a critical way, iconic Russian symbols and popular Western imagery.

MARTIN MULLER

From *Valentin Popov, FACE*, a documentary film by Celik Kayalar, 2013.

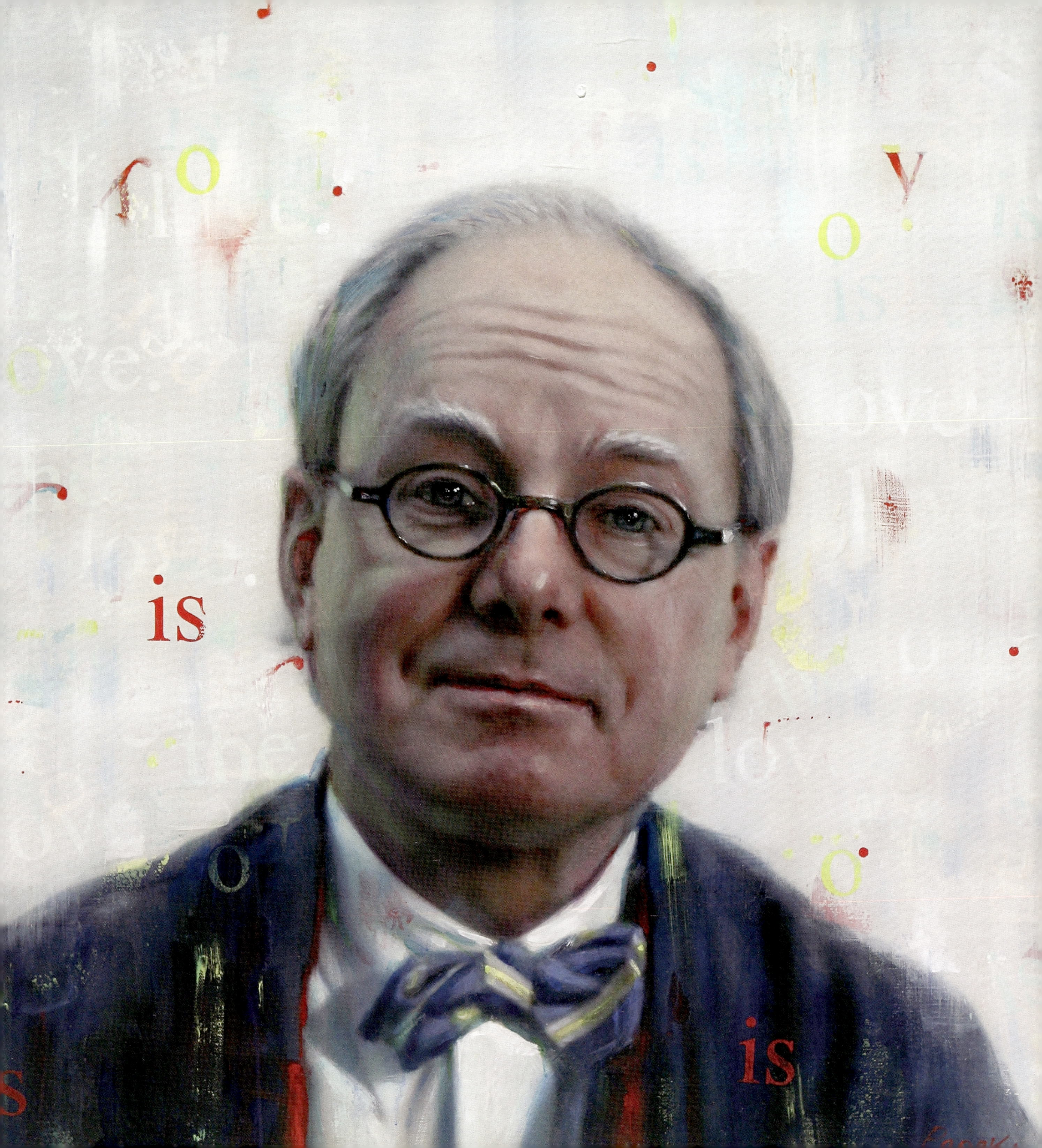
is
is

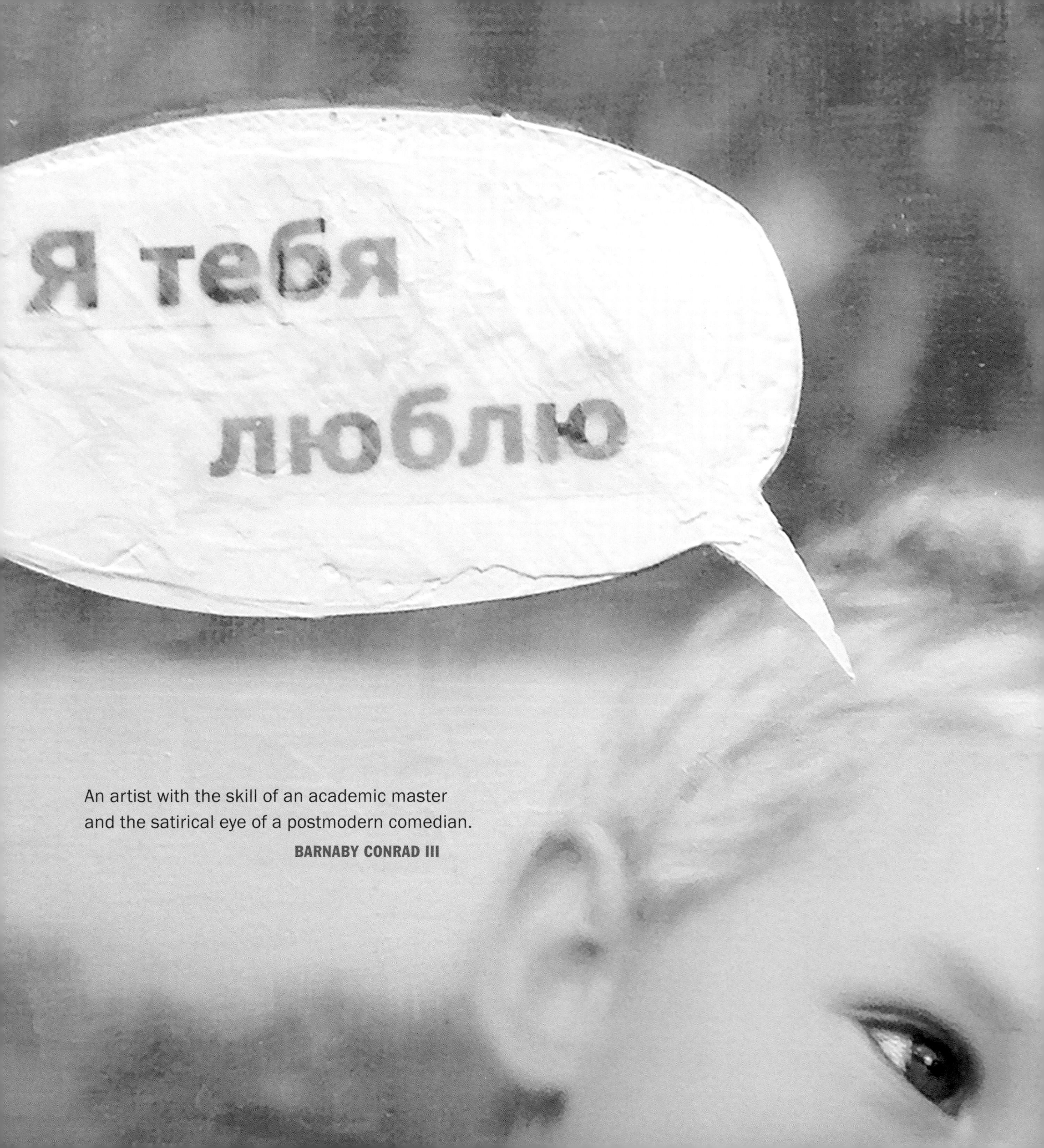

An artist with the skill of an academic master
and the satirical eye of a postmodern comedian.

BARNABY CONRAD III

JACK CONRAD, 2013
Oil on canvas, 28 × 26 in.

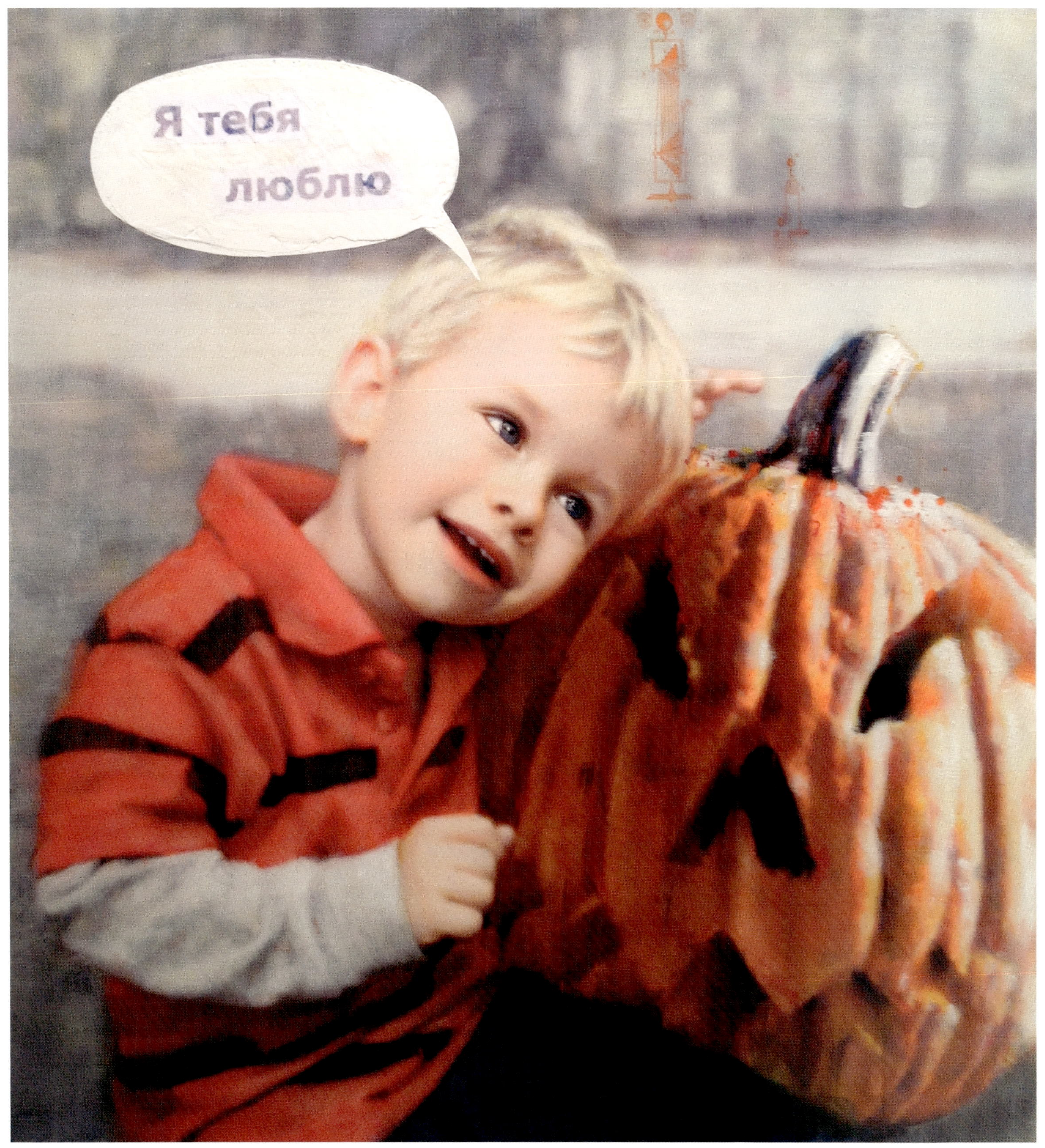

Я тебя
люблю

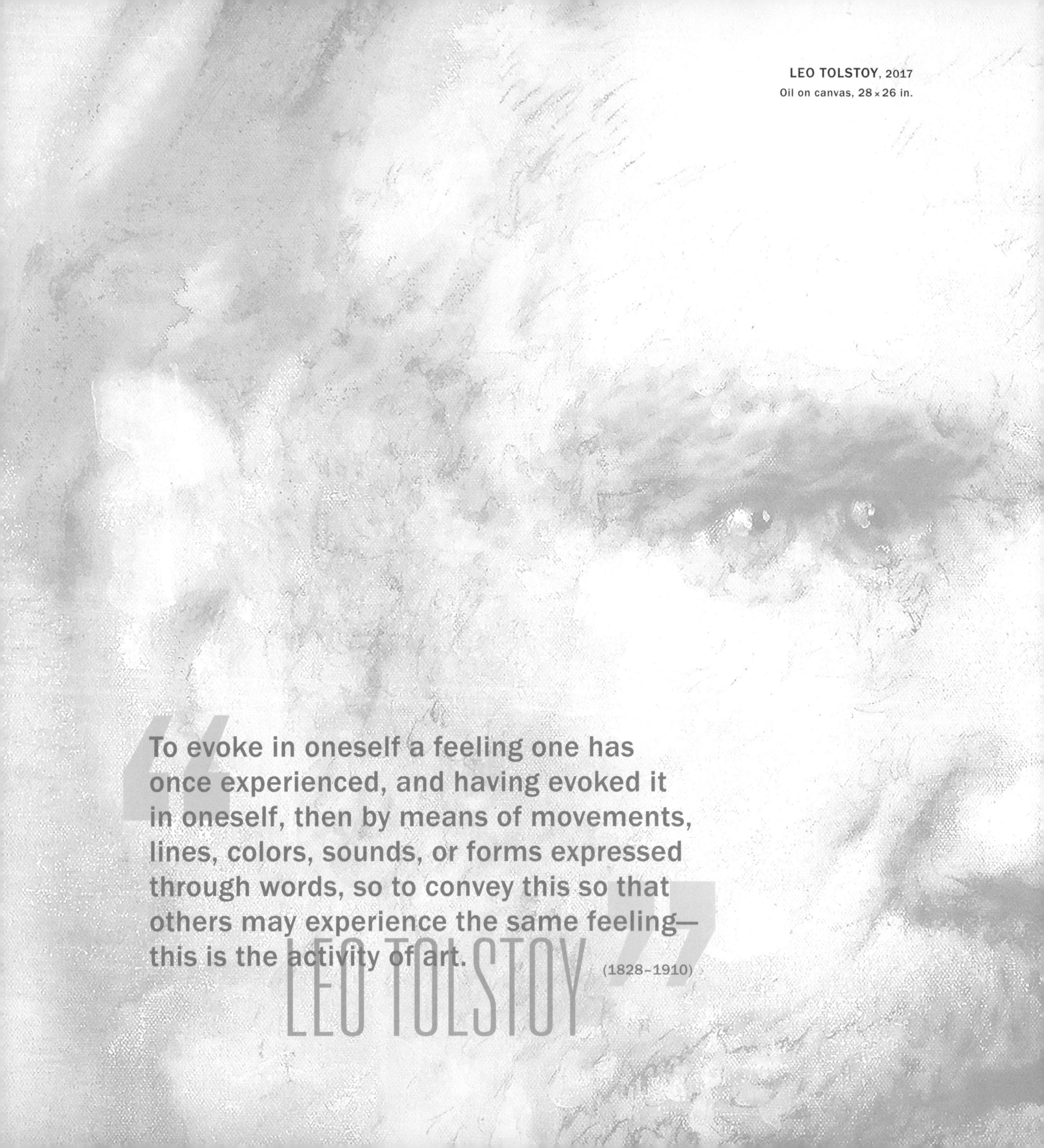

"To evoke in oneself a feeling one has once experienced, and having evoked it in oneself, then by means of movements, lines, colors, sounds, or forms expressed through words, so to convey this so that others may experience the same feeling—this is the activity of art."

LEO TOLSTOY

(1828–1910)

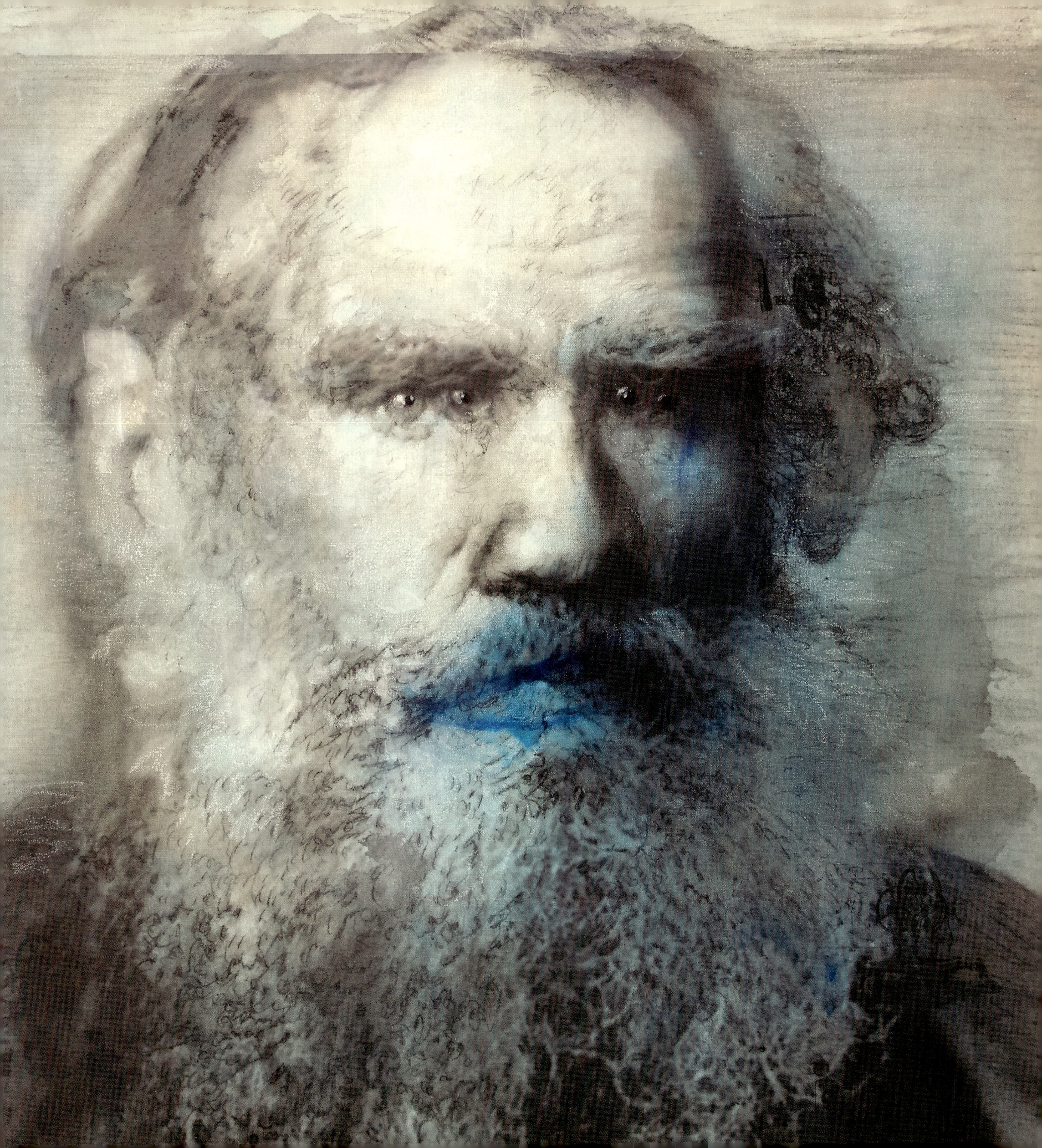

"The Universe is a dream dreamed by a single dreamer where all the dream characters dream too.

Thus, the task is not so much to see what no one yet has seen, but to think what nobody yet has thought about that which everybody sees.

Talent hits a target no one else can hit; genius hits a target no one else can see."

ARTHUR SCHOPENHAUER (1788–1860)

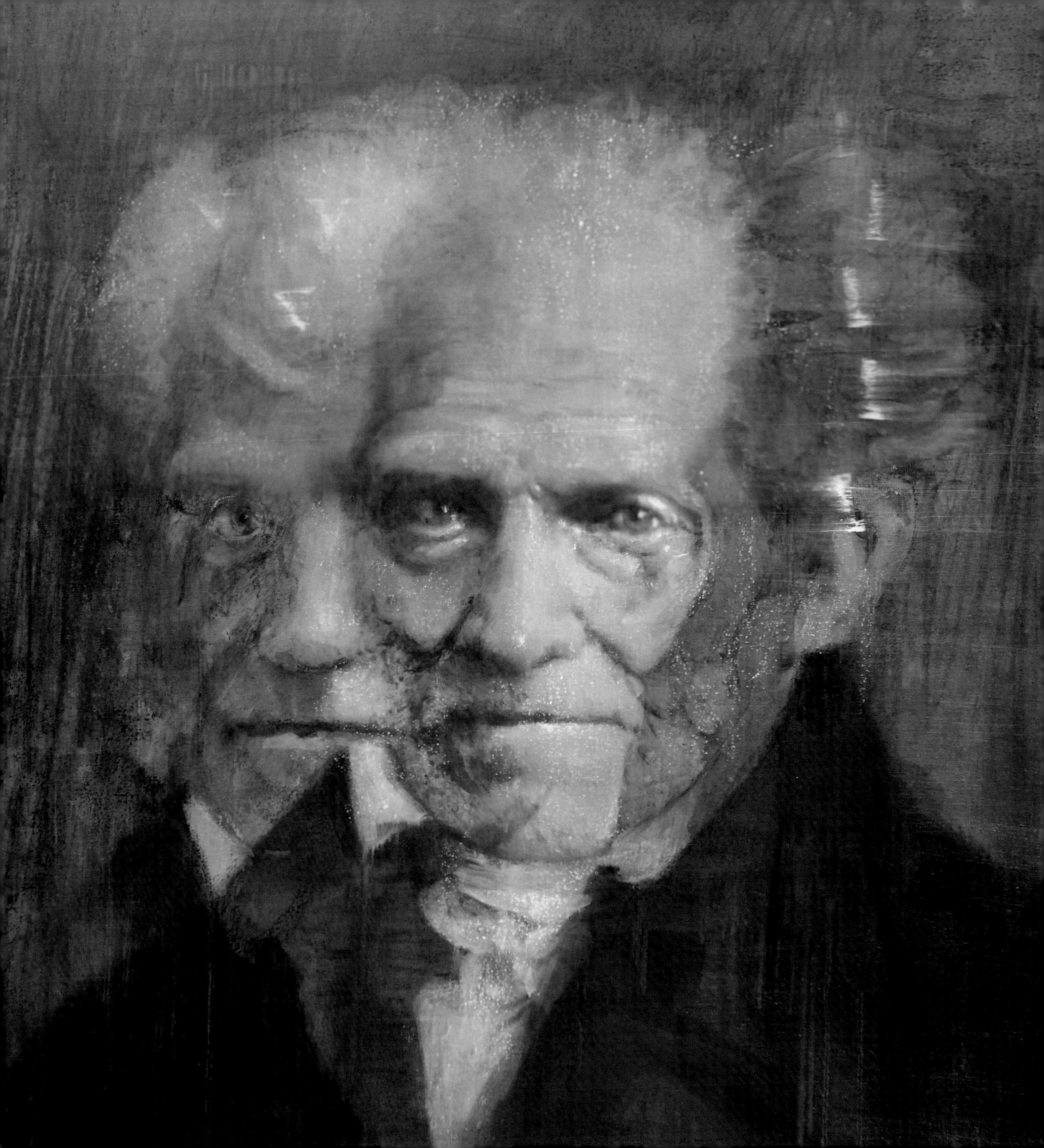

POPOV'S PORTRAITS

George Orwell said, "At fifty, everyone has the face he deserves."

Uh-oh. I was almost sixty and nobody's angel when Valentin Popov said he wanted to paint my portrait. What would he reveal? It was a sunny day when he mounted the stairs to my eighth-floor writing studio in San Francisco. Cup of tea in hand, Popov wandered around my cluttered workspace inquiring about various objects I'd gathered in my lifetime: the stuffed head of an antelope I shot in Montana, an old typewriter that had belonged to columnist Herb Caen, a penguin-shaped cocktail shaker, fishing rods leaning in a corner, and a mounted amberjack from the Gulf Stream.

Then he spotted a human skull sitting on a cluttered table.

"May I?" he asked, before picking it up. The skull's jaw was hinged with a metal spring. While gently opening and closing the mandible, he asked why I owned this classic prop for a medieval philosopher.

"*Vanitas vanitatem,*" I said. "Reminds me of the fragility of life."

He handed the skull to me. "Where did you get it?"

I confessed that I'd purchased it in a medical supply store in Paris about twenty years ago while recovering from a bad accident. While jogging in the Tuileries on a cold winter's night, I looked the wrong way and stumbled headfirst into the pedestal of a statue, breaking my jaw in two places. The surgeon wired my teeth shut, and for two months I lived on nothing but soup, milkshakes, and wine. That winter was one of the darkest of my life.

"And now life is not so bad?" Popov asked.

"Life is good now. I'm married and have a son."

While nodding empathetically—he also has a young boy—Popov began to photograph me. "Move the skull closer to your face," he coached. "Look into the darkness of the eye sockets . . . closer, closer. . . . Now kiss the skull."

"Kiss it?" I asked, hearing his camera clicking off shot after shot.

"Yes, on the mouth. . . . There. Now, move it away from your face . . . slowly . . . little by little. . . . Hold it! Think how lucky you are this skull isn't your own. You are alive!"

Within minutes Popov had all the shots he needed.

Several months later, he delivered the painting, and I unwrapped it with some trepidation. As John Singer Sargent wryly noted, "Every time I paint a portrait, I lose a friend." Popov needn't have worried. The painting seemed to capture my past, present, and future: the very real encounter with death in Paris, my current state of mind, and the inevitable fate that all of us will meet one day. The painting—from my point of view—was perfect.

Valentin Popov is not so much a portraitist as an artist who happens to paint portraits—yet, in no casual way. In less than two years, this Ukrainian-born, Moscow-trained artist produced an avalanche of over sixty portraits—enough faces to populate a small village. A portrait documents the consequences of your life and spirit—as seen by the painter. When a portrait is great, we sense a duet between the will of the artist and the spirit of his subject—as well as the zeitgeist of their age.

Photography changed painted portraiture, both helping it and hurting it. As Henri Matisse once said, "Exactitude is not the truth." A clinical record of a person's face is no more a portrait than a weather report is a poem about a summer's day. Imperfection is hardwired into all our endeavors, particularly our observations of humankind. As Sargent said, "A portrait is a picture in which there is just a tiny little something not quite right about the mouth."

Not all portraits make the sitter—or artist—happy. "Every portrait that is painted with feeling is a portrait of the artist, not the sitter," said Oscar Wilde. Winston Churchill disliked his official portrait by Graham Sutherland so much, he allowed his wife to burn it. When Lyndon Johnson saw the unflinching likeness painted by Peter Hurd (Andrew Wyeth's brother-in-law), he growled, "That is the ugliest thing I've ever seen," and sent it back. Henry Kissinger demanded a new one, while Richard Nixon craftily had his official portrait replaced with a more pleasing version years after he left the White House.

Artists sometimes have egos as large as those of world leaders. One reigning portraitist at the advent of the twentieth century was Philip de László, a dandy who sported pince-nez and a superbly tailored wit. When a grande dame he was painting snorted, "Sir, it doesn't look like me," de László replied, "Nevertheless, madame, it is the way you shall be remembered by de László."

The portrait artist walks a tightrope between two goals: achieving a good likeness and making an interesting work of art. A century from now, the owner of a portrait of his long-dead ancestor will worry less about the likeness than the overall aesthetic strength of the painting. As Édouard Manet said, "There's no symmetry in nature. One eye is never exactly the same as the other. There's always a difference. We all have a more or less crooked nose and an irregular mouth."

Valentin Popov excels at getting a likeness, but that isn't his only goal. Though he works from photographs (his own), he's no slave to exactitude. Popov photographs his sitters extensively, not just to record details, but to allow the subjects to reveal themselves in gesture and expression. He works the way a director does with an actor, concocting a mood. In our era of fast food and replication, the handmade one-of-a-kind portrait may be one of the most worthwhile aesthetic indulgences. "It's really absurd to make . . . a human image, with paint, today, when you think about it," said Willem de Kooning. "But then all of a sudden, it was even more absurd not to do it."

Advice to the sitter: spin the wheel of chance, and be a little humble. A portrait is an interpretation of you, not an identical twin. And be thankful for that.

One thing I was struck by was Valentin's command with the two most difficult
challenges in any portrait: the eyes and the mouth. If you don't have the eyes
right and you don't have the mouth right, it doesn't work. An artist can draw things
out of a person that most photography, or certainly snapshots, can't. Valentin is
particularly good at creating something new. I think that some people might even
look at their portrait afterward and say, "Not only did he capture me then,
but I might have something to live up to."   **BARNABY CONRAD III**

From *Valentin Popov, FACE*, a documentary film by Celik Kayalar, 2013.

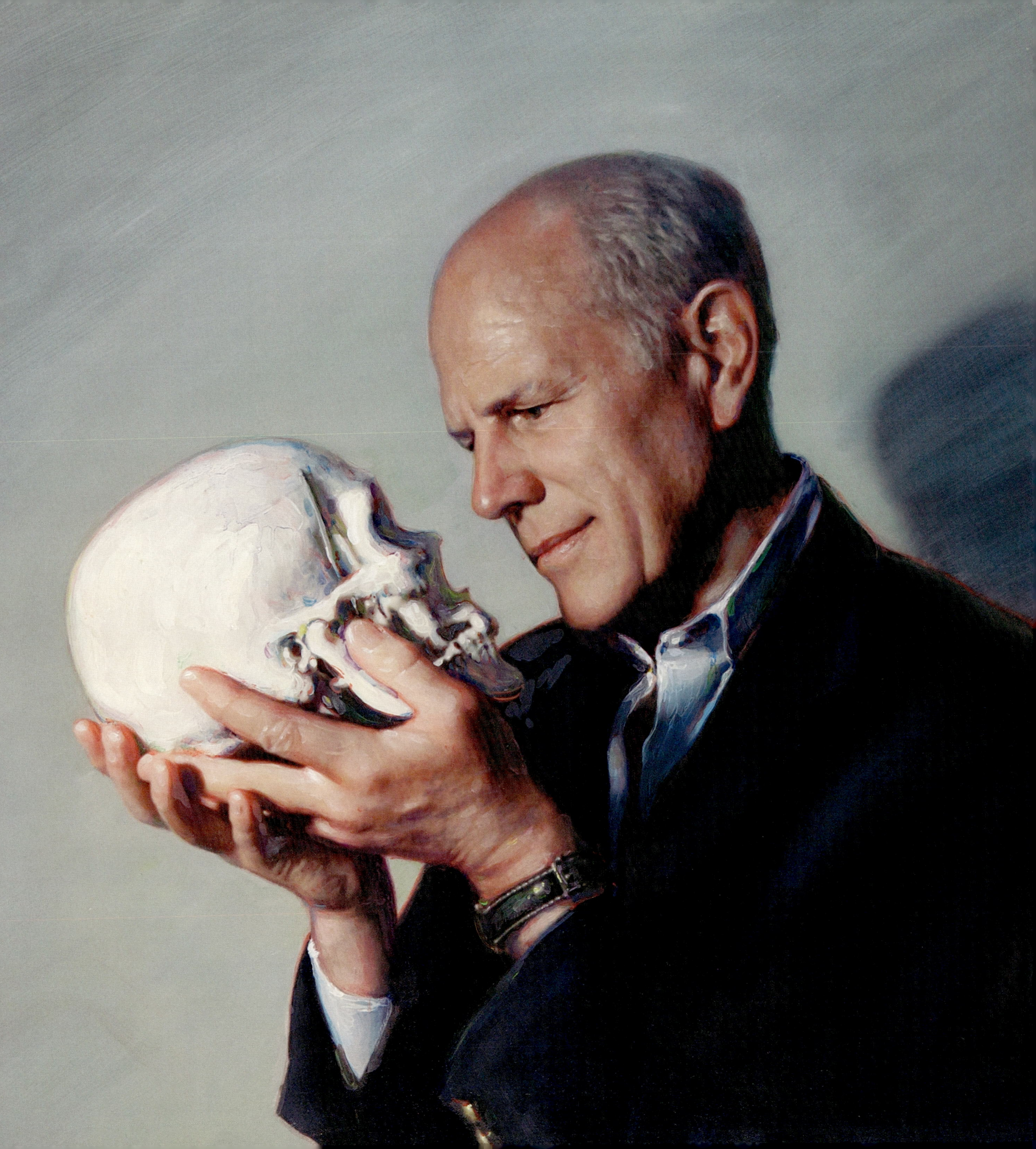

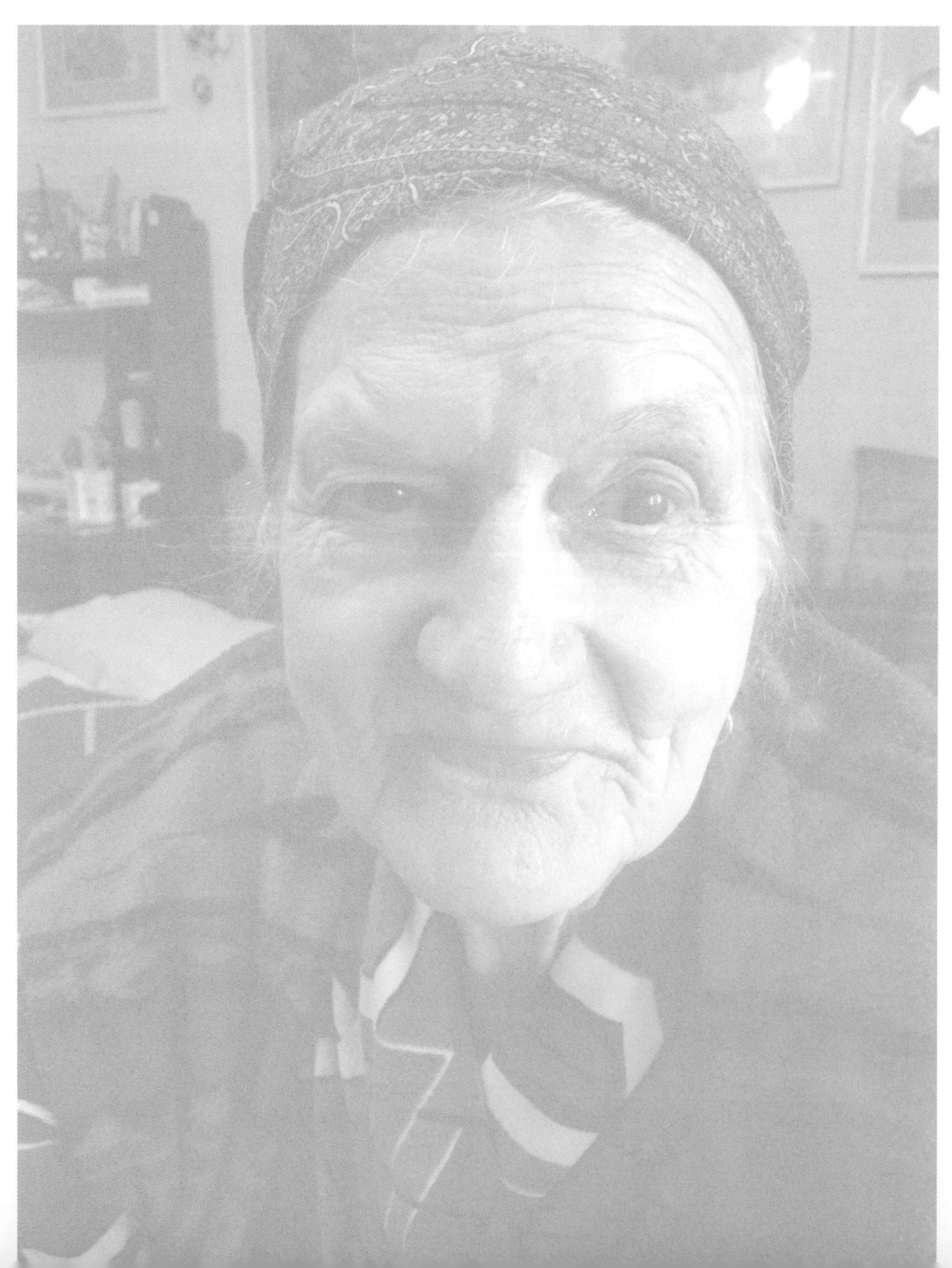

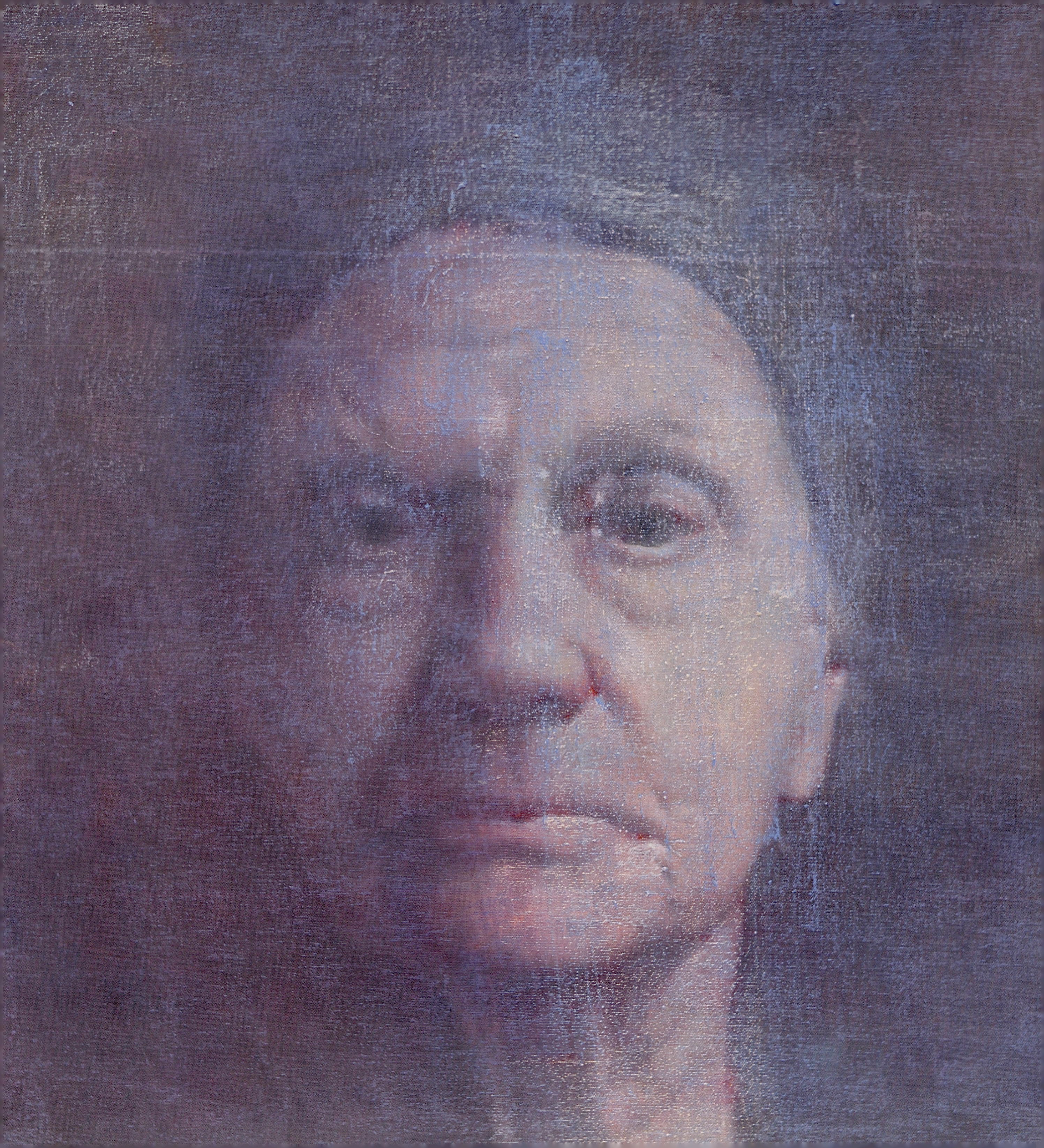

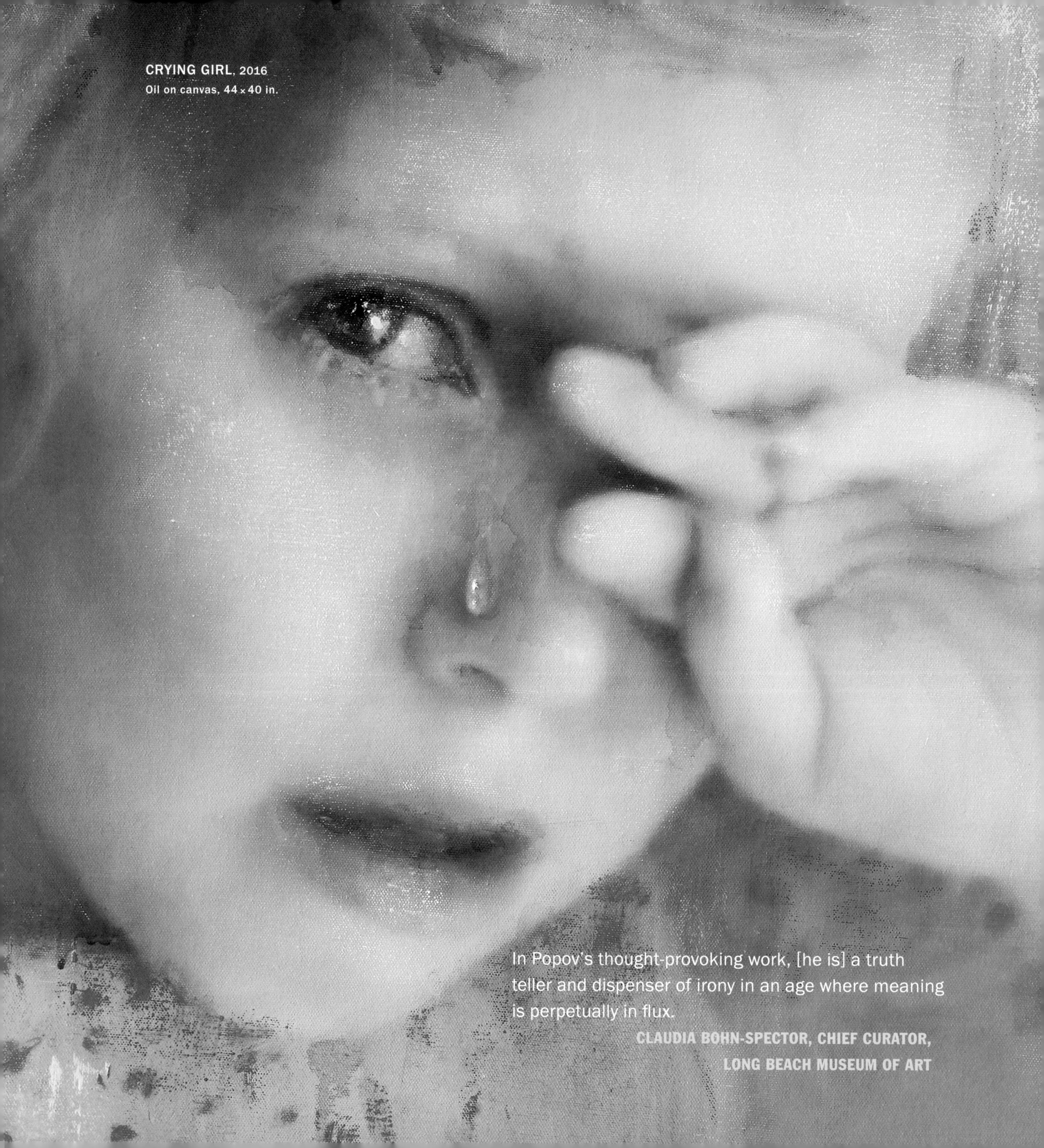

In Popov's thought-provoking work, [he is] a truth teller and dispenser of irony in an age where meaning is perpetually in flux.

CLAUDIA BOHN-SPECTOR, CHIEF CURATOR, LONG BEACH MUSEUM OF ART

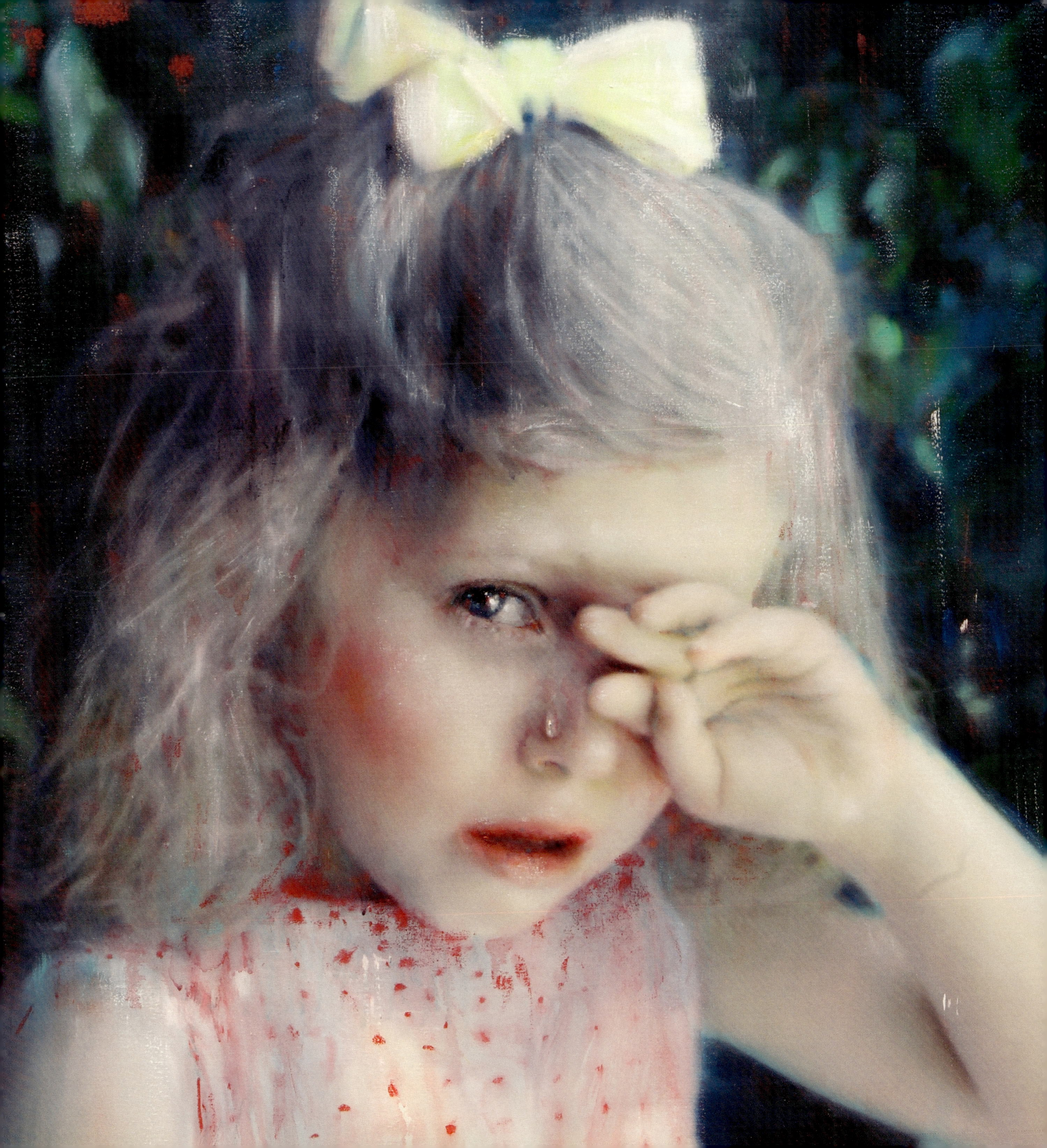

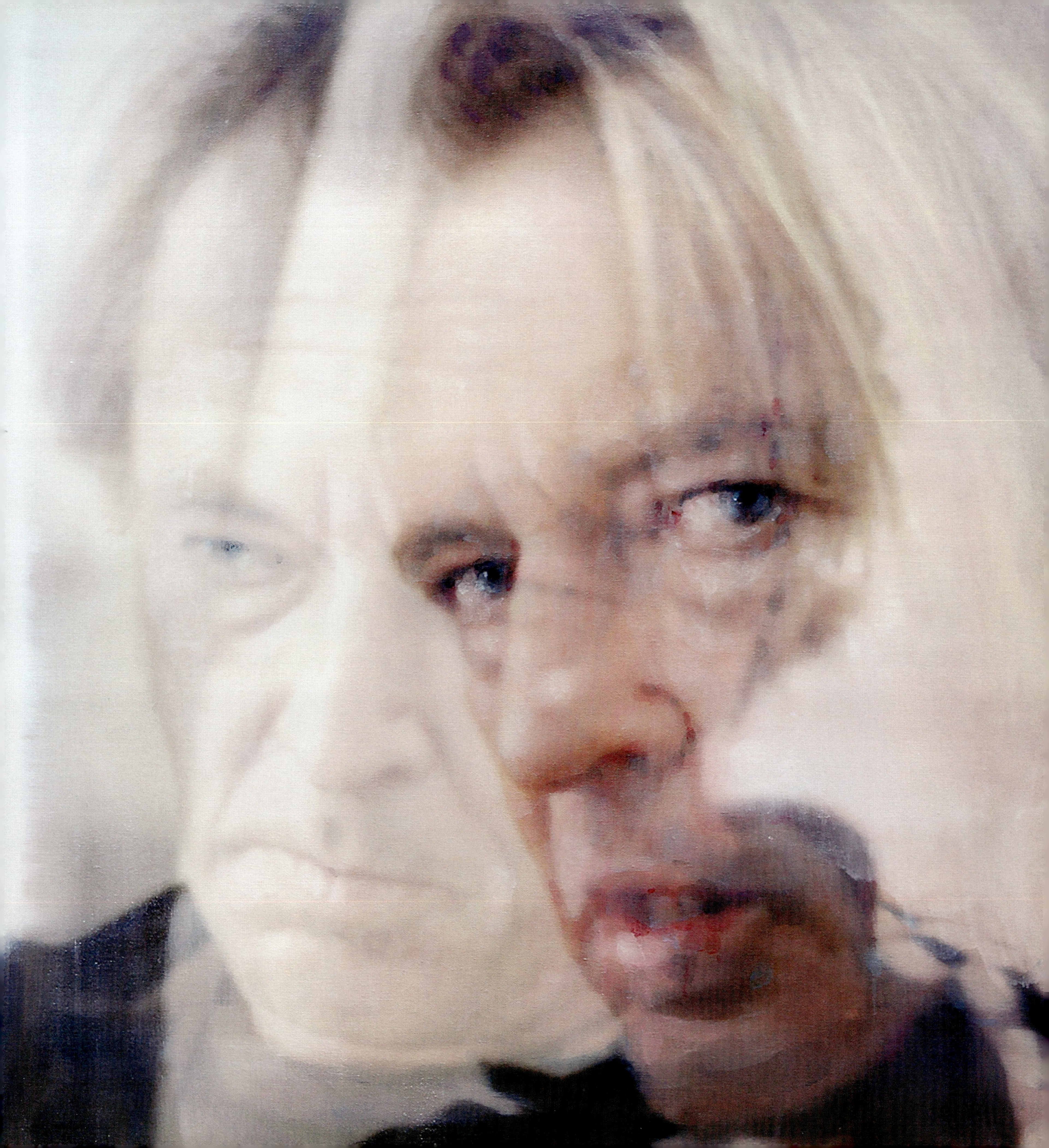

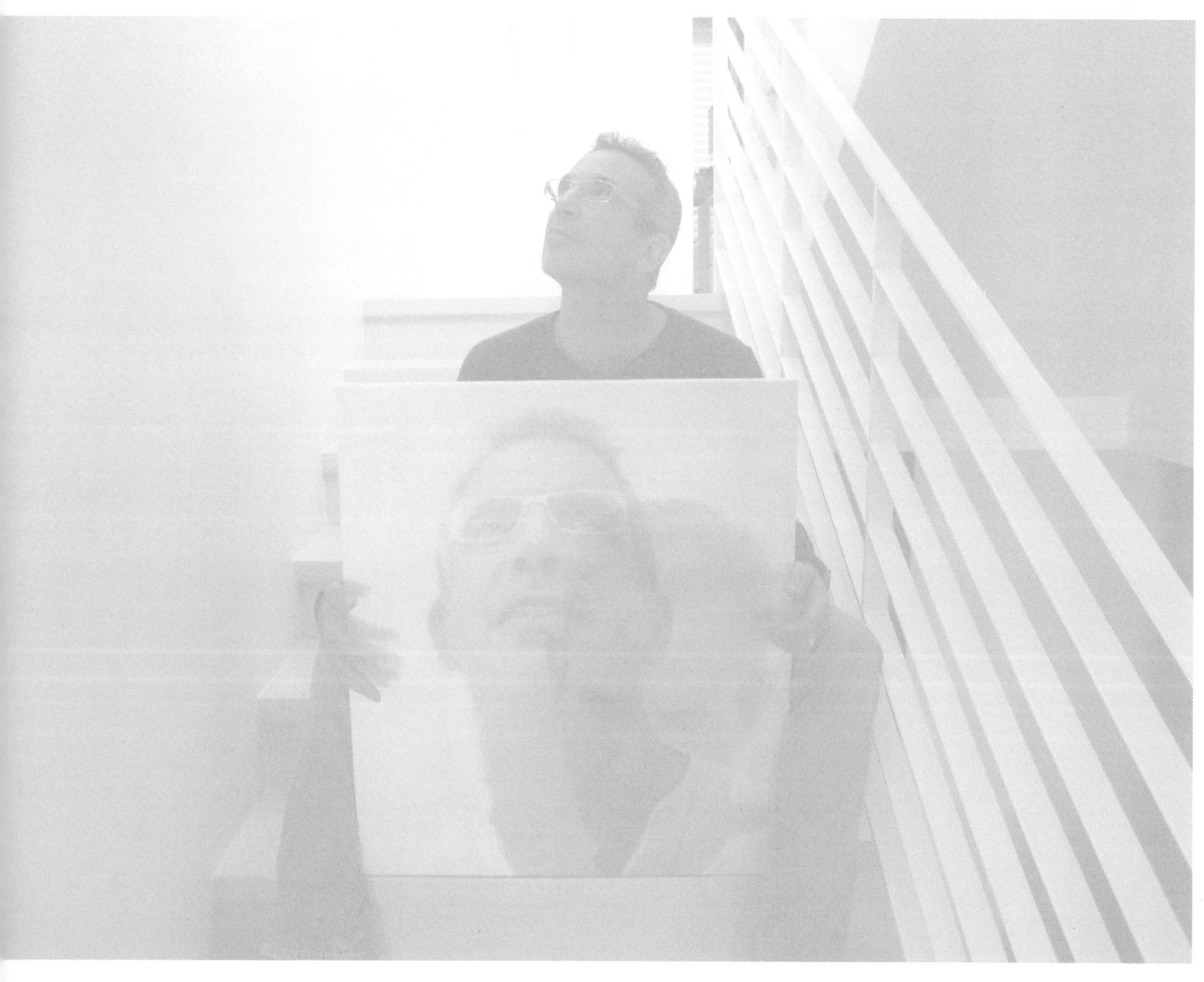

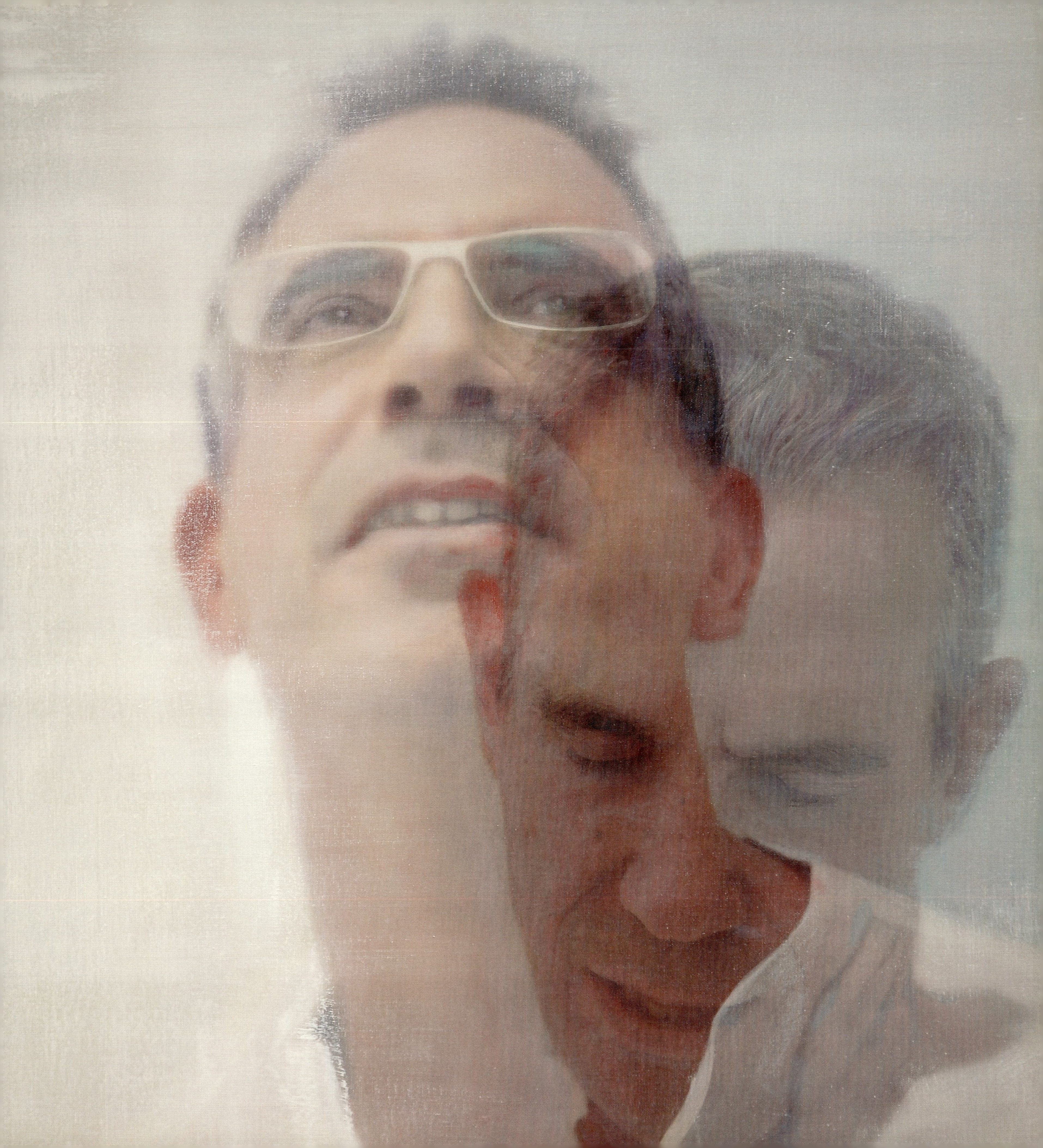

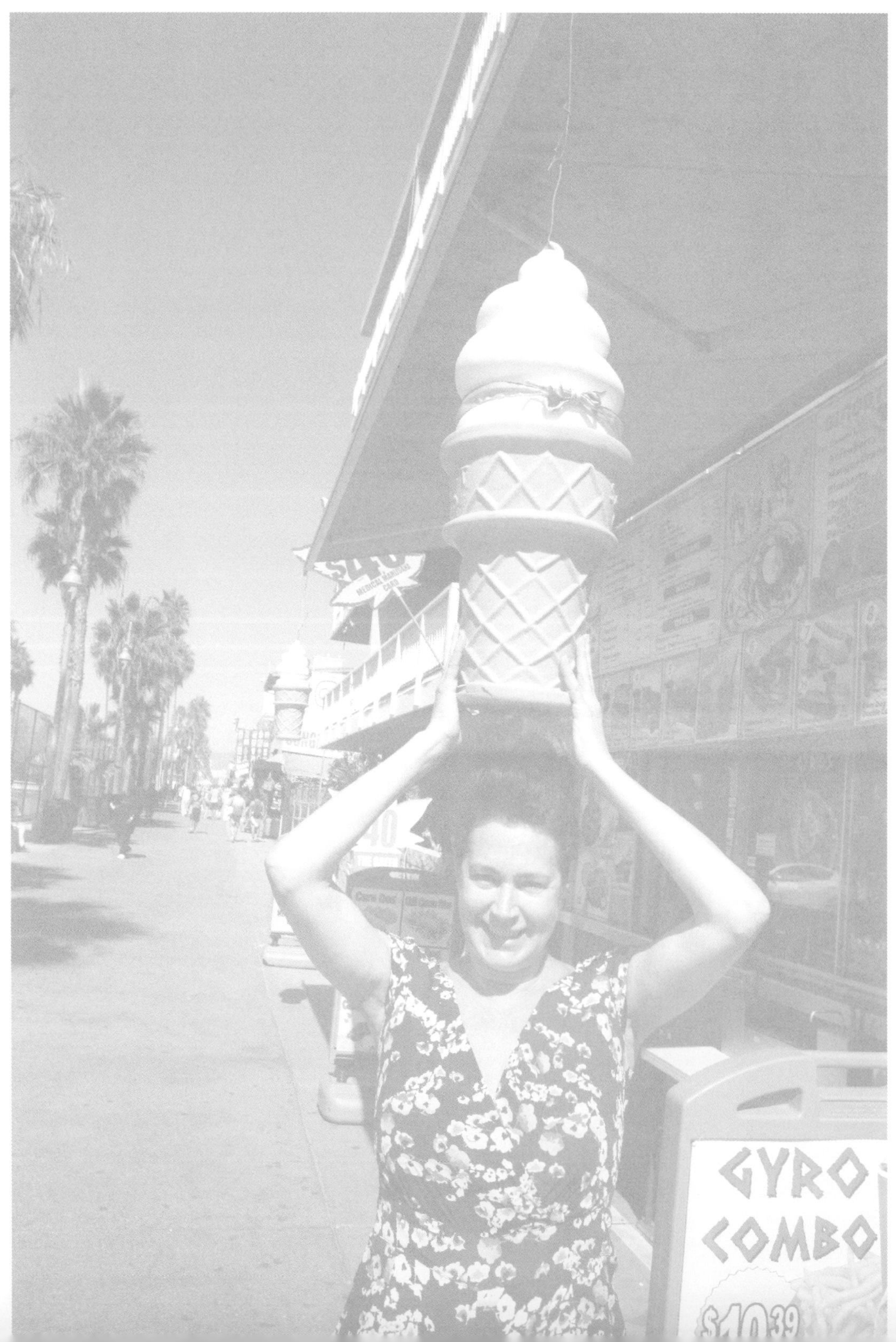
GYRO
COMBO
$10.39

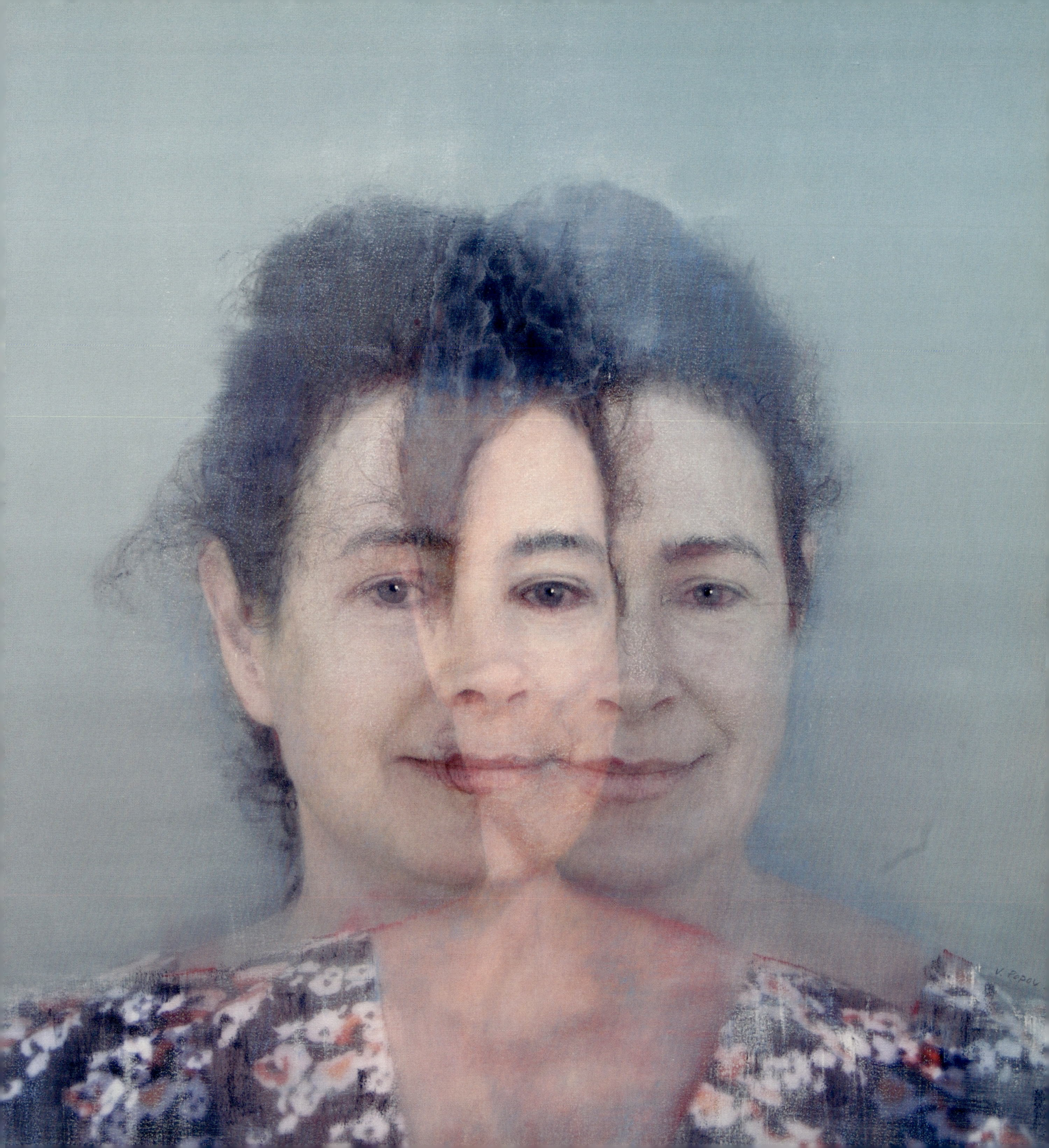

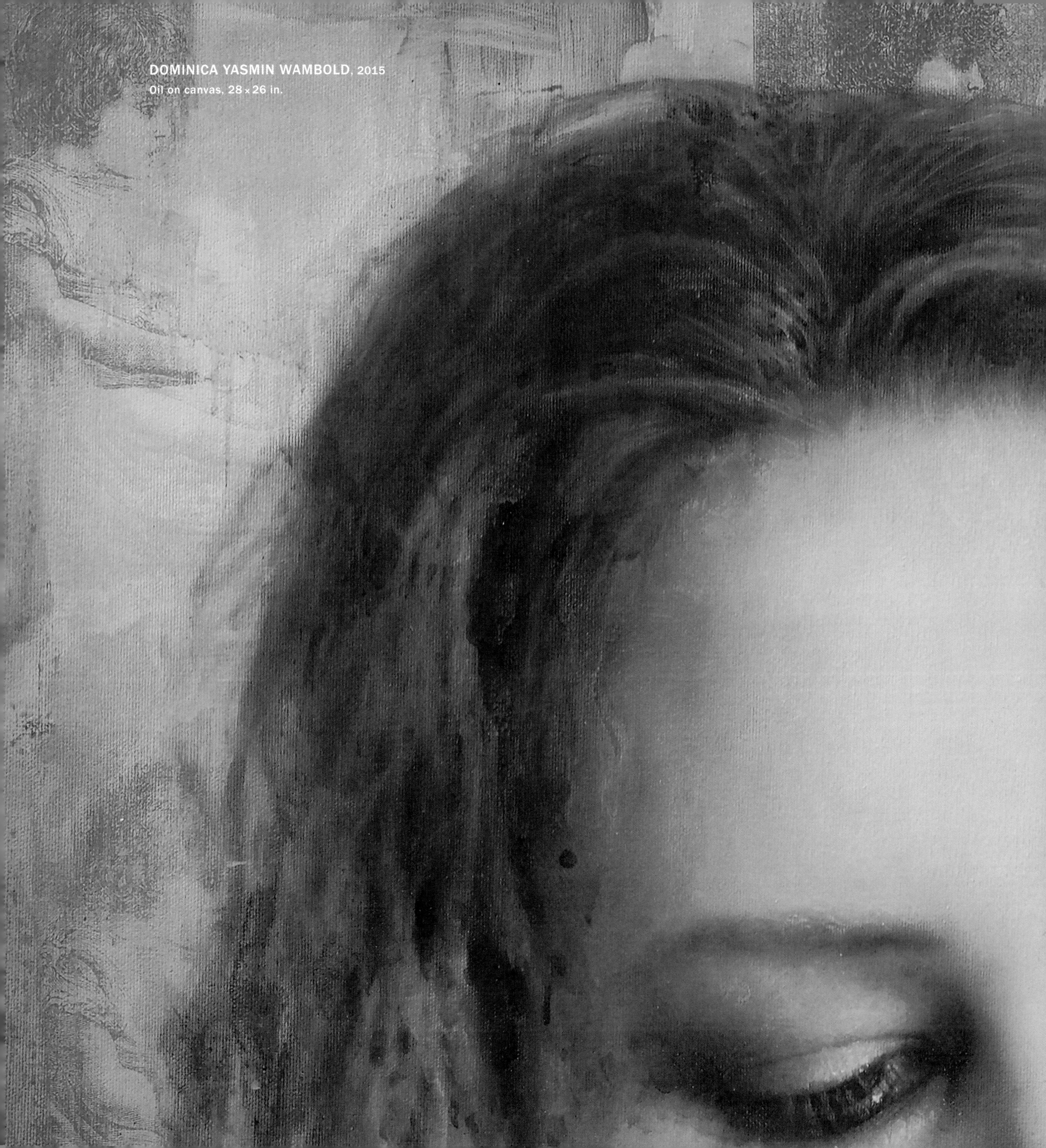

DOMINICA YASMIN WAMBOLD, 2015
Oil on canvas, 28 × 26 in.

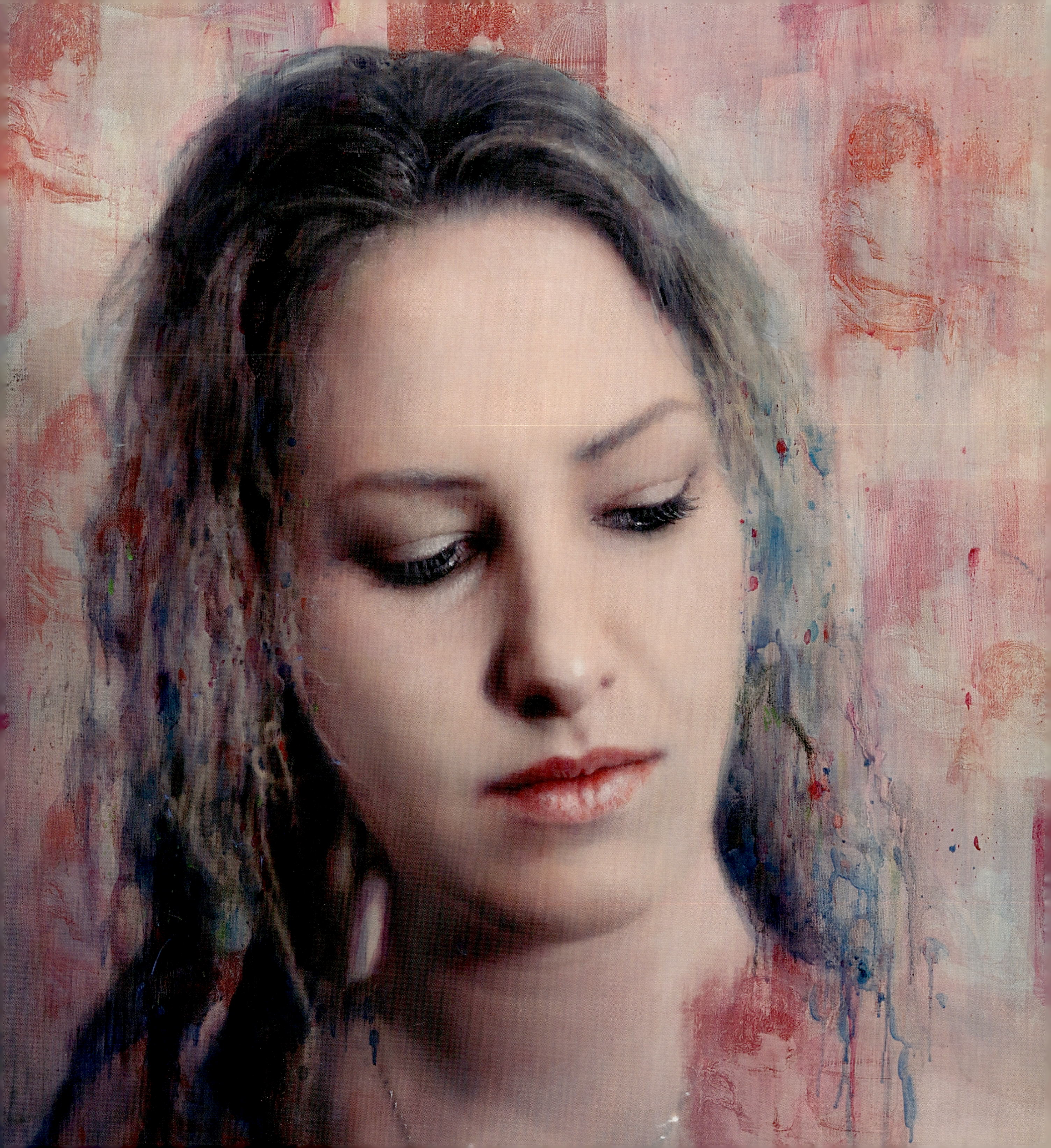

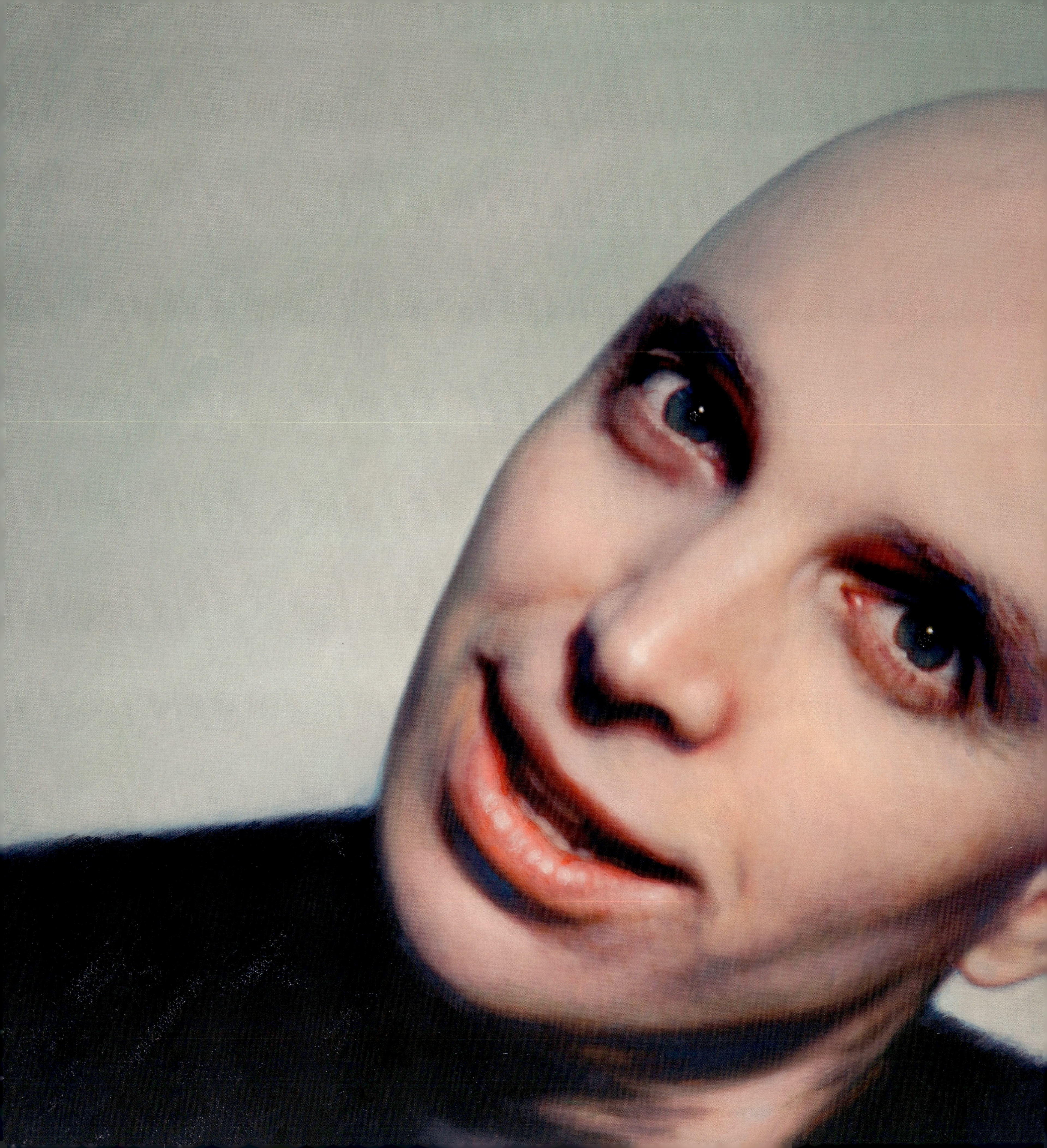

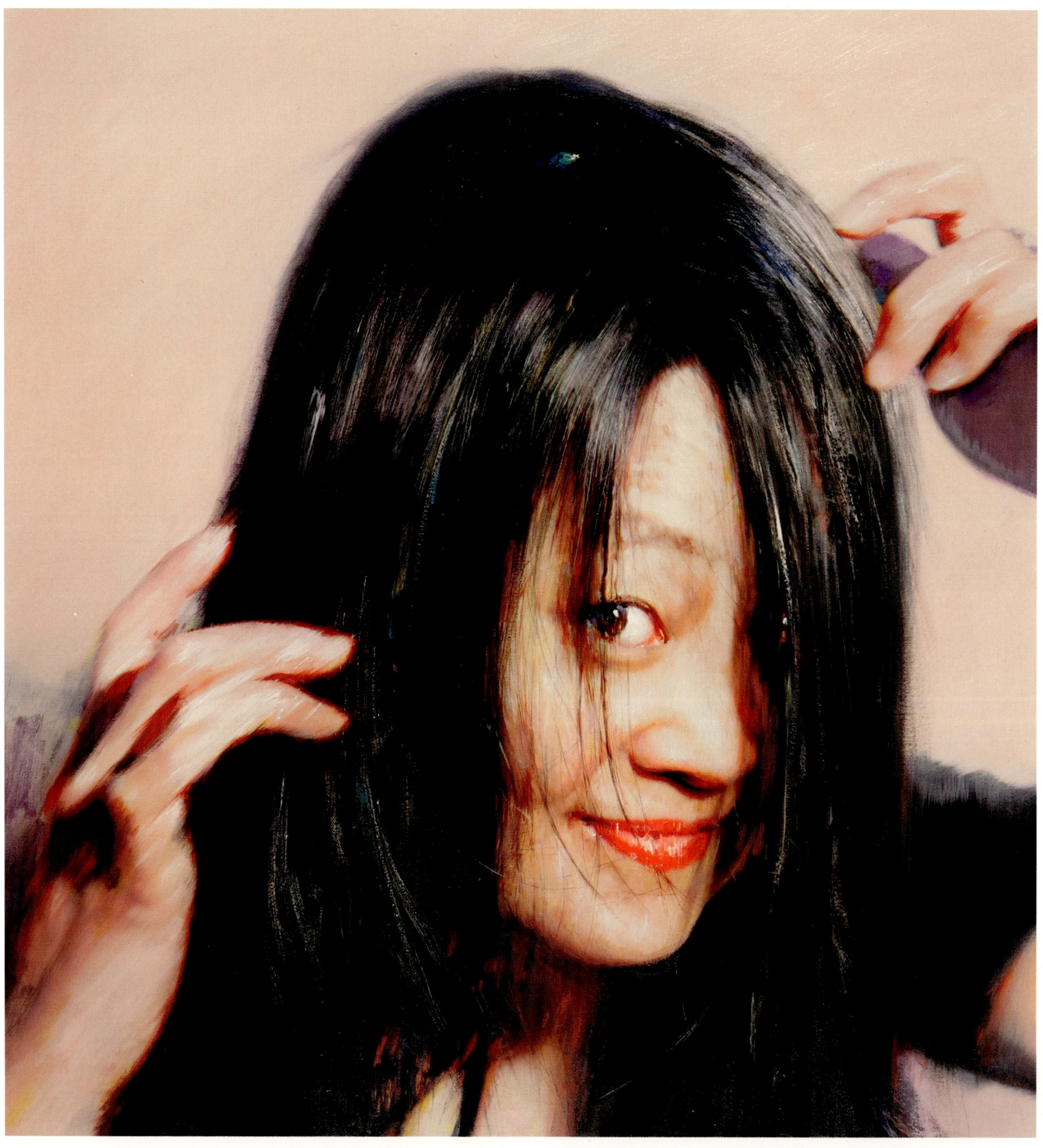

RUBINA SATRIANI, 2014
Oil on canvas, 28 × 26 in.

ZZ SATRIANI, 2013 ❯
Oil on canvas, 28 × 26 in.

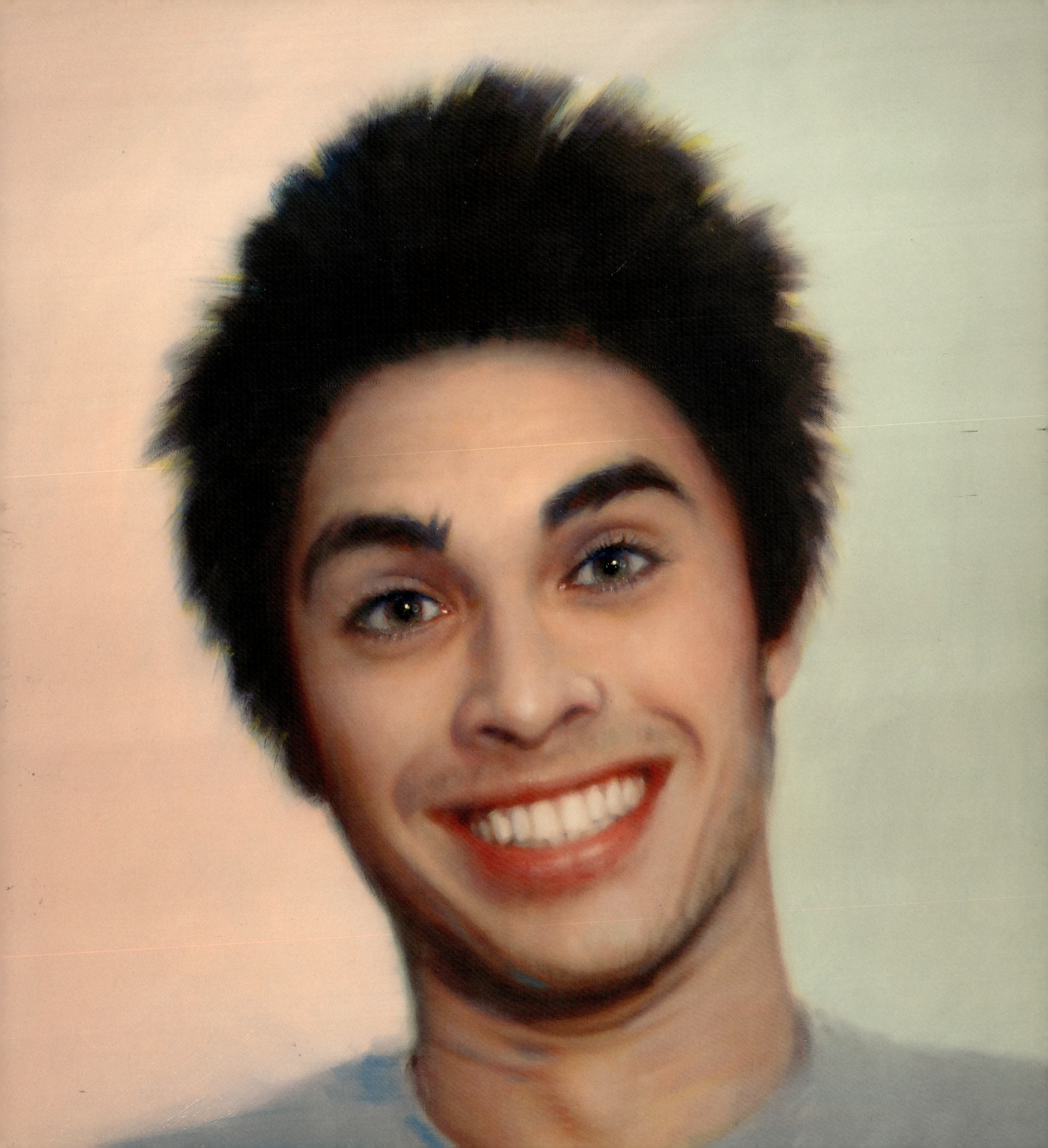

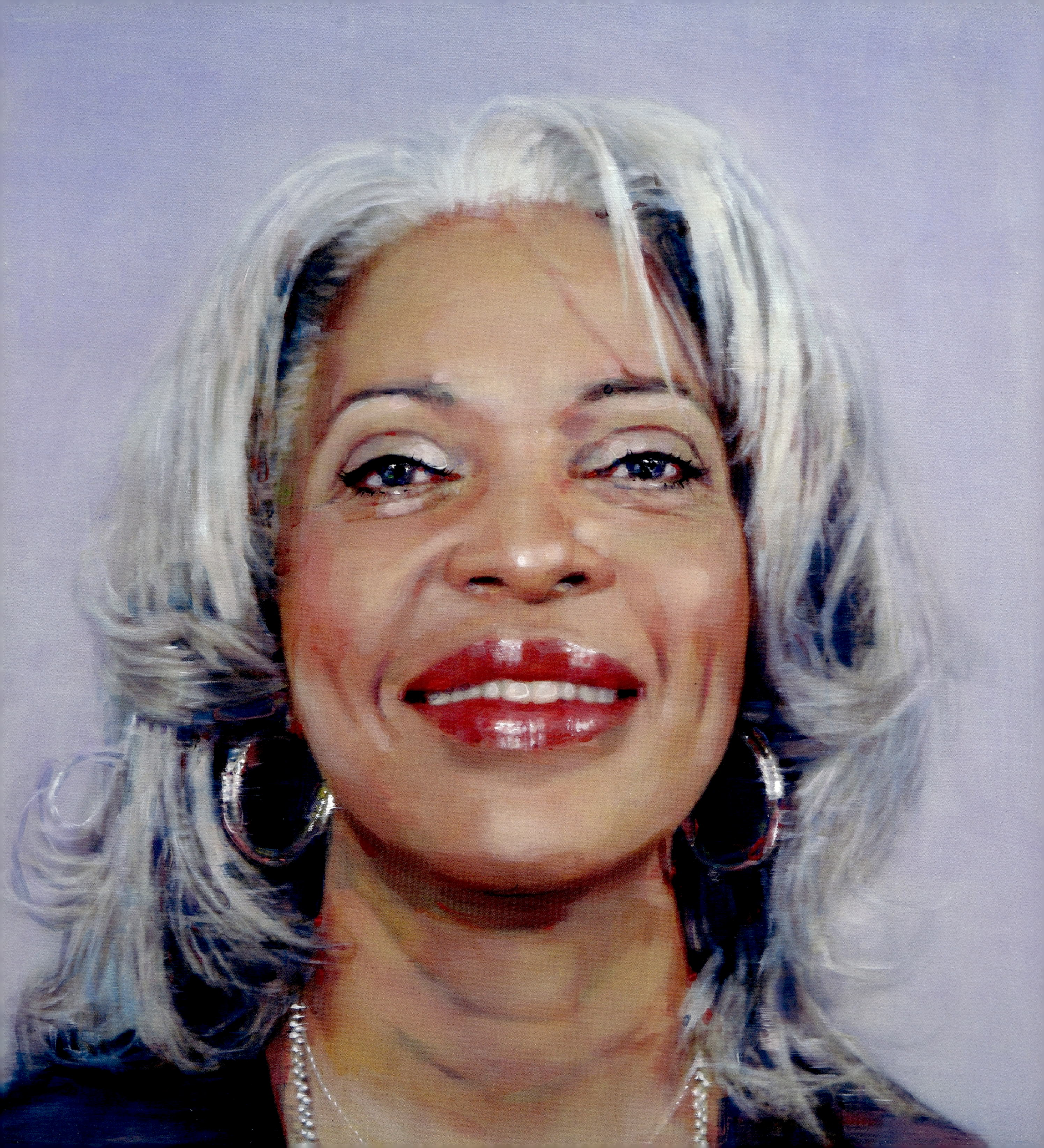

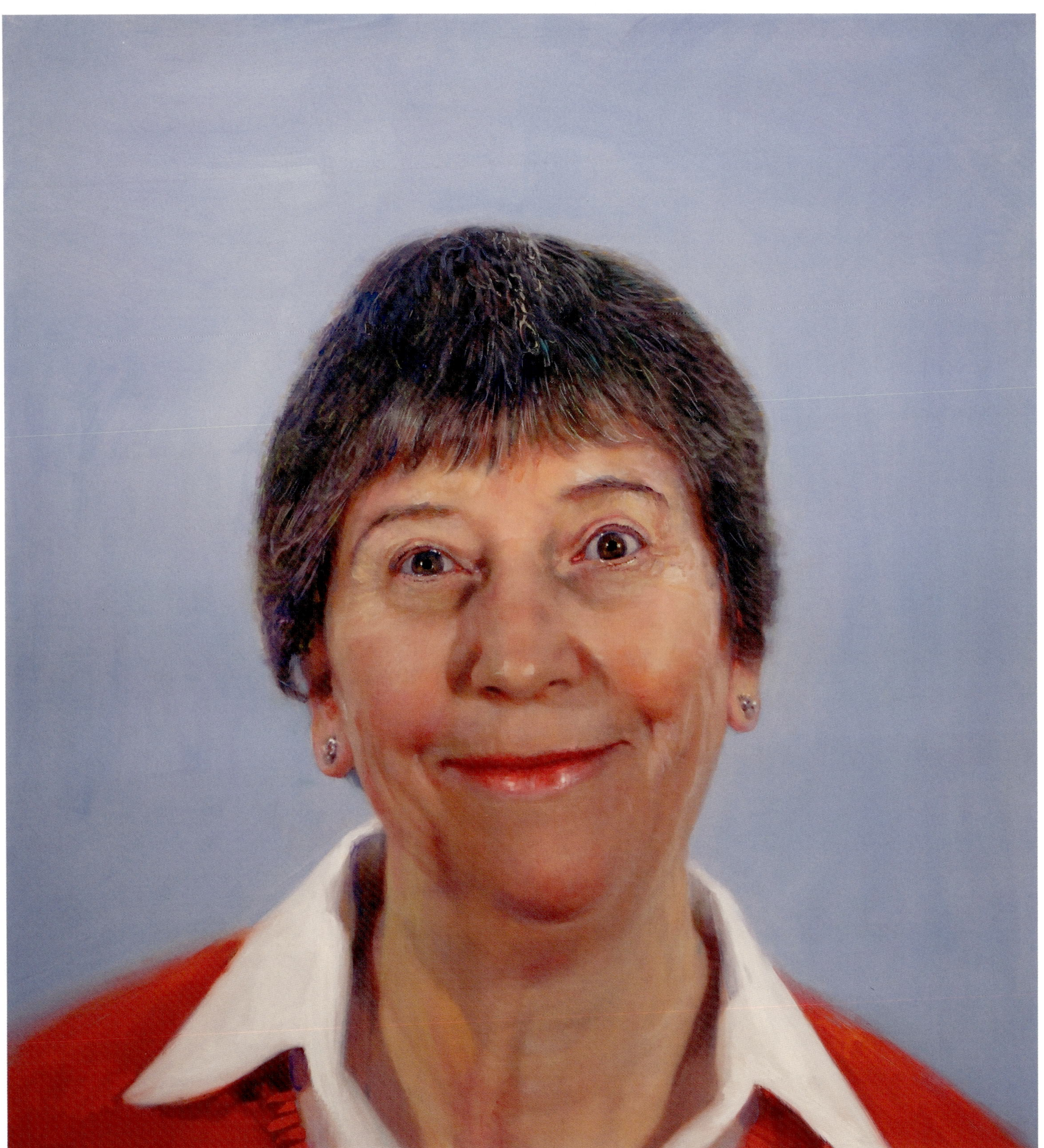

In spring 1989, my wife, Sheila Cohen, and I decided to visit Dr. Valentin Suslov, a colleague at the Urologic Institute of Kiev who shared my interest in anesthesiology and in stamp collecting. During our visit, Suslov told us that he would like us to meet a dear friend of his, the young artist Valentin Popov.

So began our friendship with Valentin. We visited his studio in Kiev and were impressed by his artwork. Despite a significant language barrier, we immediately liked Valentin and wanted to help him if we could. So we invited him to visit us at Stanford. He immediately accepted.

Valentin brought a large portfolio of about thirty works so that we could hold an exhibition in our house on the Stanford campus. When I met him at the San Francisco airport, Valentin was helping an elderly lady who could barely walk debark the Pan Am plane and find her waiting relatives. This good deed turned into a near disaster. After locating his fellow passenger's relatives, he looked for his portfolio, only to realize that he had left it on the plane. To our horror, the plane had already departed and was on its way to Los Angeles. Miraculously, Pan Am returned the portfolio the next day. This led us to believe that things would go well for Valentin in the US.　　**RICHARD I. MAZZE**

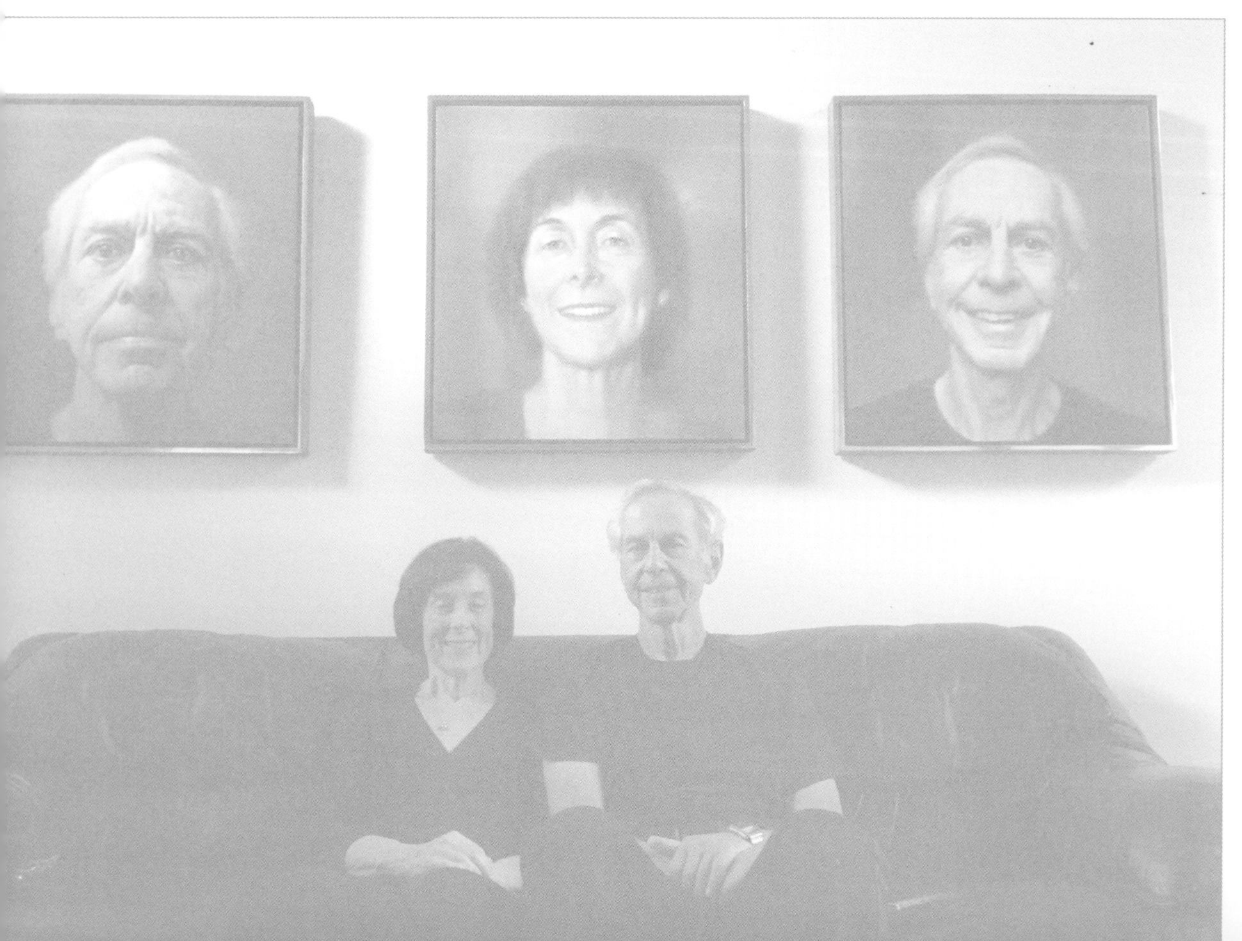

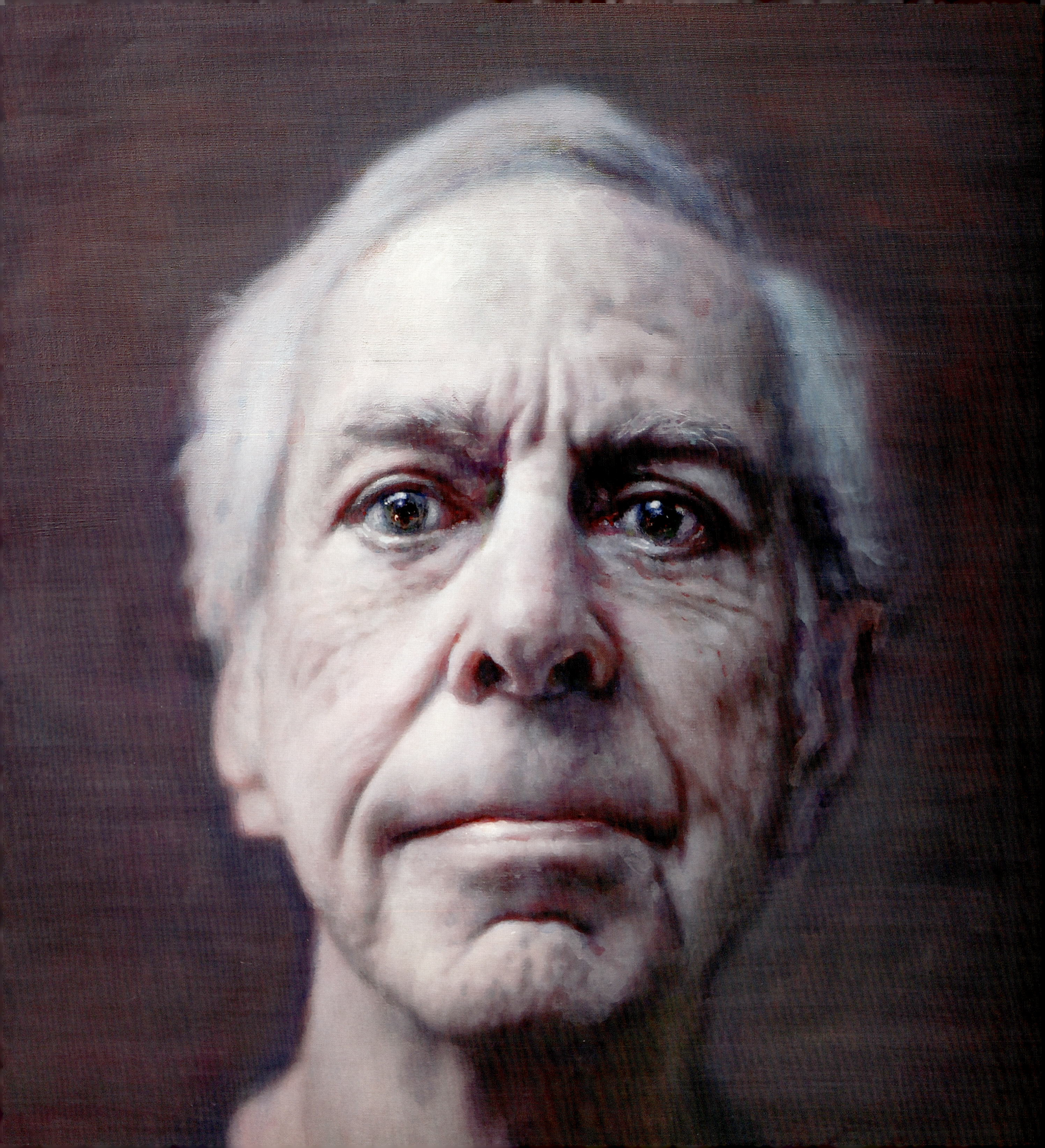

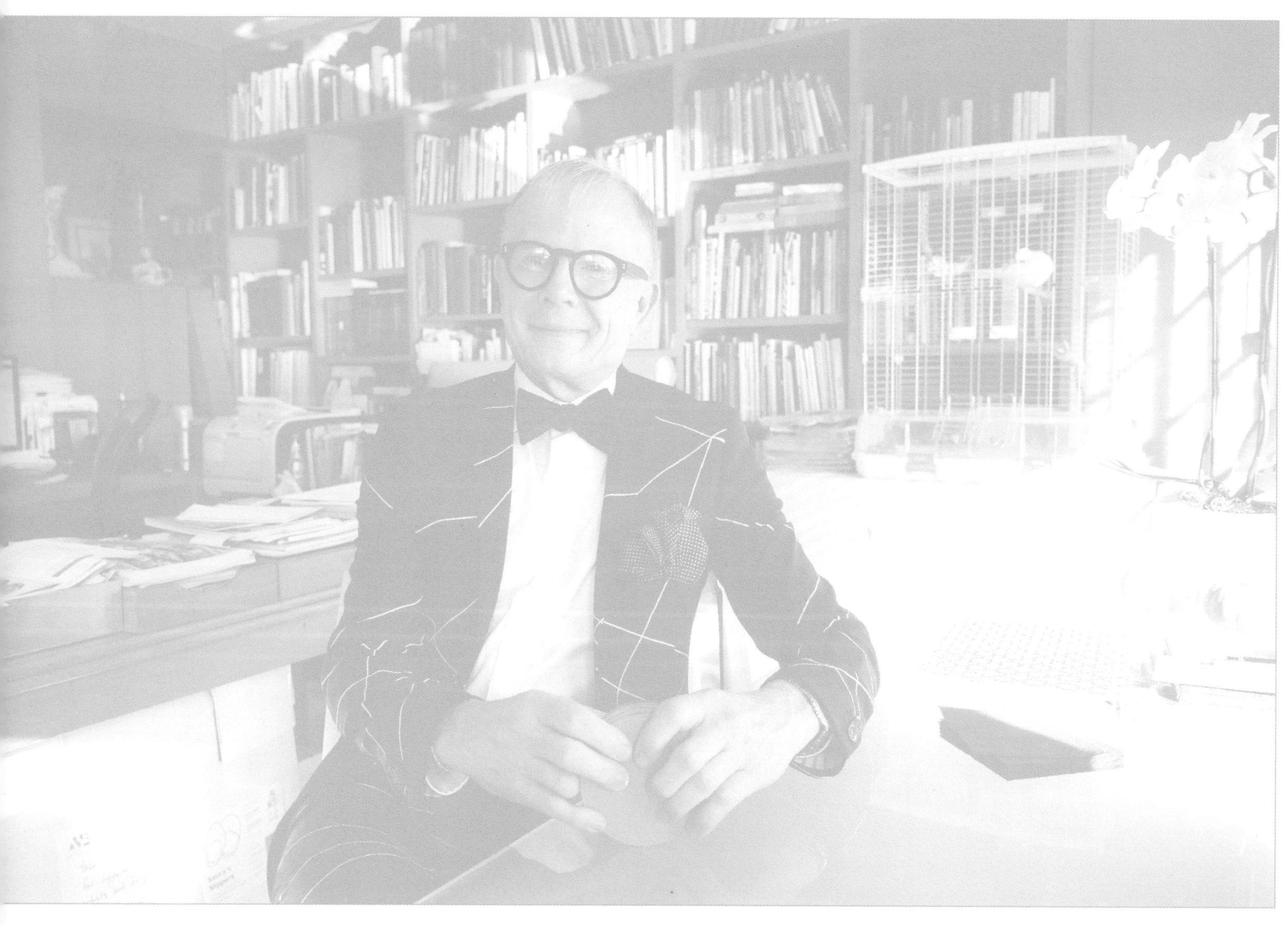

following, left: **TERRY ANTHONY 1**, 2014. Oil on canvas, 28 × 26 in.

right: **TERRY ANTHONY 2**, 2014. Oil on canvas, 28 × 26 in.

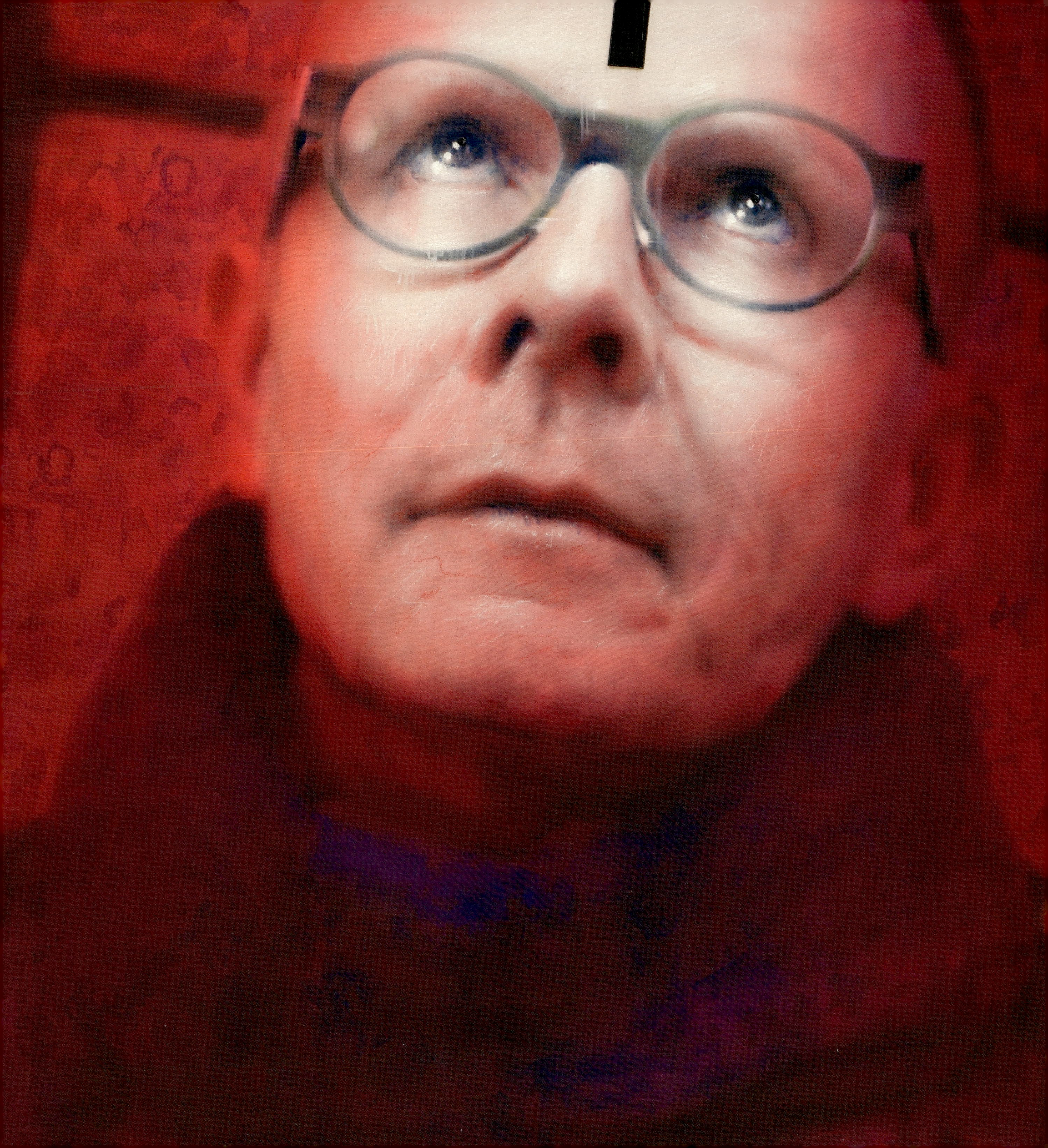

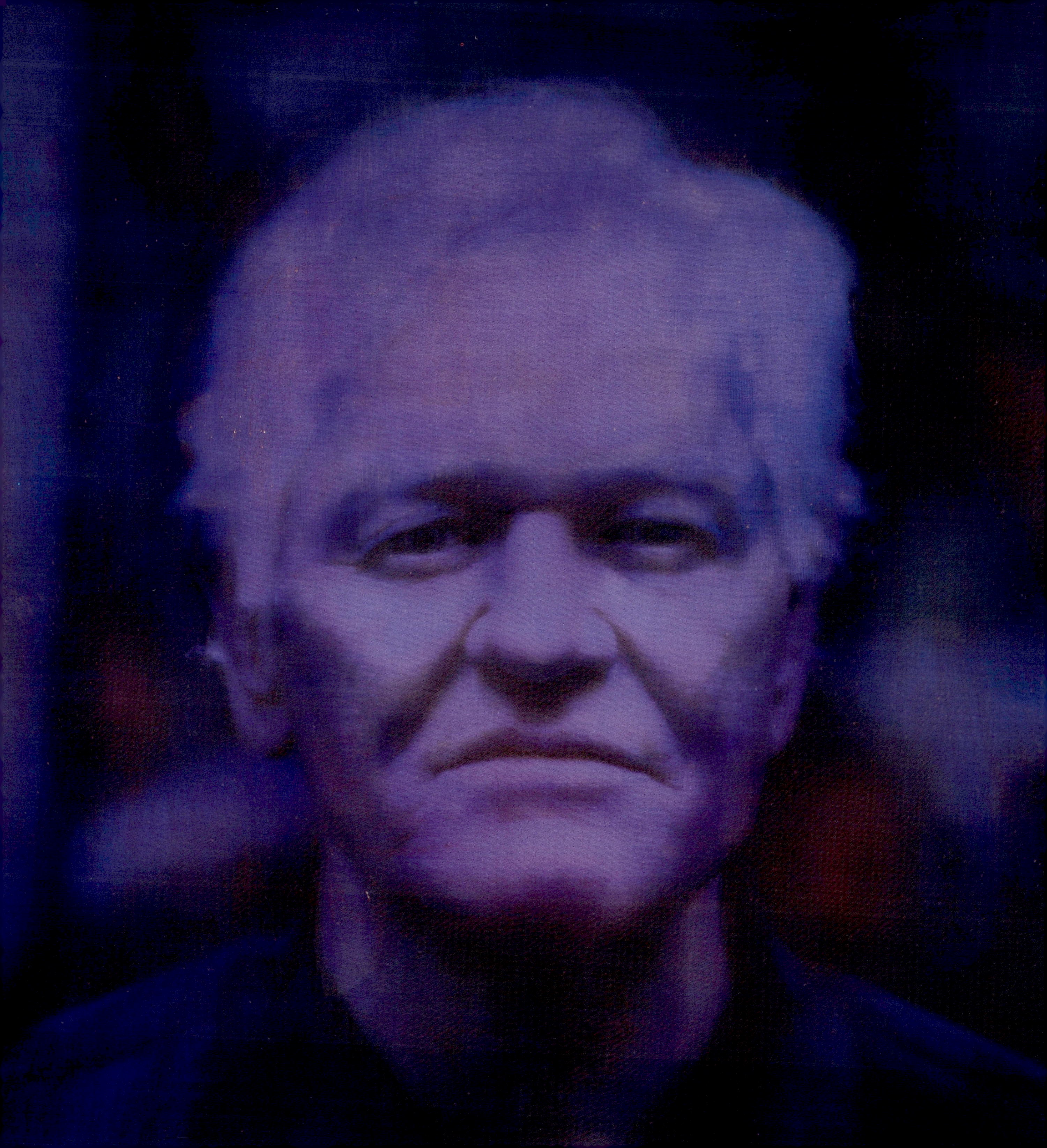

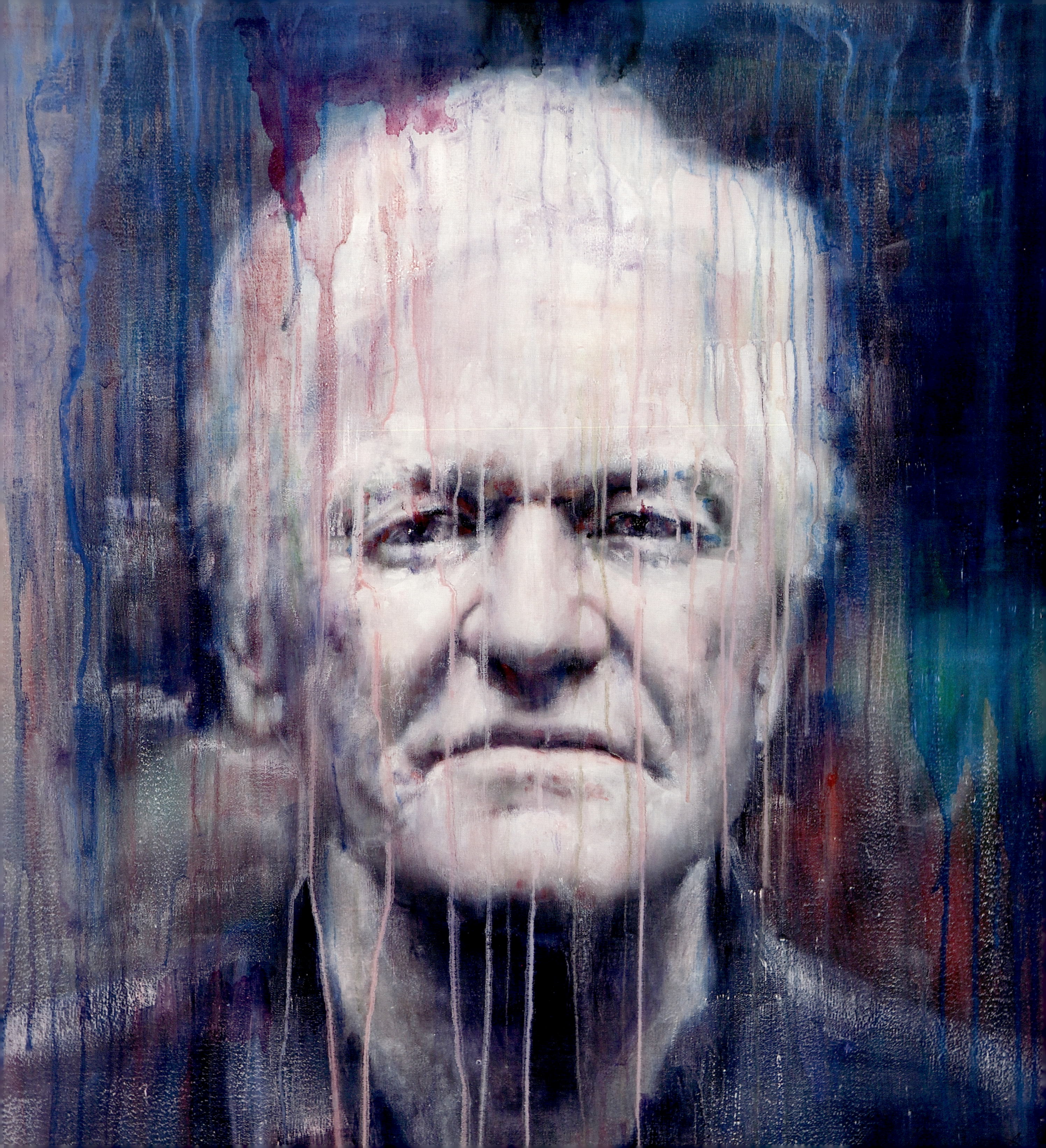

I was introduced to Valentin in 1992, after the opening of an exhibition of his etchings in Sausalito, California. As a dealer who specializes in works on paper, I was immediately impressed by Valentin's mastery of the graphic medium, but I also felt a connection with him as a fellow immigrant, he being from Ukraine and I being from Italy. I admired his resourcefulness, drive, and talent. Through the years while representing him in my gallery, we have become friends, and I continue to be surprised by his work and its impeccable technique.

PASQUALE IANNETTI

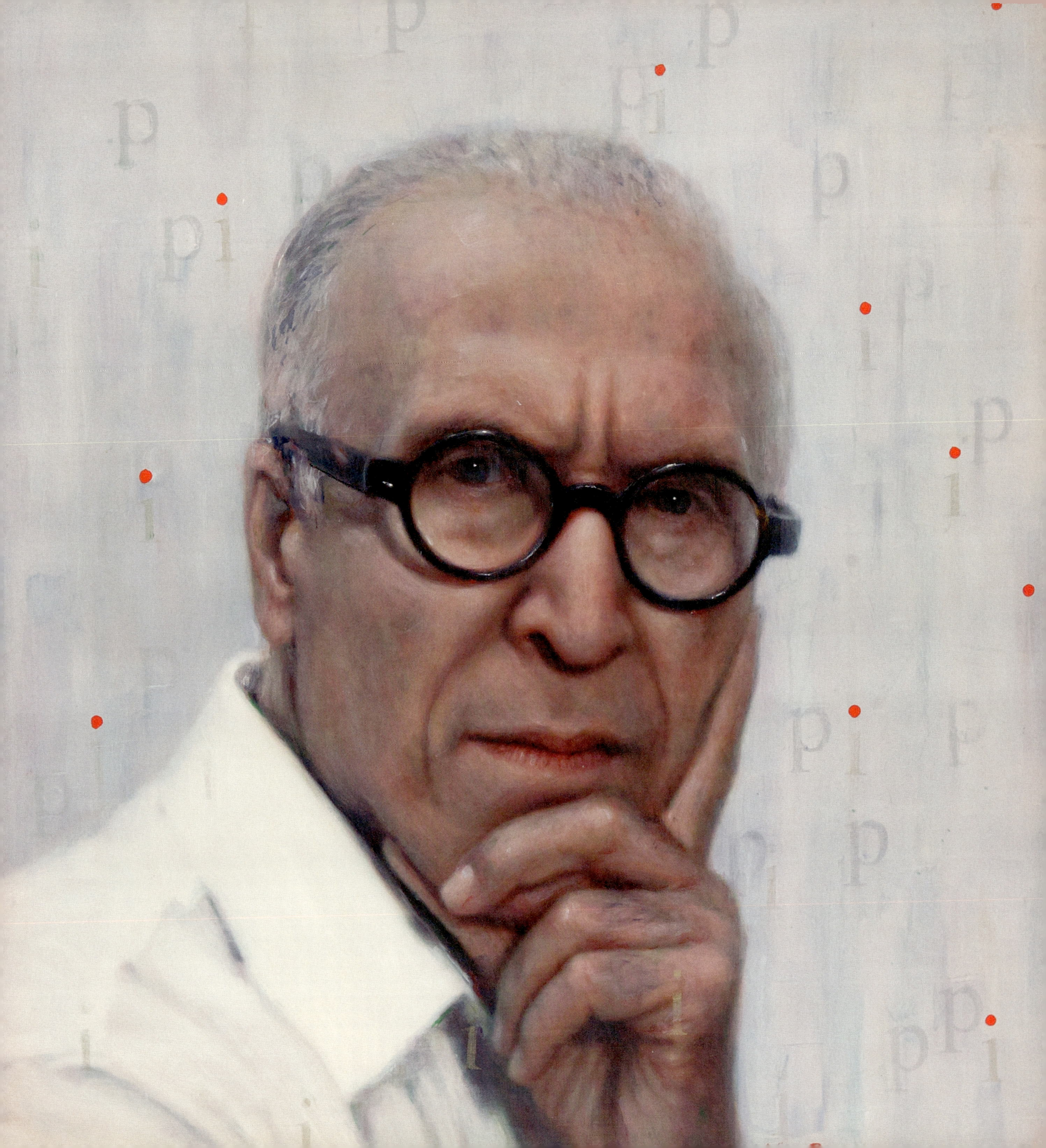

GRACE CONTRO, 2014
Oil on canvas, 28 × 26 in.

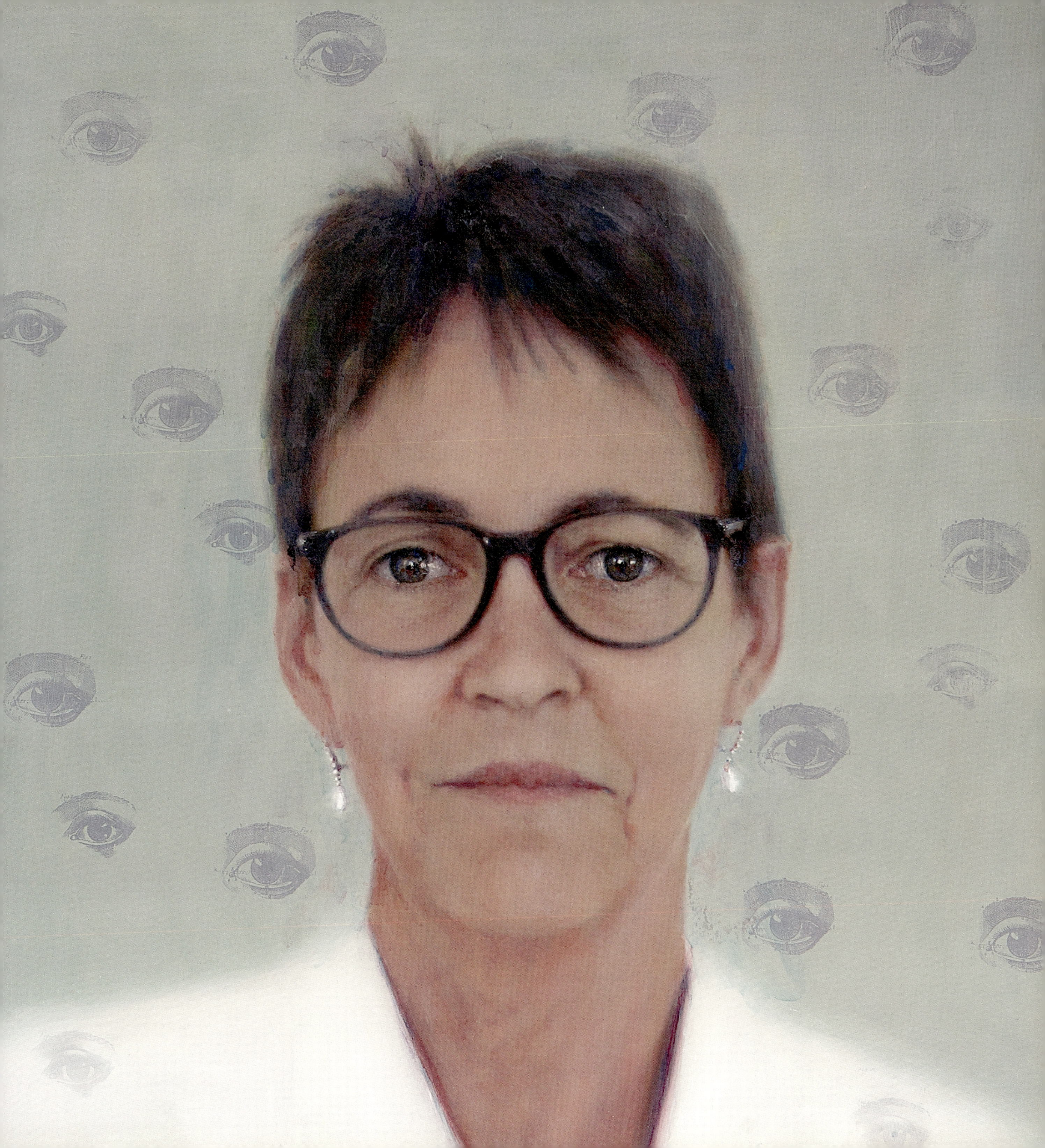

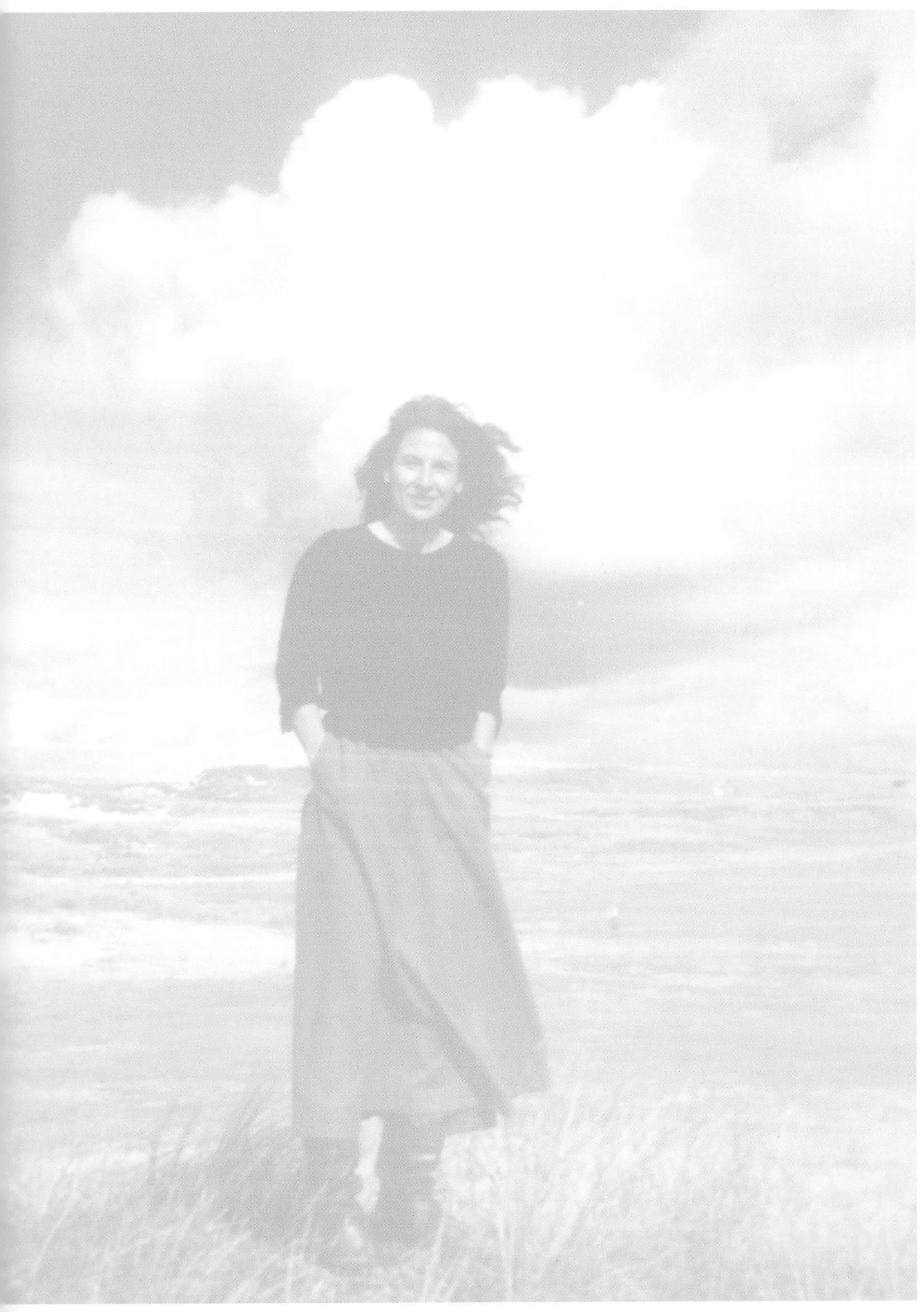

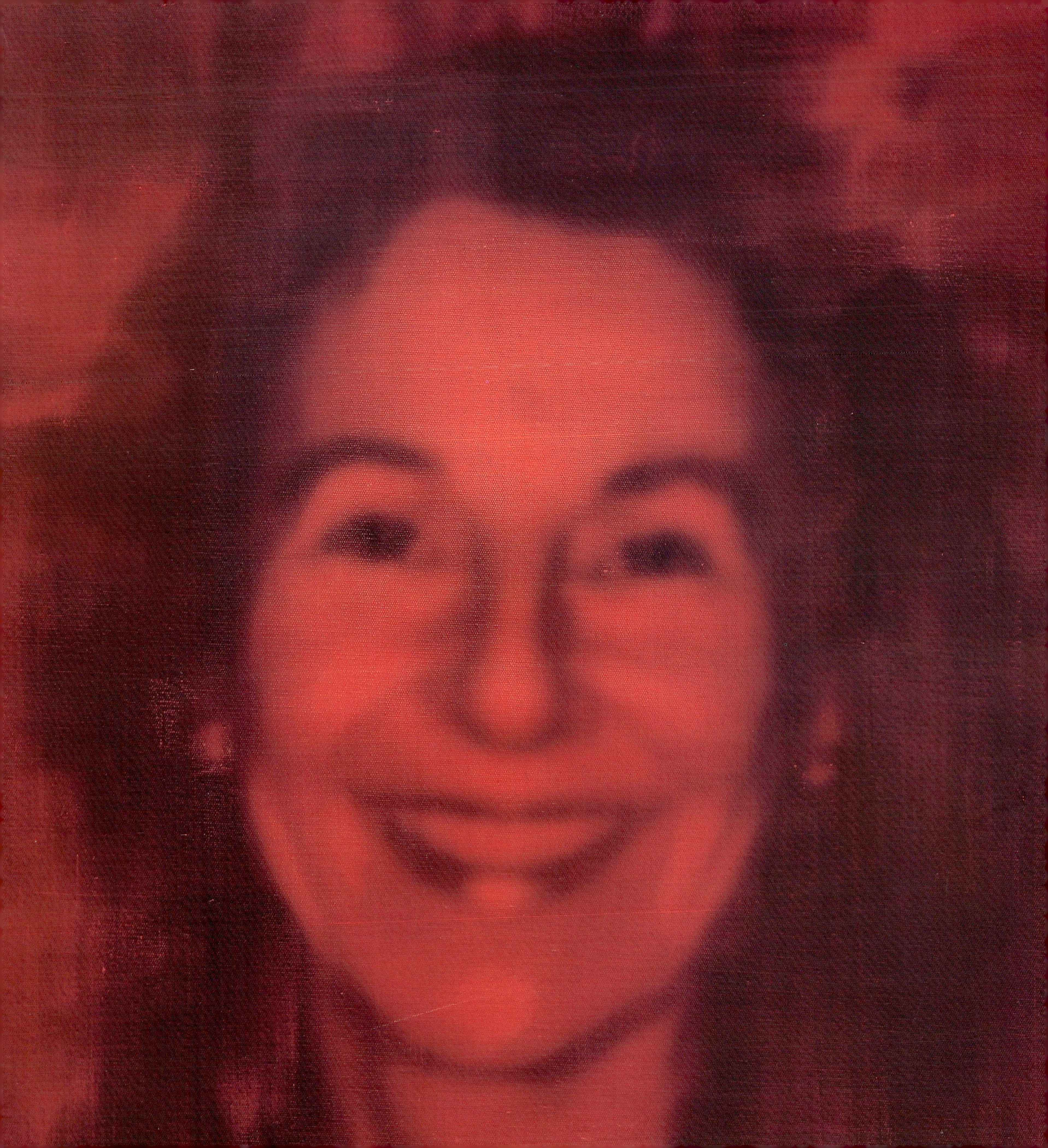

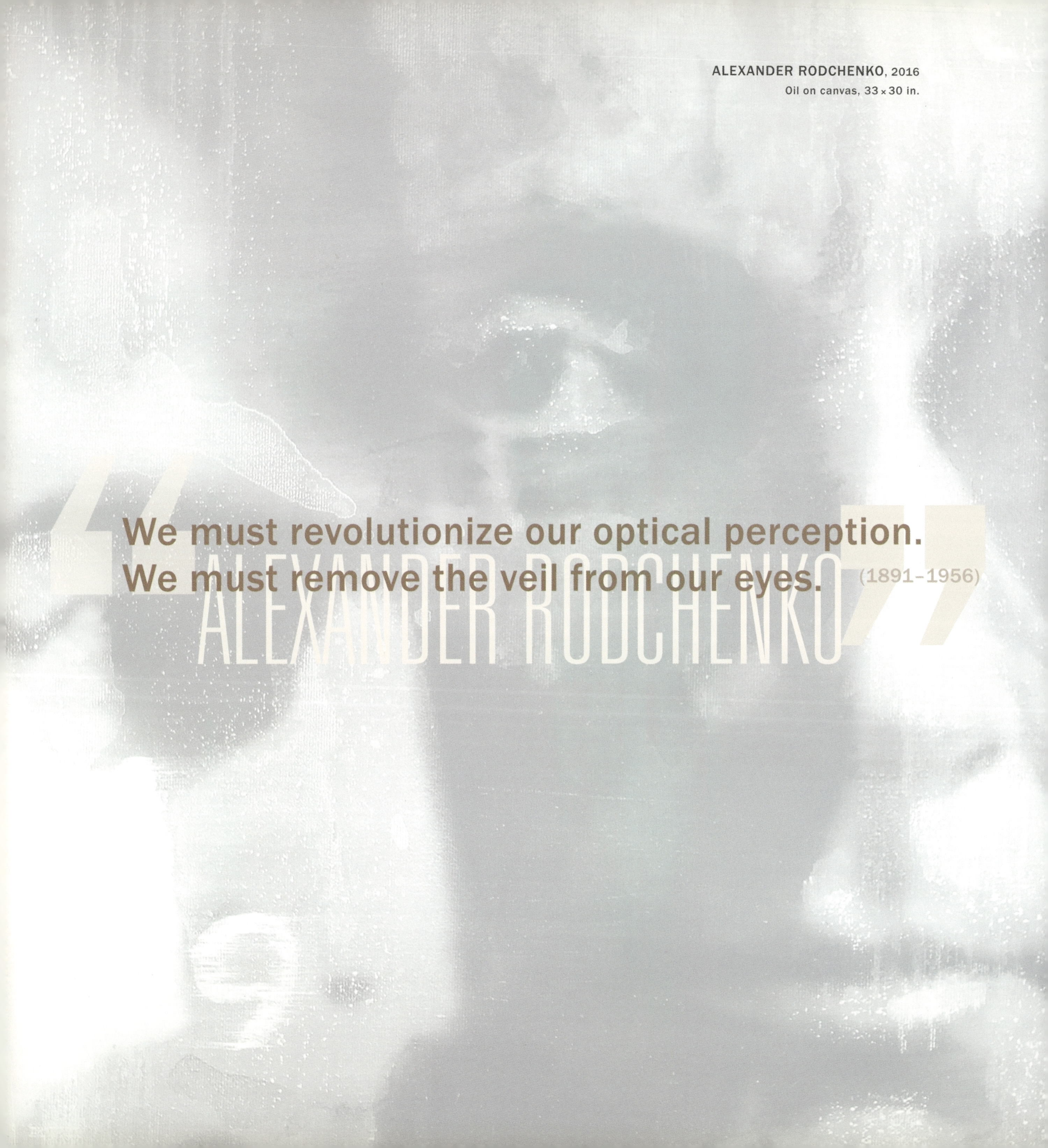

"We must revolutionize our optical perception.
We must remove the veil from our eyes." (1891–1956)

ALEXANDER RODCHENKO

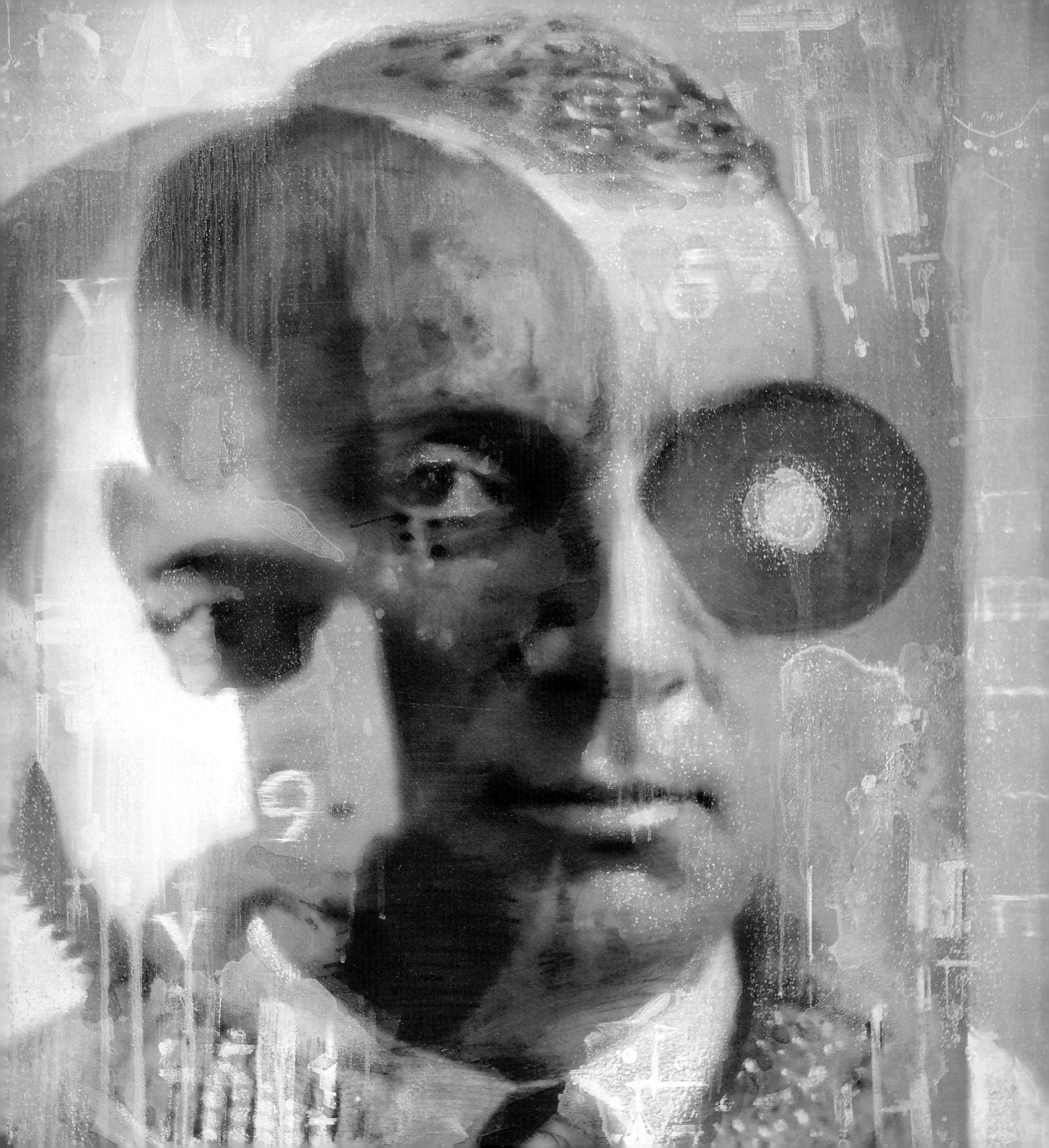

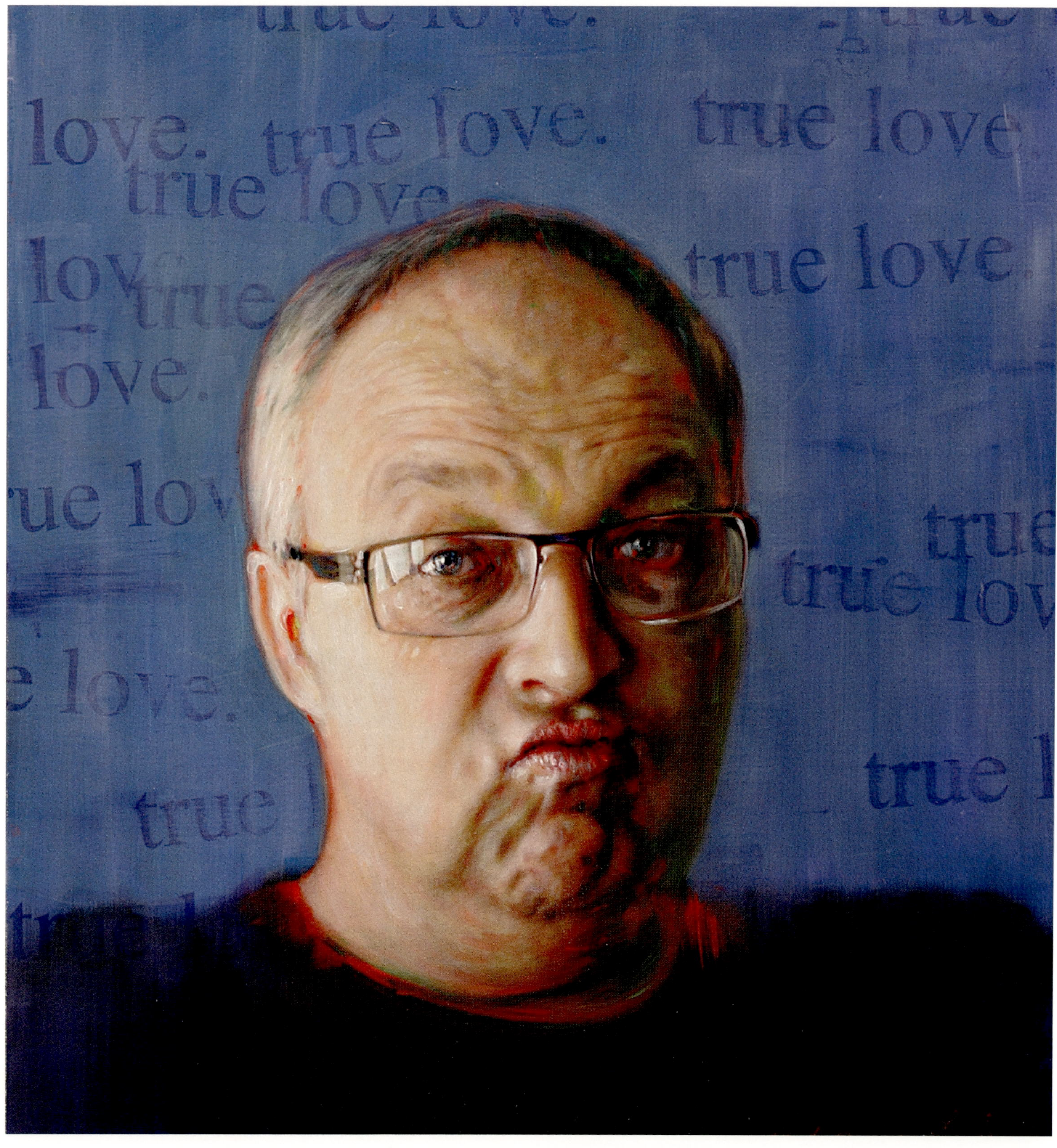

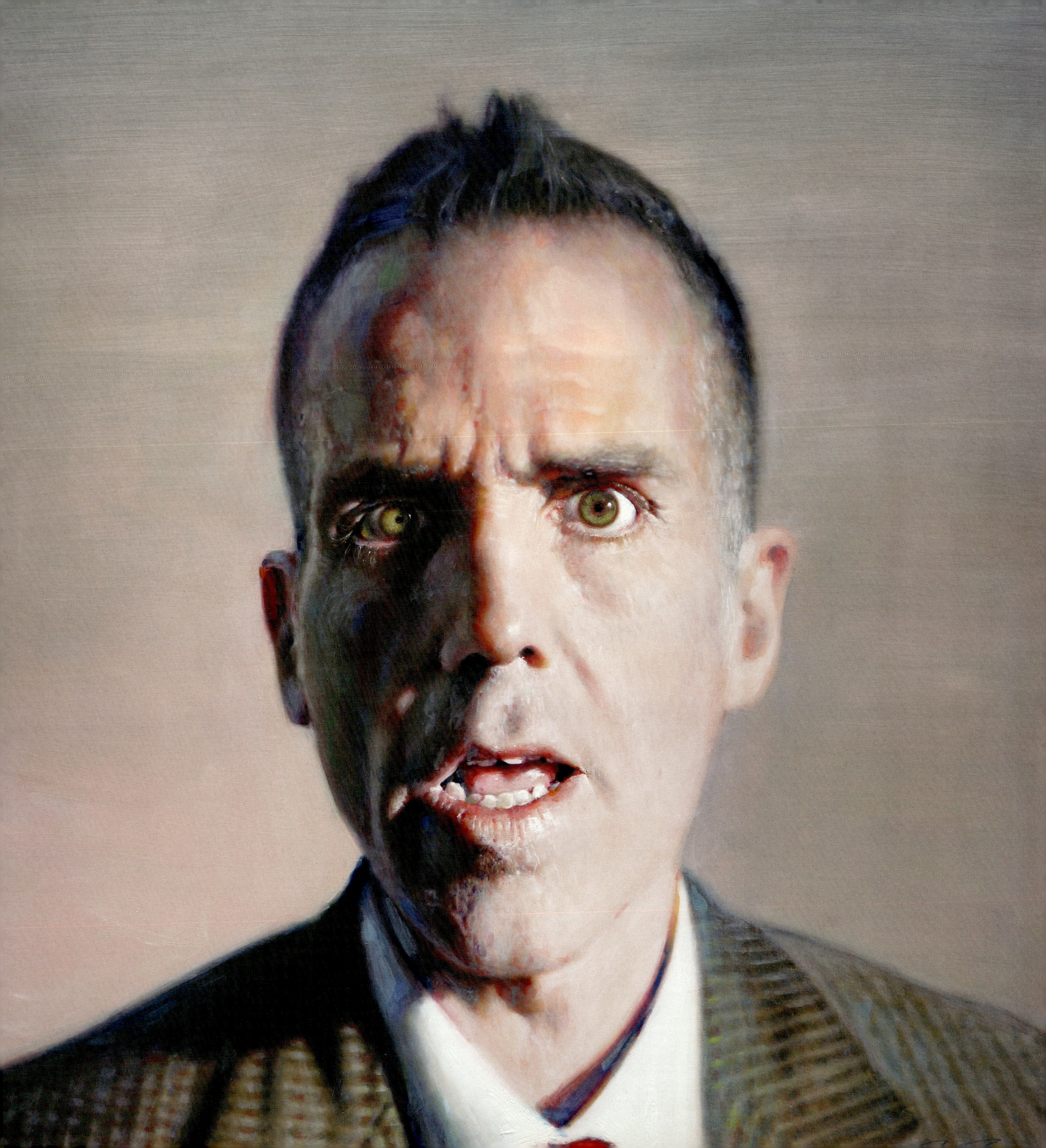

ANDREAS NOTTEBOHM, 2014
Oil on canvas, 28 x 26 in.

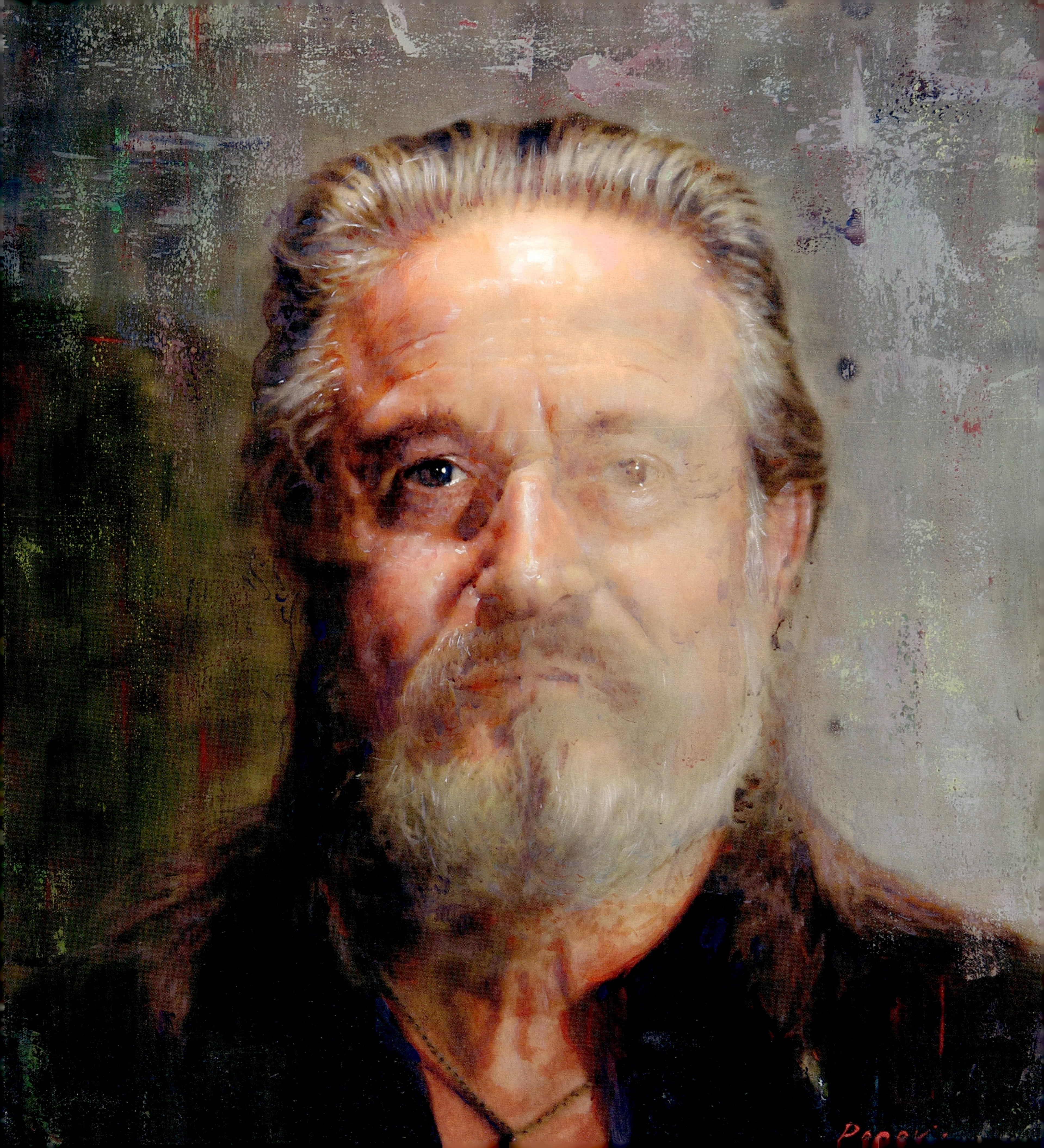

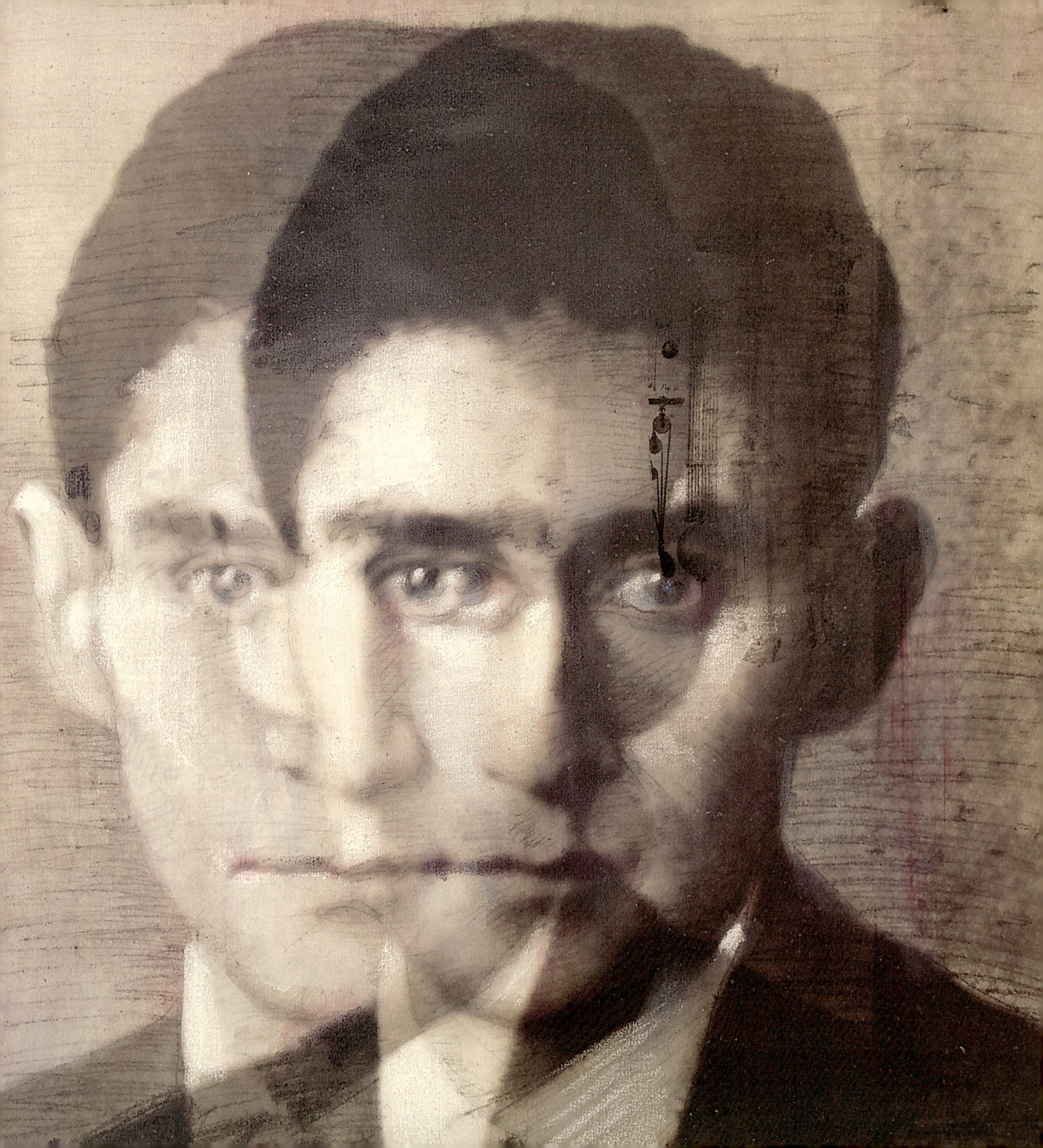

"By believing passionately in something that still does not exist, we create it. The nonexistent is whatever we have not sufficiently desired.

The truth is always an abyss. One must—as in a swimming pool—dare to dive from the quivering springboard of trivial everyday experience and sink into the depths, in order to later rise again—laughing and fighting for breath—to the now doubly illuminated surface of things.

There are some things one can only achieve by a deliberate leap in the opposite direction."

(1883–1924)

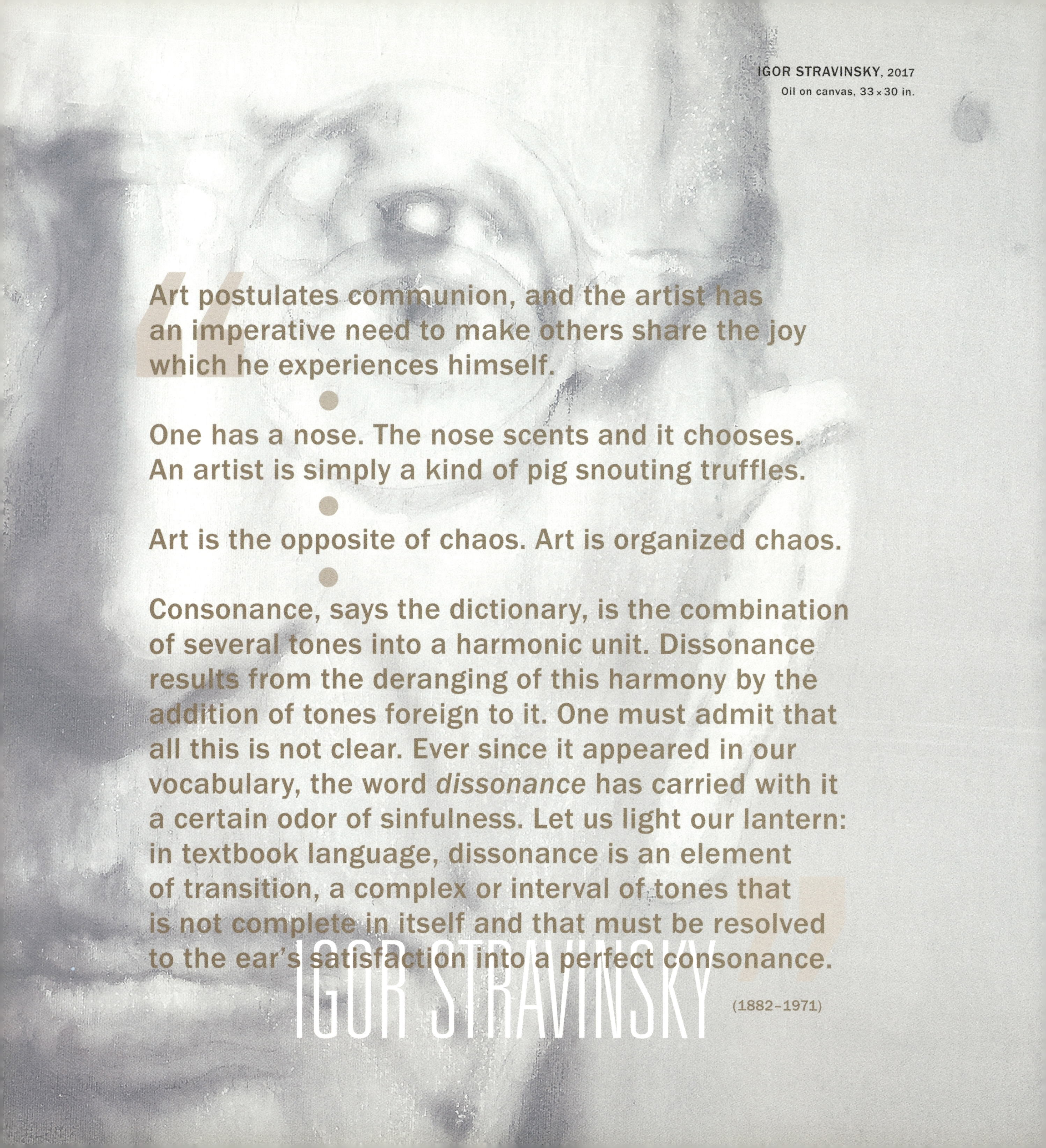

"Art postulates communion, and the artist has an imperative need to make others share the joy which he experiences himself.

One has a nose. The nose scents and it chooses. An artist is simply a kind of pig snouting truffles.

Art is the opposite of chaos. Art is organized chaos.

Consonance, says the dictionary, is the combination of several tones into a harmonic unit. Dissonance results from the deranging of this harmony by the addition of tones foreign to it. One must admit that all this is not clear. Ever since it appeared in our vocabulary, the word *dissonance* has carried with it a certain odor of sinfulness. Let us light our lantern: in textbook language, dissonance is an element of transition, a complex or interval of tones that is not complete in itself and that must be resolved to the ear's satisfaction into a perfect consonance.

IGOR STRAVINSKY

(1882–1971)

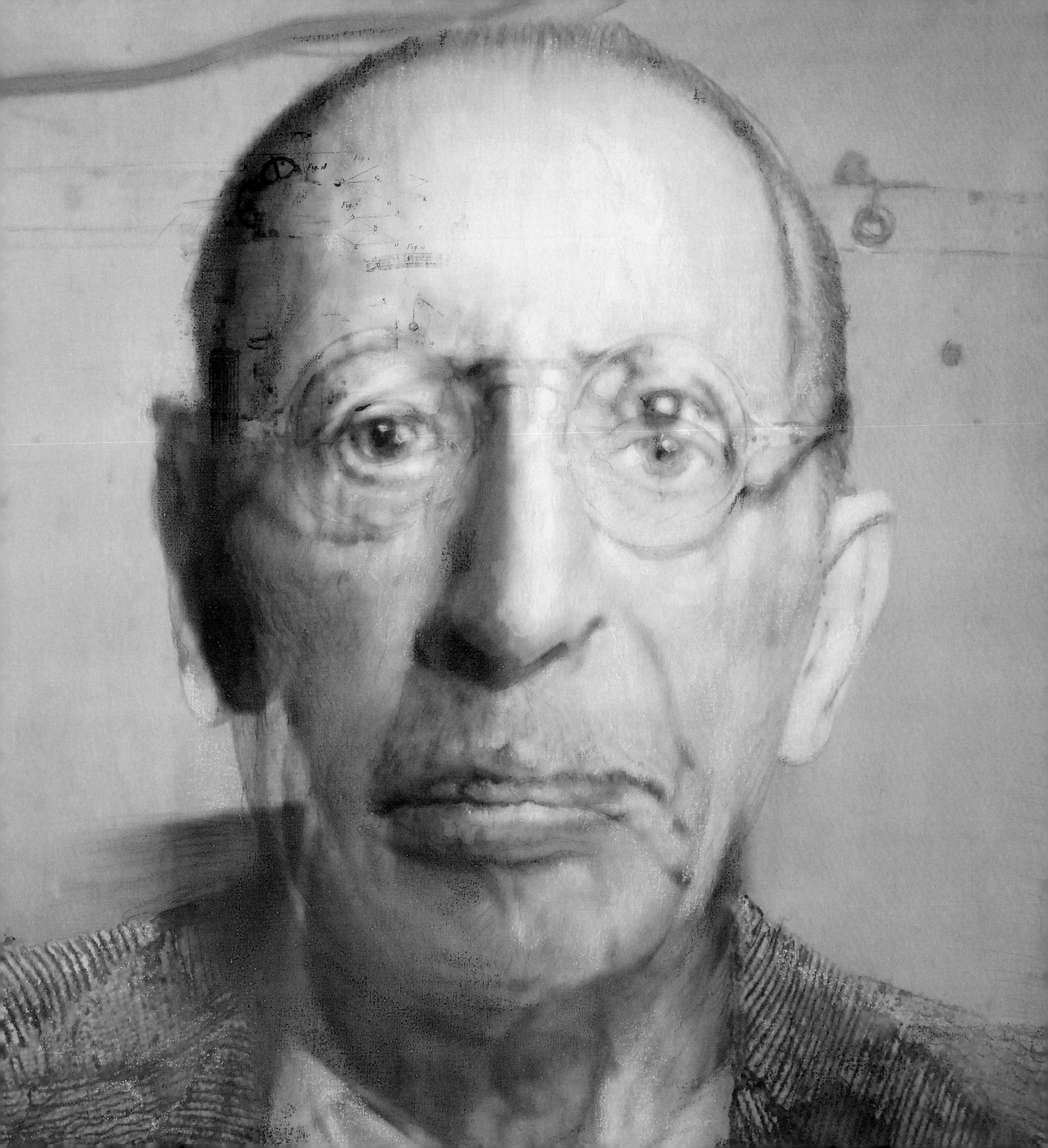

B. R. Gilbert

METAPHYSICS OF THE FACE

Portraiture is, of course, one of the most venerable genres of visual art. Although every era has had its distinctive brand, traceable by various distinctive characteristics to the period during which it was done, attempts at advancing the genre have been few. For centuries, prior to the experiments of the Symbolists, Expressionists, Cubists, and other modernists, portraiture adhered to a predictable, tacitly prescribed tradition of conventional realism, intended to capture a veristic likeness of the sitter frozen at a moment to be preserved throughout eternity, thus immortalizing its subject. In paintings and portrait busts of the Classical Period, the Middle Ages, and the Dutch Masters' halcyon, this trend persisted until the breakthrough distortions of Ensor and the asymmetrical contraventions of Picasso, Brancusi, et al. changed the prevailing standard. Popov revisits the genre from a postmodern perspective.

Evident first and foremost in Popov's portraits is the artist's customary technical virtuosity. Popov's portraits are almost photorealist, yet again they're not. They're not as slick and smugly mechanical as Andy Warhol's, nor are they marked by the same glib superficiality; they're not as precise as those done by Chuck Close; they do not possess the muted chromatic exuberance of Francis Bacon; then again, they recall aspects of all three.

Simultaneously effervescent and understated, Popov's ebullient portraits are evocative of a cross-fertilization between pop formalism and a sort of neo-tonalism. Popov's approach to his subject matter is as subtle as it is spectacular; the constituents of his canvases are carefully arranged for dramatic impact, and expressively modulated luminosity is always an integral element. Closer inspection discloses incidental details, quirks, anomalies. Popov's complex compositions bear the signature of an expert technician thoroughly in control of his medium.

Popov plays with poses and gestures. The faces of many of his sitters are counterpoised by hands, sometimes caught casually placed, as in supporting a chin, or in an attitude of contemplation, puzzlement, or reverie, at other times as if to connote some personal attribute or propensity either known to the artist or spontaneously revealing itself. Hands and, in a few instances, small props act as foils to frame or counterweight the all-important center of focus—the face. Articles of dress serve the same purpose. Popov's subjects, caught during moments of distraction, of reflection, seem enveloped by a tinge of intimacy or of confidentiality and offset by an autonomous illumination which seems to have its source in a hidden, inner light. There is a striking lucidity to Popov's faces, a mellowed metallic look.

This same subdued shininess is an effect Popov has been able to enhance in past works by painting with enamel on aluminum sheeting.

Lush pigmentation and deft, adventurous brushwork combine to masterful effect in Popov's portraits, but they are saturated with an extra ingredient—an intangible manifestation of the human essence—the vital force, the anima.

Portrait practitioners have always balanced verisimilitude with their own vision and faculties of creative interpretation, thus recreating resemblance filtered through the characteristics inherent in the medium—clay, paint, photographic film—in which the resemblance is captured. At a higher remove, portraiture does a balancing act between subject and object and between representation and abstraction. Valentin Popov takes all of this into account when rendering the human physiognomies in the present lineup. The question of identity, however costumed, is another matter.

Humanity is a profoundly social species, and, in Popov's *FACE* collection, the likenesses of individual sitters grouped together in ribbon-like tiers on the walls of the exhibition space comprise a metaphor for the social microcosm. When grouped together, this assortment of disparate heads constitutes a separate organism. Suspended somewhere between a sort of fleshly hyper-realism and Human Document School, these portraits ultimately amount to individual personality studies, not to the depiction of a cross section of a particular tribe. In certain respects, Popov is after the same attributes and shares the same goals as his august predecessors Frans Hals, Velázquez, and John Singer Sargent. He, too, is a society painter of sorts, minus the rigid formality and decorum. He is not a court painter *per se*, concerned with the pomp of hierarchies and the trappings of status and prestige, nor can he be called, as Sargent characterized himself, merely "a painter of appearances." But he does mean to survey a sampling of his contemporaries at their most insouciant and most chic and, in the process, explore their linkages and interrelationships as creatures and as cogs of society.

Popov's foray into the redoubtable realm of the portrait is more than an exercise in stylistics. A complexity of conceptual elements informs this work, centering on the elusive nature of personality. Each face has its own topography—a telltale wrinkle or crease, a twinkle in an eye, a tilt of the head, a curl of a lip, a twist at the corner of the mouth—clues to character, determinants of personality. Popov's portraits witness a range of emotions and other indicators of psychological makeup. Personality is the hidden entrance to the hall of human identity, penetrable by way of the *eyes*; the heart of the face is the eye. Popov has constructed an Argus of multiple eyes peering from the gallery wall: connection occurs through reciprocating retinae—*I'm looking at you looking at me looking at you*. The well-delineated eye is a Popovian signature. The eye is a two-way vestibule through which we see others at the same time as we see ourselves reflected. The eye is both a window and a mirror.

Is the portrait, then, a person or a thing? How does a painted portrait differ from a photograph? The face to be reproduced in a portrait is a chemical enigma as elusive and ultimately irreducible as the quality of identification itself. Portraiture is, to a great extent, an intricate game of visual semantics aimed at defining terms of human individuality. The task Popov has assigned himself is nothing less than expanding the parameters of the portrait genre. For all the excellence of execution evident in this series, *FACE* still remains a matter of form over content.

There is a poetry, a lyricism to these semblances. They are fraught with implied narrative, and in them can be read a secret language of the face. No key can unlock the whole of their mystery nor fathom the paradox of their function as masks or guises—for, in the end, they conceal as much as reveal.

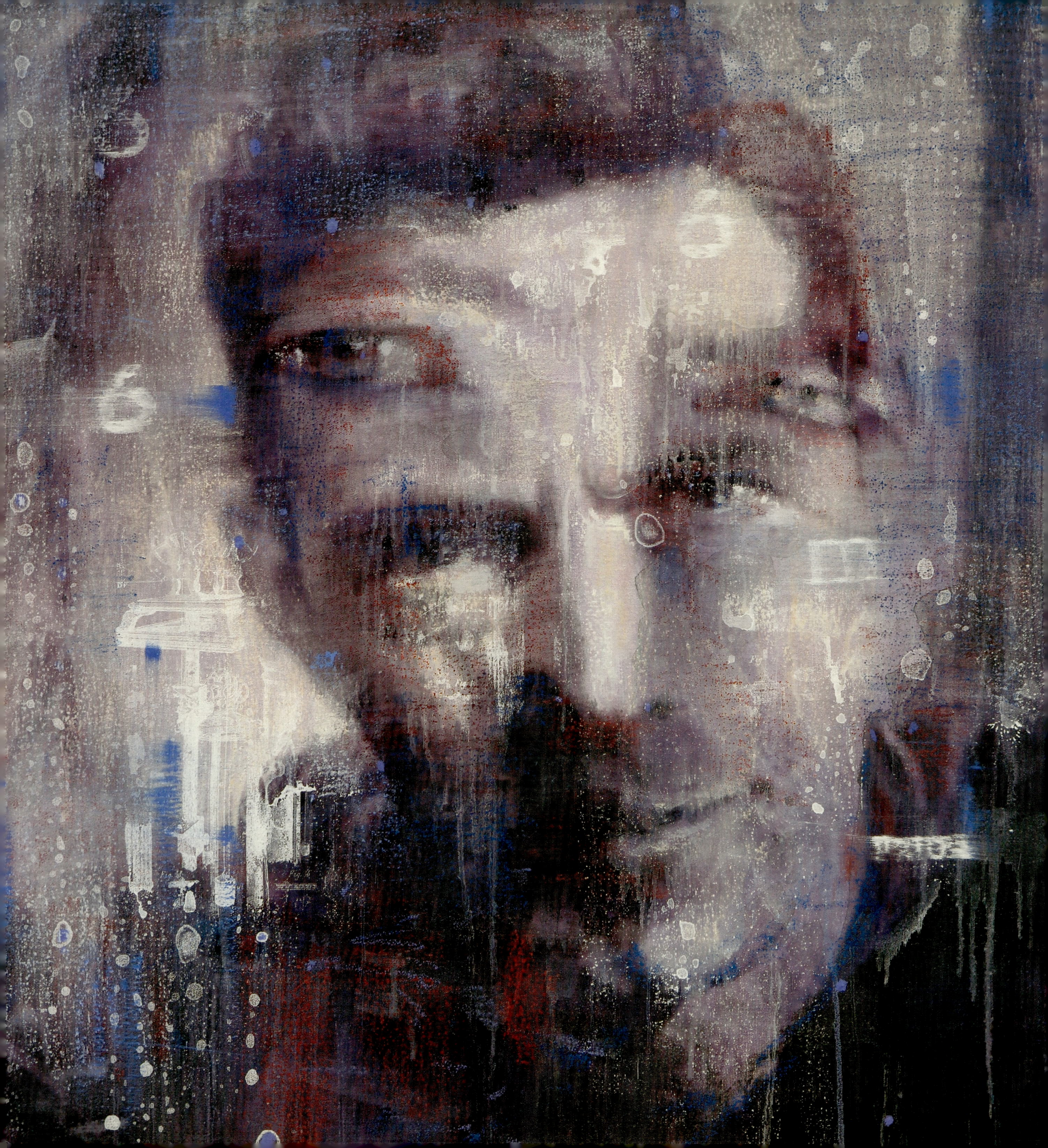

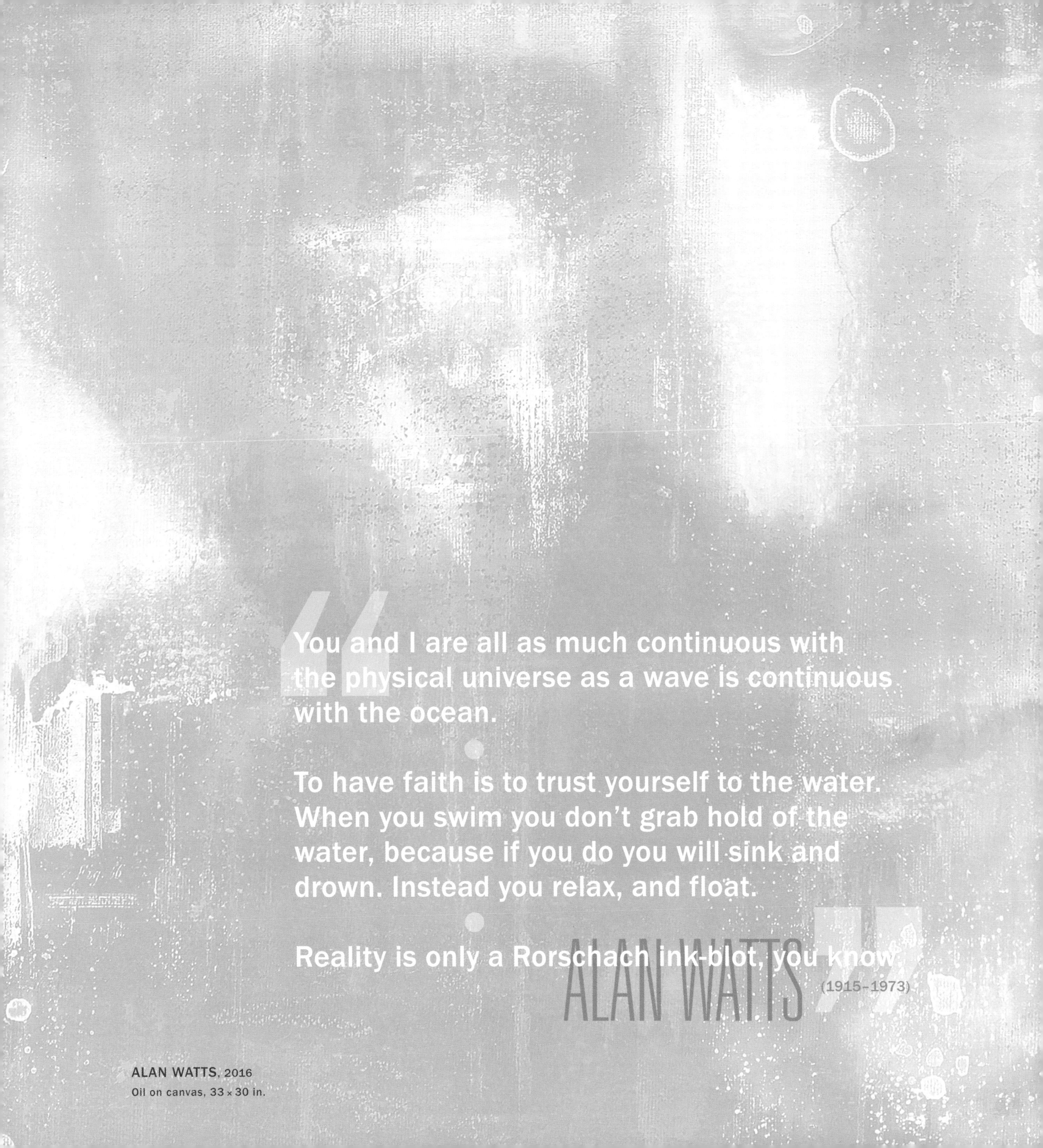

ALAN WATTS, 2016
Oil on canvas, 33 x 30 in.

JORGE LUIS BORGES, 2016
Oil on canvas, 33 × 30 in.

"The worst labyrinth is not that intricate form that can entrap us forever, but a single and precise straight line."

JORGE LUIS BORGES (1899–1986)

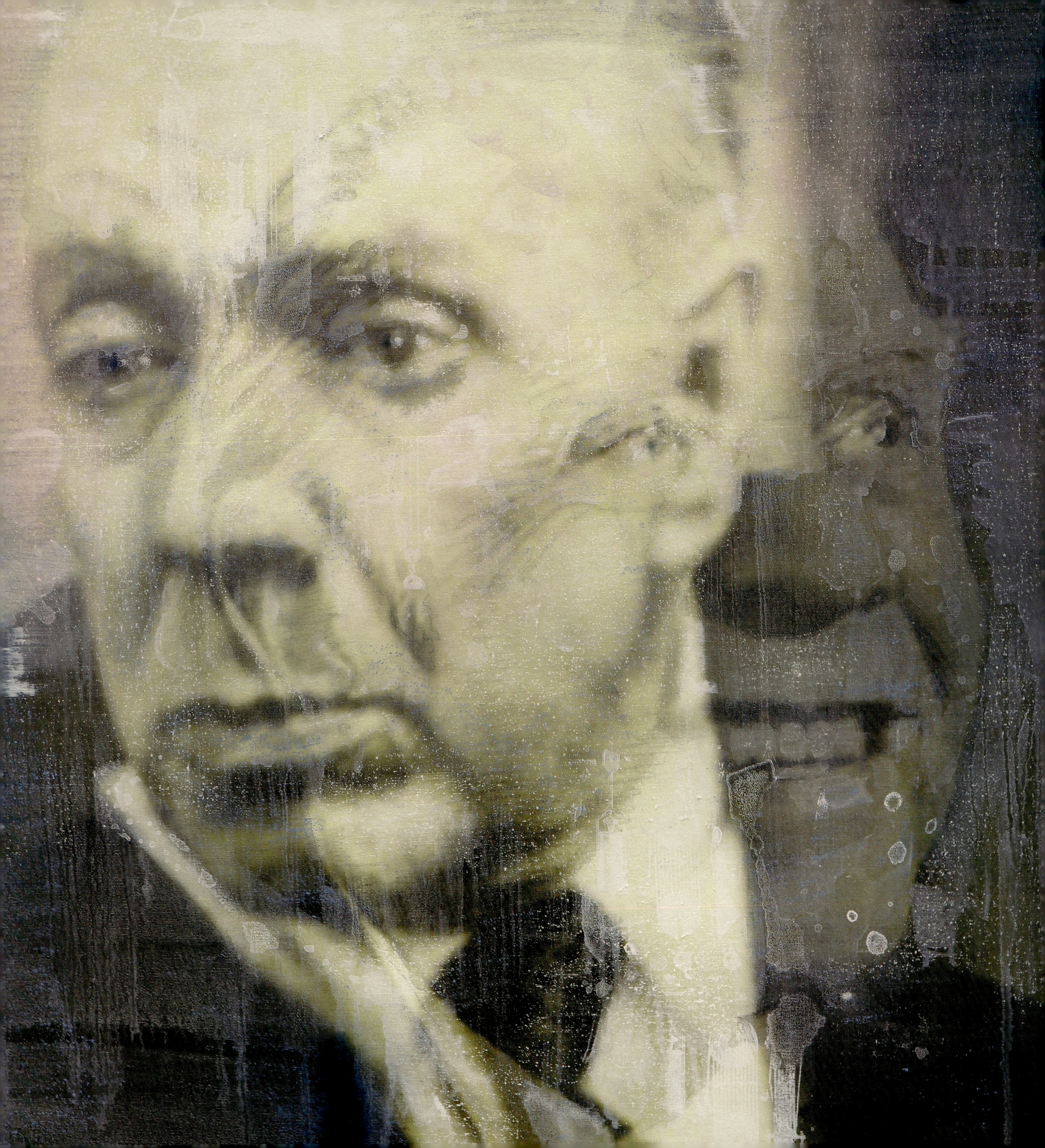

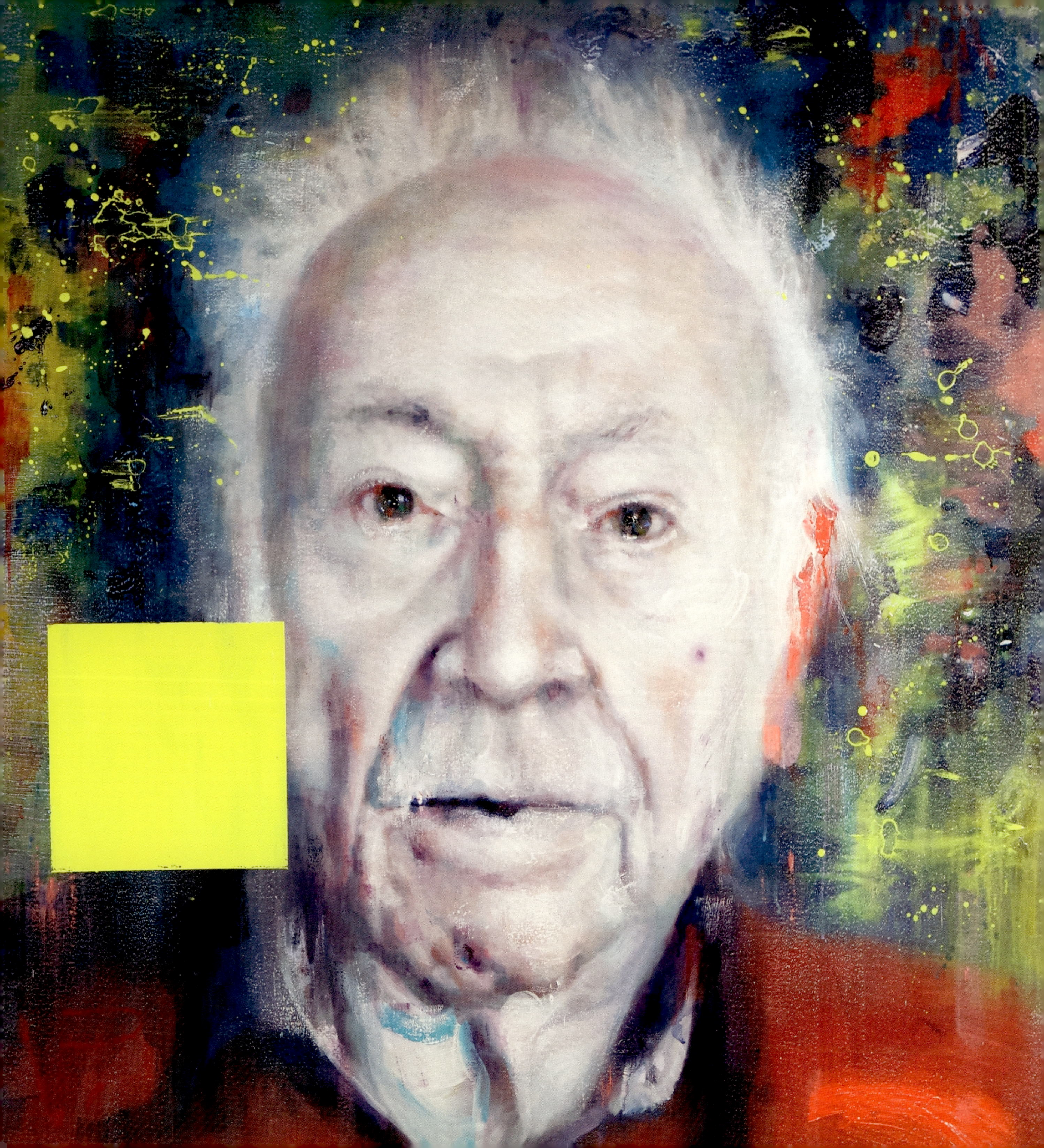

CONCERNING
VALENTIN POPOV'S PORTRAIT OF PETER SELZ

PAUL KARLSTROM I think it's a striking portrait, and I like it better the more I sit here and look at it. "Fragile . . . here is a fragile Peter Selz," Carol [Selz] just said. At first I thought, *Well, although she knows him much better than I, why is Carol using that term?* Fragility—or vulnerability, perhaps. I can see that now, but the portrait strikes me somewhat differently. The way I read it is mainly bewilderment. To me you look bewildered, and this could be extended into a much bigger life interpretation. At any rate, that's my take. Then there's a surprise— that aura, that halo of hair shooting up like this, as if electricity is being generated—and then again bewilderment. It's as if you're thinking: *What is this? What's happening? I'm getting older, I'm getting old; how has life changed?* So, Peter, I see this kind of psychological aspect to your portrait. But as an art historian, what strikes me immediately is the presentation of you as an eminent professional surrounded by the accoutrements of your occupation and other visual references to the milestones of your distinguished career. This is the perfect modernist art portrait of somebody who was one of the pioneers in the study of modernist painting. Conceptually, it's perfect because the pictorial elements that surround you allude to modernist art. Among the things that jump out—and almost jarringly in some ways—is that yellow square, which I immediately read as your lifelong interest in and appreciation of hard-edged painting. It perfectly reflects a highlight of your career as an interpreter and champion of geometric abstraction, Abstract Classicism, and the Non-objective School—and that whole area of modern art. On top of this, the central composition is framed by explosions of color and the splatterings of Abstract Expressionism. So you have these multiple points of reference. . . .

PETER SELZ Oh, very good.

PK This blend of ingredients renders the portrait for me very, very effective—intellectually satisfying and thoroughly complete. The viewer sees not just a likeness, but a personality profile and a summation of a life devoted not just to a special subject but to a consuming enthusiam for art.

PS I have to agree. I think the portrait captures not only my appearance but encapsulates many aspects of my life. I like the yellow square very much, because it makes you aware that, although you are looking at a largely realistic painting on a two-dimensional surface, there are hidden depths that wouldn't be revealed, or even suggested, were it absent. And then there are all the things bespangling the sky—all these scraps and iterations and different colors—I like these, too.

Conversation between Paul Karlstrom and Peter Selz filmed by Celik Kayalar in Berkeley, California, 2015.

PETER SELZ, 2015
Oil on canvas, 44 × 40 in.

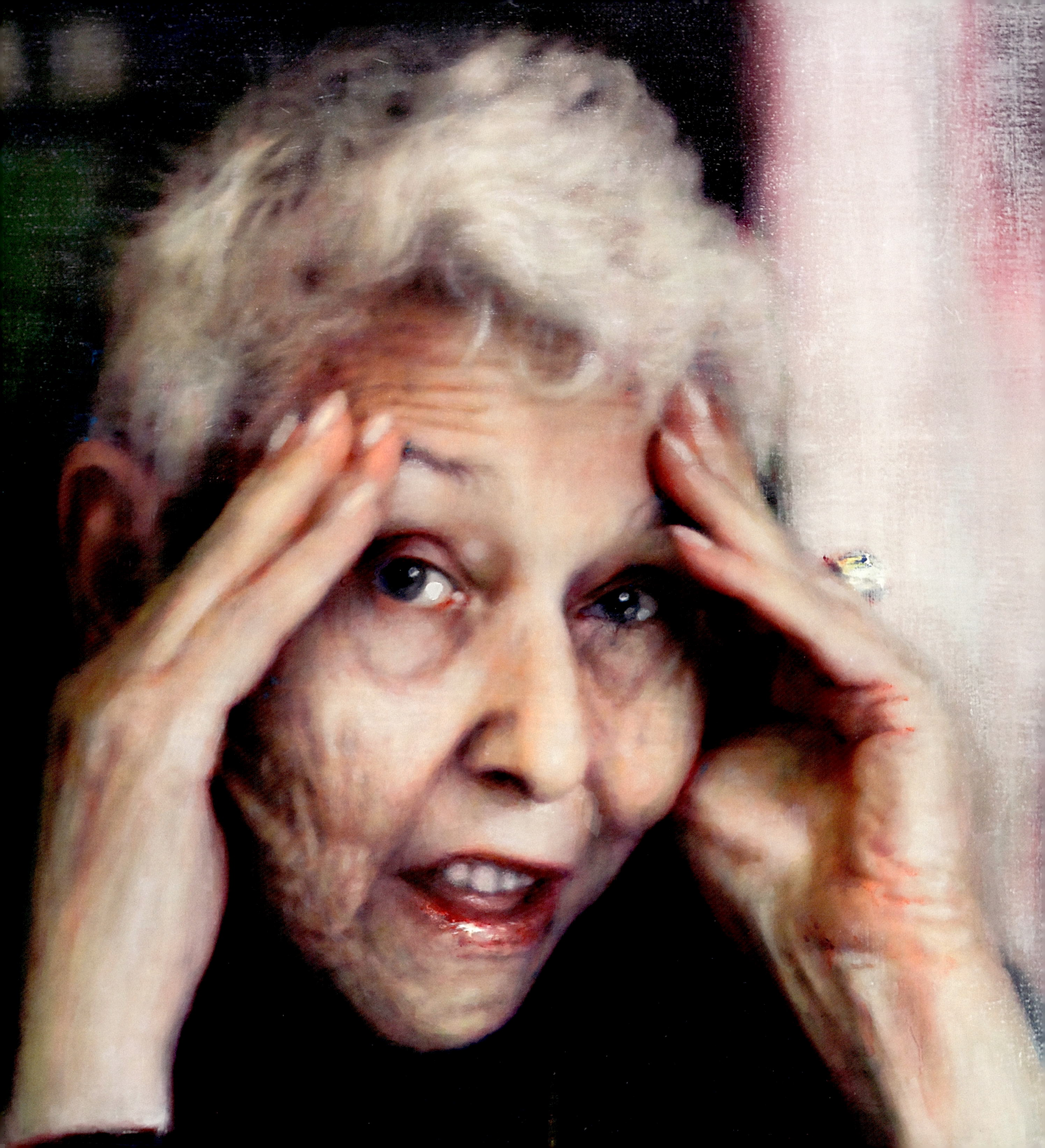

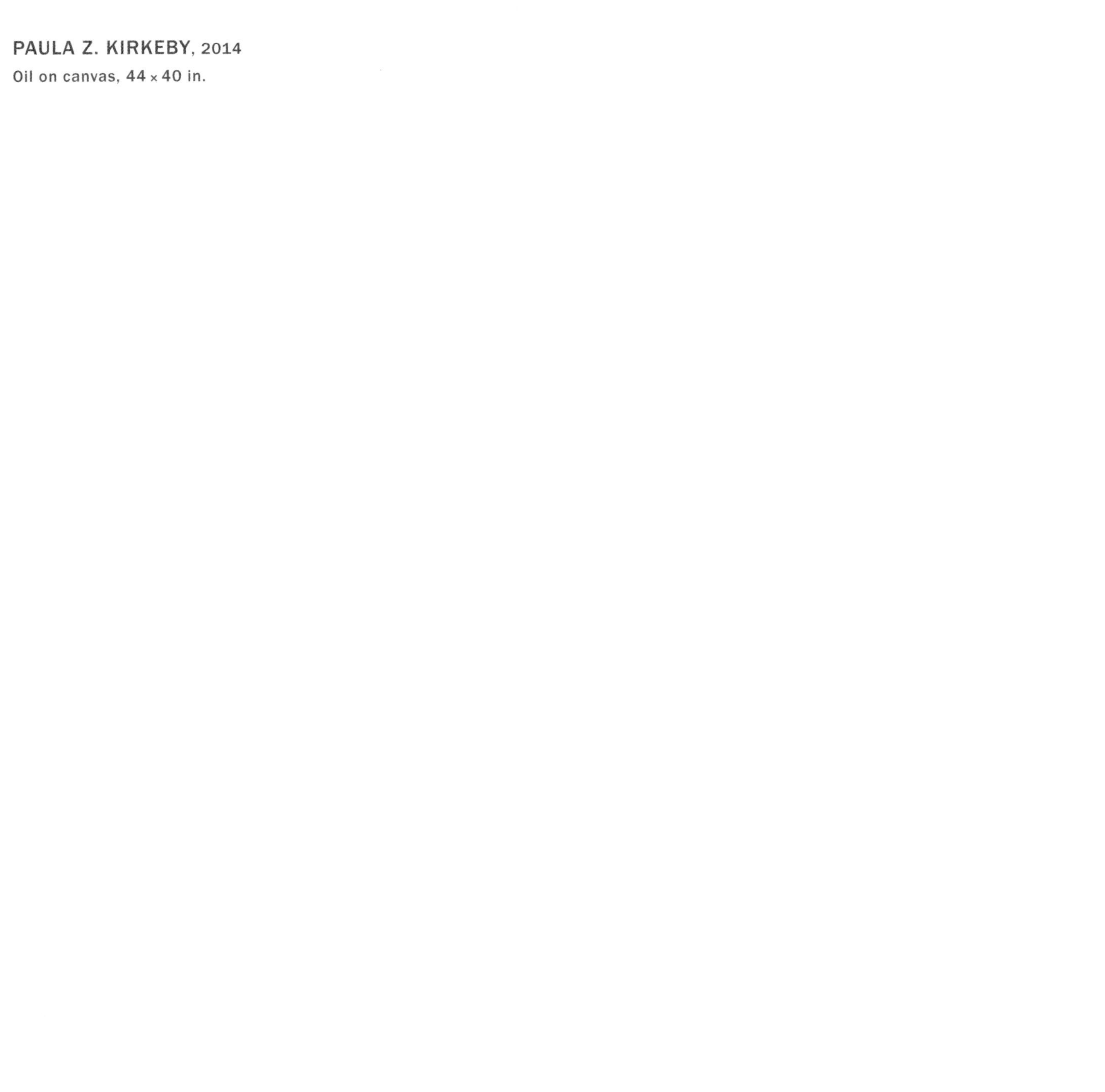

It's all magic. Everything that happened between Valentin and me is pure alchemy. There you have it. That's the height of magic. **PAULA Z. KIRKEBY (1934–2016)**

From *Valentin Popov, FACE*, a documentary film by Celik Kayalar, 2013.

I'm Valentin's very close friend and art supplier. This interaction between the artist and the art supplier is way beyond what you could imagine. All the process . . . starts from the material, from the pigment itself. It's so particular, it's so difficult, you know? . . . Sometimes it's surprising because it's very, very precise as to what he needs. So it's a good challenge for him—so at some point I help him, but also he helps himself to evolve.

•

What I see in Valentin is he is always reinventing himself—he's always pushing the envelope. . . . And I know it because the supply side, it's very, very challenging. I don't know where he's going exactly, because it's always a surprise, but what I can promise you is that he's not going to stay still, he's going to surprise us, and he's going to make everybody interested in his work.   **PIERRE-YANN GUIDETTI**

From *Valentin Popov, FACE*, a documentary film by Celik Kayalar, 2013.

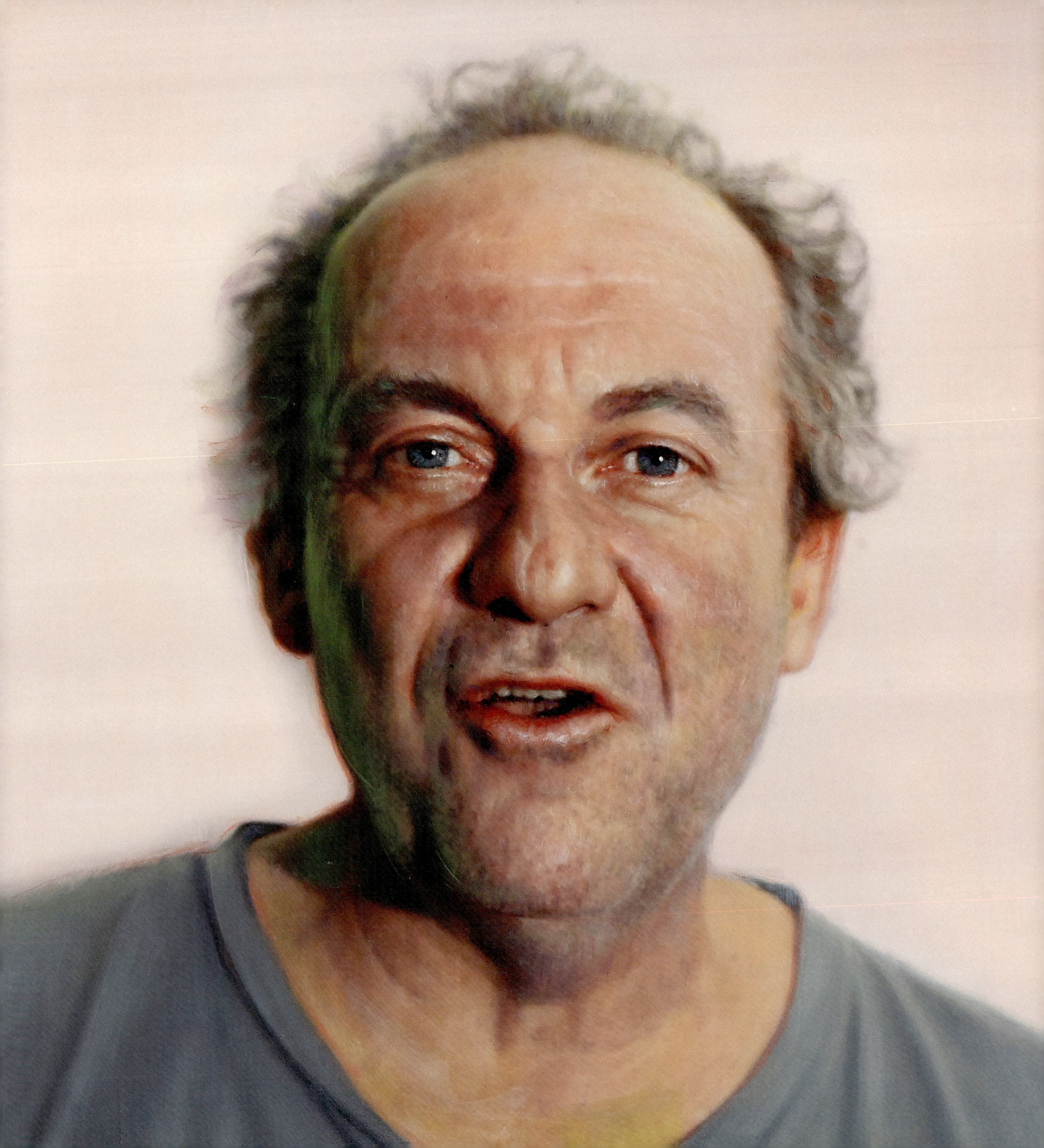

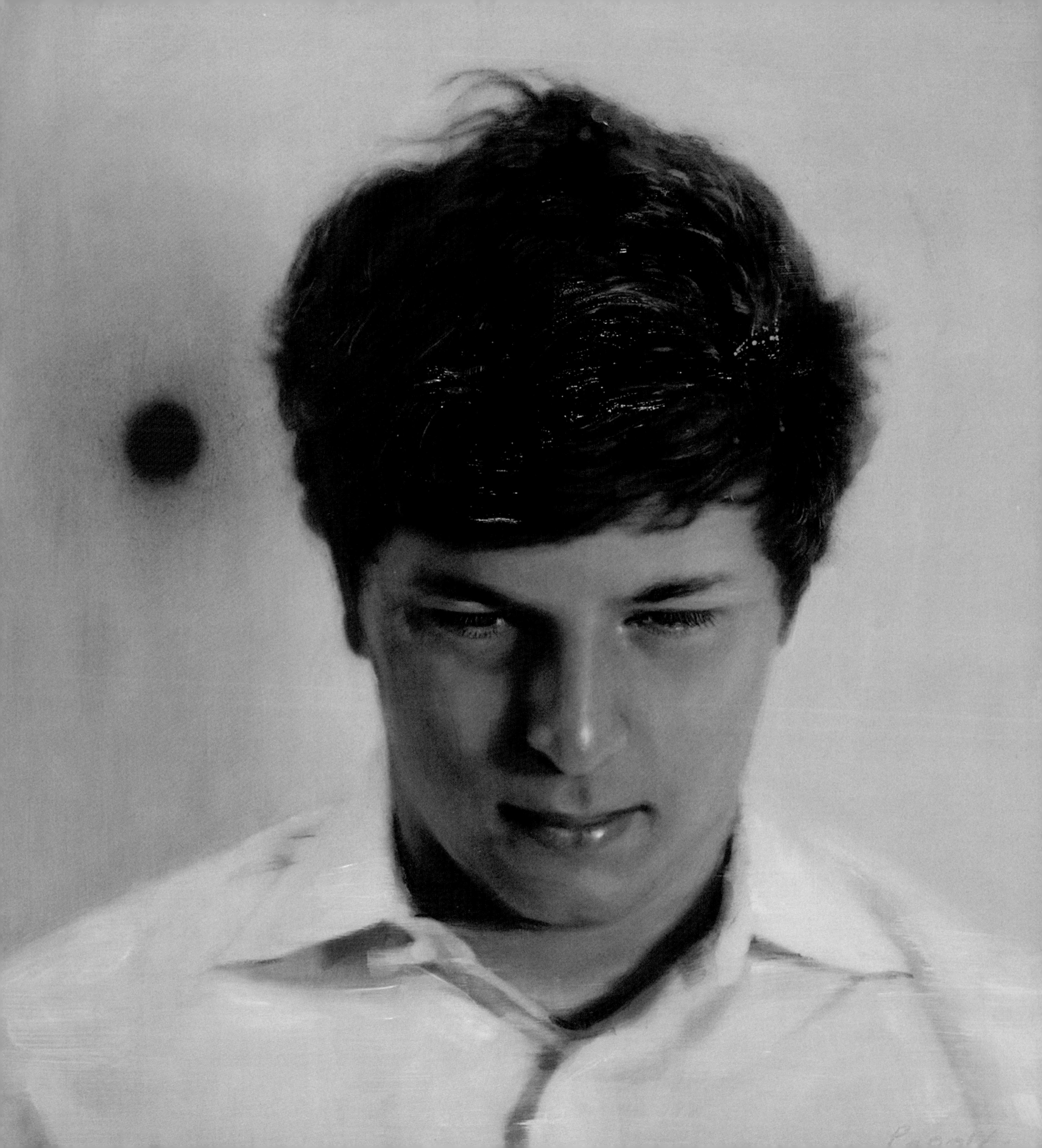

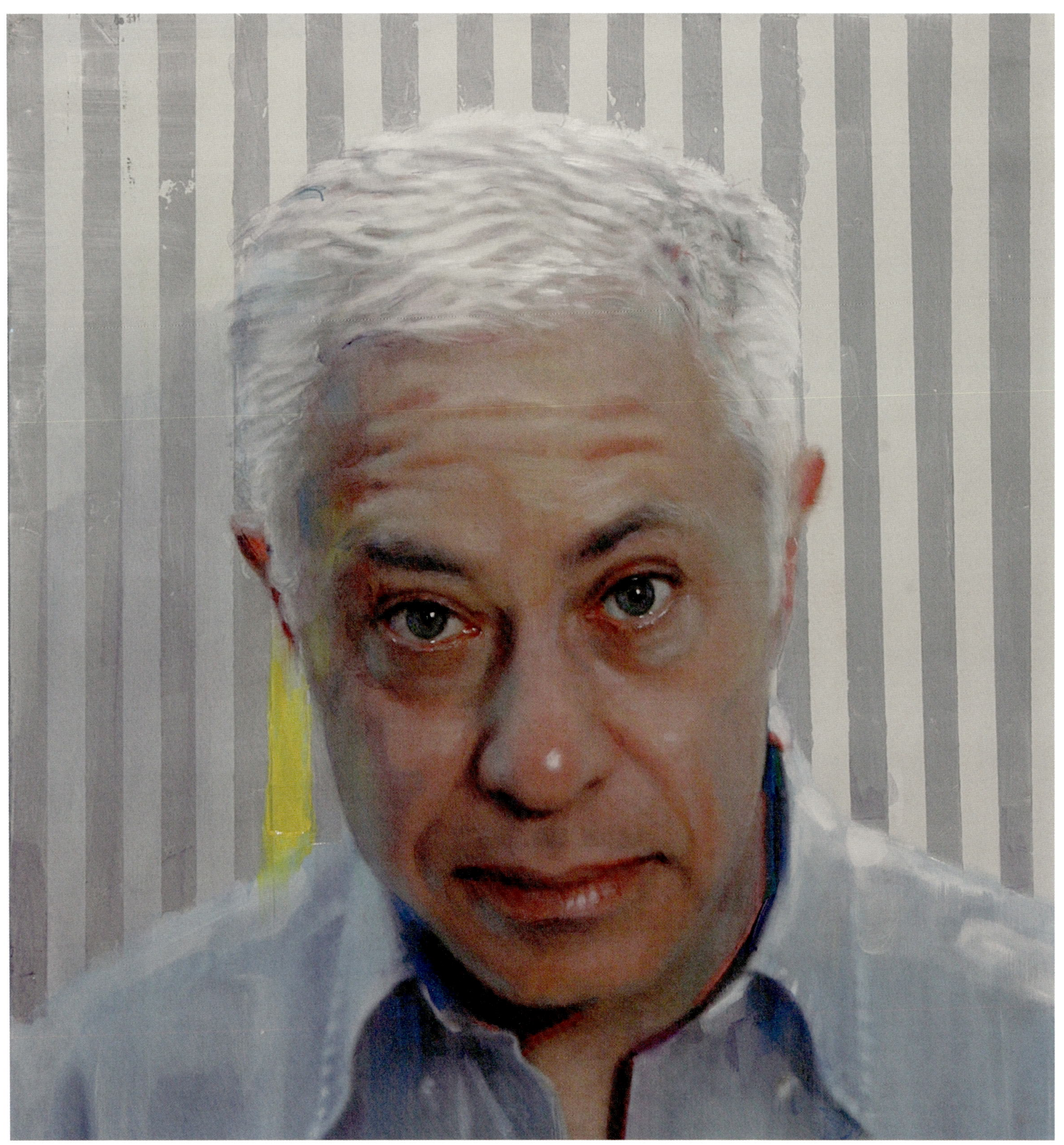

CHARLIE WINTON, 2016
Oil on canvas, 44 × 40 in.

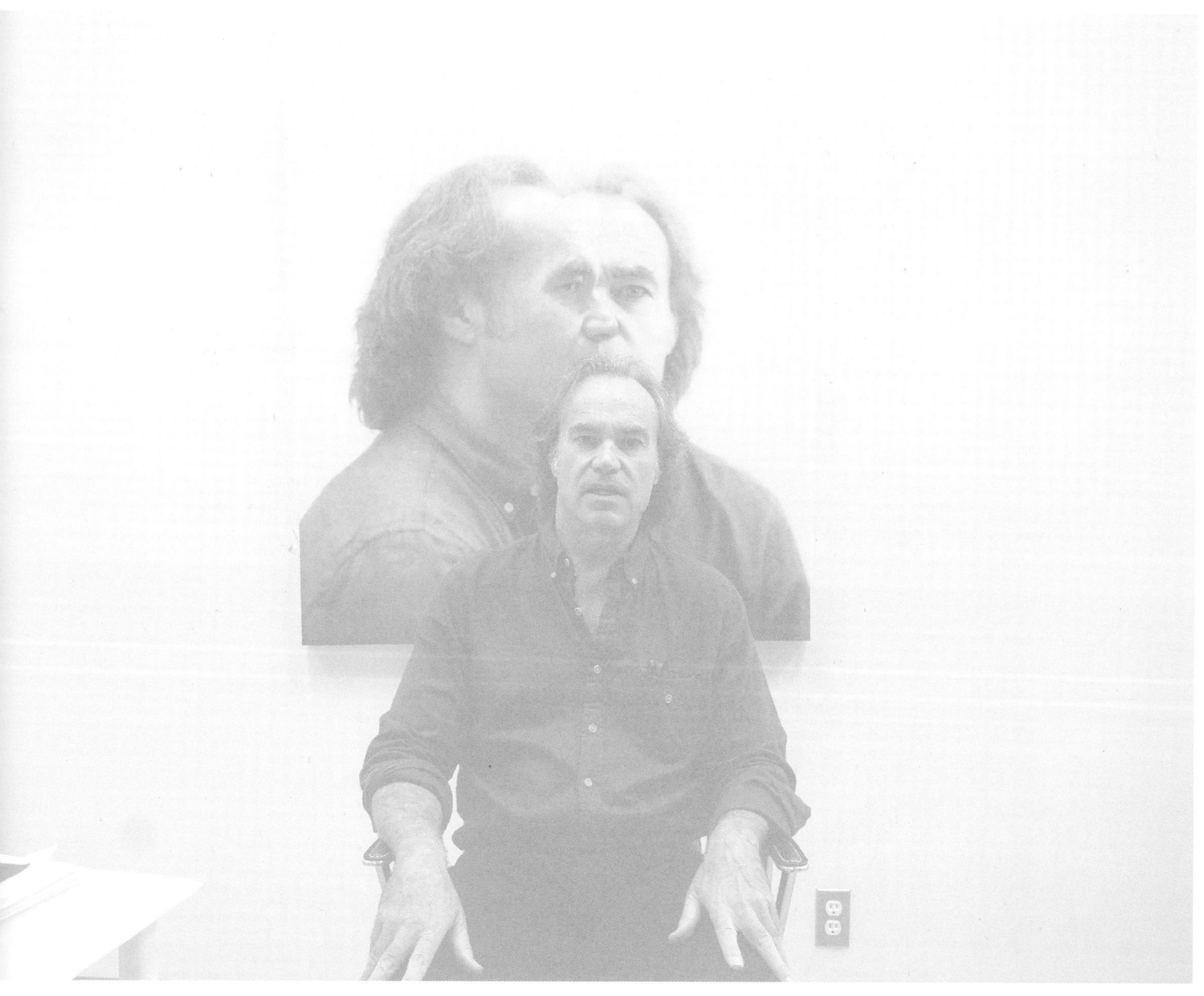

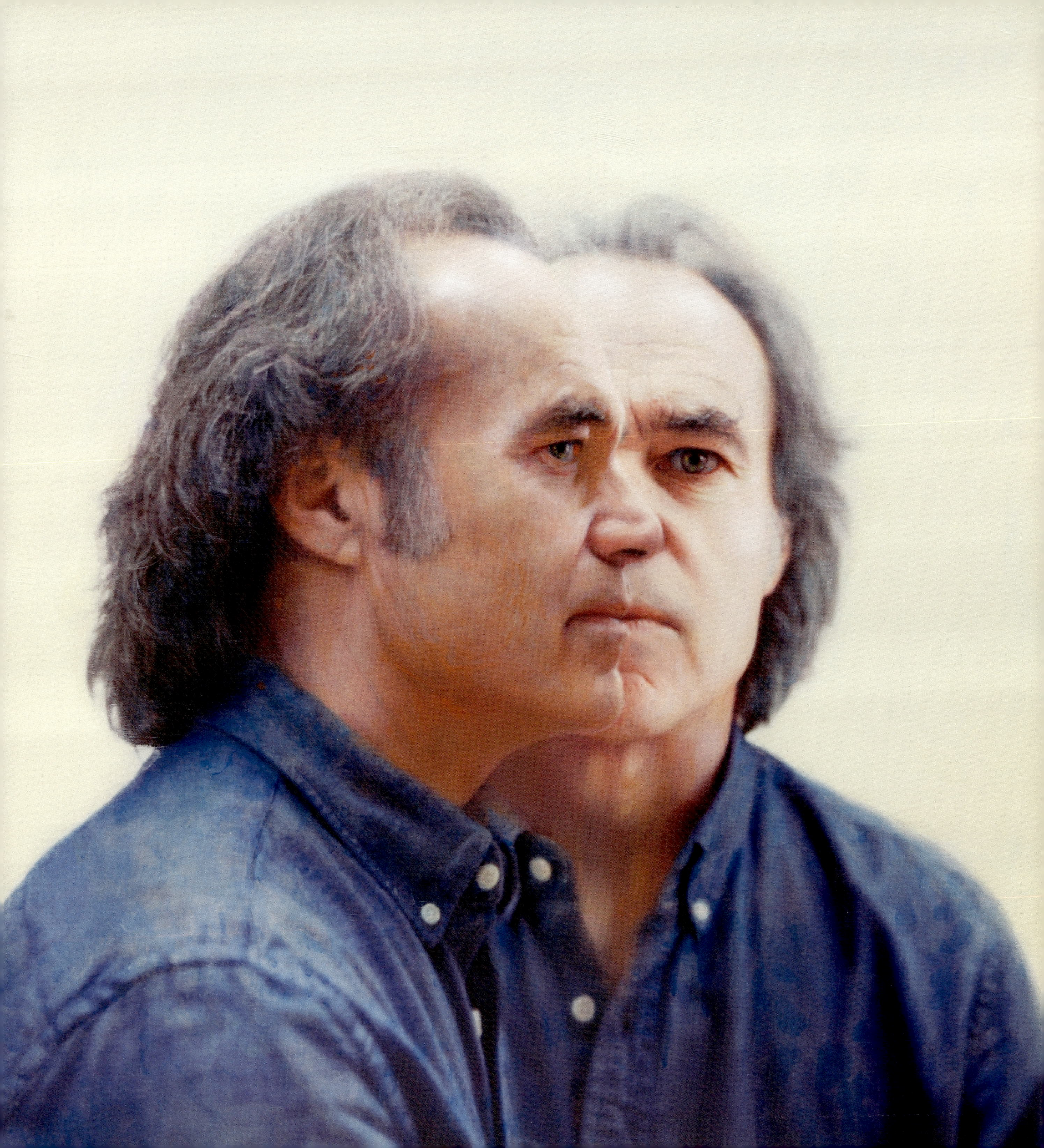

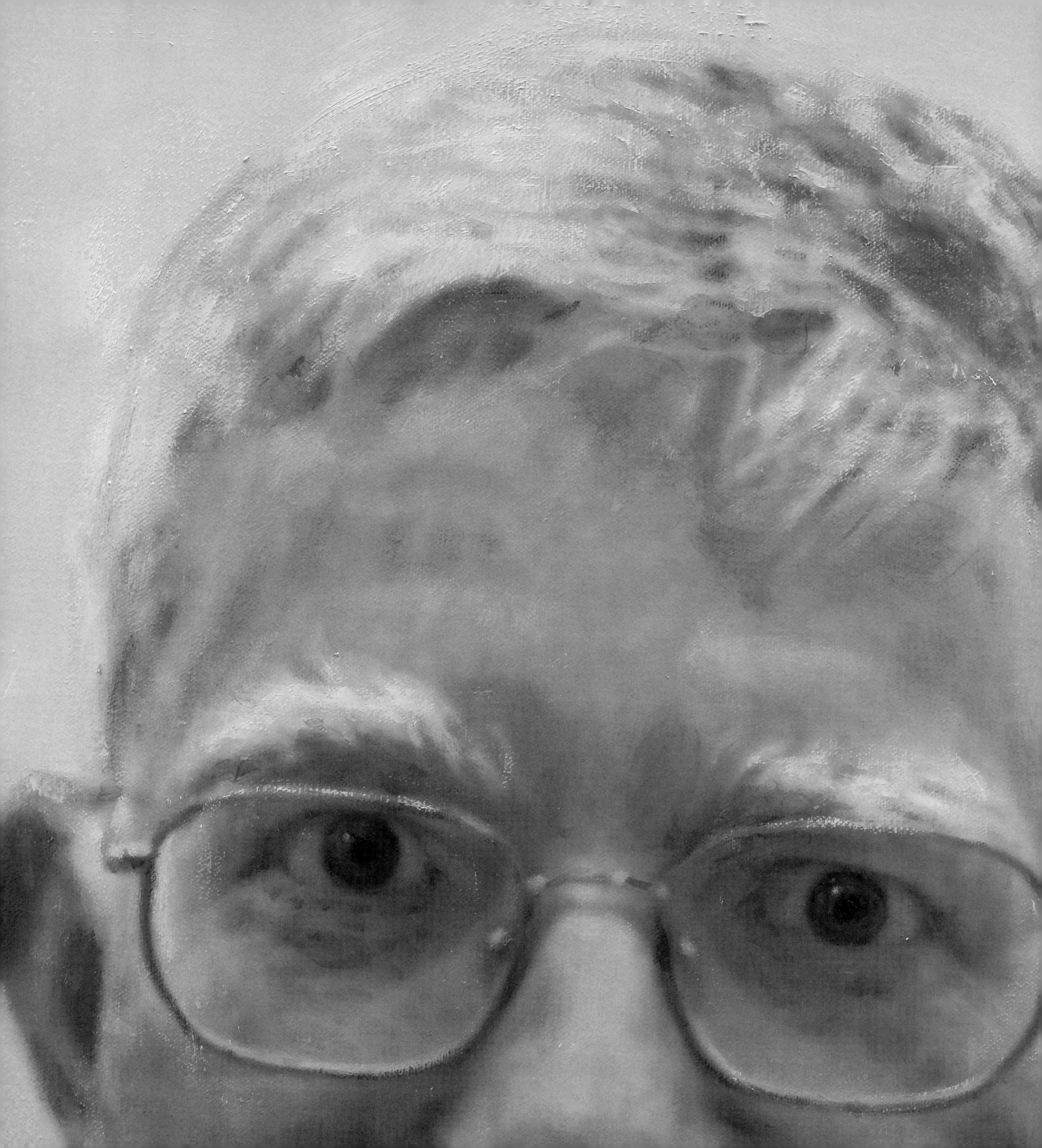

LEROY WILSTED, 2011
Oil on canvas, 28 × 26 in.

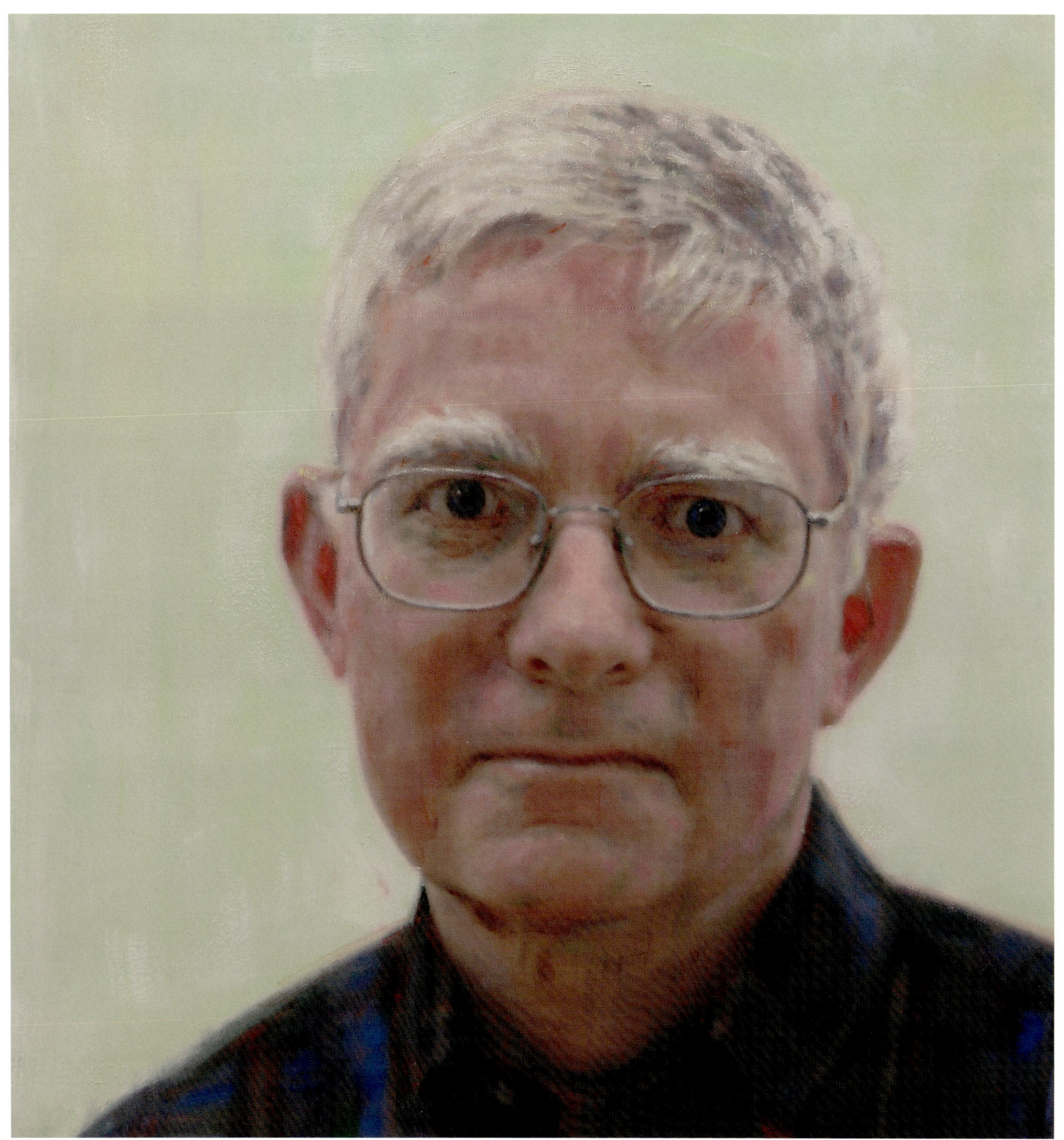

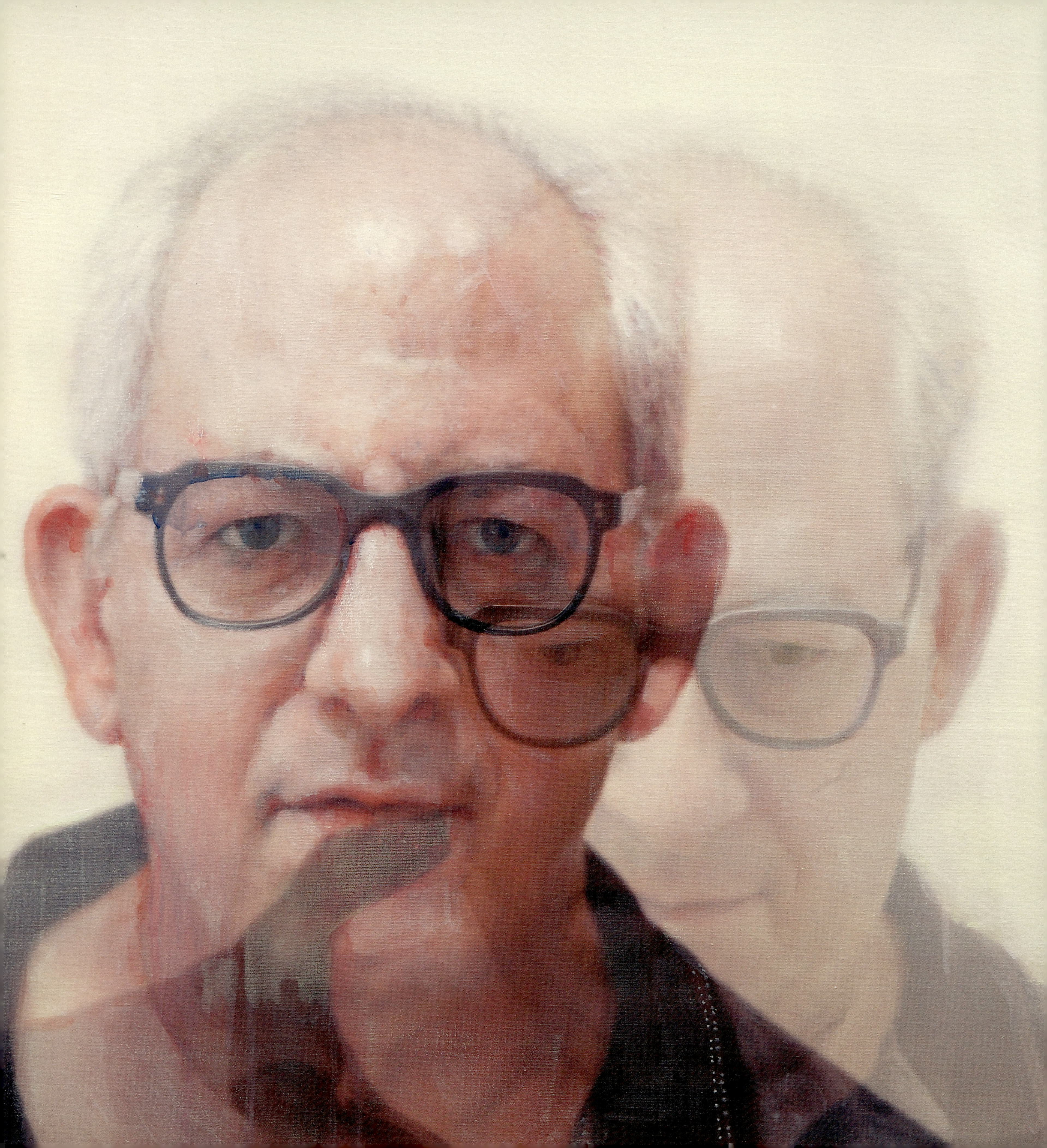

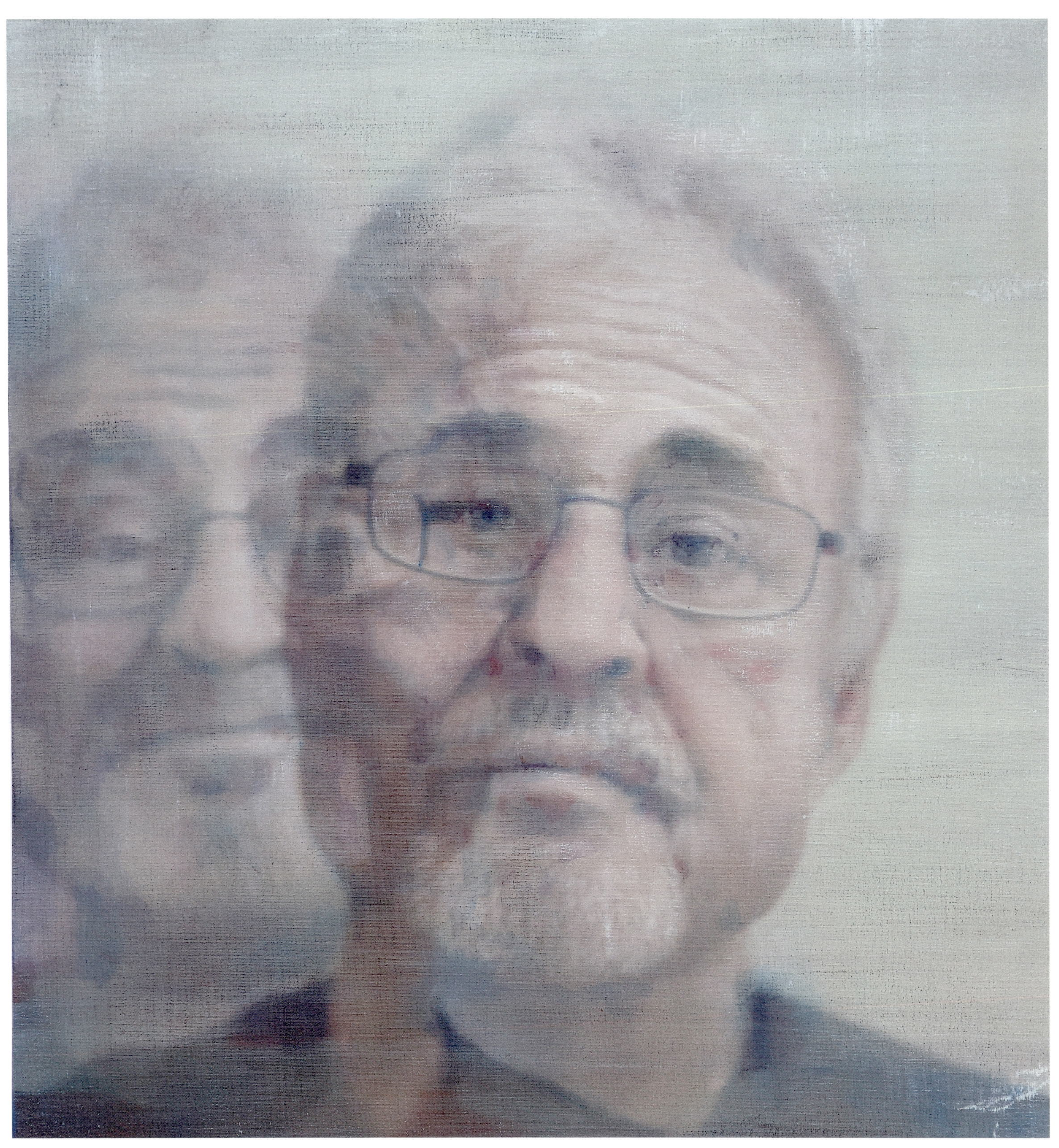

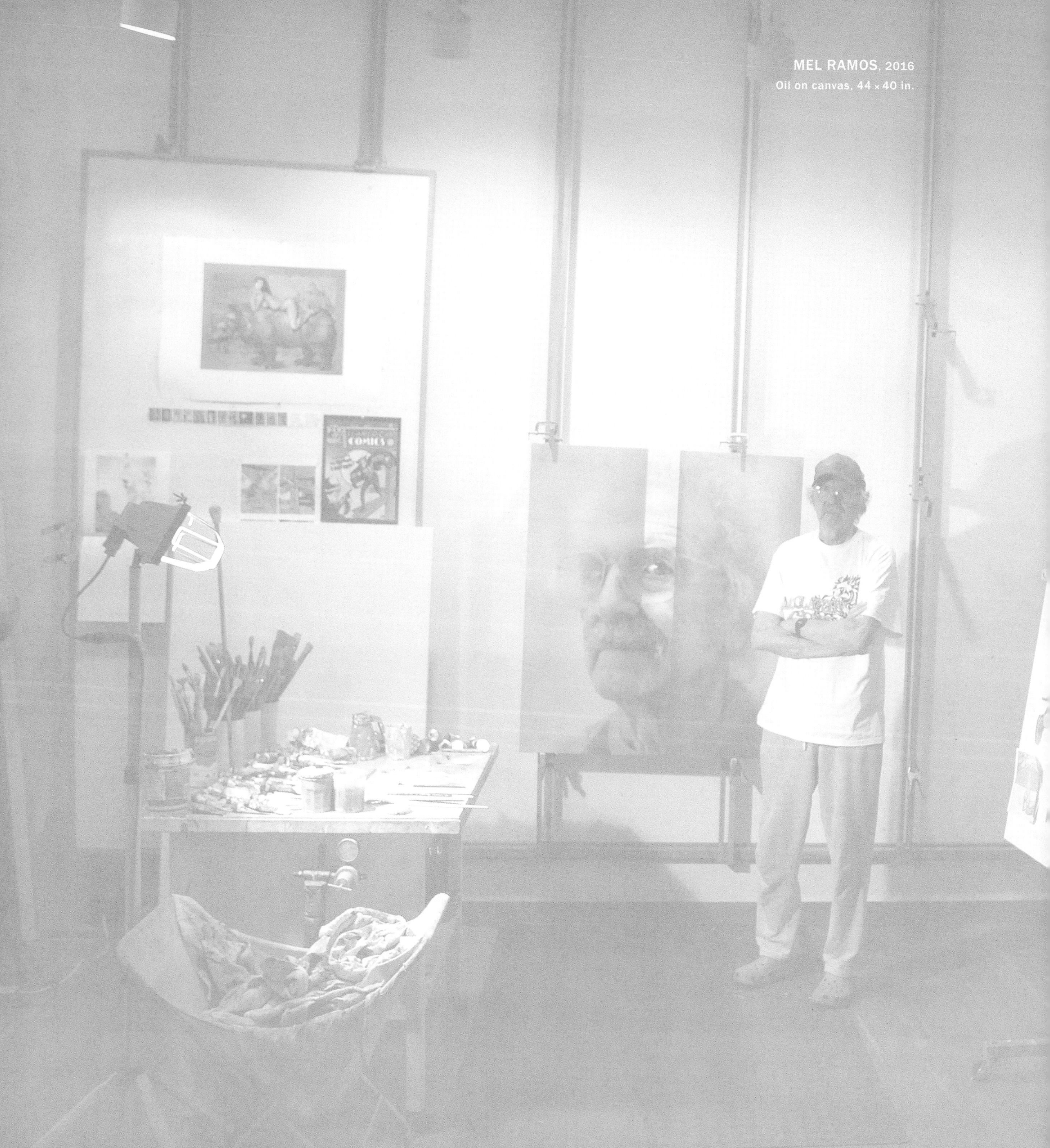

MEL RAMOS, 2016
Oil on canvas, 44 × 40 in.

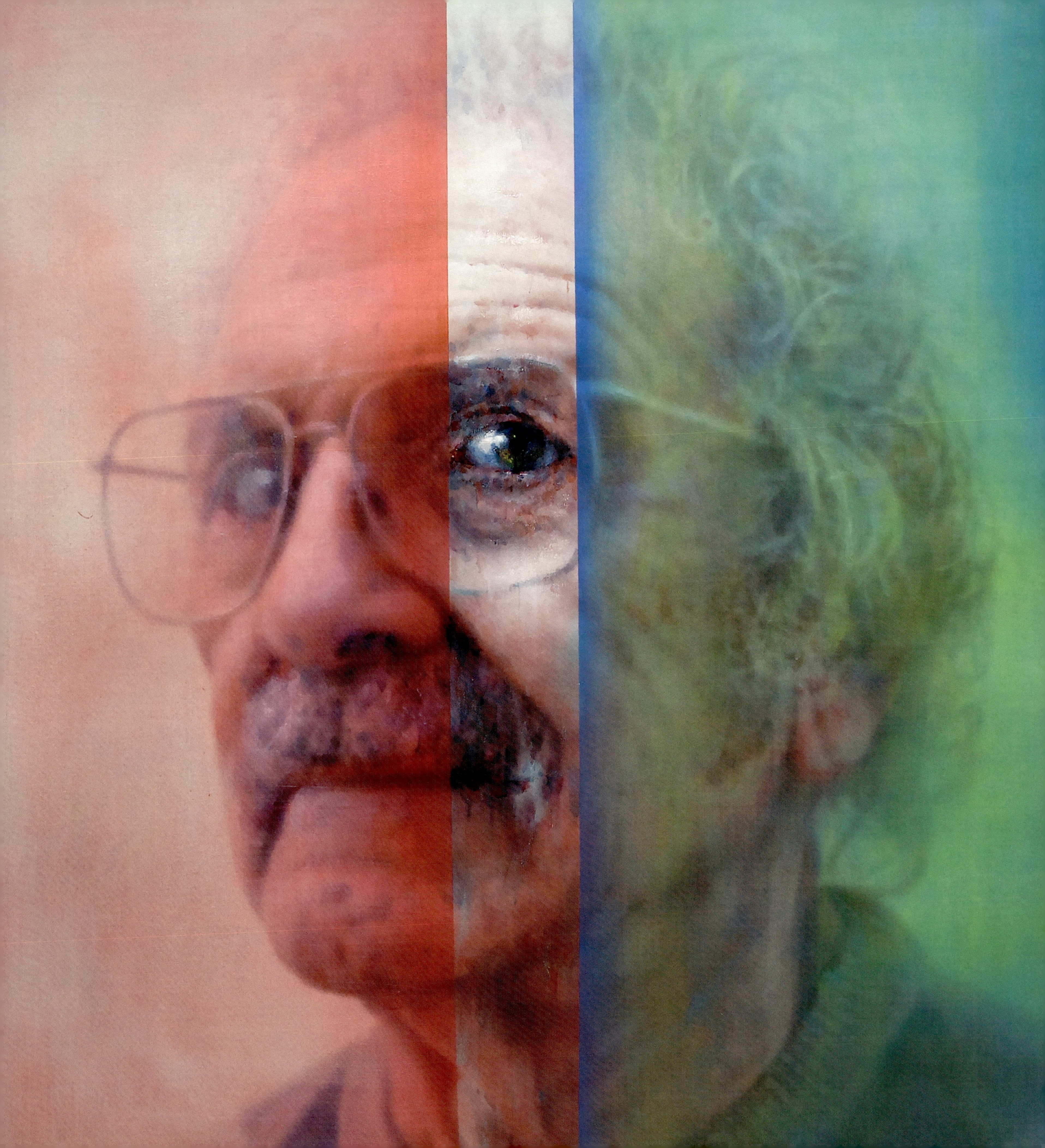

The skillful art of Valentin Popov is a mix of the academic and the anarchistic.

ROBERT FLYNN JOHNSON, CURATOR EMERITUS, ACHENBACH FOUNDATION
FOR GRAPHIC ARTS, FINE ARTS MUSEUMS OF SAN FRANCISCO

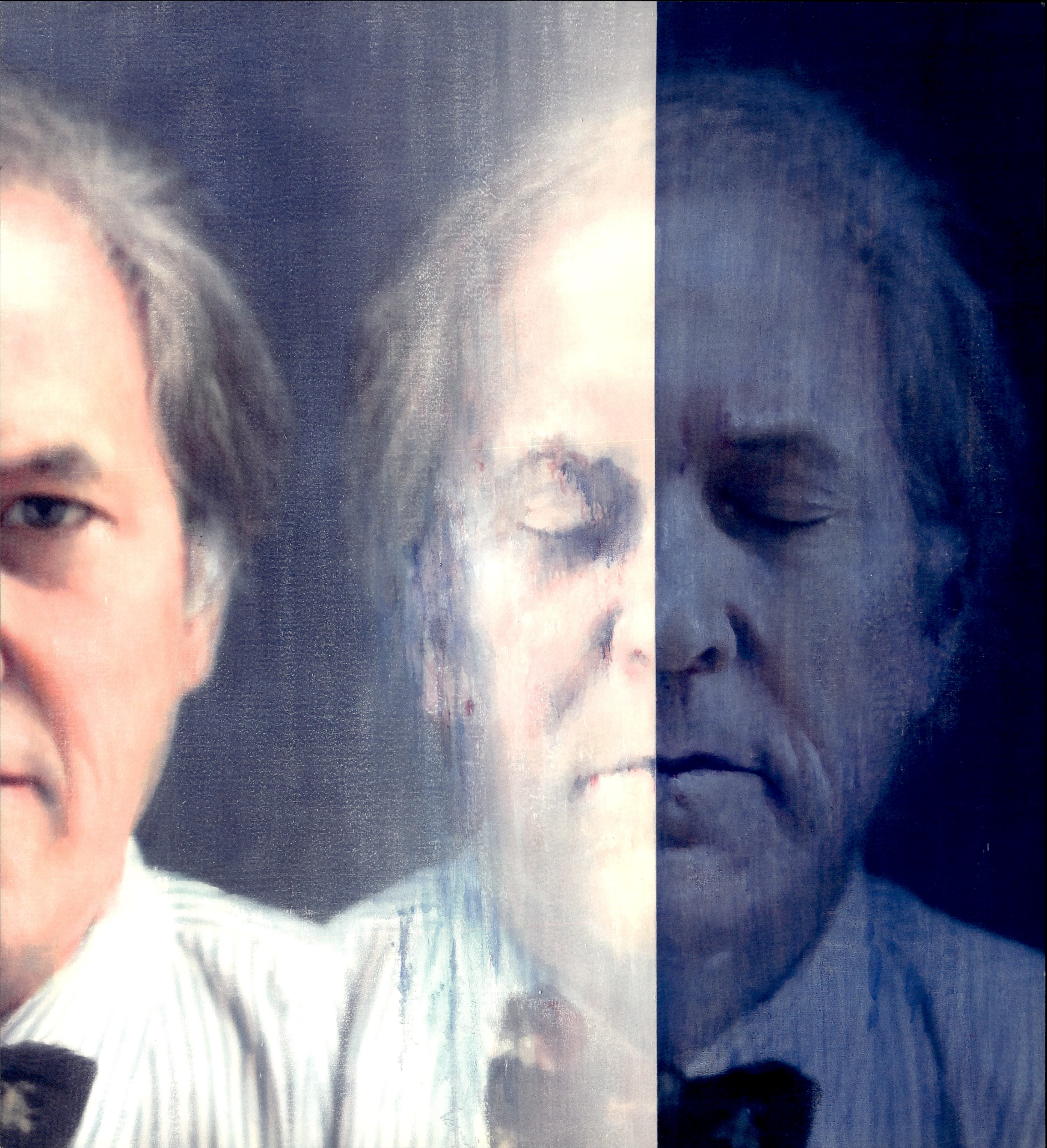

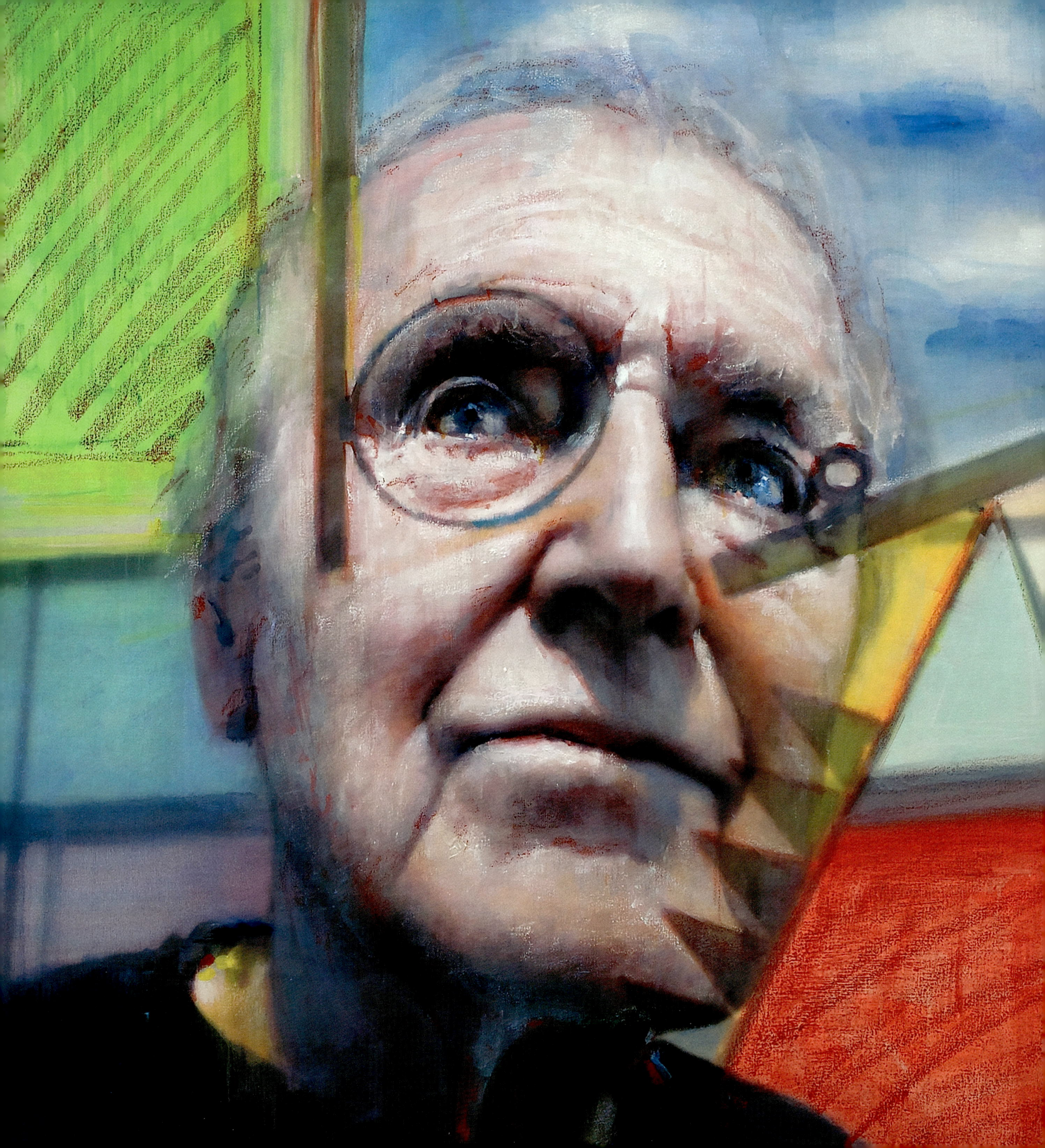

FLETCHER BENTON, 2016
Oil on canvas, 44 × 40 in.

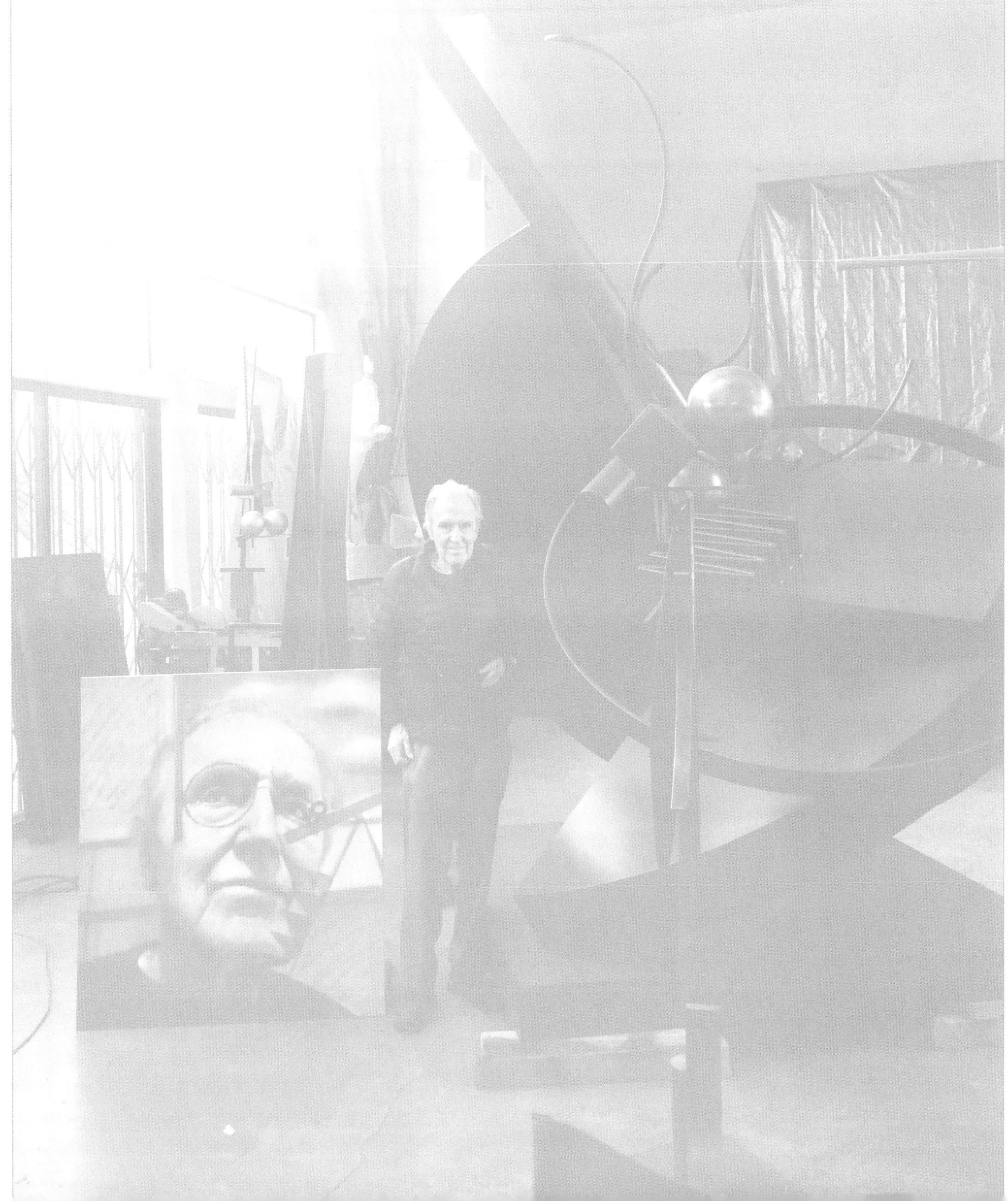

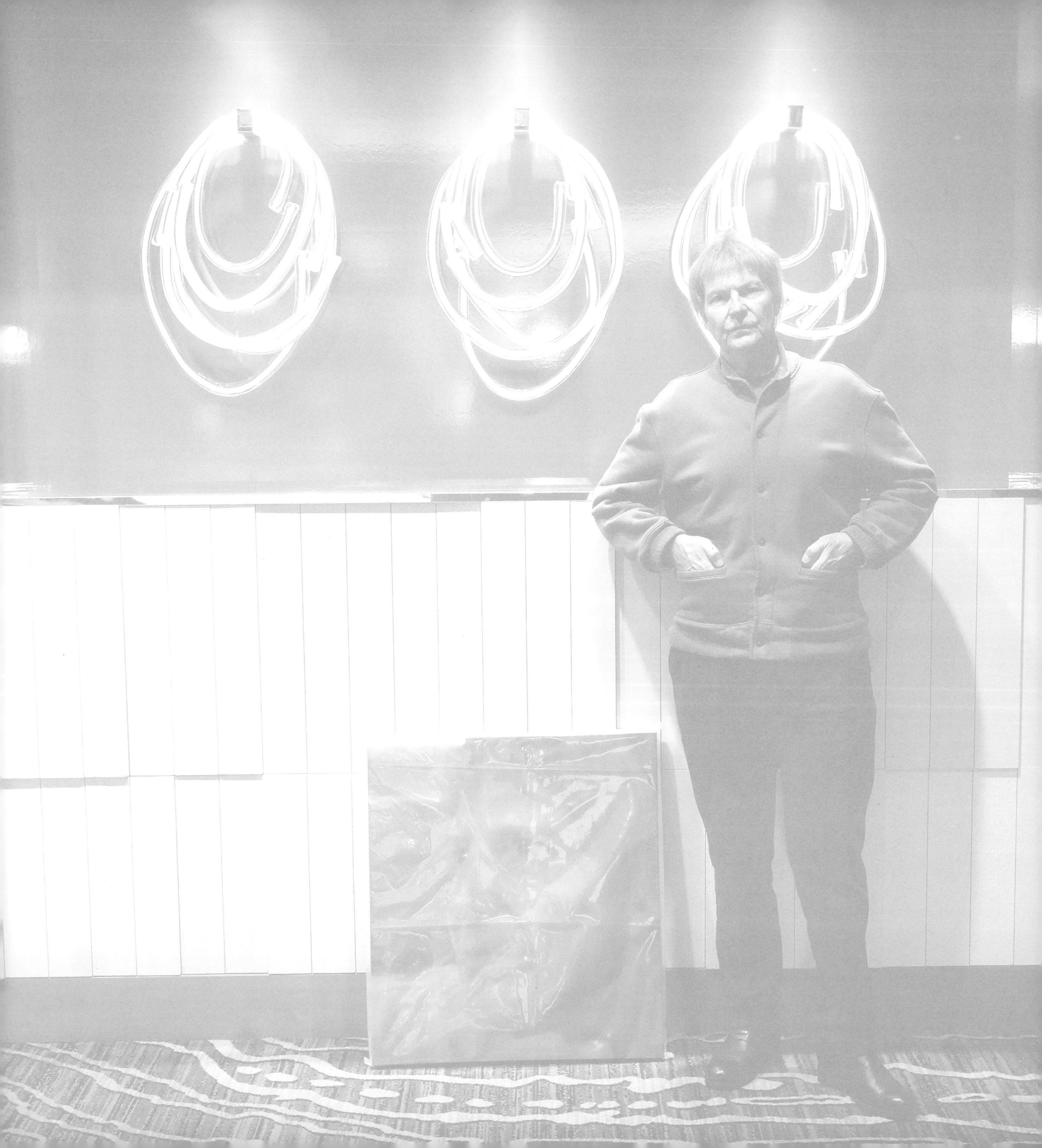

RICK GILBERT, 2013
Oil on canvas, 28 × 26 in.

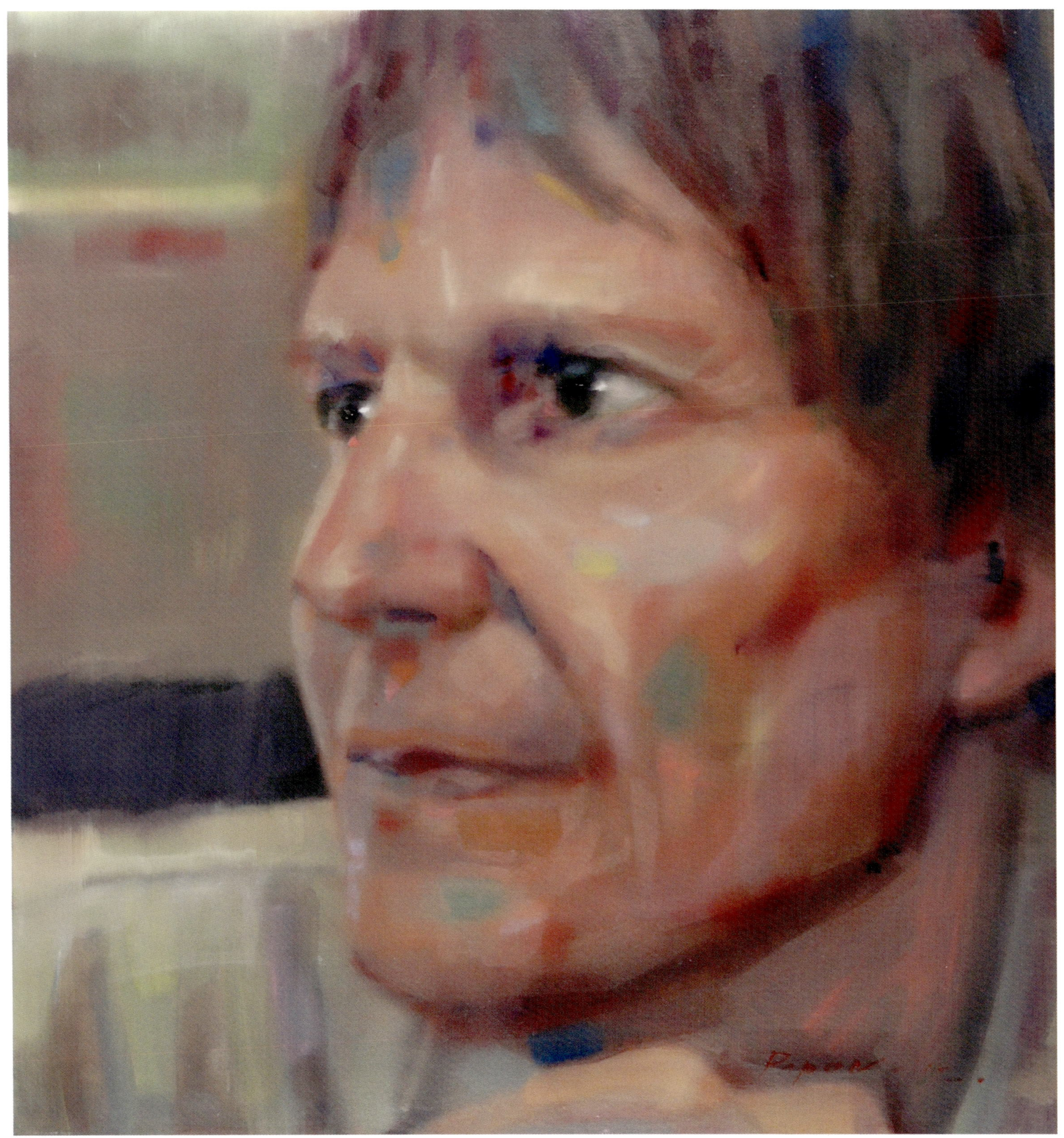

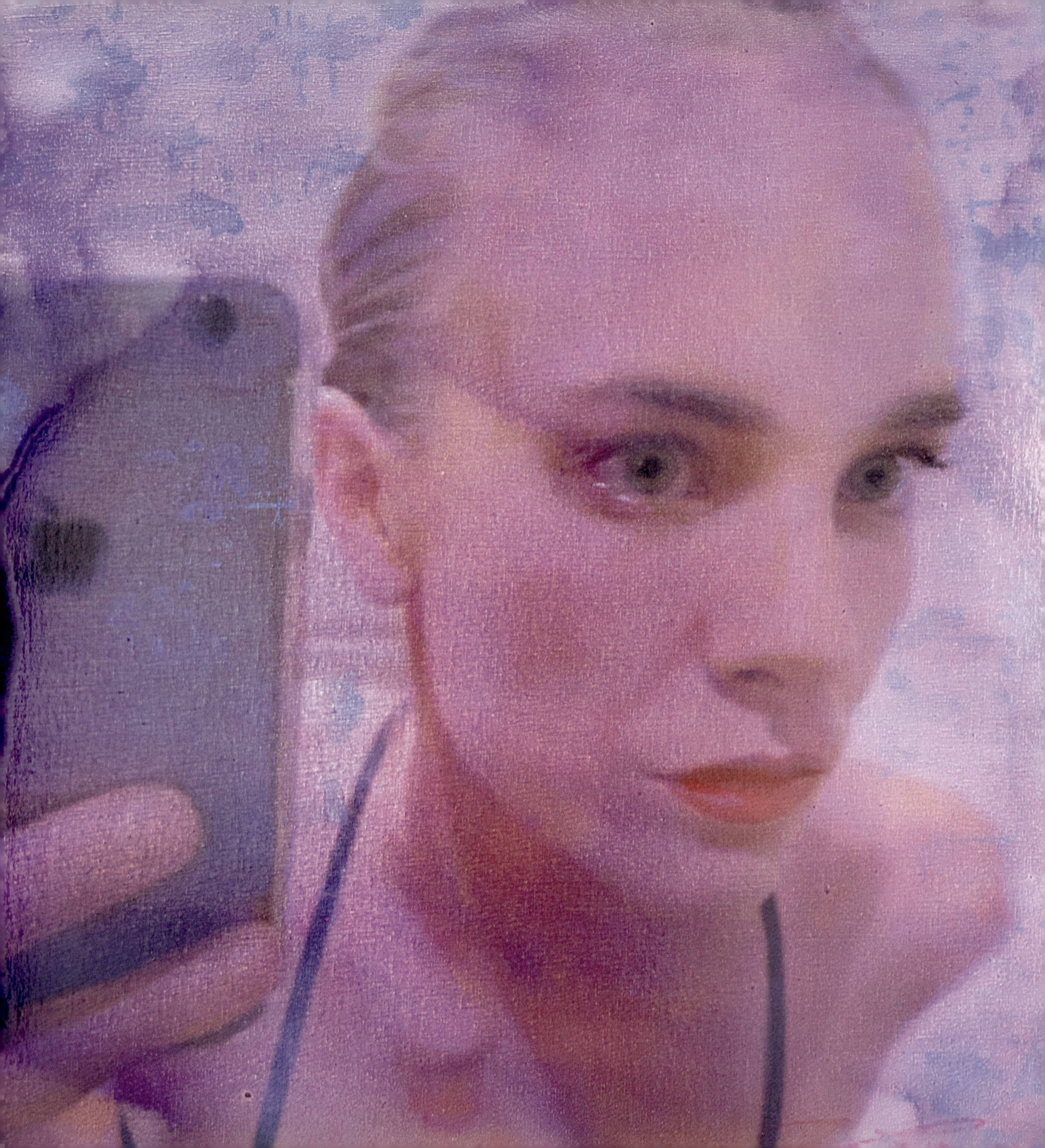

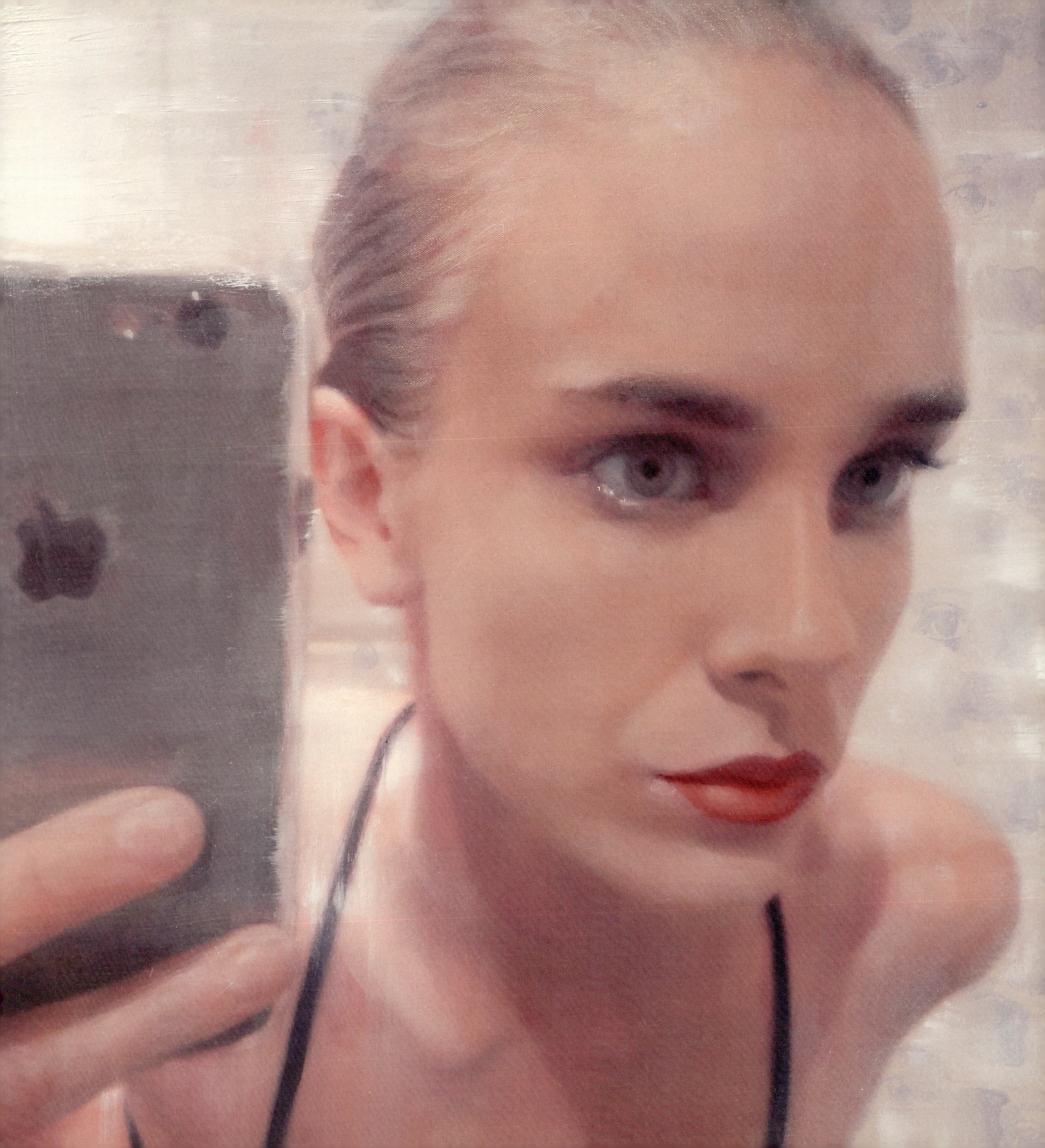

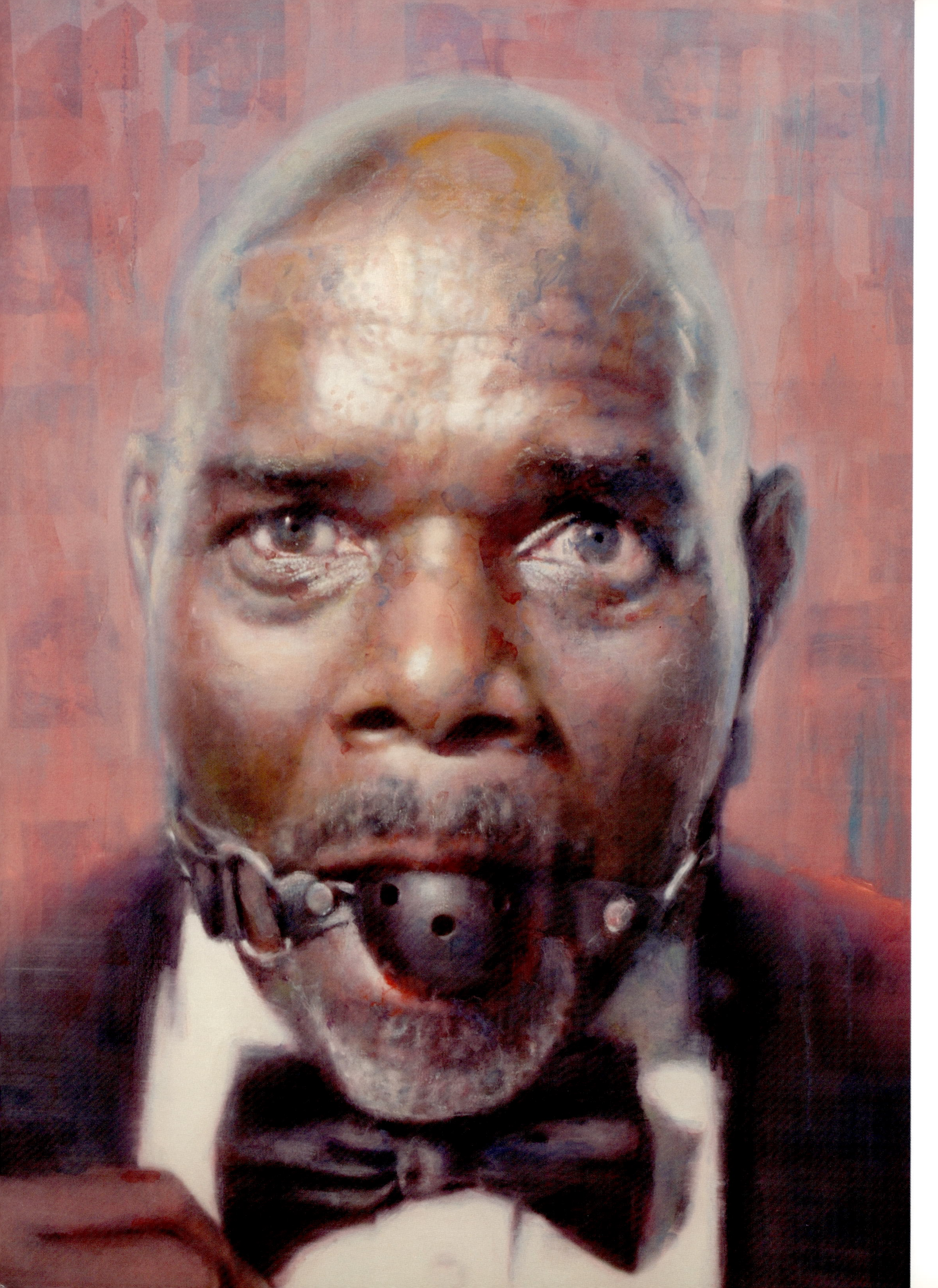

OLIVER WITH GAG 1, 2017
Oil on canvas, 70 × 52 in.

OLIVER WITH GAG 2, 2017
Oil on canvas, 70 x 52 in.

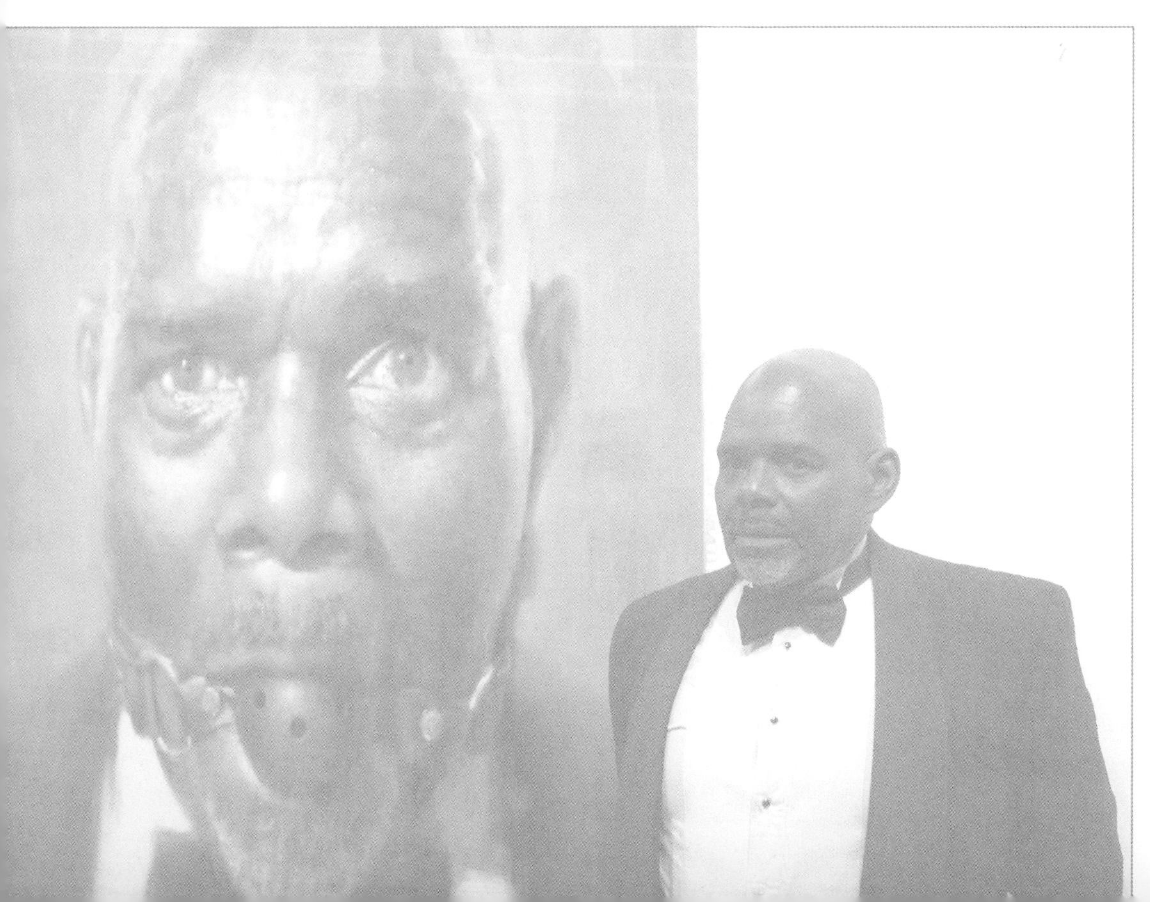

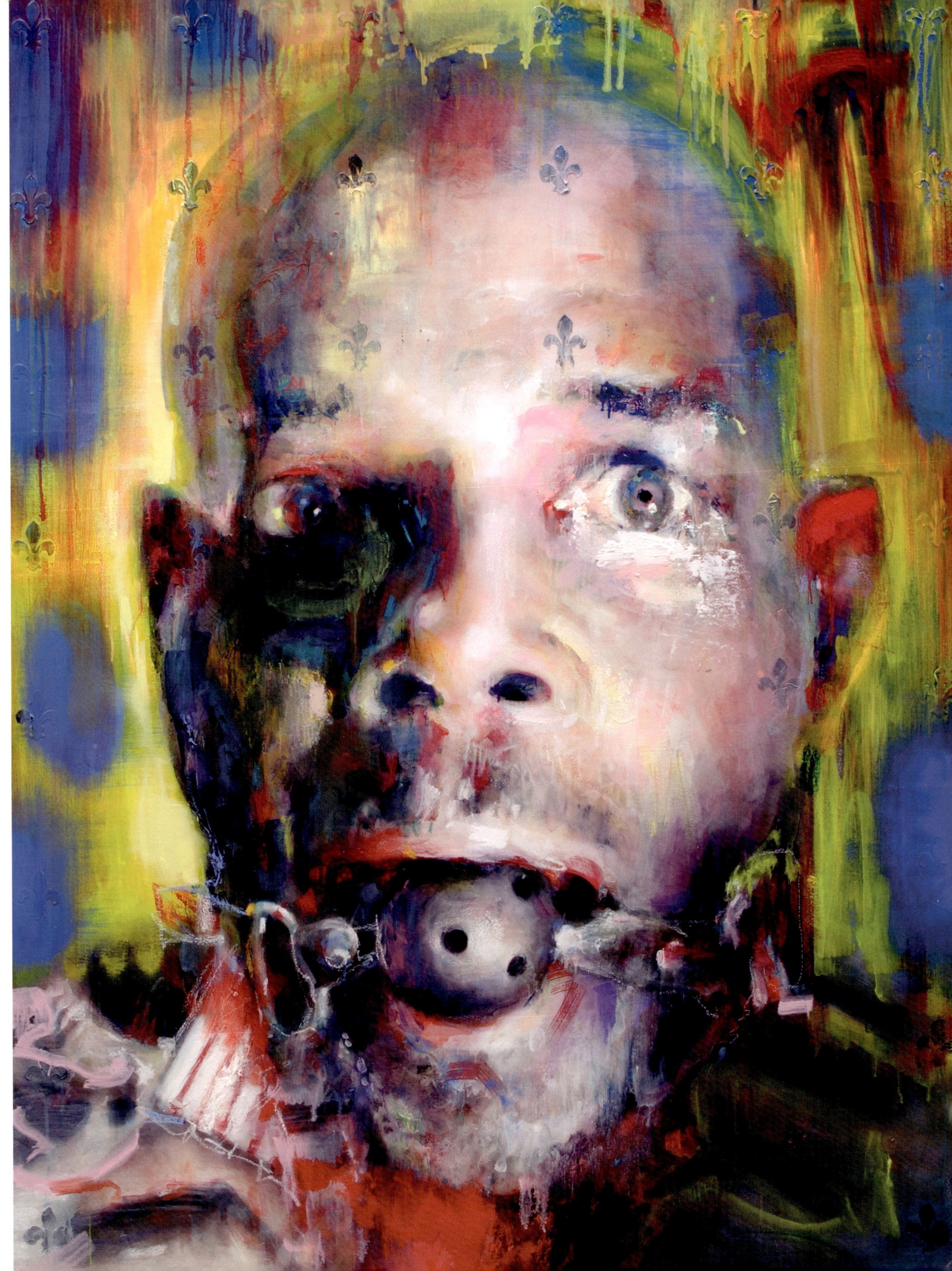

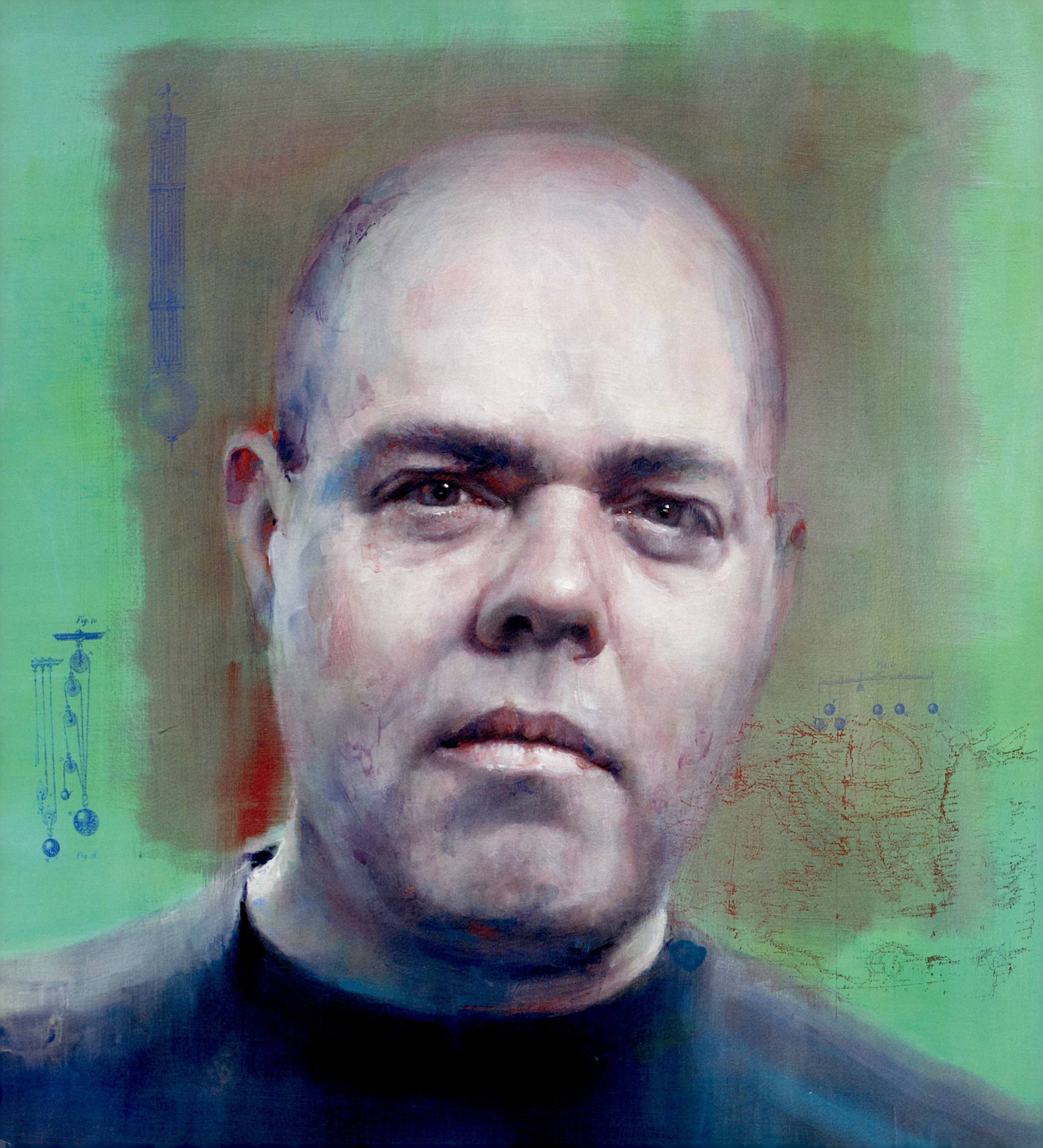

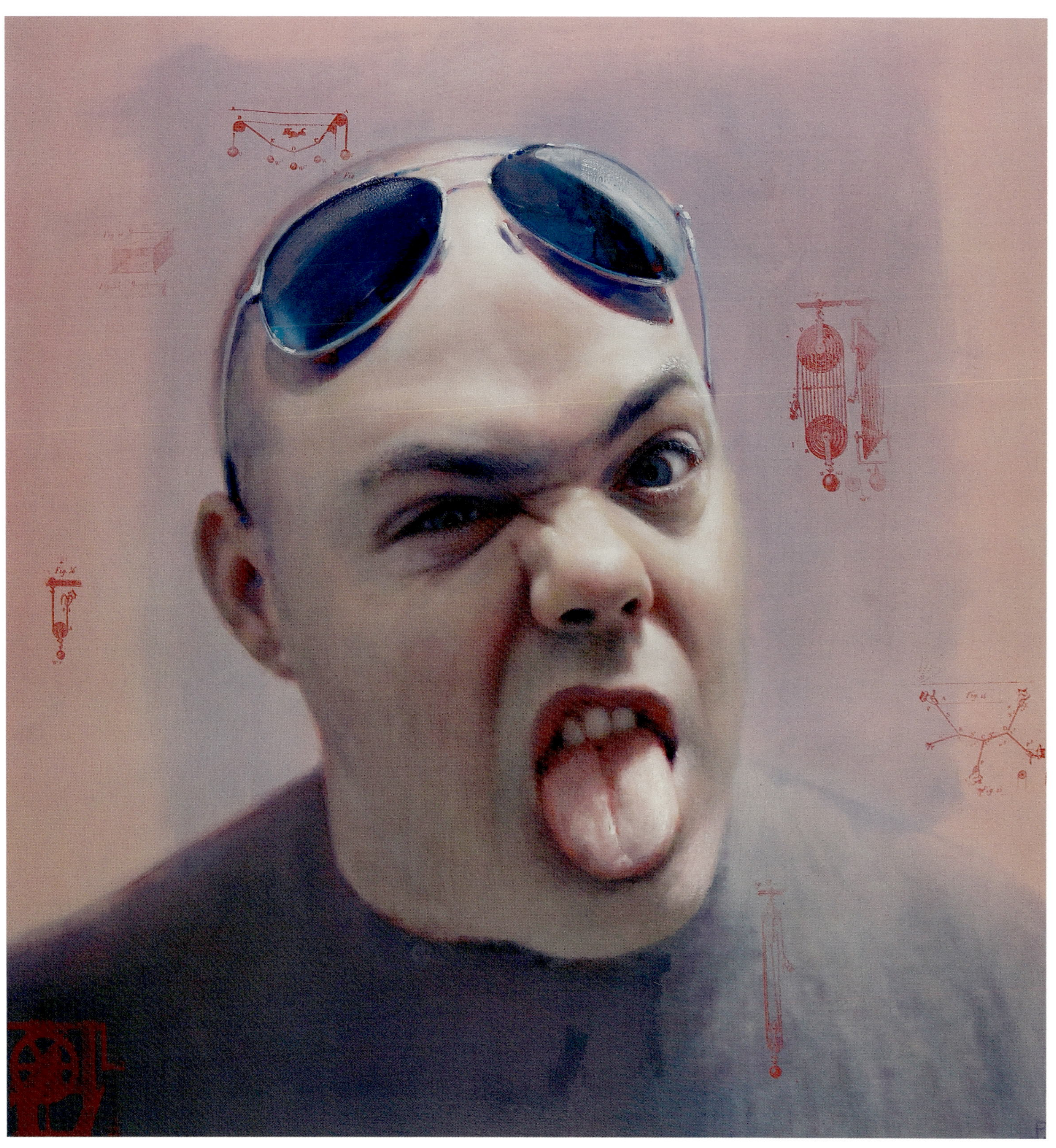

CECILIA DE CERVANTES, 2015
Oil on canvas, 28 × 26 in.

XAVIER CERVANTES, 2015 ›
Oil on canvas, 28 × 26 in.

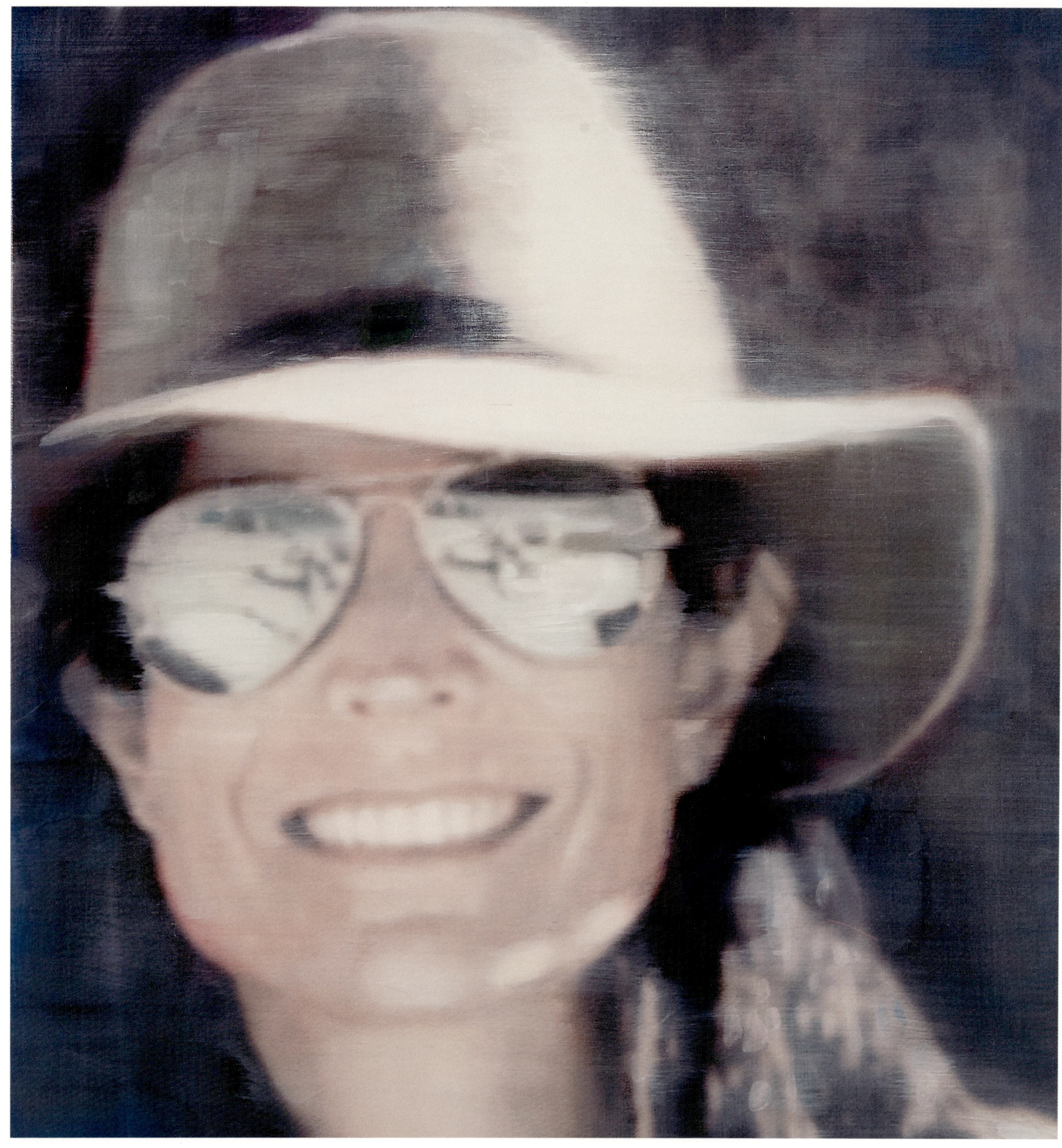

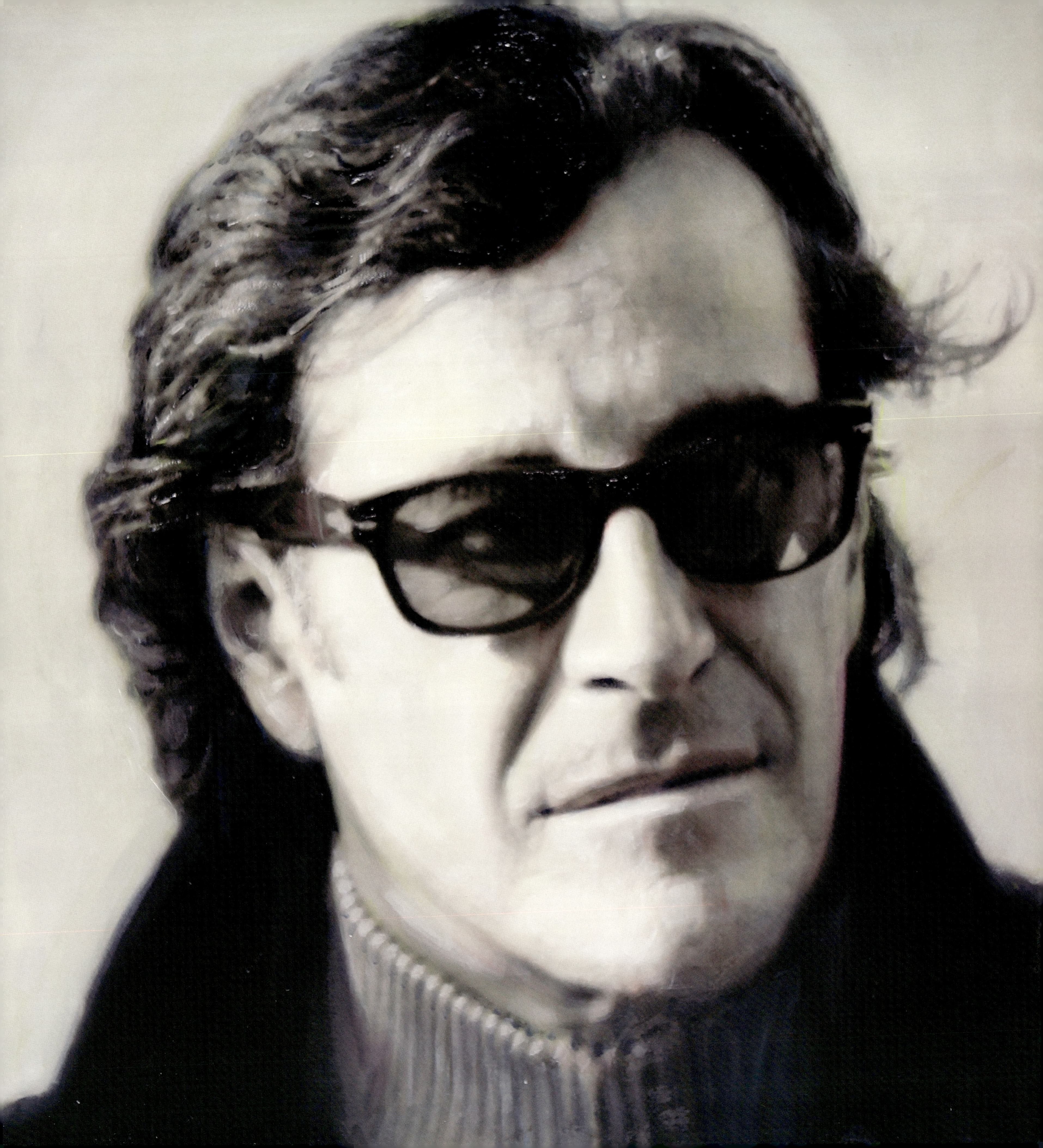

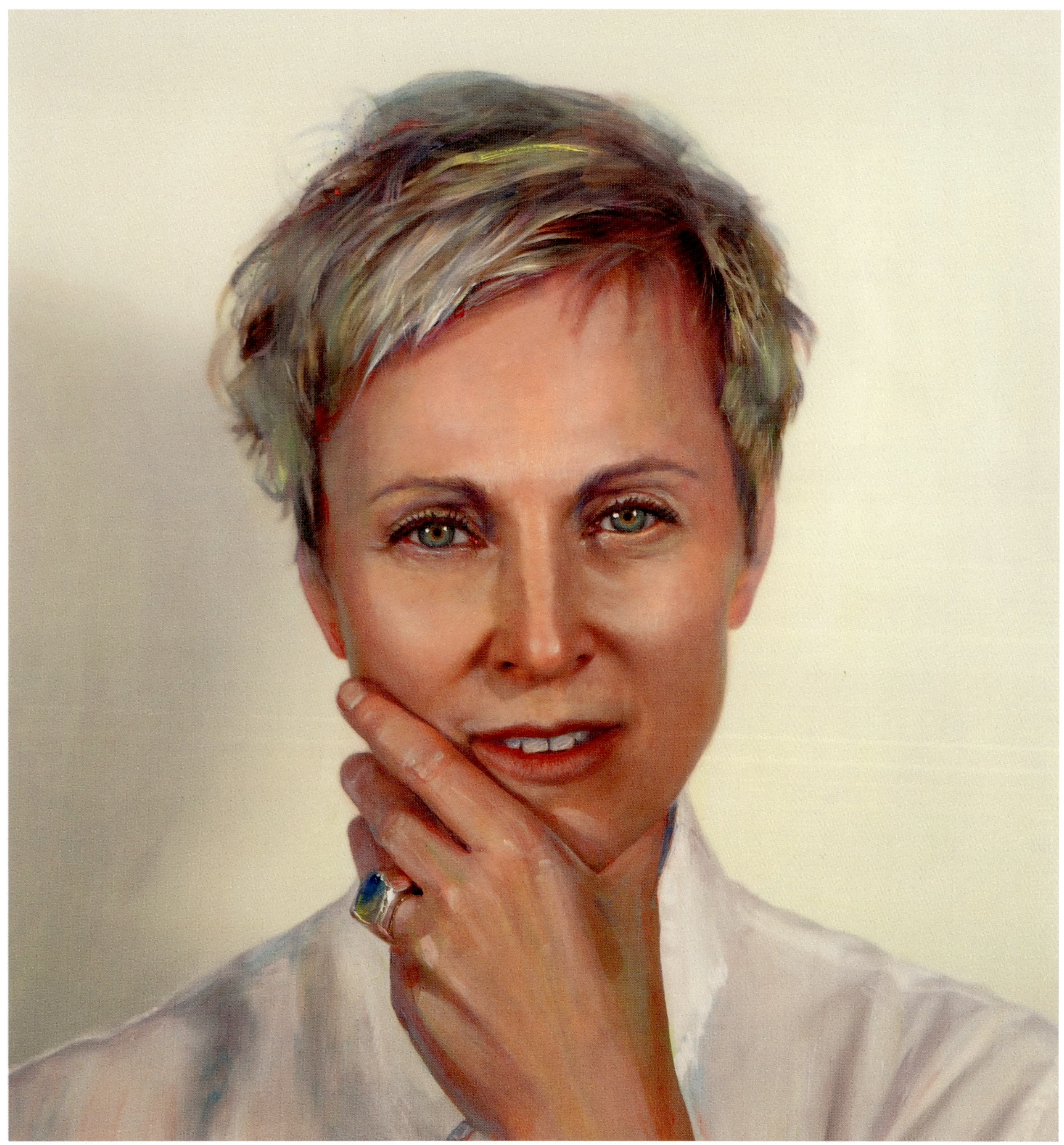

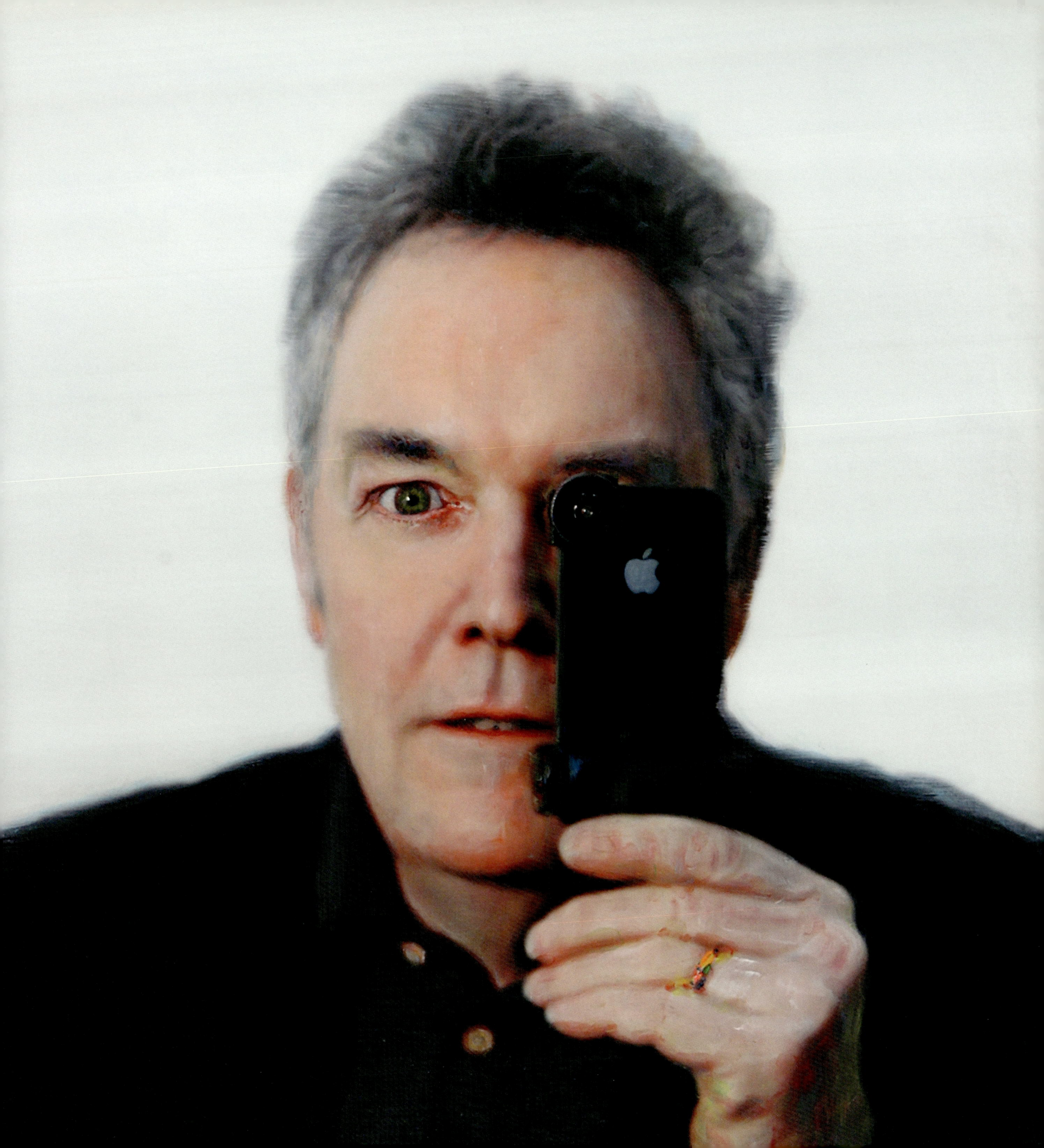

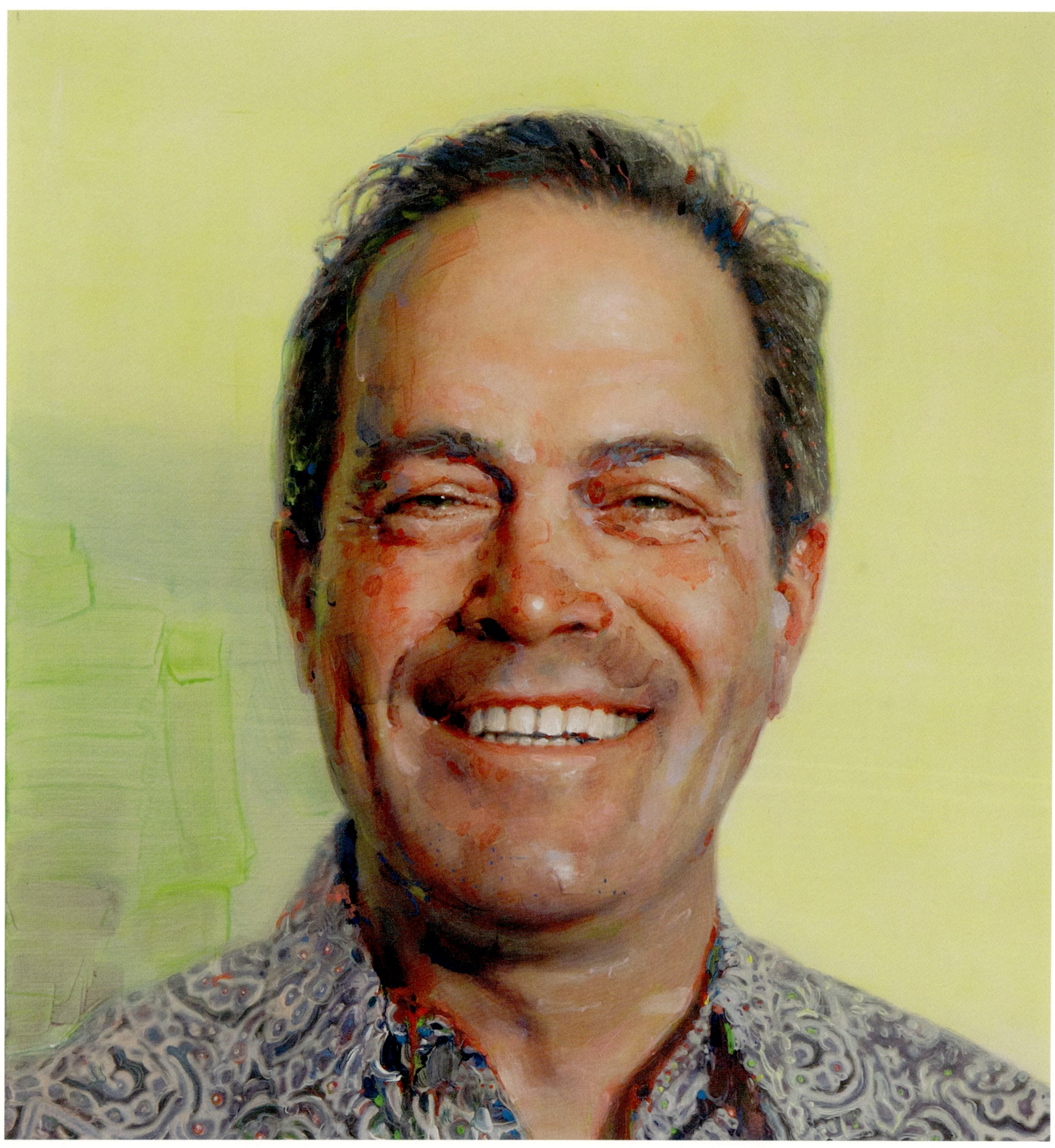

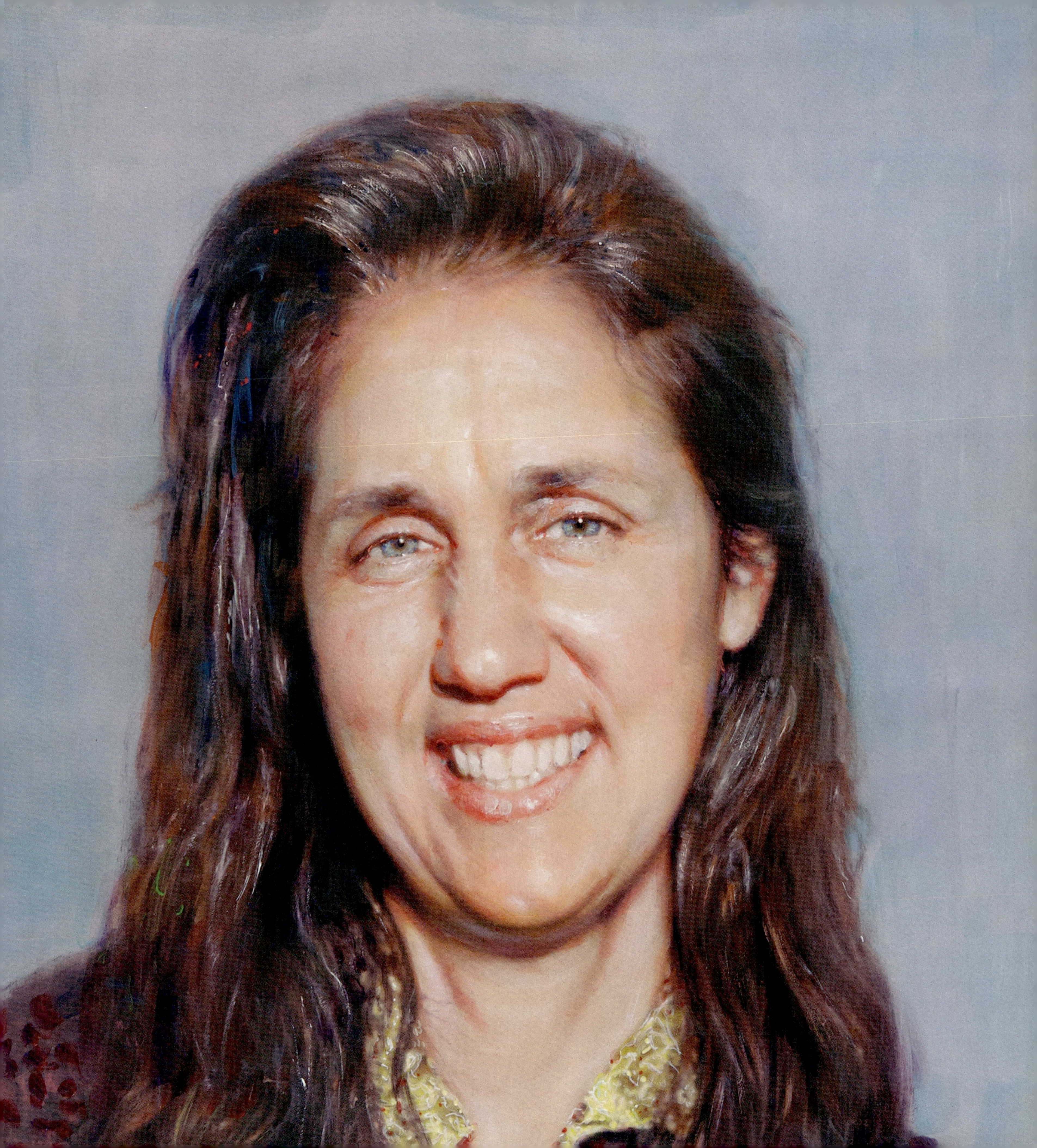

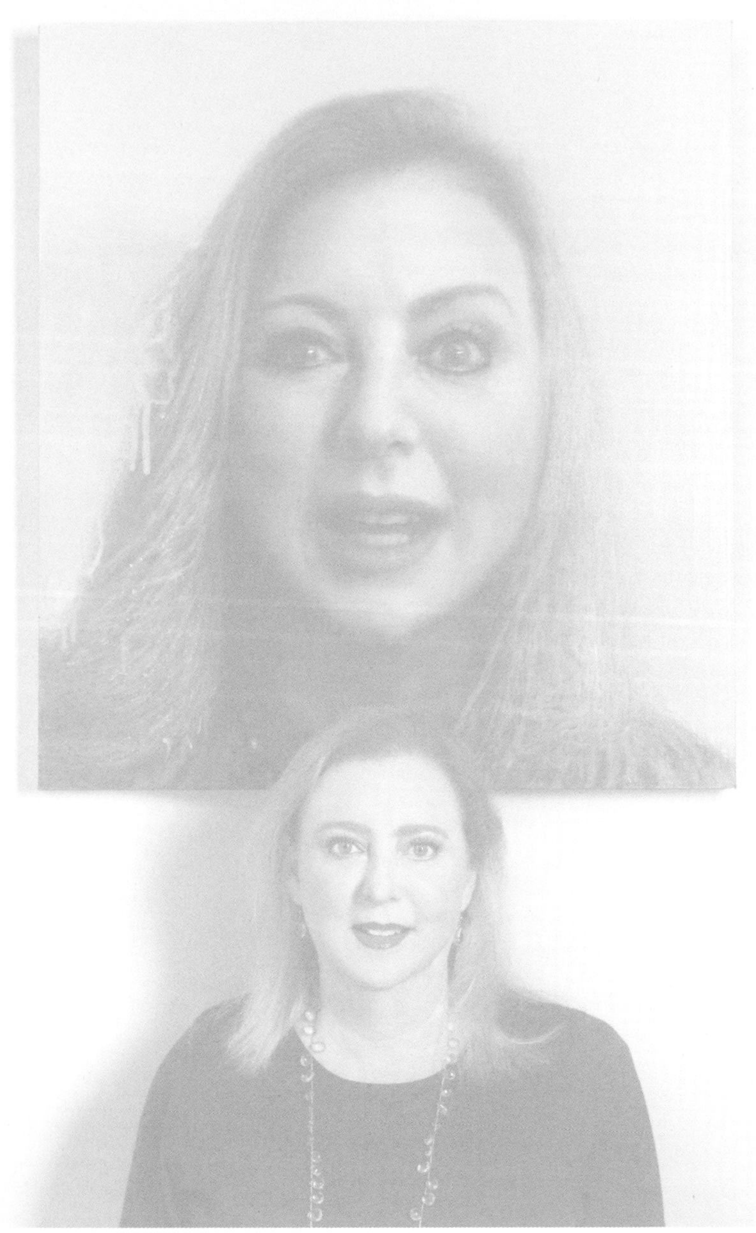

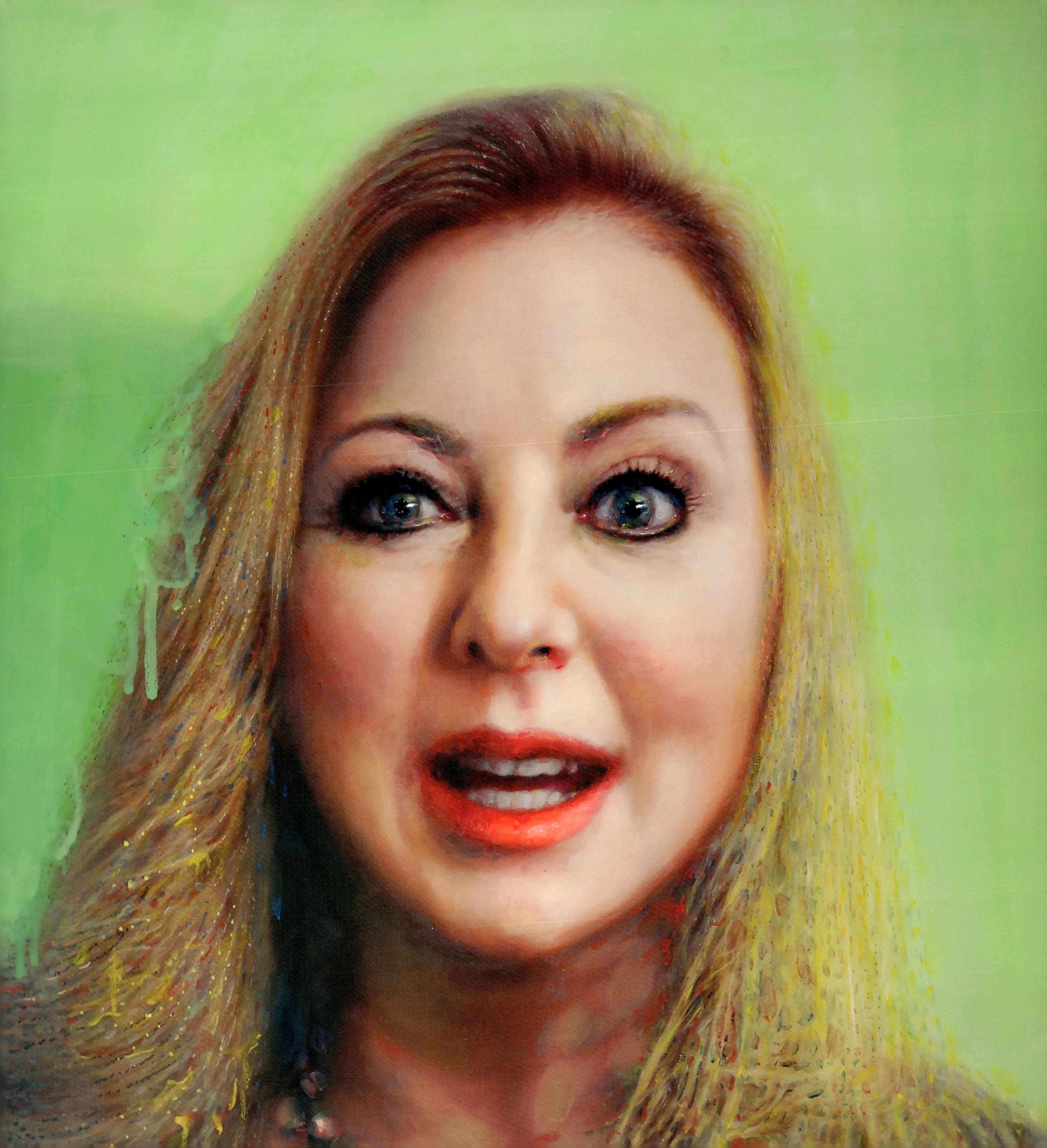

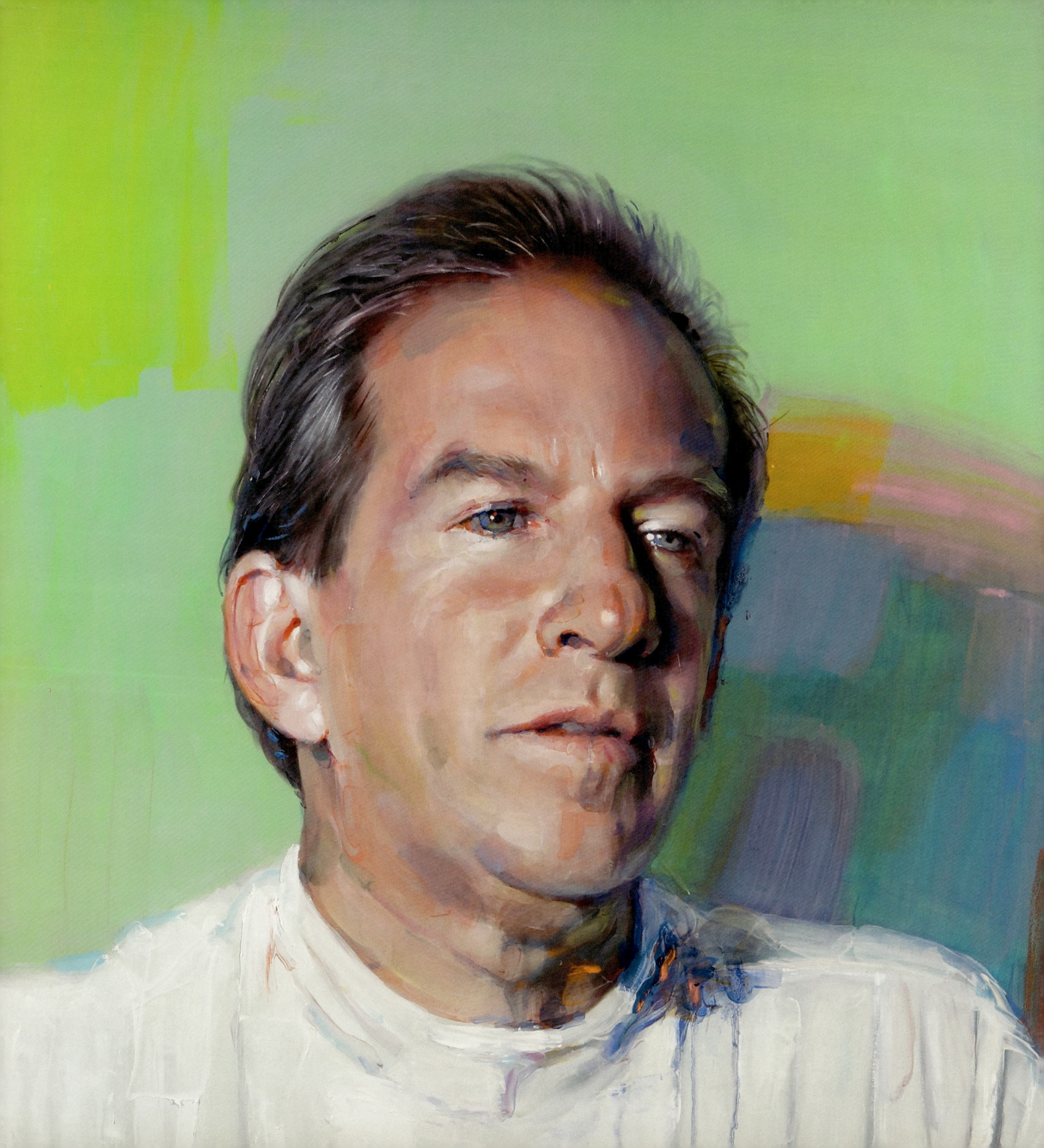

Popov's is a deft and elegant handling of his specific medium.

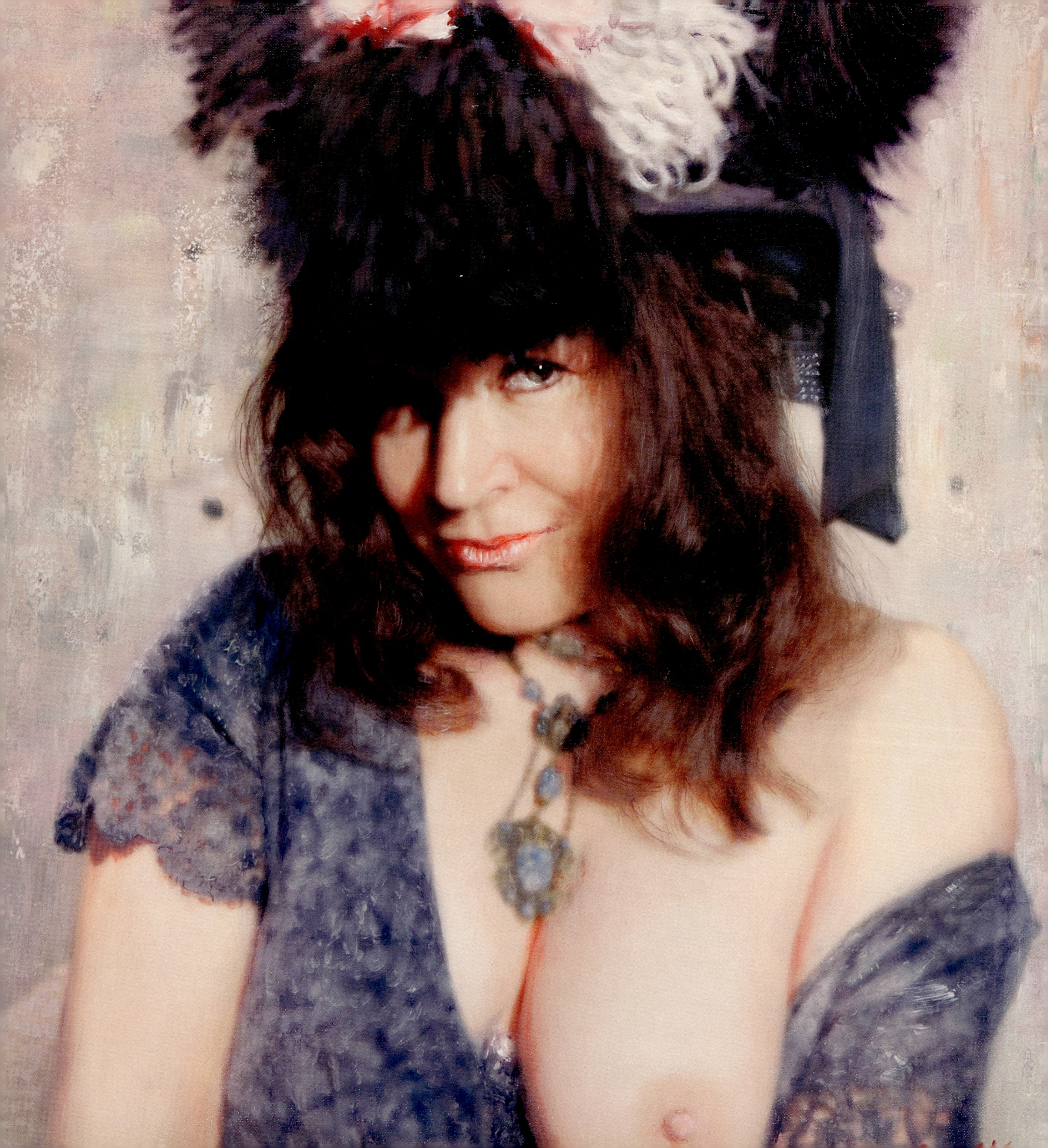

TESS NOTTEBOHM, 2014
Oil on canvas, 28 × 26 in.

following, left: **ROSEMARY MCNEELY 1**, 2016. Oil on canvas, 28 × 26 in.

right: **ROSEMARY MCNEELY 2**, 2016. Oil on canvas, 28 × 26 in.

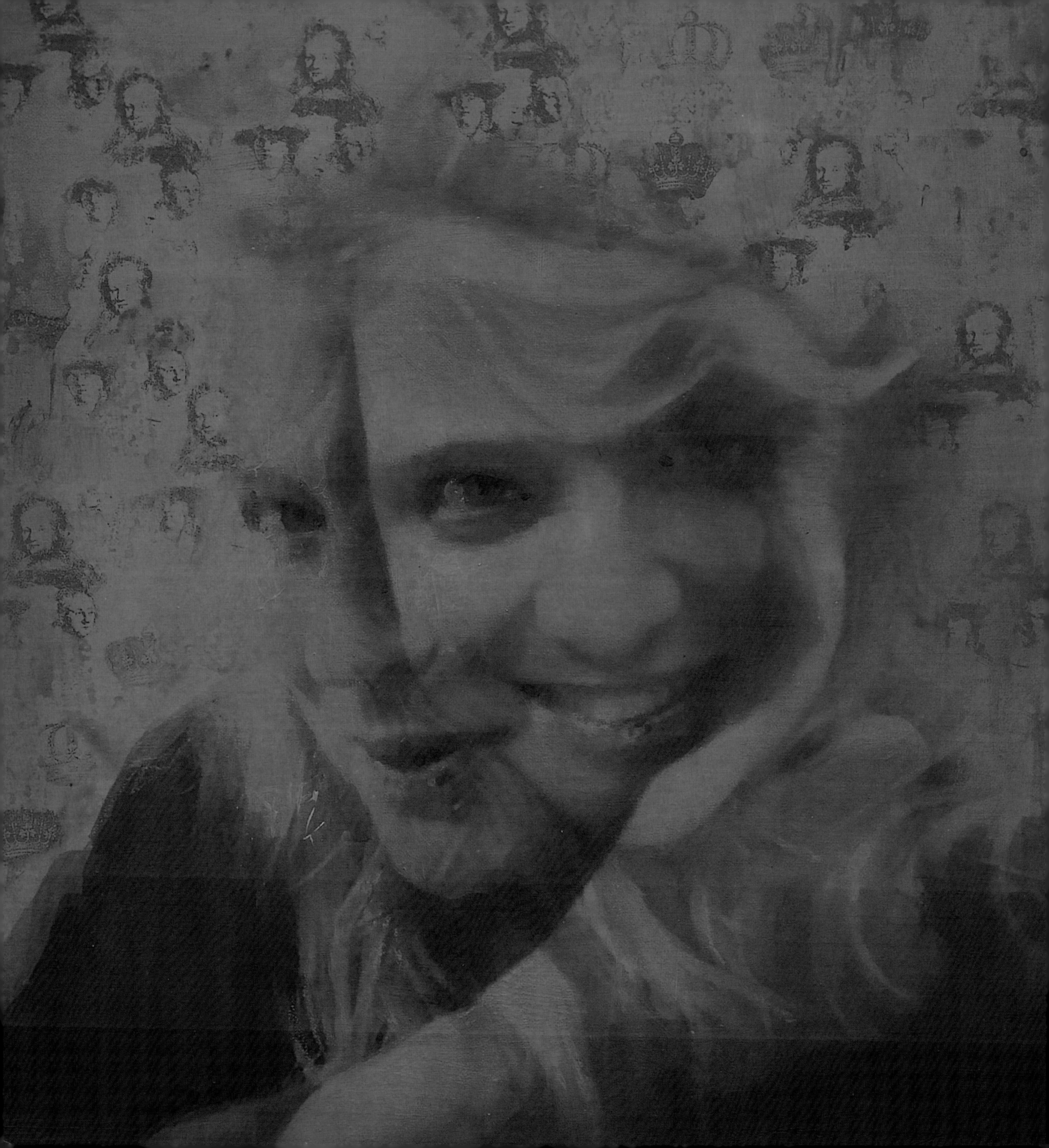

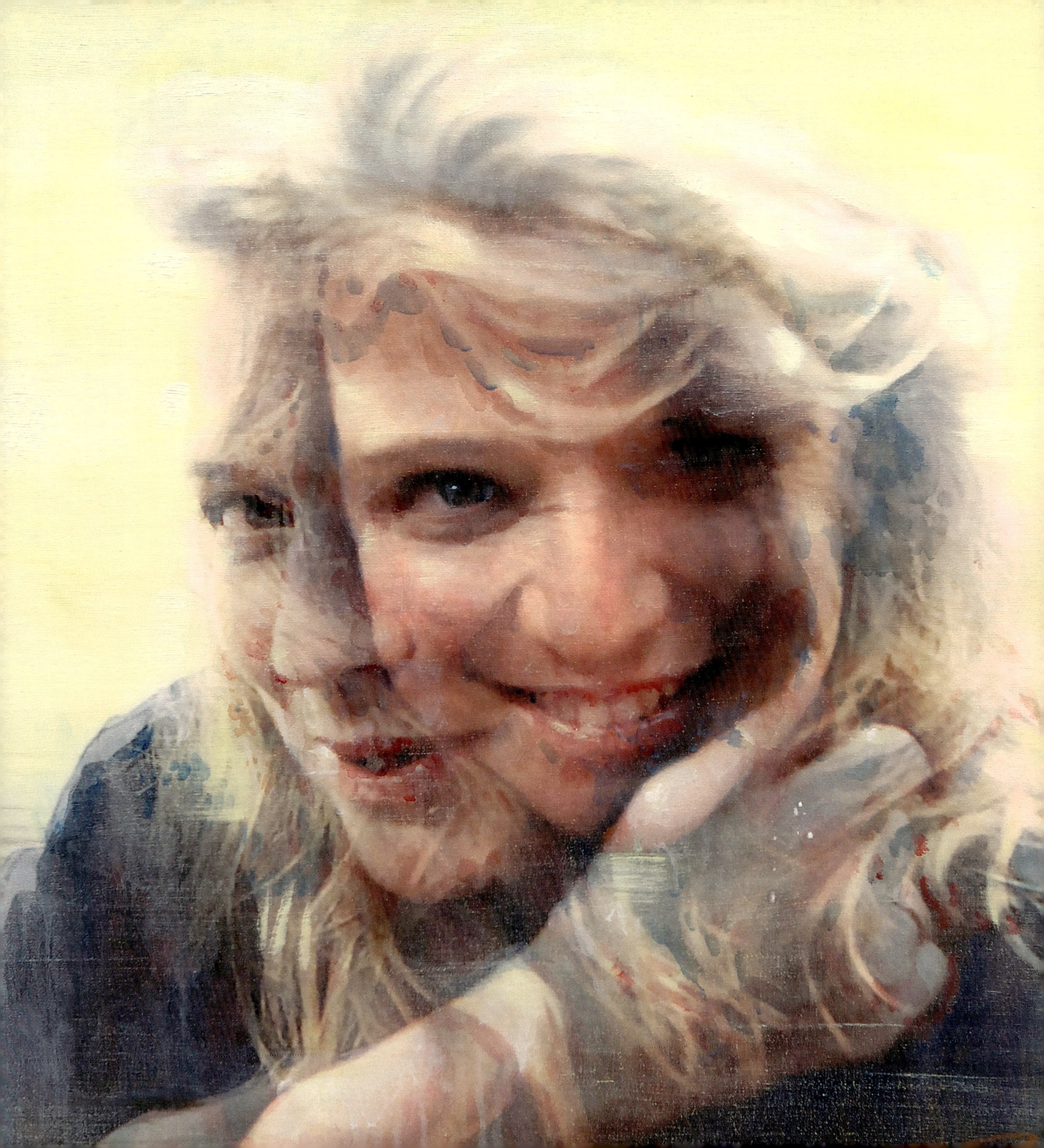

To sit for a Valentin Popov portrait is slightly narcissistic, exciting, revealing, and ultimately very gratifying. The atmosphere of his magnificent studio space is matched by his ever-flowing creativity and energy. He moves around you ubiquitously as he clicks his digital camera at a machine-gun pace, capturing your every mood and facial expression. When he feels he has enough photographic images to work from, you are invited to go downstairs to enjoy a delicious dinner.   KEVIN W. MCNEELY

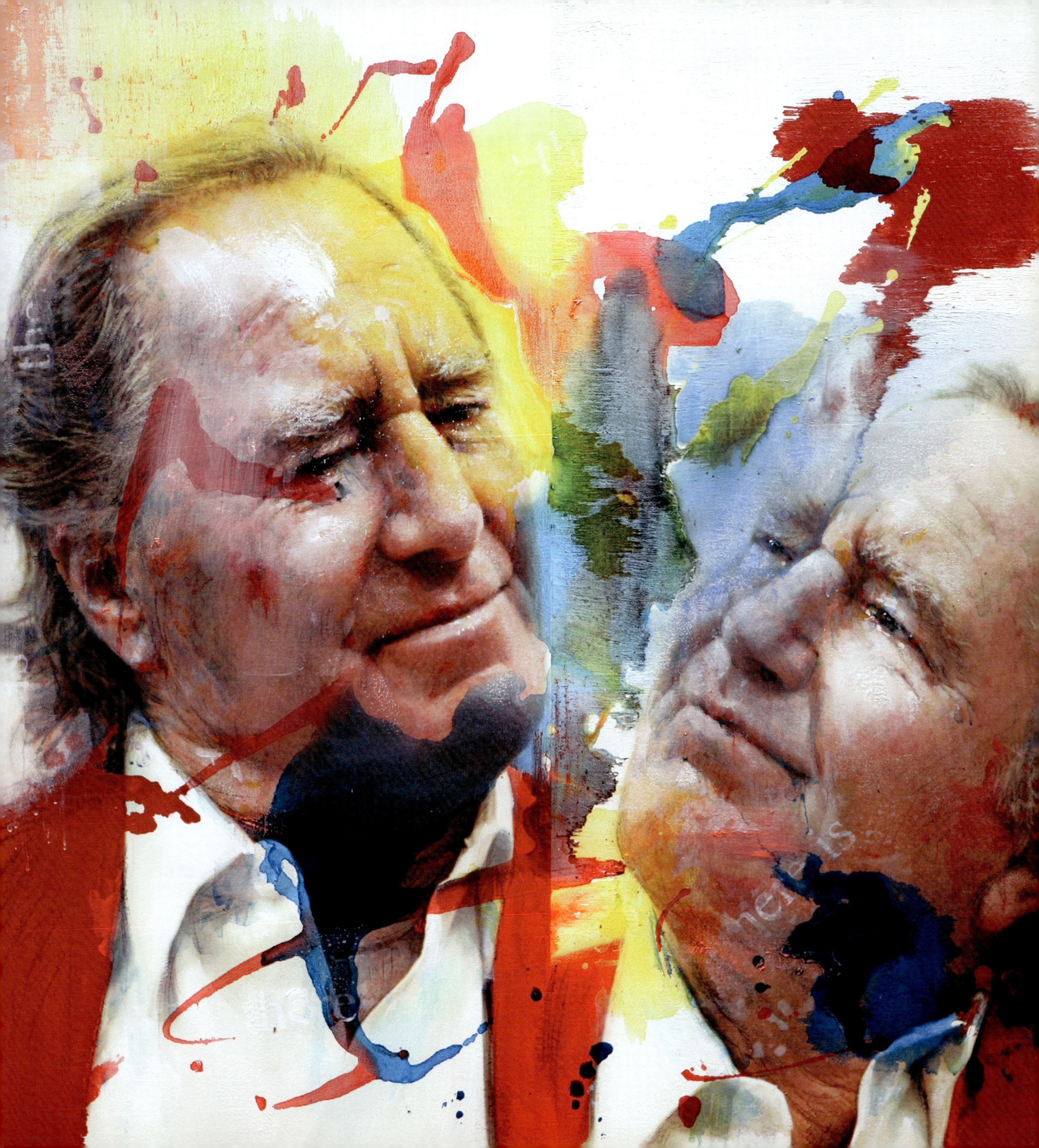

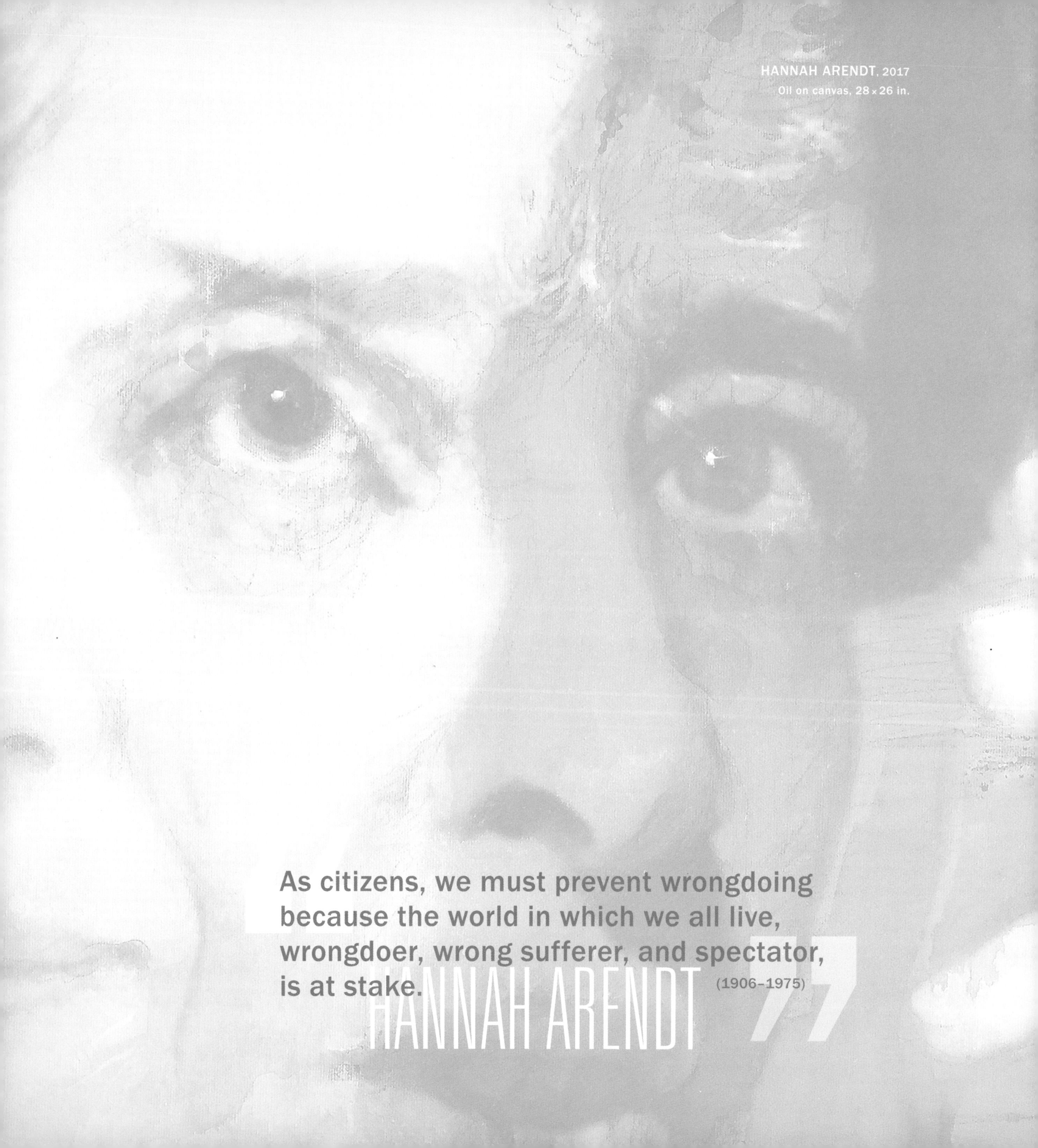

HANNAH ARENDT. 2017
Oil on canvas, 28 × 26 in.

As citizens, we must prevent wrongdoing
because the world in which we all live,
wrongdoer, wrong sufferer, and spectator,
is at stake.

HANNAH ARENDT (1906–1975)

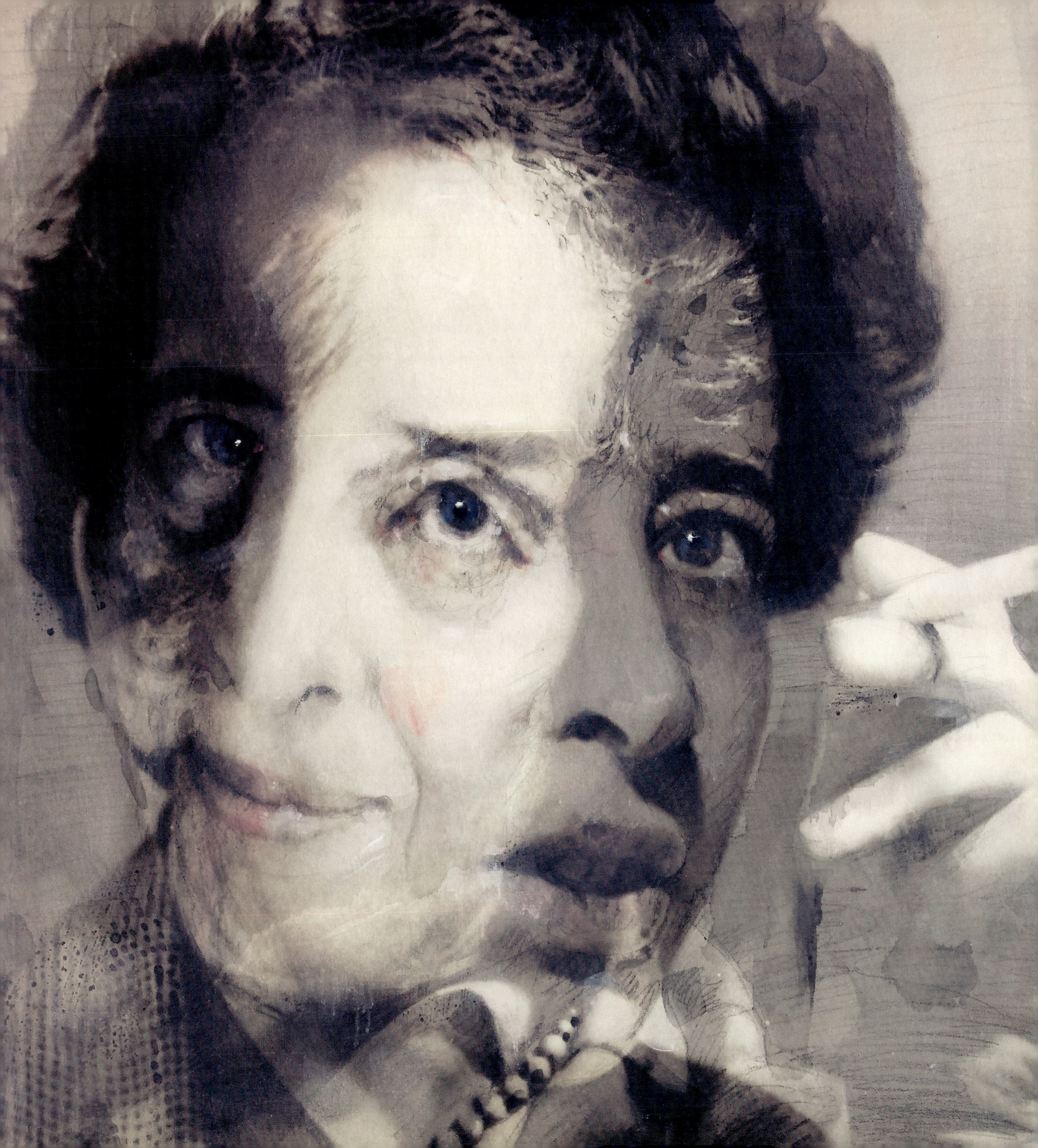

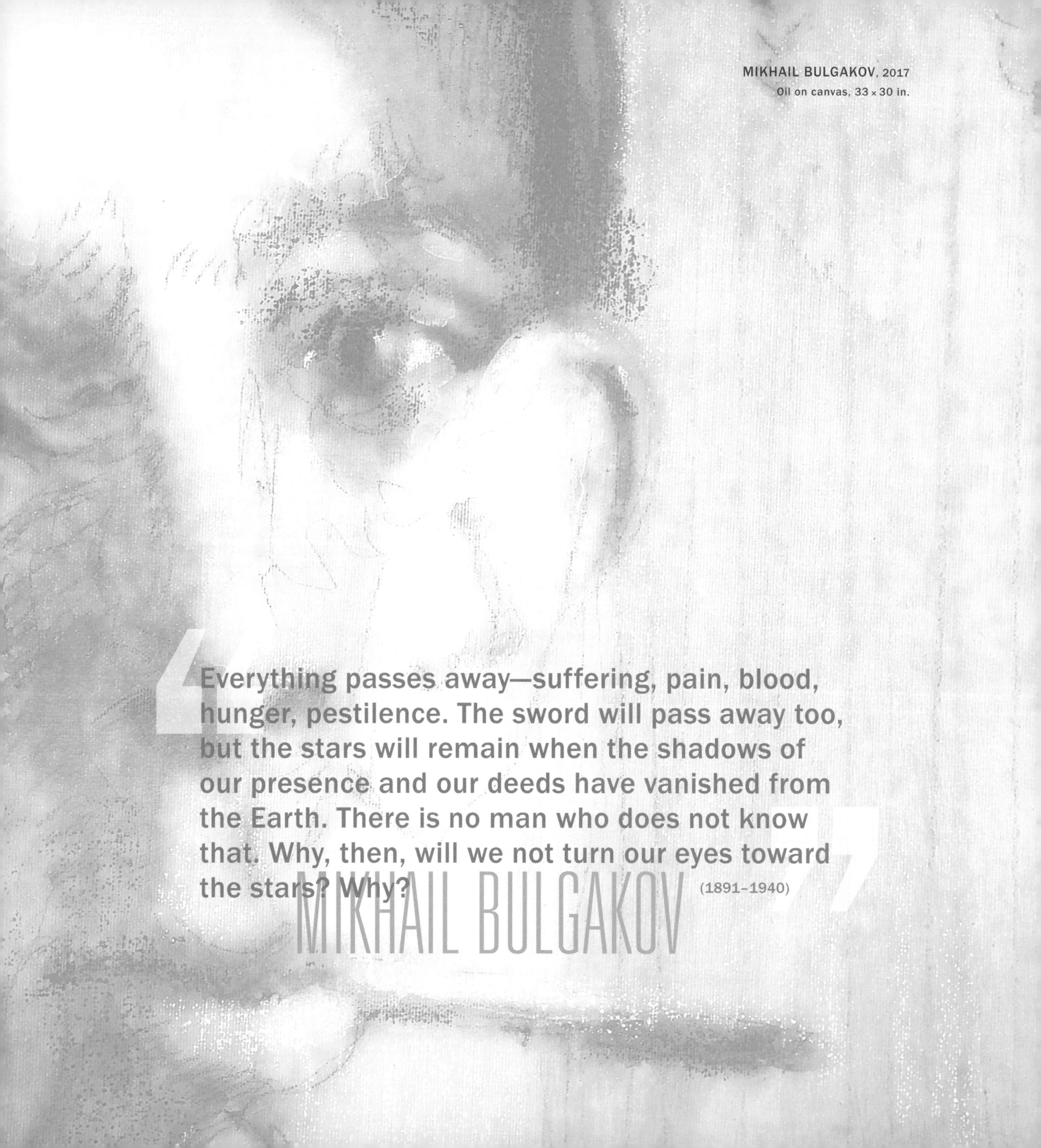

"Everything passes away—suffering, pain, blood, hunger, pestilence. The sword will pass away too, but the stars will remain when the shadows of our presence and our deeds have vanished from the Earth. There is no man who does not know that. Why, then, will we not turn our eyes toward the stars? Why?"

MIKHAIL BULGAKOV (1891–1940)

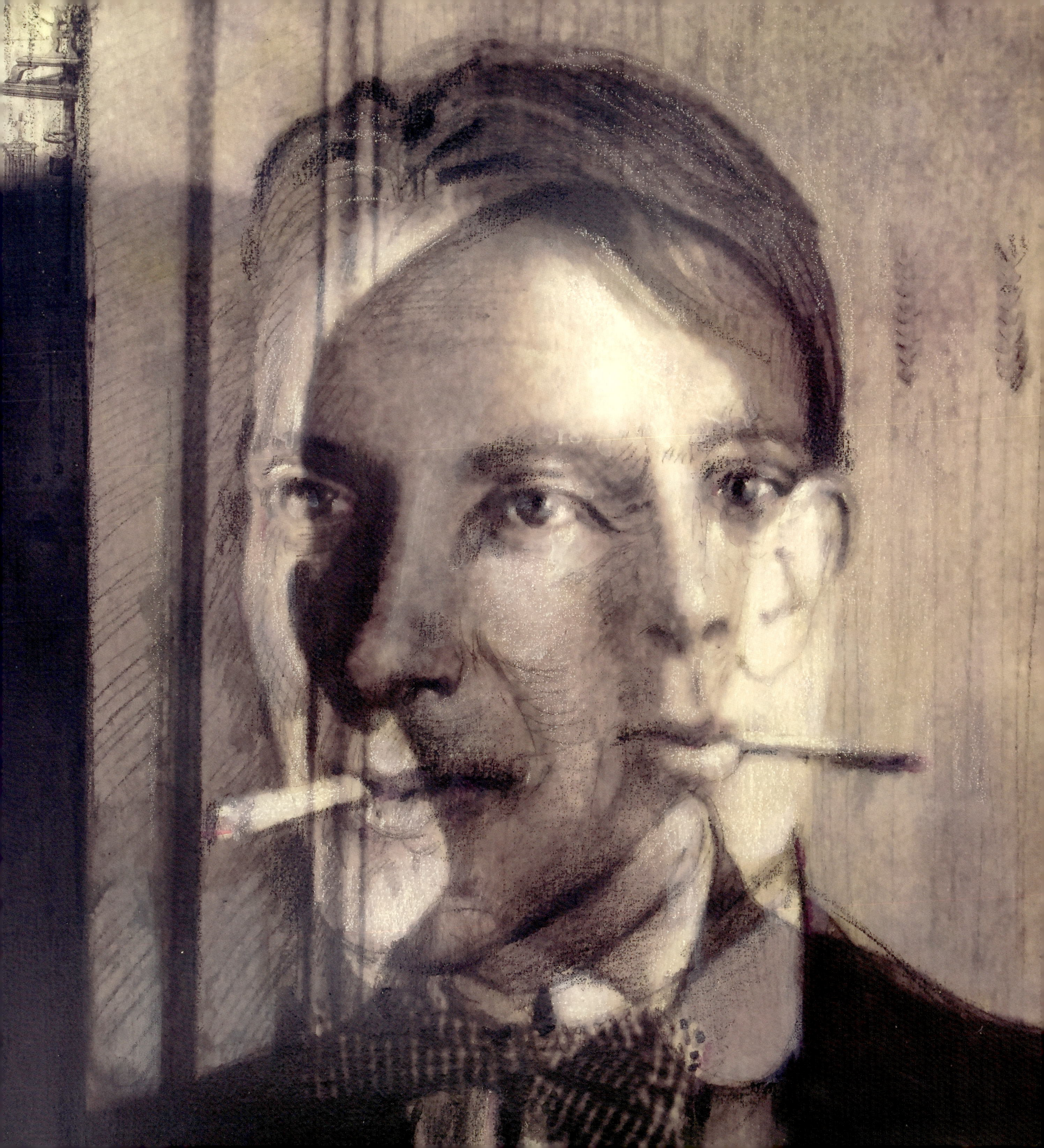

B. R. Gilbert

SEEING DOUBLE
A WOOZY GLIMPSE AT THE PARATACTIC PORTRAITS OF VALENTIN POPOV

Plurality is a constant in the work of artist Valentin Popov. In his *Batman* constructs and in his richly inventive satires and allegories, with their implied narratives, the dualistic footprint of righteousness and wickedness, light and darkness, is omnipresent. Popov routinely acknowledges that, like magnetic poles, the contrasting aspects of man's dual nature hold him in moral and metaphysical abeyance. Popov's evocation of this postulate is a nod to a principle of duality so pervasive that it has long been a subset of formal philosophy pondered by luminaries the likes of Descartes and Leibniz down to the scientific materialists of the present day. In philosophical thought, dualism is a theory or system that considers reality to consist of two irreducible elements or modes, particularly as expressed in the religious doctrine that the universe contains opposed powers of good and evil, seen as balanced equals.

In his portrait work, Popov adopts a variety of departure points. In the case of the conventionally presented portraits, they are mostly drawn from the artist's immediate social coterie—old friends, fresh acquaintances, and a collegiate circle of art professionals—critics, curators, and other custodians of culture. In the case of the double, compound portraits, most are historical personages, selected because of spiritual associations. With the compound or "double" likenesses, we're no longer in conventional portrait territory; we've trespassed into a new, not easily defined area where fragmentation, juxtaposition, and superimposition hold sway.

In Popov's historical portraits, the viewer is usually confronted by a profile presented in juxtaposition to a frontal view. The frontal view is the popularly known image candidly presented to the world; the profile is the immortalized, official likeness preserved for the ages—or a contrary, subversive version of the personality we thought we knew, but to whom the artist's prism of multiple perspective has now lent an ulterior significance.

Fragmentary portraiture has manifested in Cubism, Futurism, and Surrealism. In the case of these historic movements, the motivation for fragmentation was to recognize, as in Duchamp's *Nude Descending a Staircase*, that any totality is a composite of myriad particles or actions; or, more broadly, to expose what lurks beneath the surface of things and to affirm that reality is not what it seems, and that appearances can be deceptive. Contrast and counterpoint are everywhere evident in Popov's portraits, both solo and duo. But these are only technical incidentals of visual presentation. The deeper drama lies in the psychic life suggested by these flourishes of coloration, shading, and bravura display of special effects.

Preservation for posterity is the principal purview of portraiture. Popov's portraits of historic personages differ from those he has made of his contemporaries in one important respect: they are portraits of personages who are already deceased. Having departed this earthly plane, these subjects cannot be painted from life, but must be depicted according to the artist's imagination and interpretive faculties coupled with a process of rendering dependent on past portraits and archival images such as photographs. This set of circumstances affords the artist free rein to indulge in a freewheeling dialog between subject and object, viewer and viewed.

Because of their mythic stature and the long train of lore associated with them, it is natural that they should be seen as multidimensional and larger-than-life. Honored occupants of the sacred precincts of history, these illustrious individuals may be, and have been, portrayed with some latitude in variation, in any number of fashions over the course of time. Popov takes the matter of free interpretation a step further by creating *infratwins*—composites consisting of a primary sitter paired with a doppelgänger—a second self or hallucinatory double. These ghostly doubles haunting their familiar counterparts throw us off base to suggest the fragility of accepted consensus and the ultimate unknowability of history. What begin as stark frontal views reminiscent of mug shots are impinged on by overlapping and transitional convergences of imagery, then splintered, compartmentalized, and rapidly dissolved into a skein of fractal duplications. Enhaloing each portrait on the periphery is a plurality of tangents echoing and re-echoing the dominant theme and fringed by a frenzy of optical subtleties of every sort—fogs, mirages, and eidetic phenomena.

Yet, however novel the approach to the venerable portrait genre, the perennial problem of scope remains. By means of what technique can the *gestalt* of a person be encompassed in a portrait? What quality invests a portrait with the greatest accuracy of essence? The question persists because the human face, like the personality which it encases and which it sometimes conceals and sometimes reflects is, in all its complexity, ultimately inapprehensible and unmappable. How ironic that the shallow human epidermis should serve as the modulus of deepest recognition and identification among individuals! When appraising the human face and all its power and mystery, we are reminded of the incisive words of William Blake: *What immortal hand or eye could frame thy fearful symmetry?*

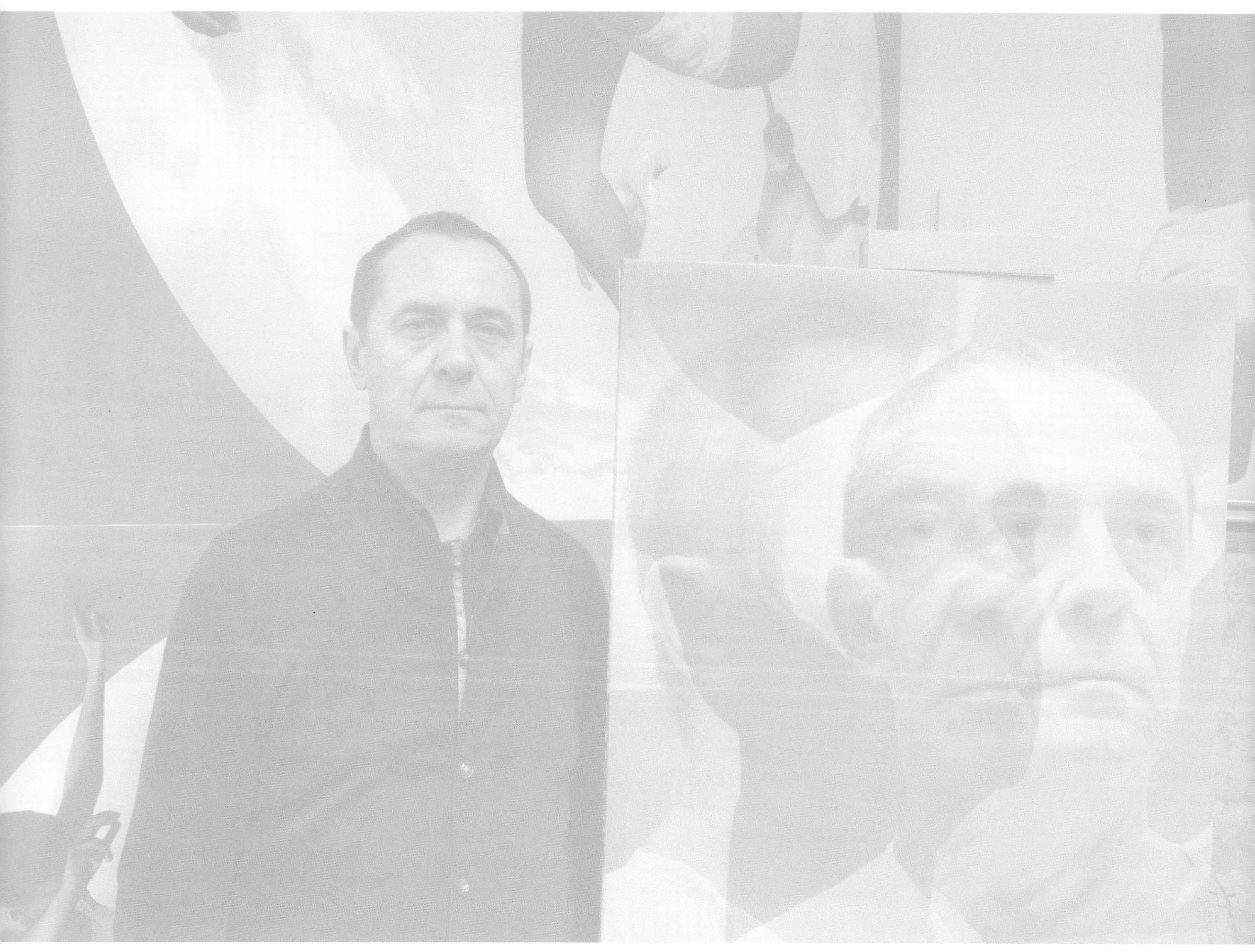

following, left: **TWO JAKES**, 2015. Oil on canvas, 28 × 26 in.

right: **JAKE**, 2014. Oil on canvas, 28 × 26 in.

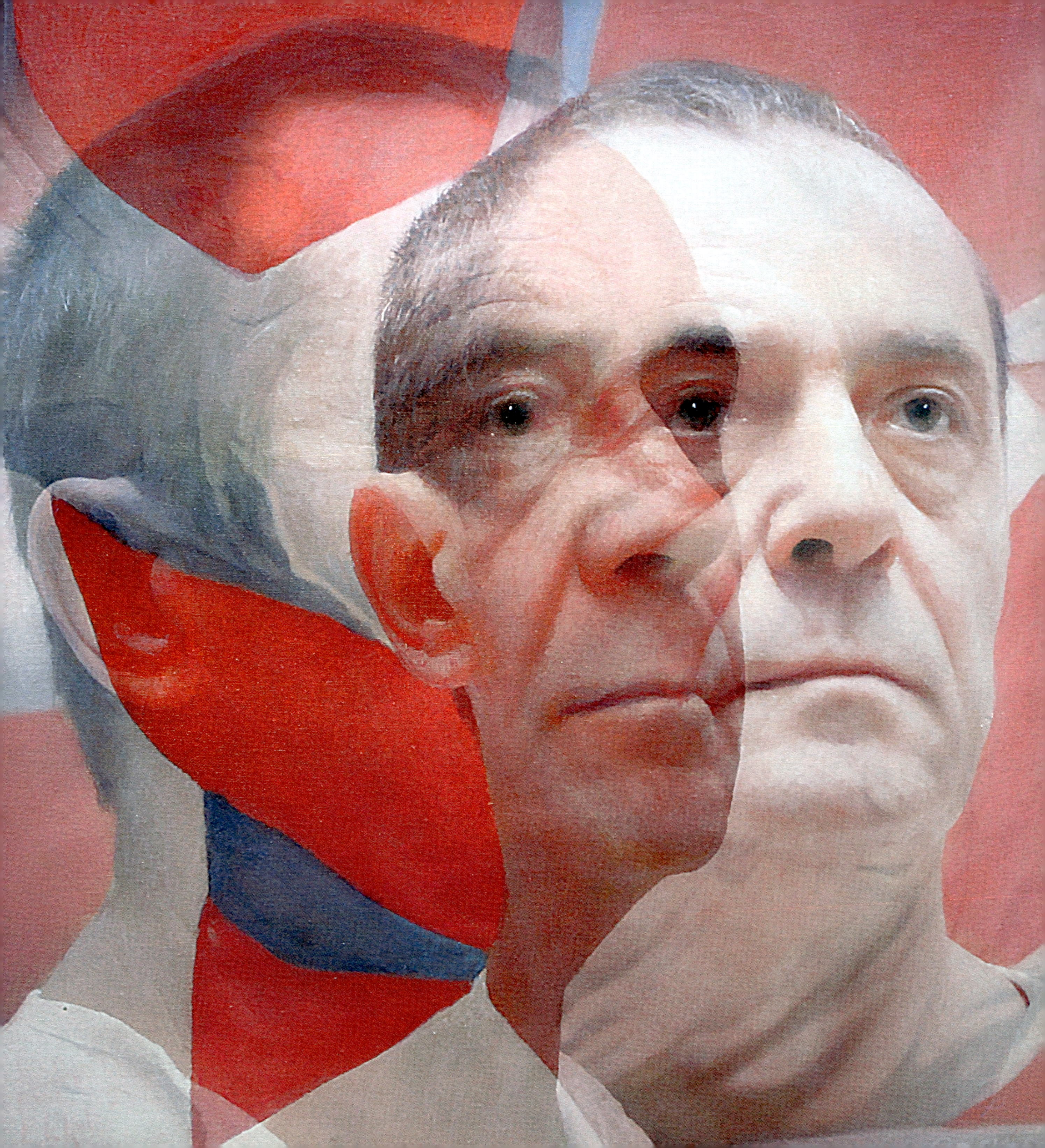

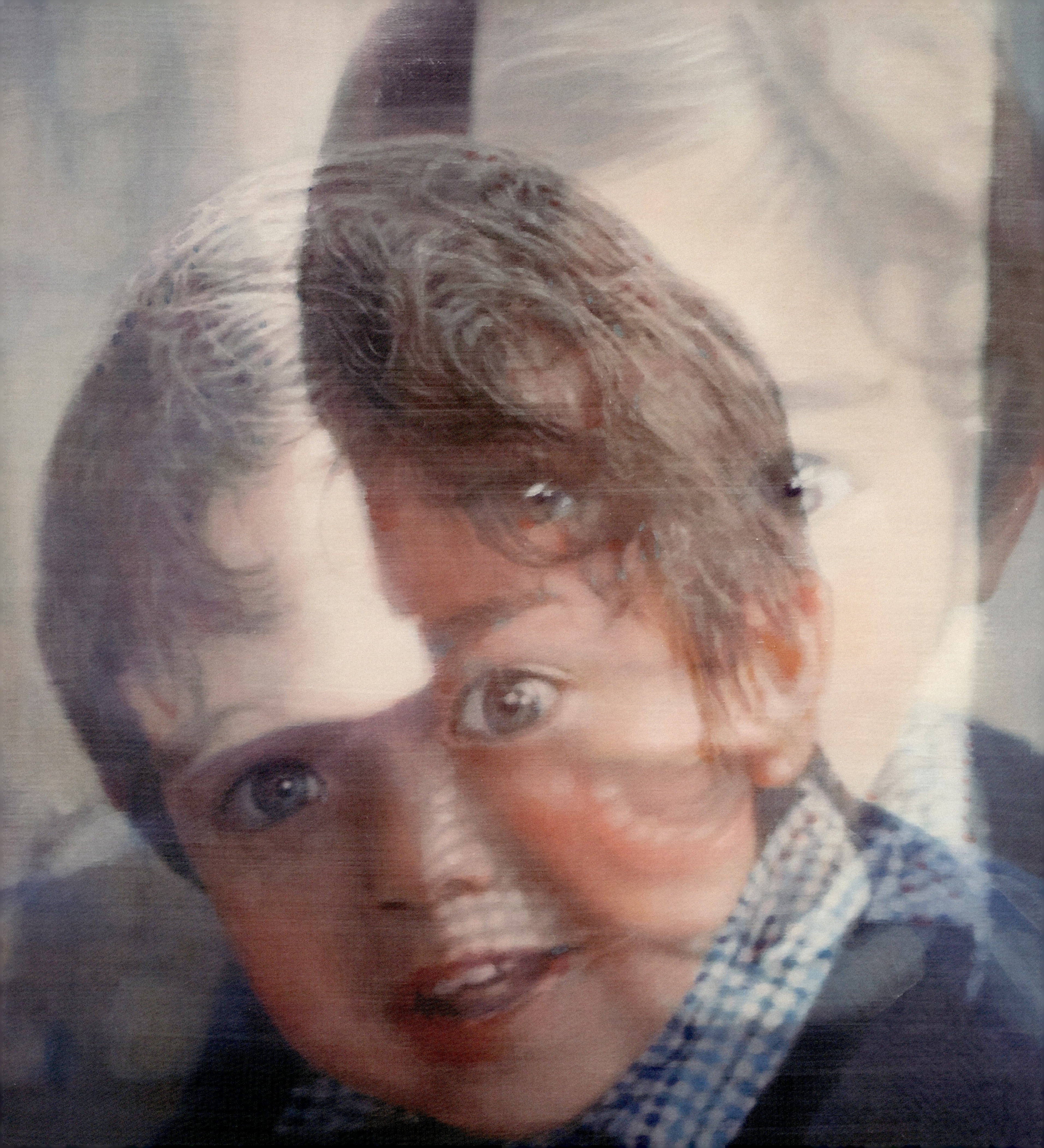

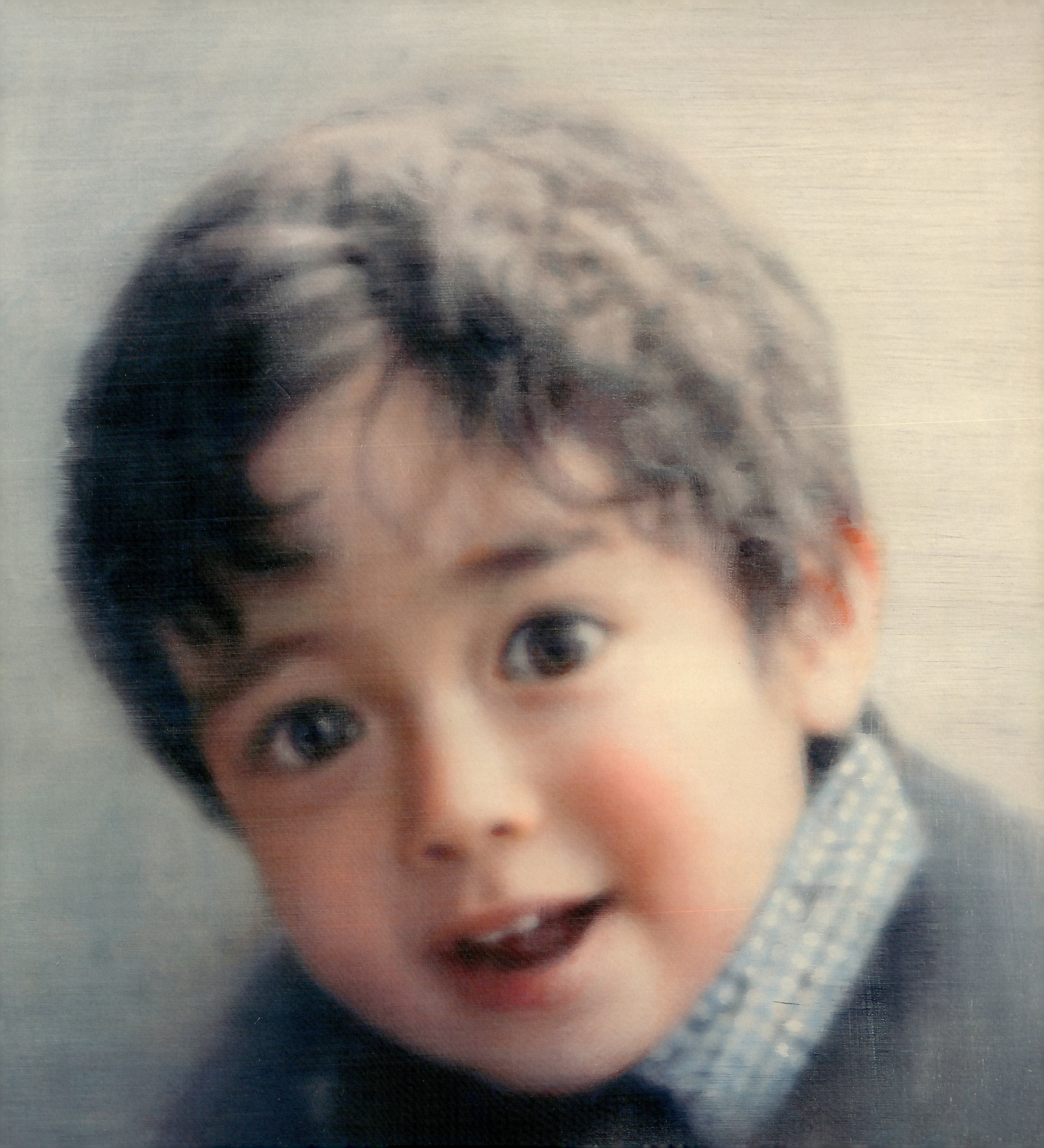

ZENKO AFTANAZIV, 2016
Oil on canvas, 28 × 26 in.

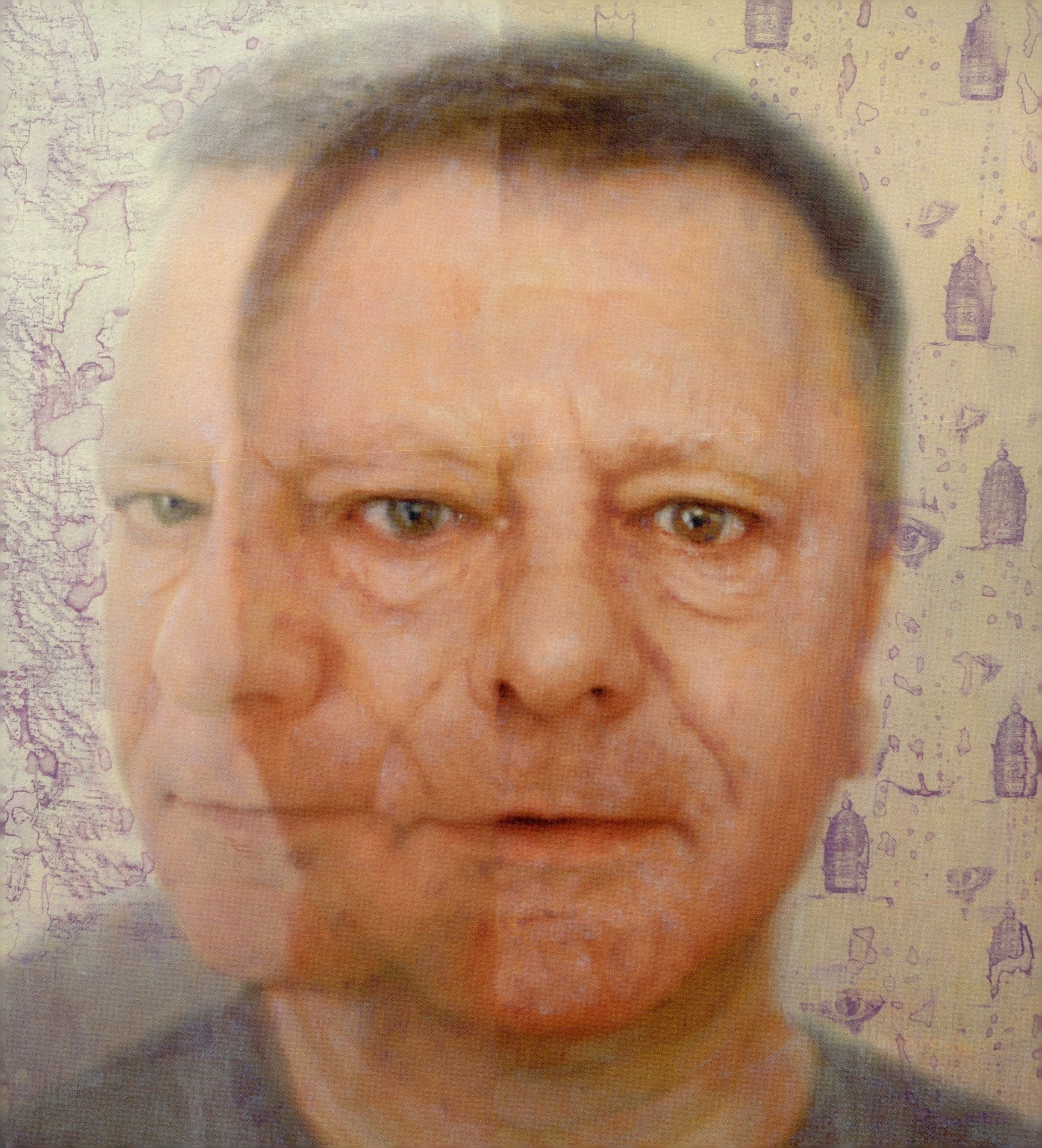

YANA AFTANAZIV 1, 2016
Oil on canvas, 70 × 52 in.

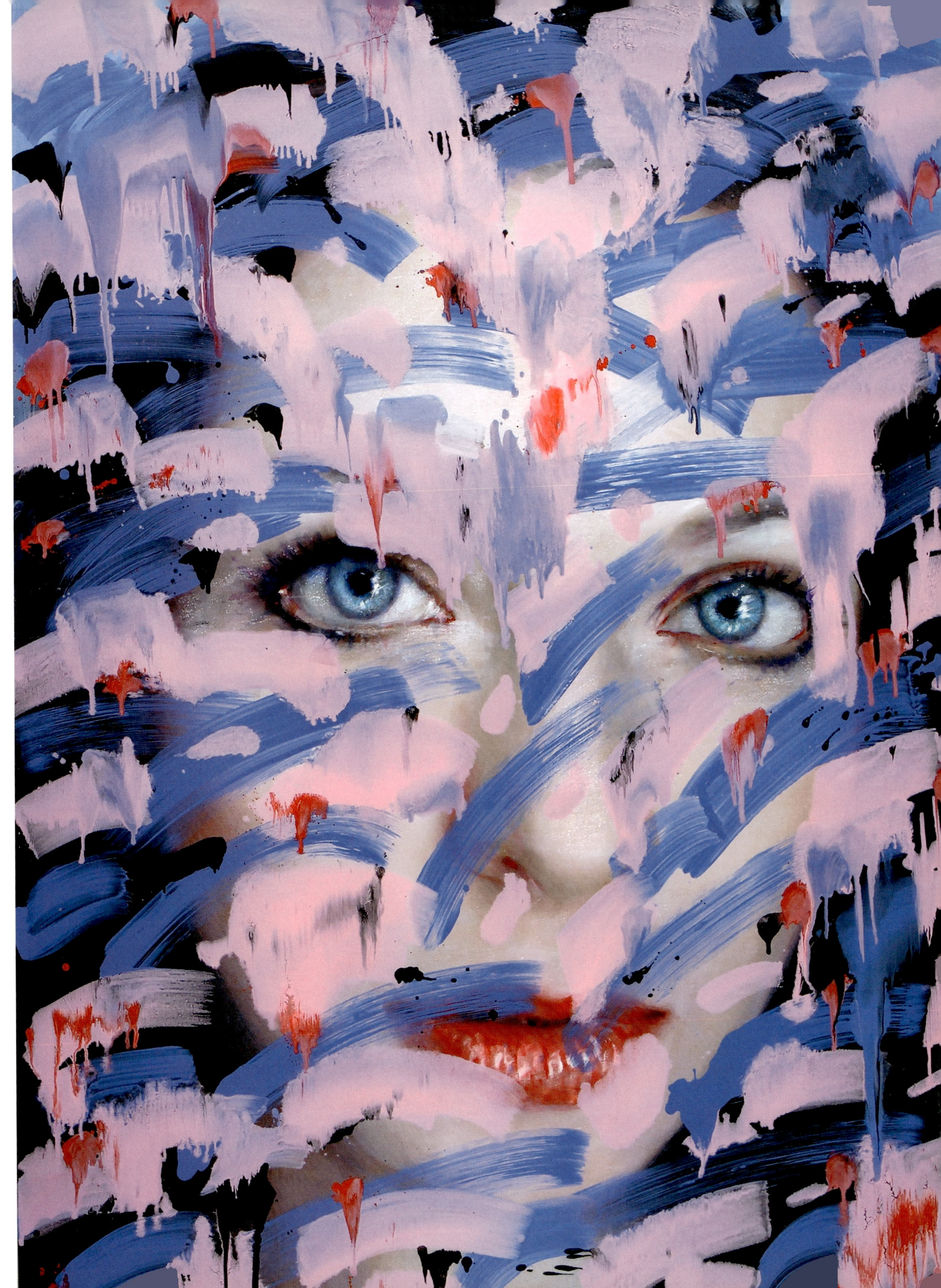

YANA AFTANAZIV 2, 2016
Oil on canvas, 70 × 52 in.

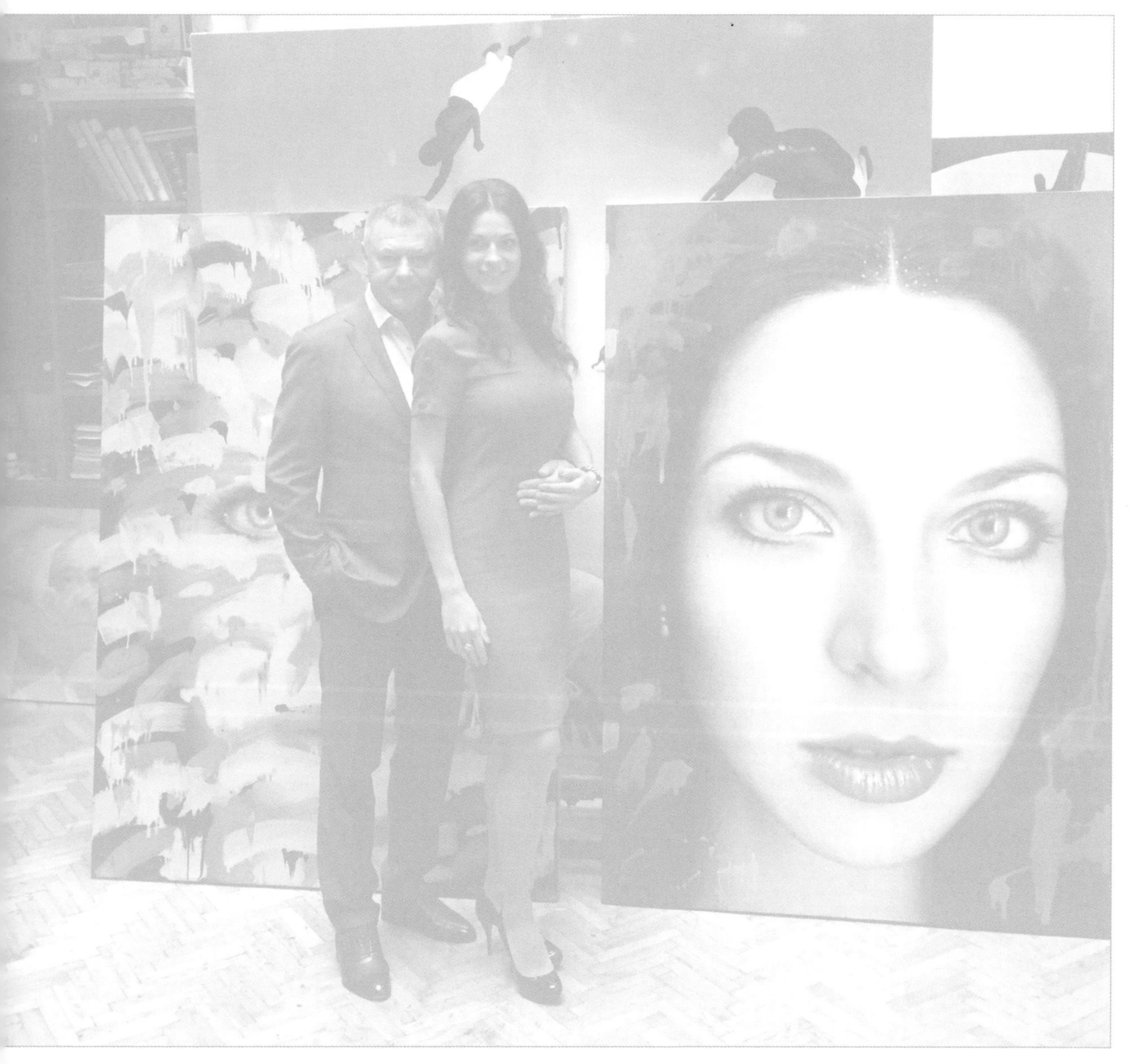

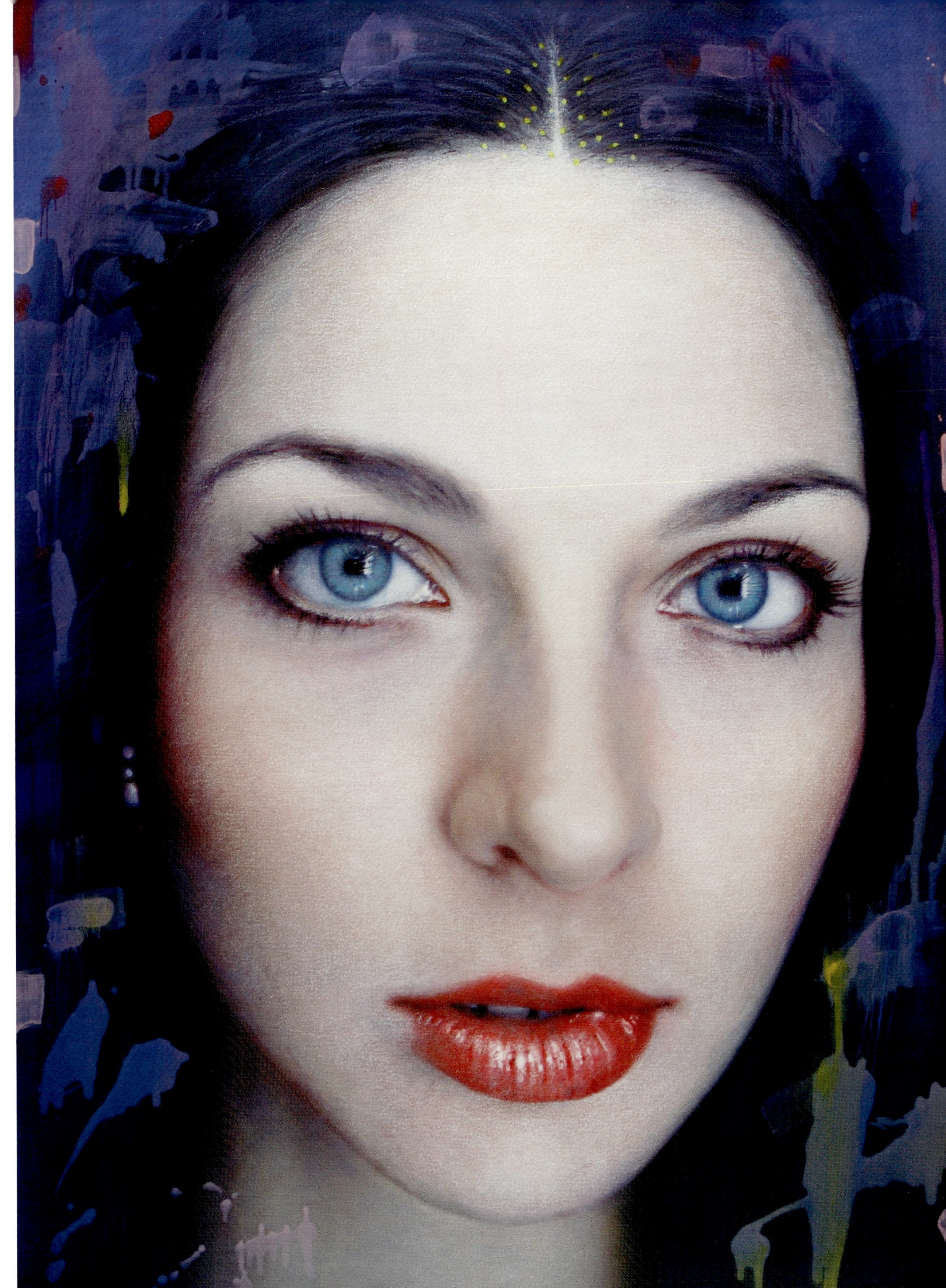

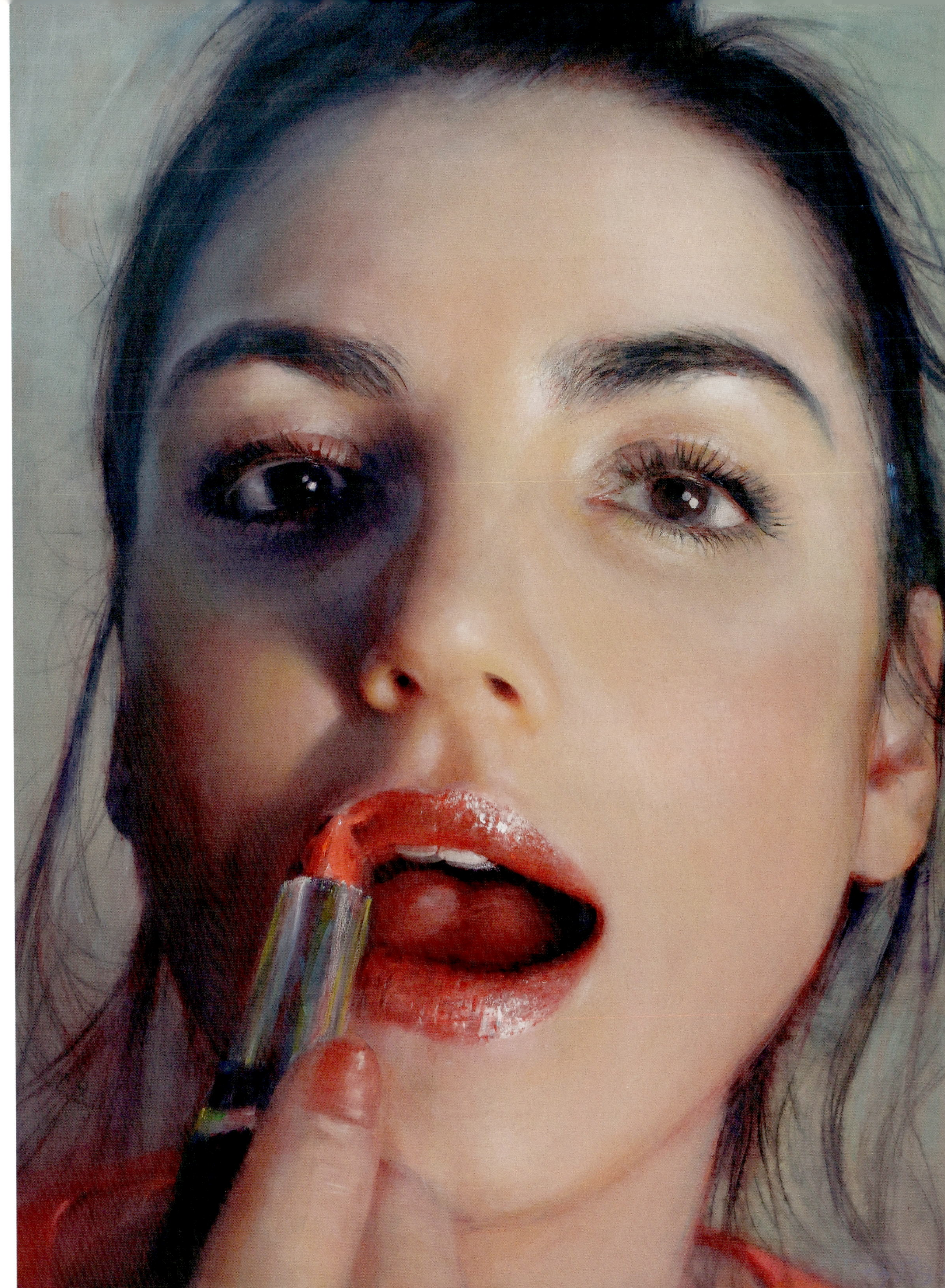

LIPSTICK 2, 2015
Oil on canvas, 70 × 52 in.

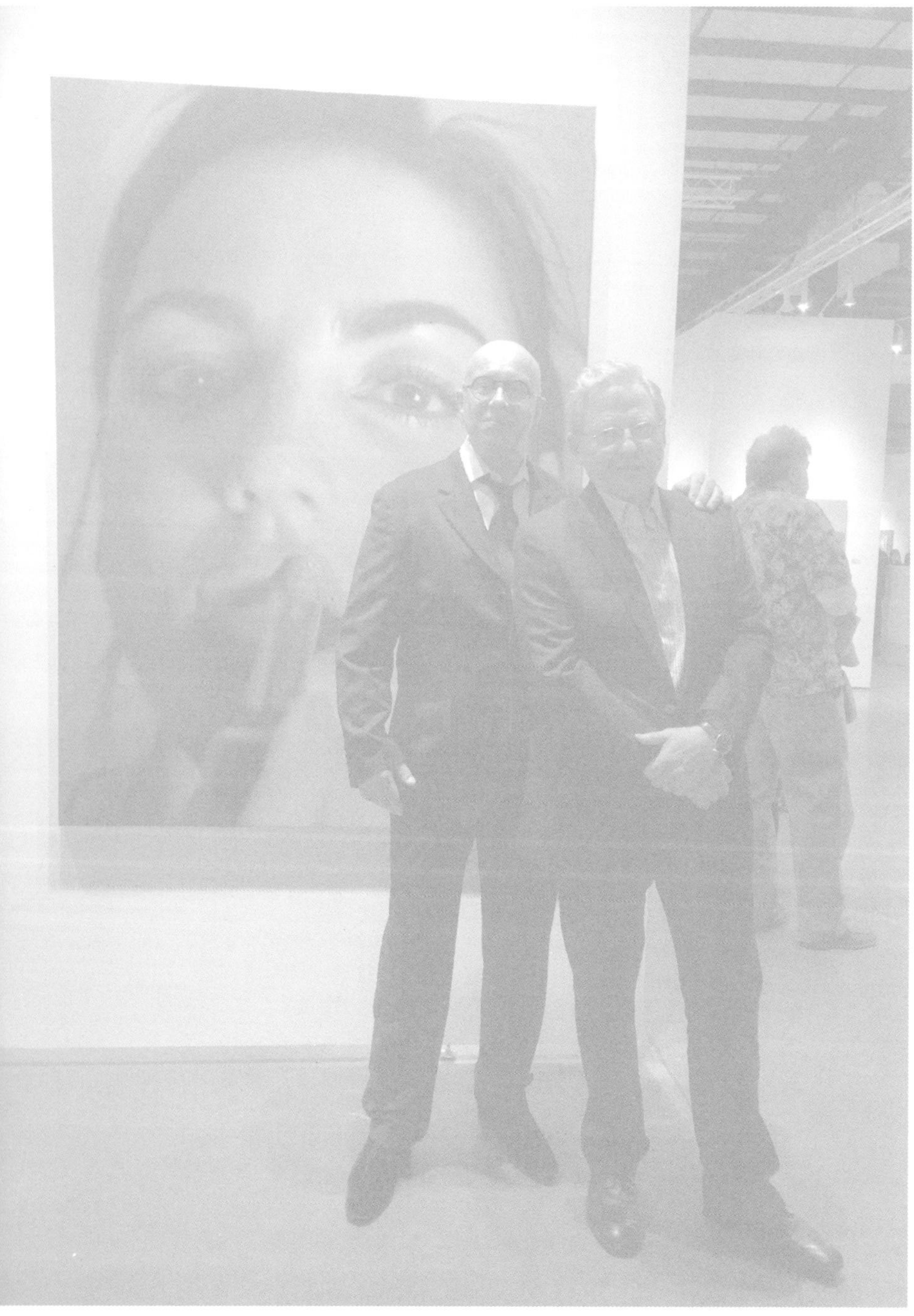

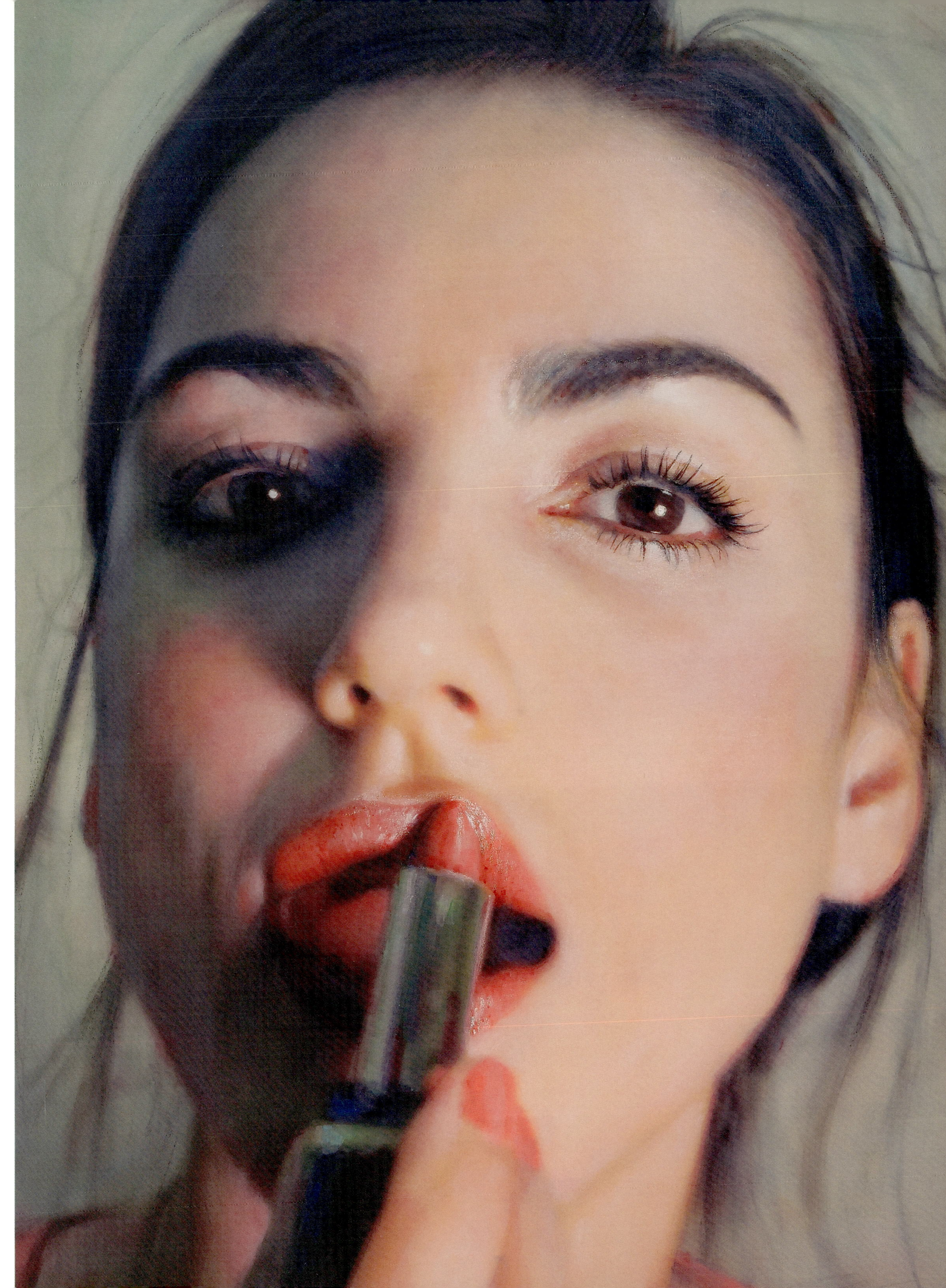

DAVID TERRY, 2013
Oil on canvas, 28 × 26 in.

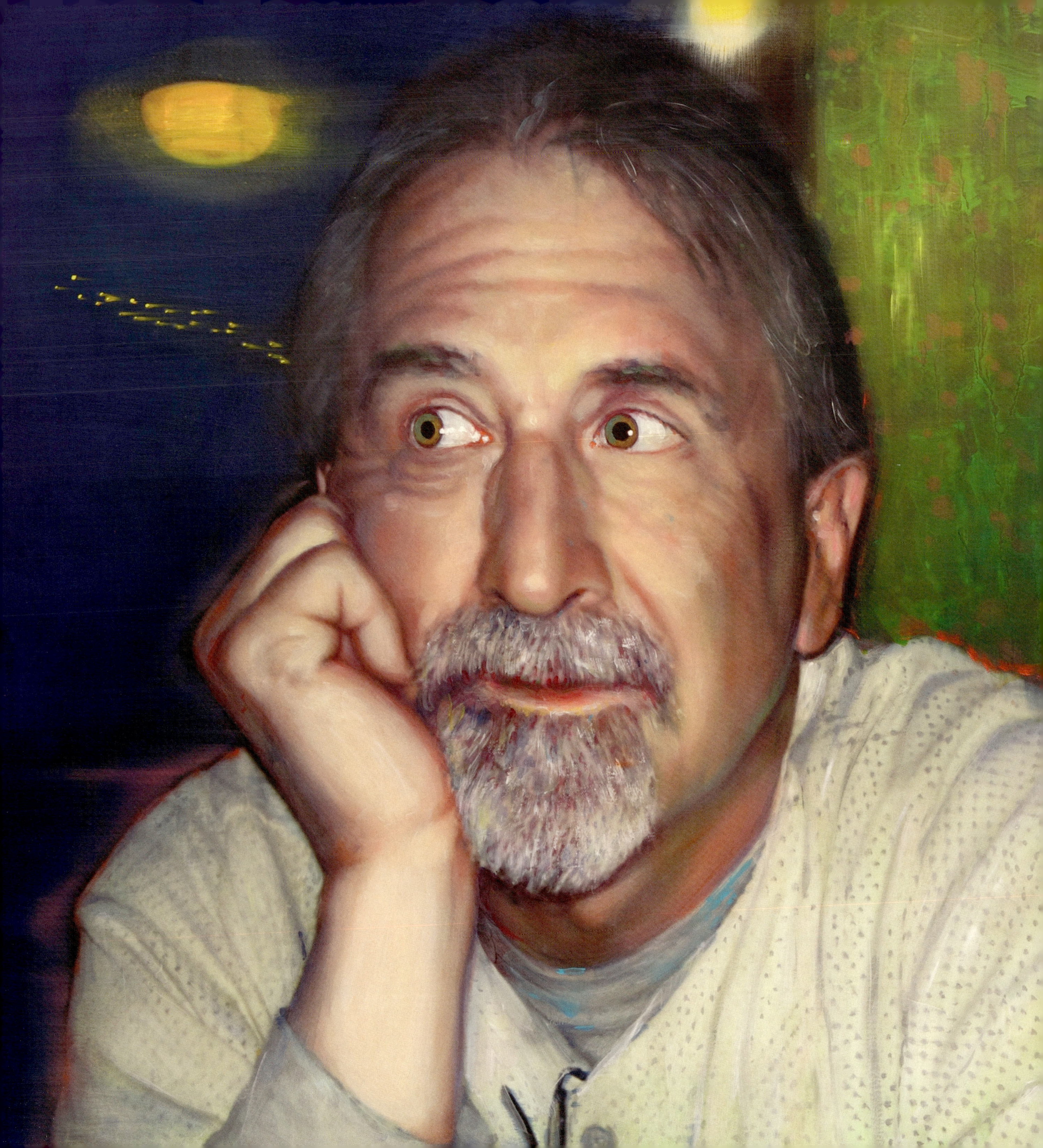

There is a lot of skill and technique involved in his unique compositions.

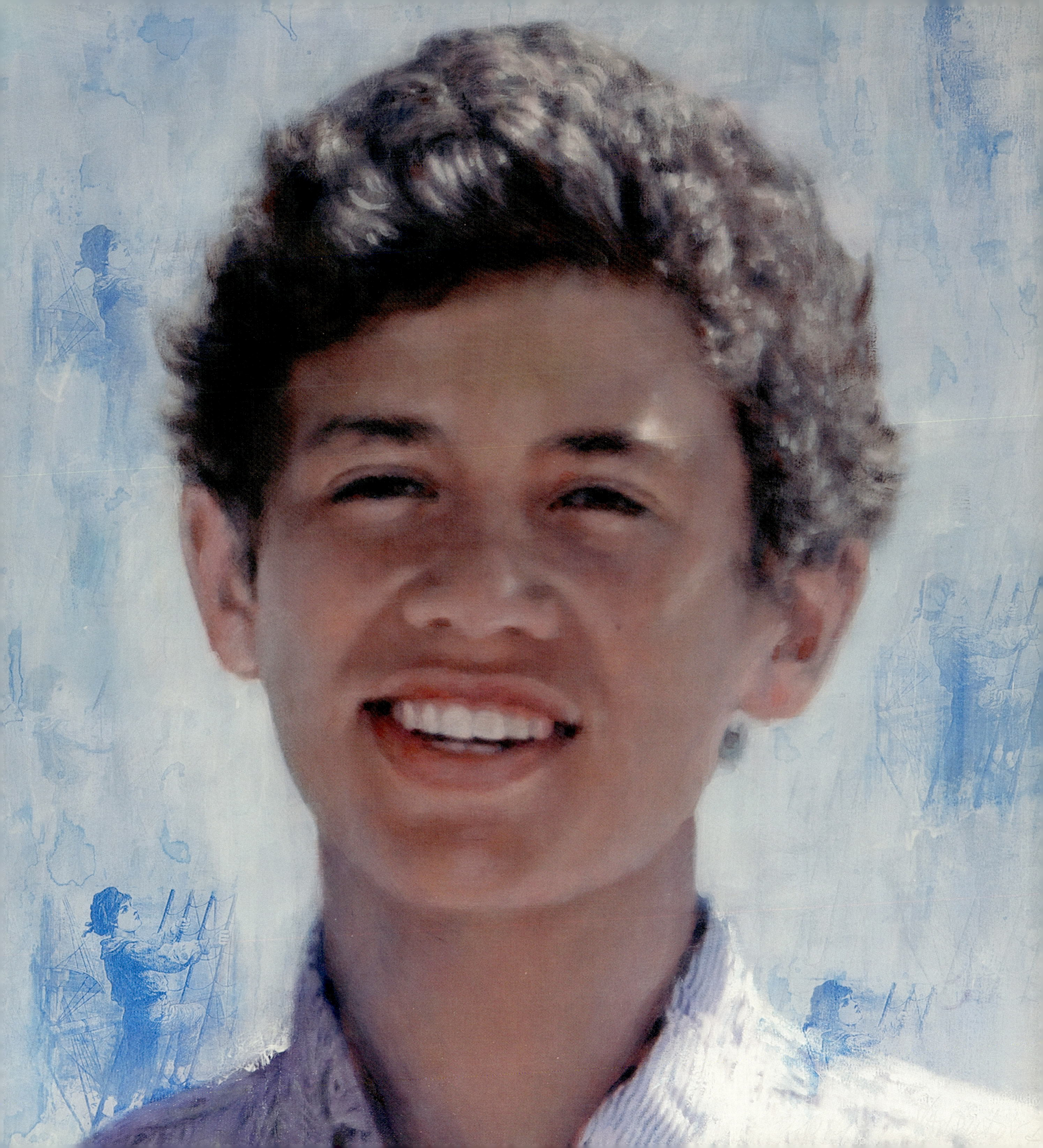

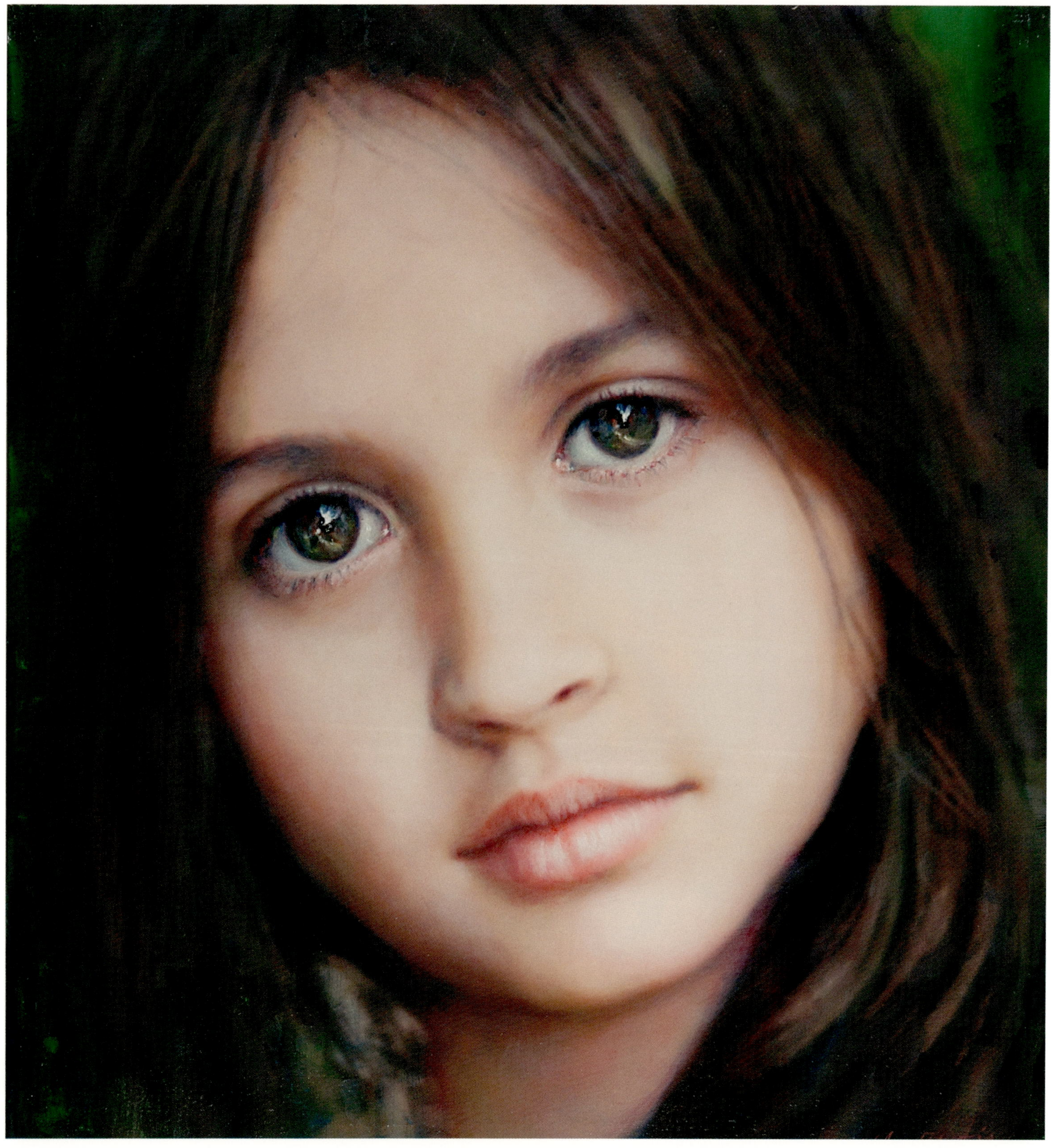

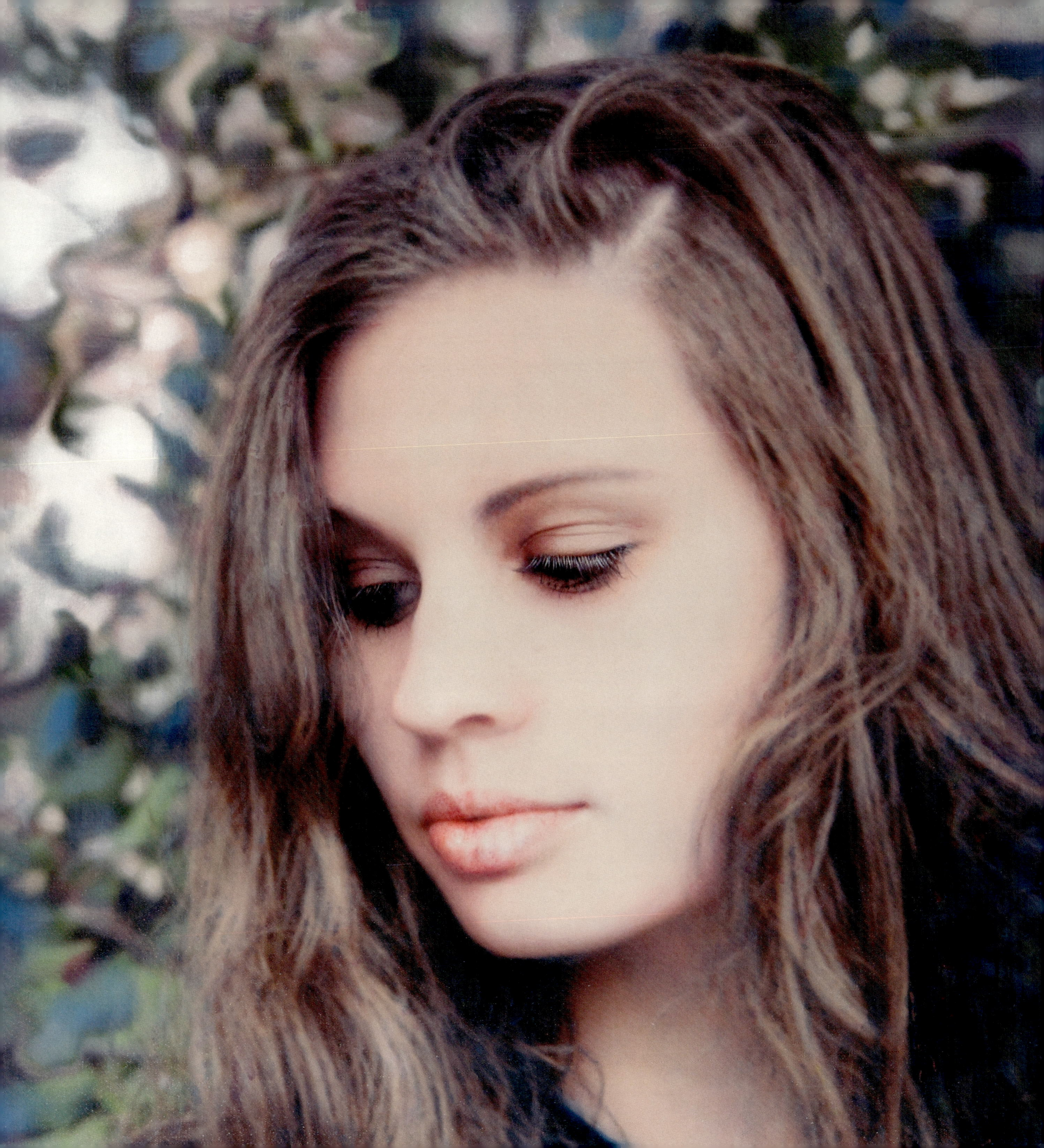

JOHN LYDDON (MORNING), 2016
Oil on canvas, 44 × 40 in.

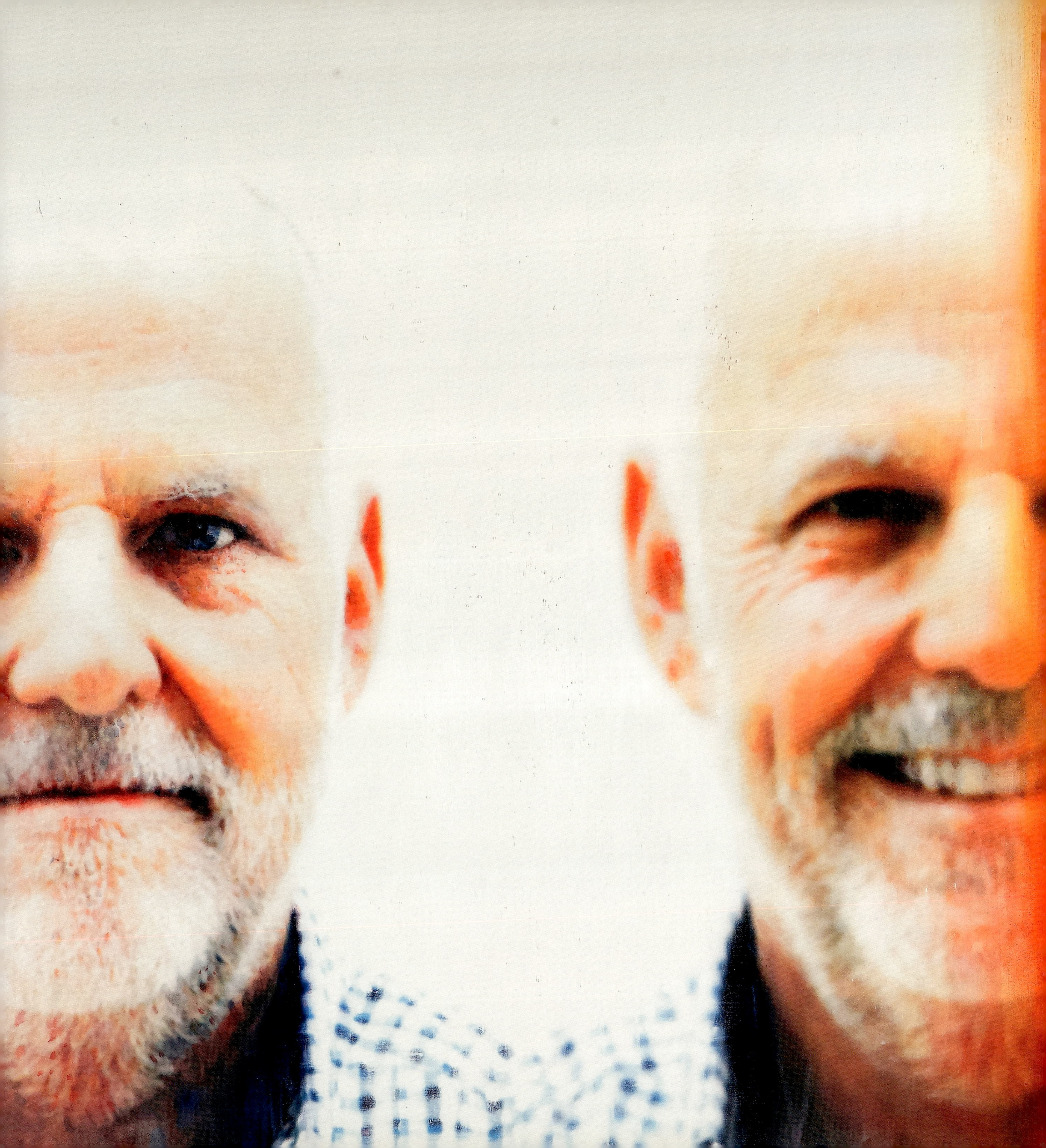

JOHN LYDDON (NOON), 2016
Oil on canvas, 28 × 26 in.

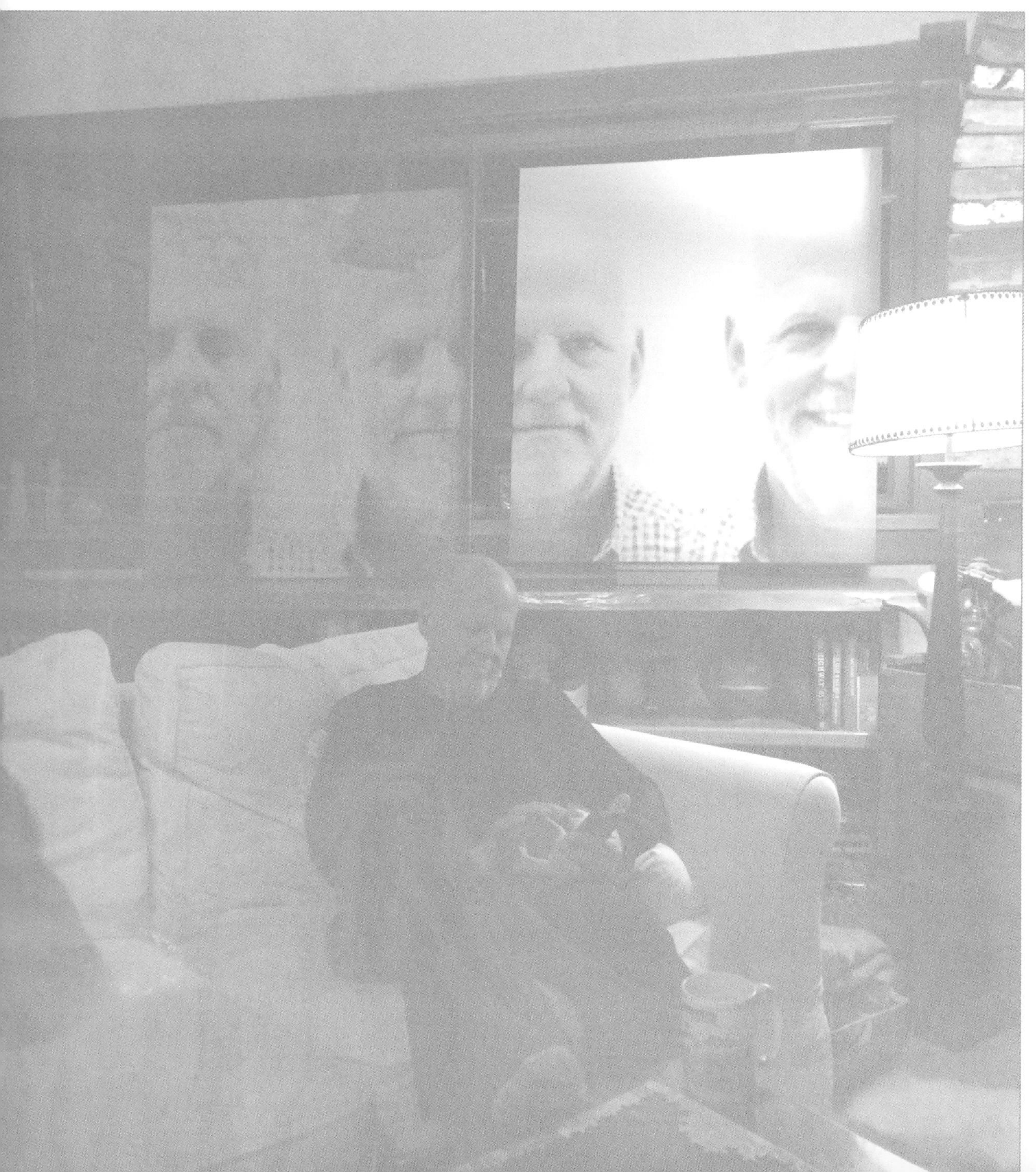

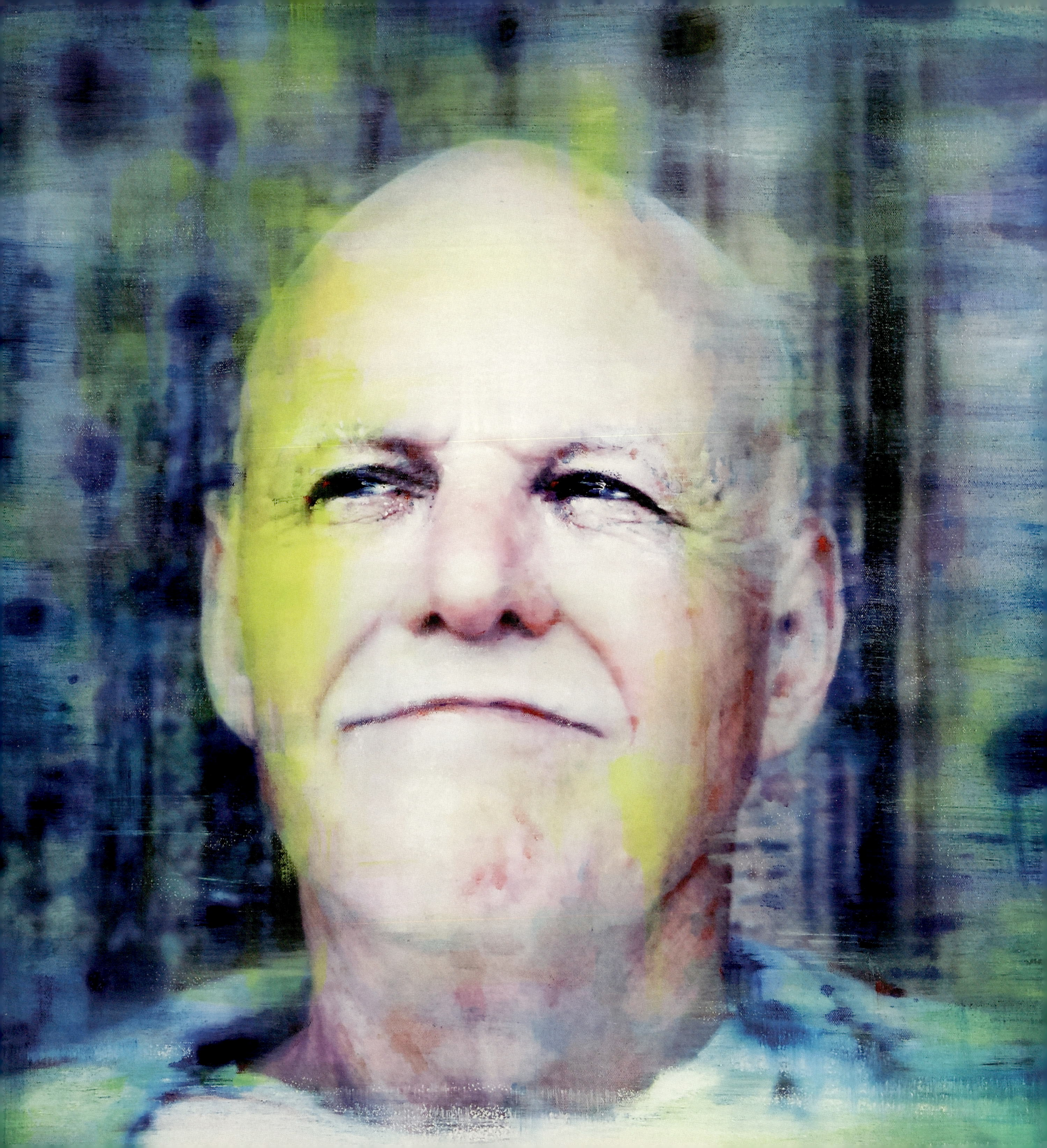

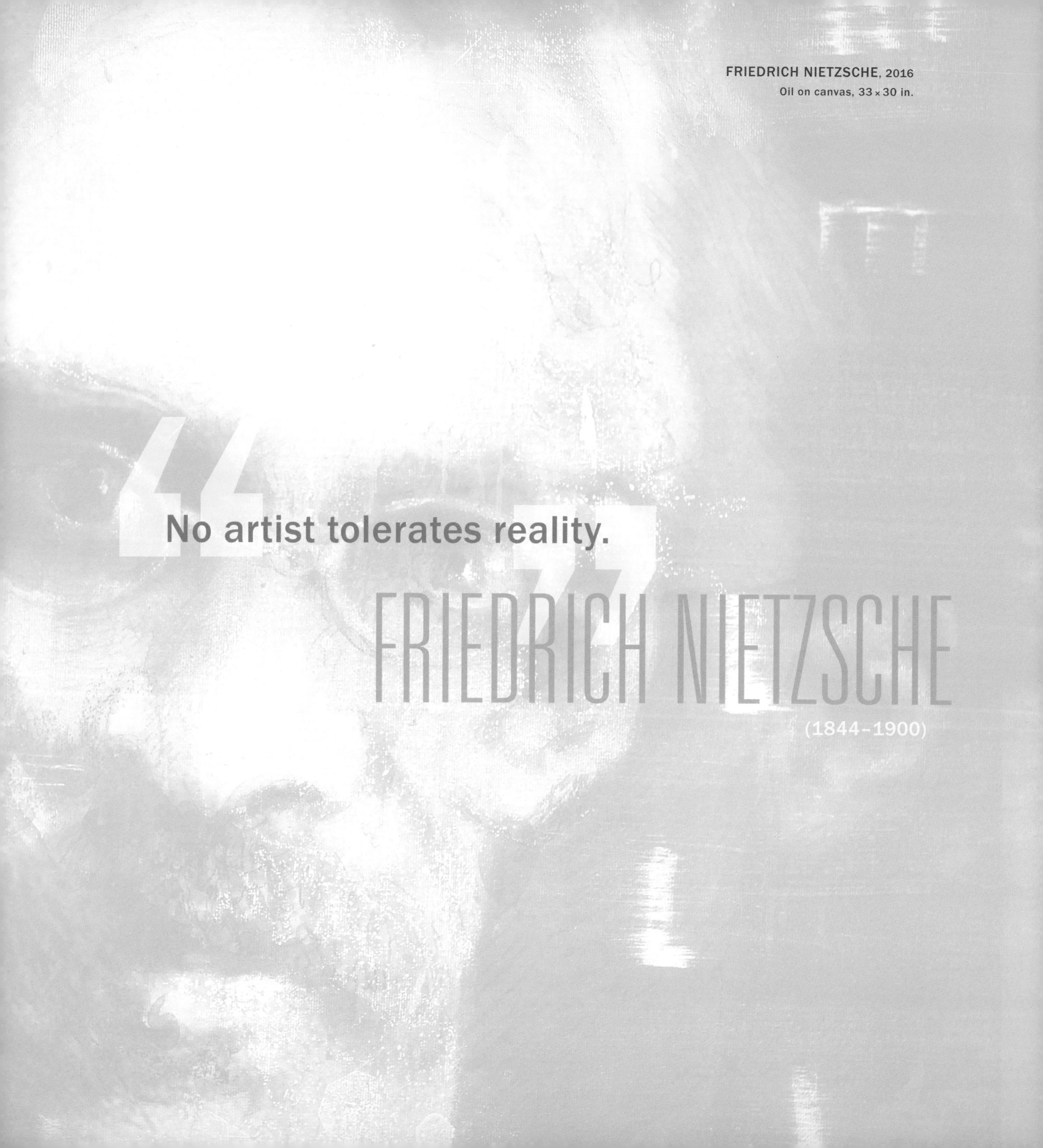

"No artist tolerates reality."

FRIEDRICH NIETZSCHE
(1844–1900)

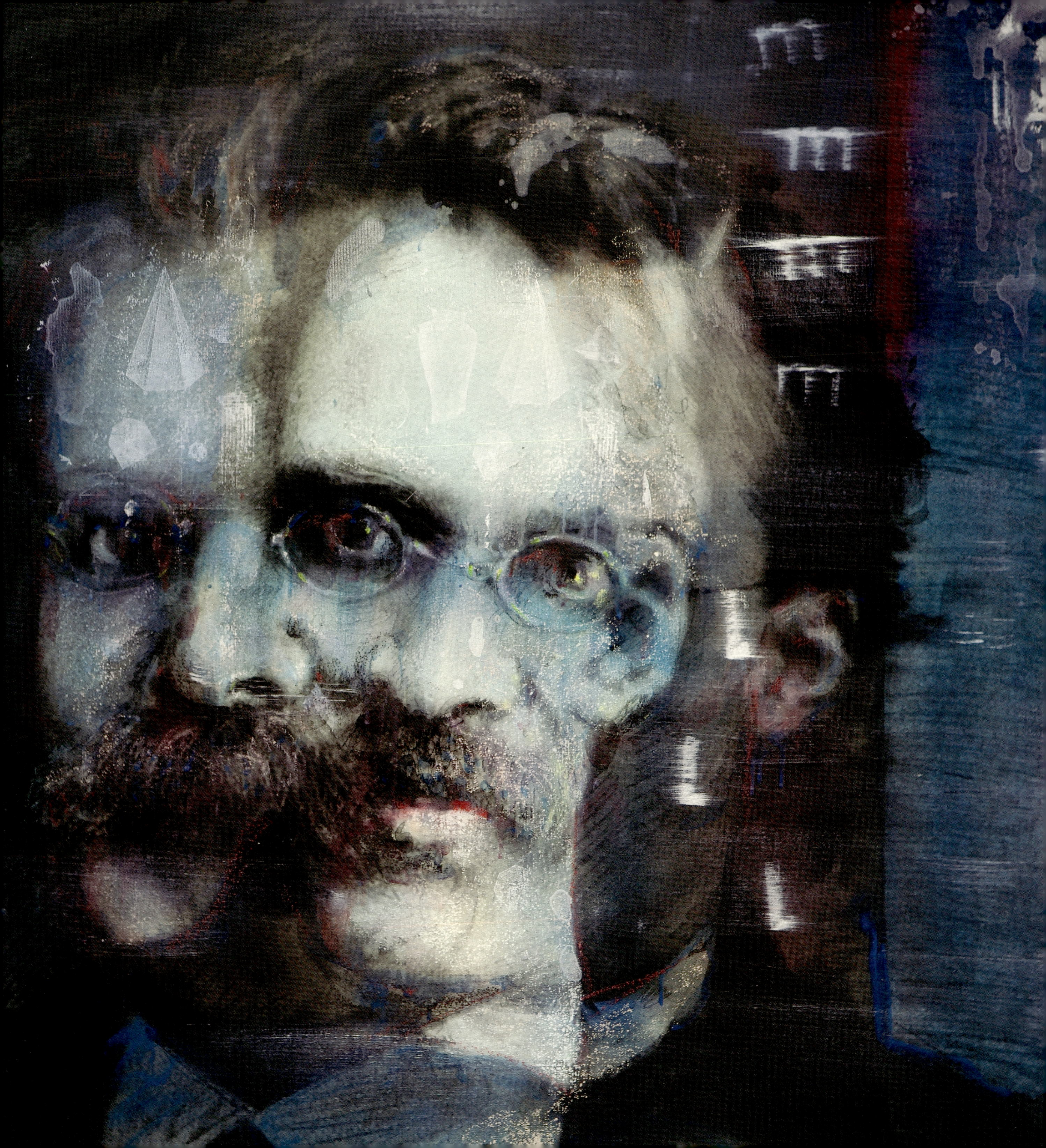

Andrei Ustinov

POPOV'S IDENTIFICATION
ON VISAGE AND VISION

You got lucky as well; where else, save in a portrait perhaps,
will you forever remain free of wrinkles, lithe, caustic, vivid?
Having bumped into memory, time learns of its impotence.
Ebb tide; I smoke in the darkness and inhale rank seaweed.

JOSEPH BRODSKY, "BRISE MARINE"

Through the glass of the portholes, I observed the same faces: they were waves that escaped.

ANDRÉ BRETON AND PHILIPPE SOUPAULT, *LES CHAMPS MAGNÉTIQUES*

Valentin Popov's *FACE*(s) is a magnificent construction. It is assembled as carefully as a very personal collection, and this is exactly how it occurs. When the "faces" were presented at the de Saisset Museum very close to each other, they induced associations with a Lepidoptera collection, where each frame looks like a box, while the walls look like bigger boxes that contain rare butterflies.

This catalog, however, evokes a comparison with an herbarium from Popov's childhood, when kids collected plants, dried them in a book, and glued the most precious flowers on separate pages, adding descriptions of taxa. Here Popov did not choose his portraits simply to present a personal collection. He assembled *FACE* to tell his personal story of the human condition through the faces of children, women, and men, whose qualities and deficiencies are caught by the artist with empathy, zest, often with a touch of irony, and not without an enigma.

Popov tells his story of the human condition with almost inhuman optical precision. Such is the caveat of hyperrealism or photorealism, monikers that are called to describe an extremely high level and utmost sophistication of painting technique. It is not important which term is used, as long as one recognizes the immeasurable attention displayed in all aspects of that artistic expression: composition, line, foreshortening, vector, detail.

Popov goes back to his juvenilia, created when he practiced his drawing by learning from the works of old masters, such as Albrecht Dürer, Rembrandt, and Mstislav Doboujinsky. Barnaby Conrad once exposed Popov's inspirations while paying a visit to the artist's abode in Montclair: "Inside, the walls are decorated with original prints by Dürer, Rembrandt, Piranesi, and Goya. 'These artists certainly inspired my work,' [Popov] says, 'but so did many others, from Velázquez and Rodchenko to Picasso and Hockney.'"

Popov used his formative years to conquer etching, a severely exhausting and meticulous technique, which convinced him that the line should be considered the most important element in any artistic expression, whether figurative or abstract. This technique also taught him the extremely important concept of artistic economy, the essence of which is quite simple: a painting contains an exact number of lines (and colors), just enough to fully convey artistic vision. Anything else may become excessive and could easily dilute that vision. It requires tremendous discipline, and Popov strictly adheres to this principle, as if he was not a bohemian, but a Zen monk. It is especially challenging to bring artistic economy to depicting faces, because artists have always sought to recreate visage in a portrait.

On the other hand, when looking at portraits, one is compelled to search not solely for similarity, but also for verisimilitude. This is where technique comes into play, since an artist carries limited artistic license when it comes to portraits. Technique can therefore annihilate or elevate the painted visage, because, after all, this is exactly what the artist's vision aligns to his subjects' hopes to recognize themselves. Yet, Popov did not choose these faces just to display his artistic technique or his mastery of hyperrealist imagery, although there is no doubt of the latter.

If we knew who these people were, we would have recognized them immediately.

One portrait is of Sean Young. Despite all the changes, her face inevitably carries that powerful aura of her breakthrough character Rachael in Ridley Scott's magnificent film *Blade Runner*. Here is Peter Selz, a famous art historian who authored the classic and still unsurpassed exposé *German Expressionist Painting* and served as a project director for Christo and Jeanne-Claude's *Running Fence* in the Marin and Sonoma hills. And here is Paula Kirkeby, who sadly passed away recently. She remains alive here, her face brimming with the wit and wisdom she kindly shared with her friends and collaborators. Paula was very generous in life, and in particular to Popov, giving him a real chance by curating his first exhibit in America. Paula's portrait is that of reciprocity, and her generosity is captured forever.

The very genre of portrait invites recognition and possibly identification of the subjects depicted on canvas. Collective portraits, be it Domenico Ghirlandaio's *La Visitazione* (*Visitation*, from *Stories of St. John the Baptist*, 1486), Rembrandt's *De Nachtwacht* (*The Night Watch*, 1642), or Max Ernst's *Au Rendez-vous des amis* (*At the Friends' Reunion*, 1922), are even more complicated. Each collective portrait requires a list of those faithfully depicted, and in Ernst's case, such a list is provided as an innocuous part of the canvas.

If we treated *FACE* under such auspices, it is possible to fathom this catalog as a collective portrait of a local art scene, or, to be precise, a behind-the-scenes view of local mechanics of art as a commercial endeavor. The subjects are those who are essential for the art scene to exist, people who are supplementary in promoting art as a venture—gallerists, curators, art writers, and, most important, *marchands*, a nickname given to Paul Guillaume, the greatest art dealer of them all.

Then there are also patrons, part of a tradition that originated with Lorenzo de' Medici, Il Magnifico. Patrons who commissioned their depictions are responsible for a majority of portraits in the history of art. Most of them have been forgotten: very few have a story that comes along, like that of the Viennese socialite depicted in the notorious *Portrait of Adele Bloch-Bauer*, which took Gustav Klimt three years to complete. These people compose the art scene, but not Art itself, as the art scene appears at the very margins of Art. The patrons are significant only to any particular artist and, in general, are marked for obscurity, thus carrying a certain degree of anonymity. Accordingly, Popov does not want to burden us with direct identification of people generally unknown.

Such anonymity denies the biographical nature of but denotes the visionary aspect in each of Popov's portraits, making viewers perceive *FACE* as a sampling of human types or, in more general terms, as a selection of manifestations of human visage. In this regard, it is worth looking at the series of paintings prepared specifically for this catalog. Their genre could be best described as "imaginary visage." This series brings to the proscenium a collective portrait of Popov as an artist. The works are dedicated to those who had a defining influence on him, first as a young man, and then as an accomplished artist.

This is quite a cosmopolitan jet set: writers Lev Tolstoy, Franz Kafka, Mikhail Bulgakov, and Jorge Luis Borges; poets Vladimir Mayakovsky and Daniil Kharms; philosophers Arthur Schopenhauer, Friedrich Nietzsche, Hannah Arendt; Russian-French-American composer Igor Stravinsky; and local exegete of Zen Buddhism for Western minds Alan Watts, who lived on a houseboat in Sausalito and died in a cabin on Mount Tamalpais. Popov could not have known any of them personally, but he has been, and is still, having imaginary dialogues with them, similar to the never-ending discussions between Pontius Pilate and Yeshua

Ha-Notsri, the main protagonists of a "novel about Jesus" within his favorite prose, Bulgakov's *The Master and Margarita*, written between 1928 *and* 1940.

Popov confessed his love for this novel in a conversation with Barnaby Conrad: "Bulgakov was from Kiev, and I used to walk by his former house as a child. Later my art studio was three hundred yards away. His masterpiece, *The Master and Margarita*, was a great influence on me. It was written in 1940 under Stalin's rule and was a great satire of life at that time. It stars the Devil himself, who comes to St. Petersburg for a visit. . . . But the book wasn't published until 1966. . . . People went crazy for it. Some of Bulgakov's mix of satire, reality, and parable appears in my paintings. At least I hope so."

Another literary inspiration that certainly dictates the fantastic on the verge of nightmarish in Popov's other paintings is *Novellas and Parables*, by Franz Kafka, in Russian translation. Opening with *The Trial*, followed by "The Metamorphosis" and other novellas from *The Punishments* (1915), this little black book of selected Kafka works was published in Moscow in 1965 and was impossible to find. The very same year, the works of Daniil Kharms (1905–1942), poet, playwright, performance artist, and profound interpreter of the absurd in Leningrad of the 1930s and '40s, were discovered and unveiled in the samizdat, having a major influence on the generation of nonconventional and mostly underground Soviet poets, artists, and humanitarians.

Another Kiev connection to Popov's past is Kazimir Malevich, the founder of Suprematism, and along with El Lissitzky, one of the ubiquitous creators, dynamic proponents, and undisputed stalwarts of the Russian experiment in art. These two leading figures of the avant-garde are the only artists included in the series, and their presence is paramount when it comes to *FACE*. Previously, Popov engaged in a long-term dialogue with Malevich in a different artistic project, *Figures*, where he reconstituted the Suprematist *Peasants* on double canvases. Cutting through the first layer of paintings with a razor in the manner of Lucio Fontana, he added a third dimension to the Malevich originals.

In *FACE* he picks up on the celebrated poem of the Russian avant-garde, Velimir Khlebnikov's "Op. No. 13" ("Bobehobi, the lips were sung"), much revered by Malevich, which directs a new perspective of seeing visage and articulating it in words: "Thus on a canvas of some correspondences / Beyond dimensions there lived the face." Similarly, articulating the face on canvas intends to undermine viewers' expectations and give it life beyond established artistic dimensions.

The paintings in *FACE* reflect on Popov's conversations with his predecessors. This is why the portraits implement a double exposure as an artistic device, at the same time communicating Popov's dialogue with these protagonists and addressing early avant-garde discoveries in photography. El Lissitzky experimented with multiple exposure, treating it as the only possible approach to adequately introduce a person. This is exactly how he created memorable portraits of Kurt Schwitters and Hans Arp. By now, multiple exposure has become a standard in artistic photography. However, when it comes to painting, it is by no means a triviality. "There's a dialogue," confesses Popov, "but the imagery does most of the talking."

Indeed, some of the portraits draw special attention, because there may be a certain artistic shifter, some element injected by the artist that shatters a viewer's perception. That would be a yellow square juxtaposed to a seeming nimbus of Peter Selz's silver hair, which steals the viewer's attention and at the same time suggests Van Gogh's yellow color, Malevich's black and red squares, and the palette created by Franz Marc and Wassily Kandinsky for The Blue Rider. A skull in Barnaby Conrad's palm mesmerizes us and leads to the subject's pensive eyes, which convey *memento mori* better than any still life done in this cautionary genre.

Although these portraits create an impression of immediacy, as if paraphrasing Joseph Brodsky's verse—"O beautiful moment, hold! You are not as marvelous, as absolutely unique"—the true essence of Popov's *FACE* has a different impetus. In spite of his contemporary instrumentarium, he remains an old soul when it comes to Art. The magisterial idea of Art, which is to save each and any of us, all of us, from oblivion, remains defining for him, guiding his work. We become subjects for portraits at artists' discretion, and because of Art, we are given a chance to escape oblivion. This is the epilogue, if not the last sentence, of Popov's story of the human condition.

I know this, because I am here, and I see how the visage transforms into the artist's Vision.

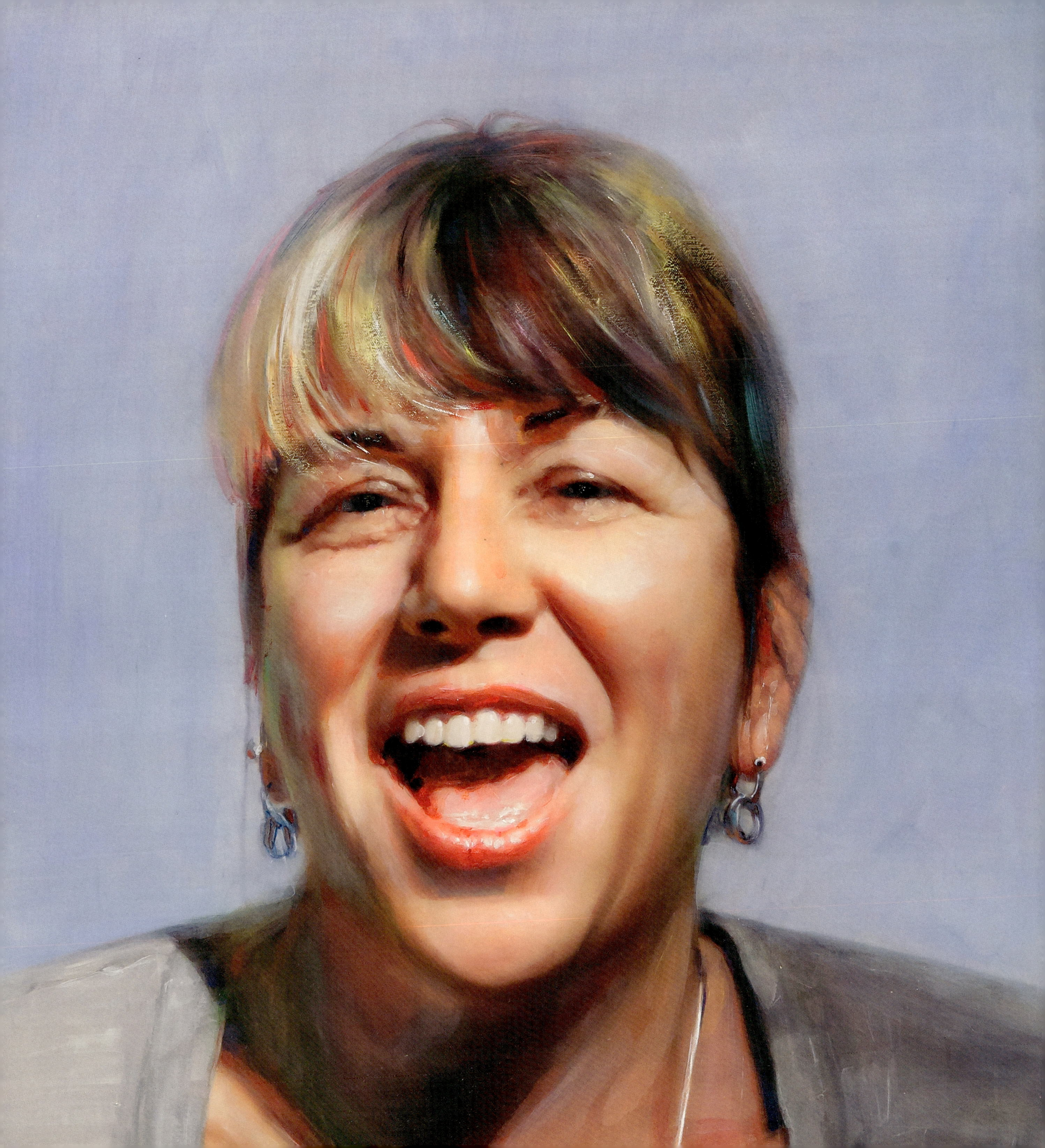

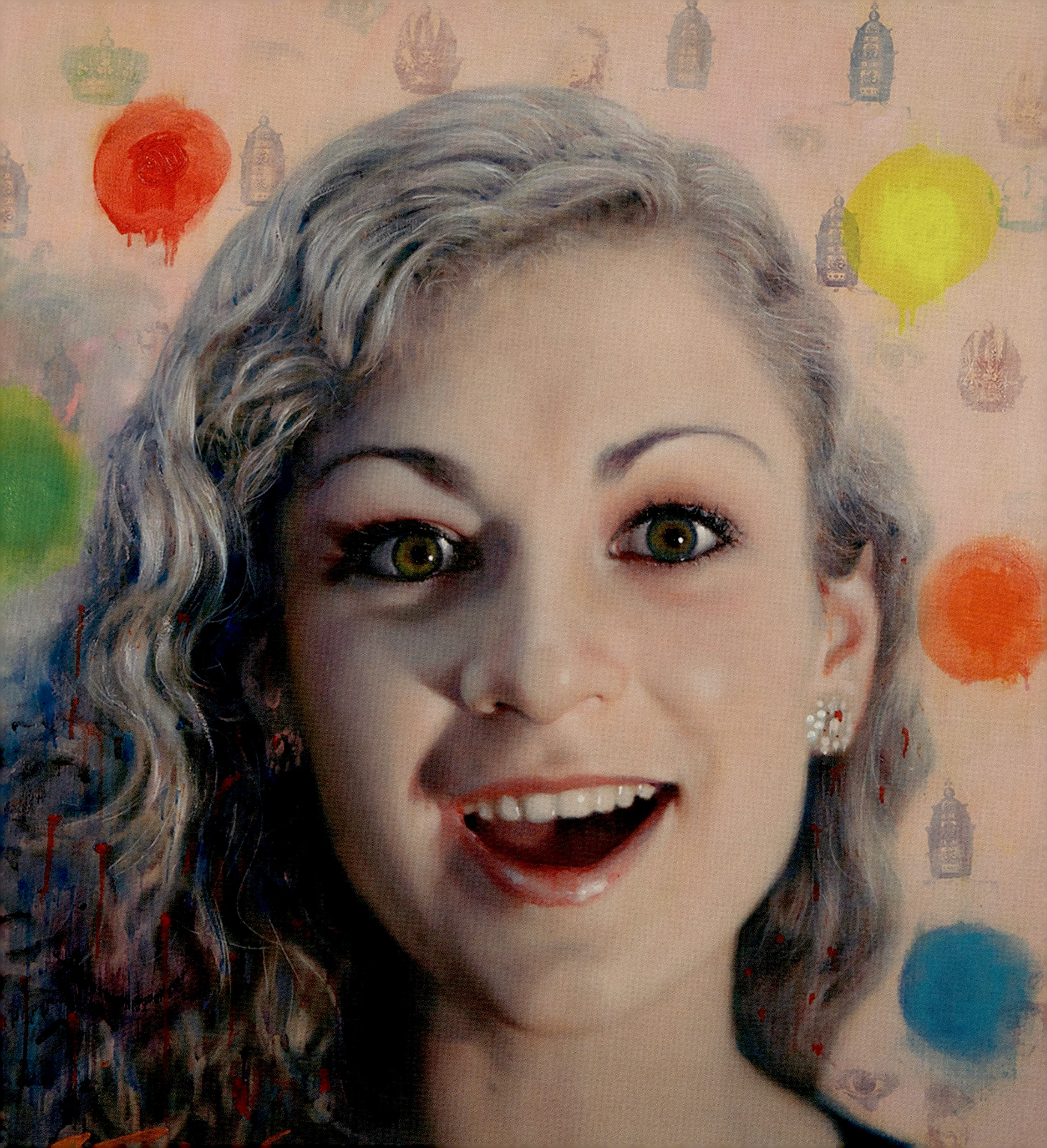

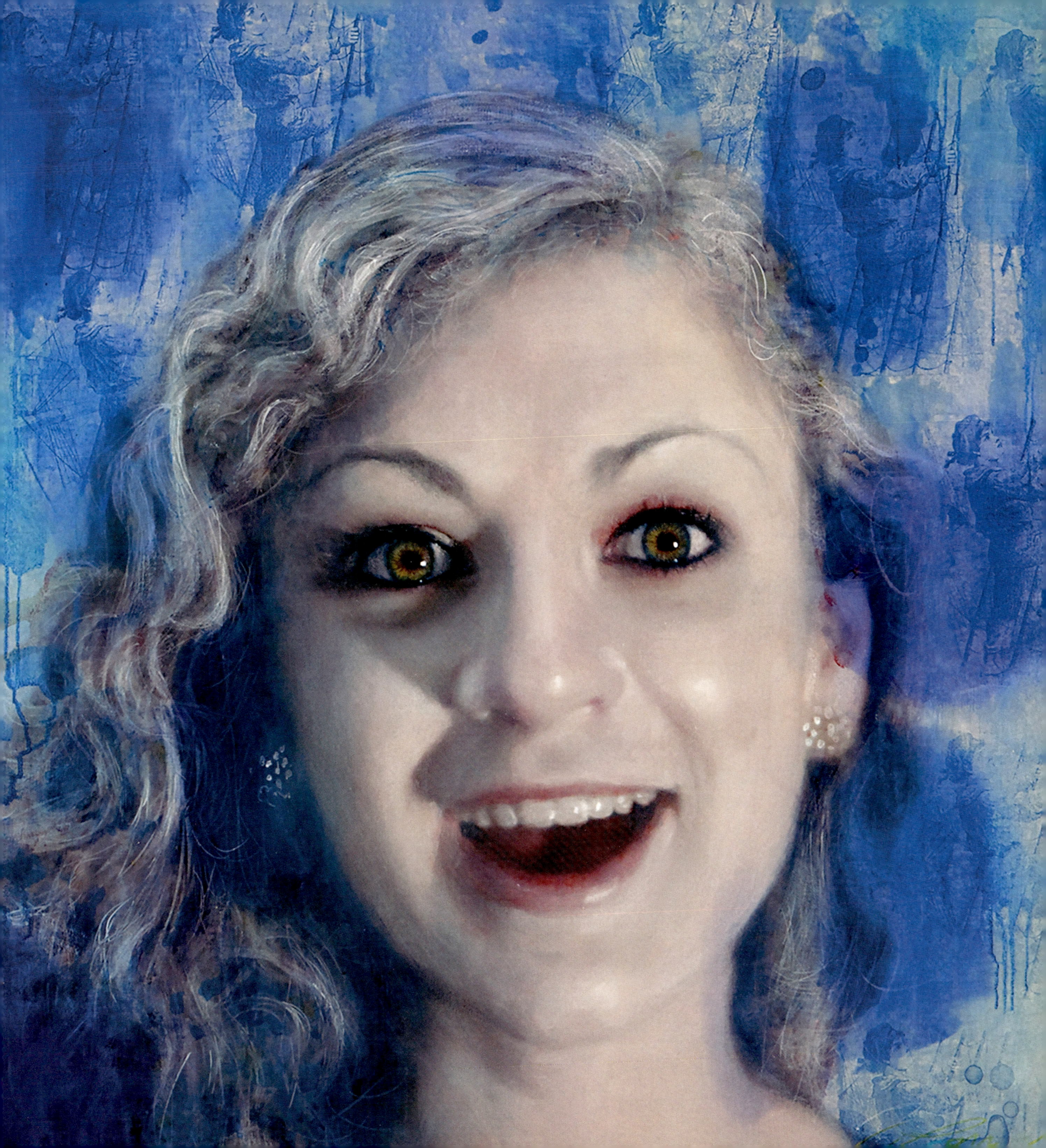

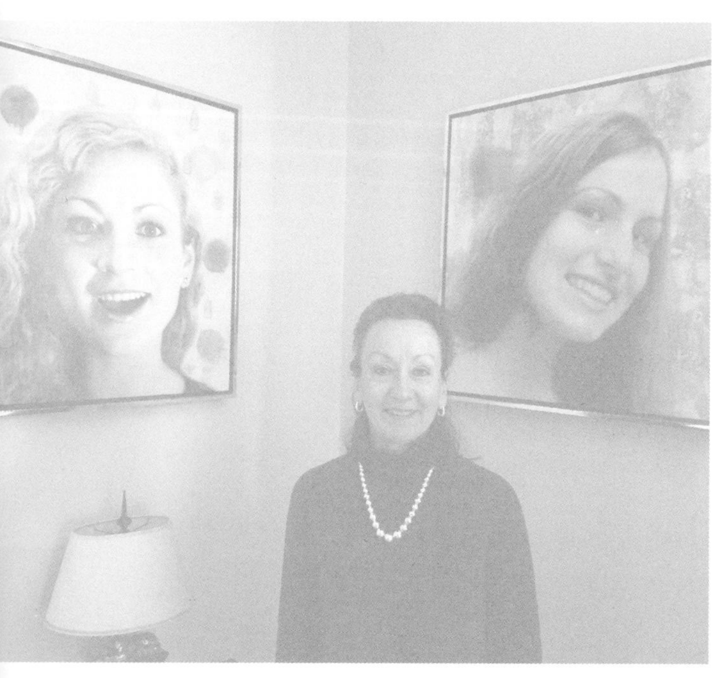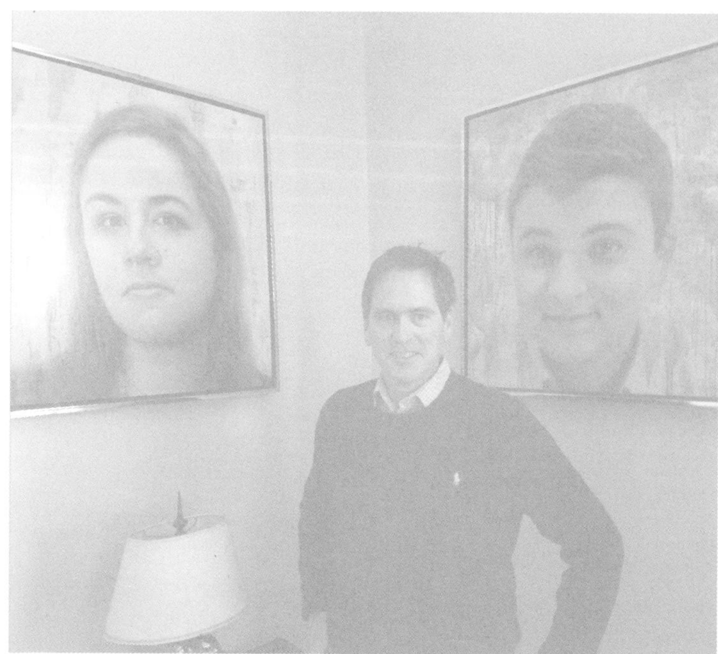

previous, left: **MICHELLE RODRIGUEZ (PINK)**, 2014. Oil on canvas, 28 × 26 in.

right: **MICHELLE RODRIGUEZ (BLUE)**, 2014. Oil on canvas, 28 × 26 in.

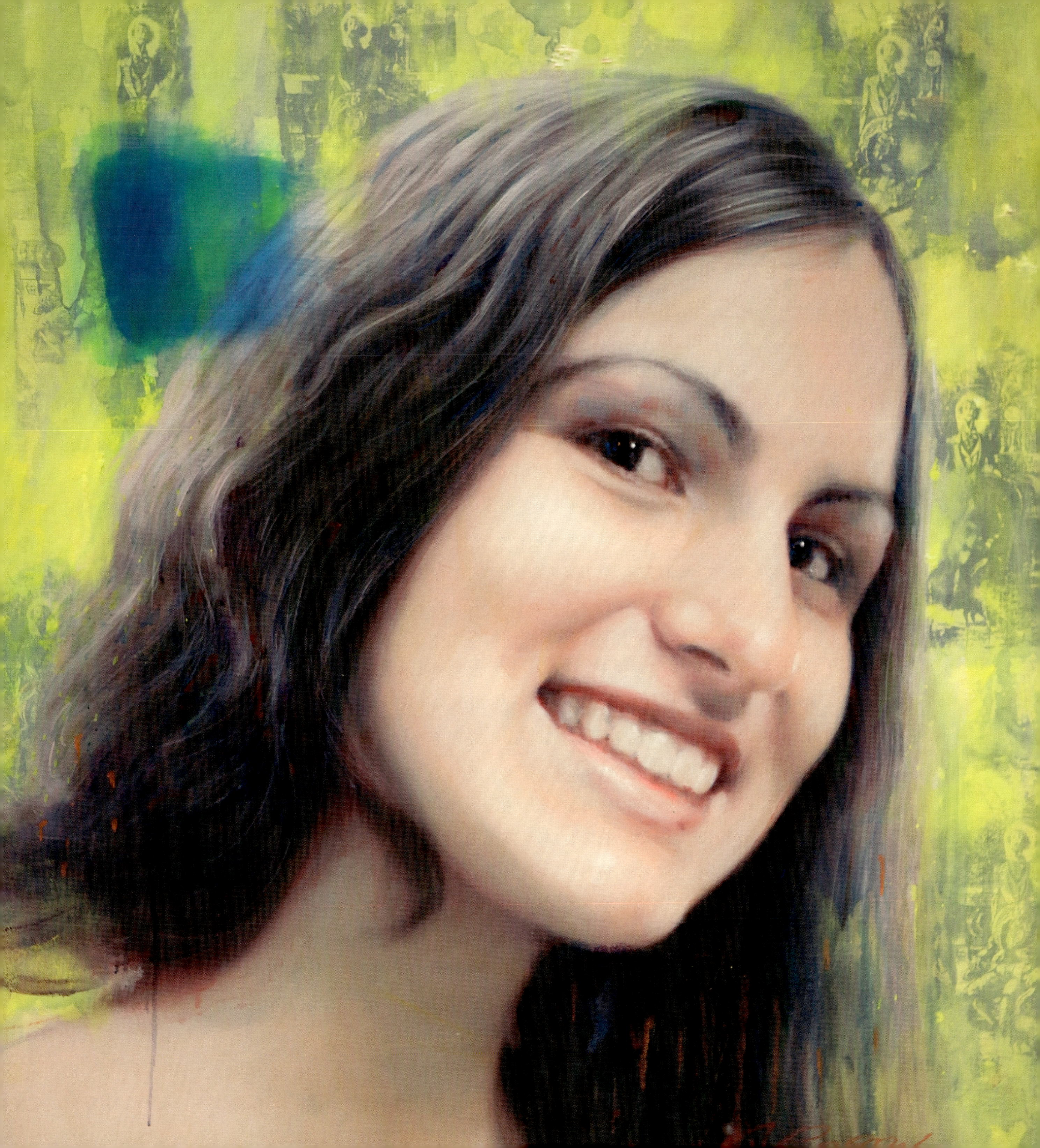

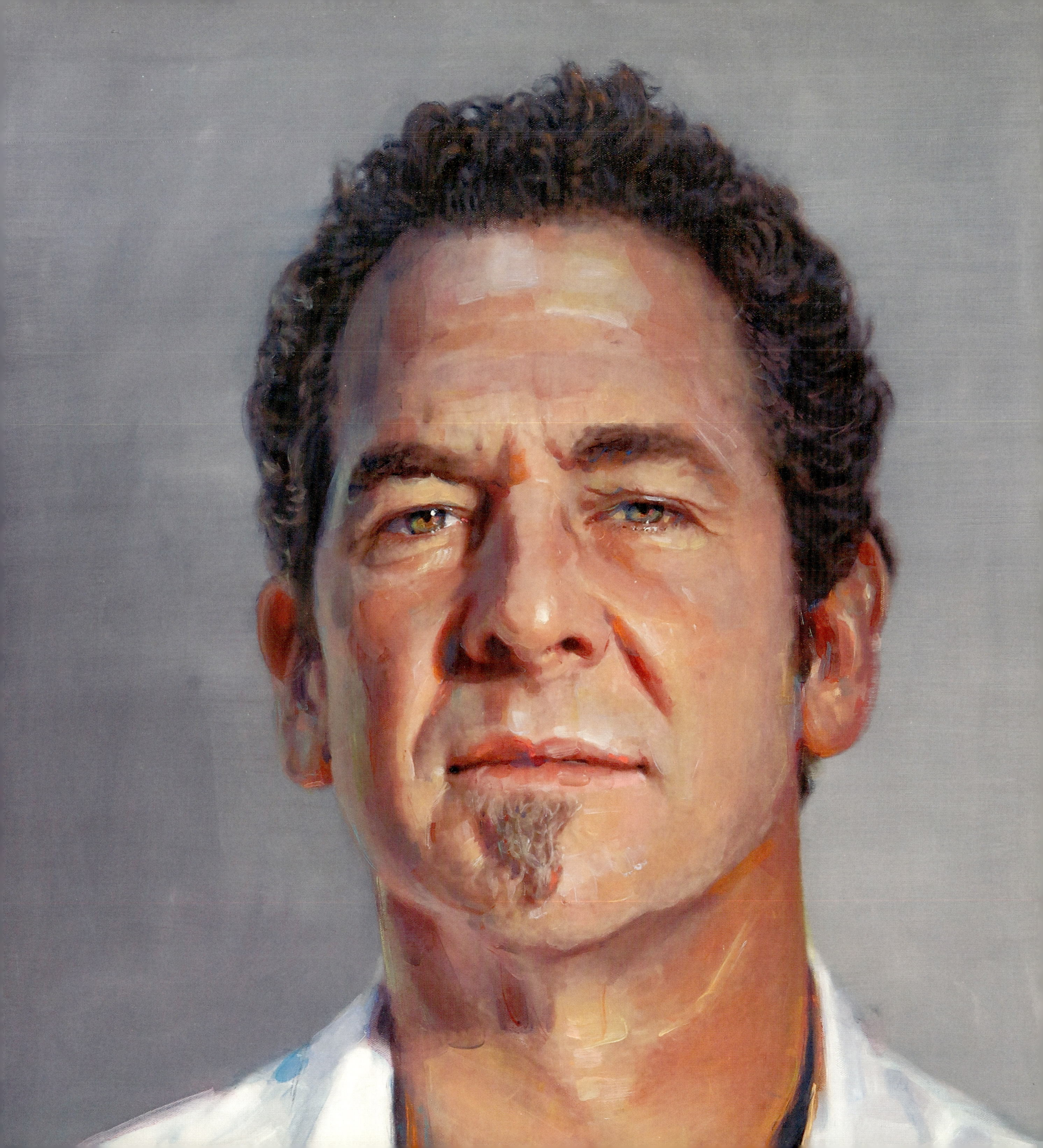

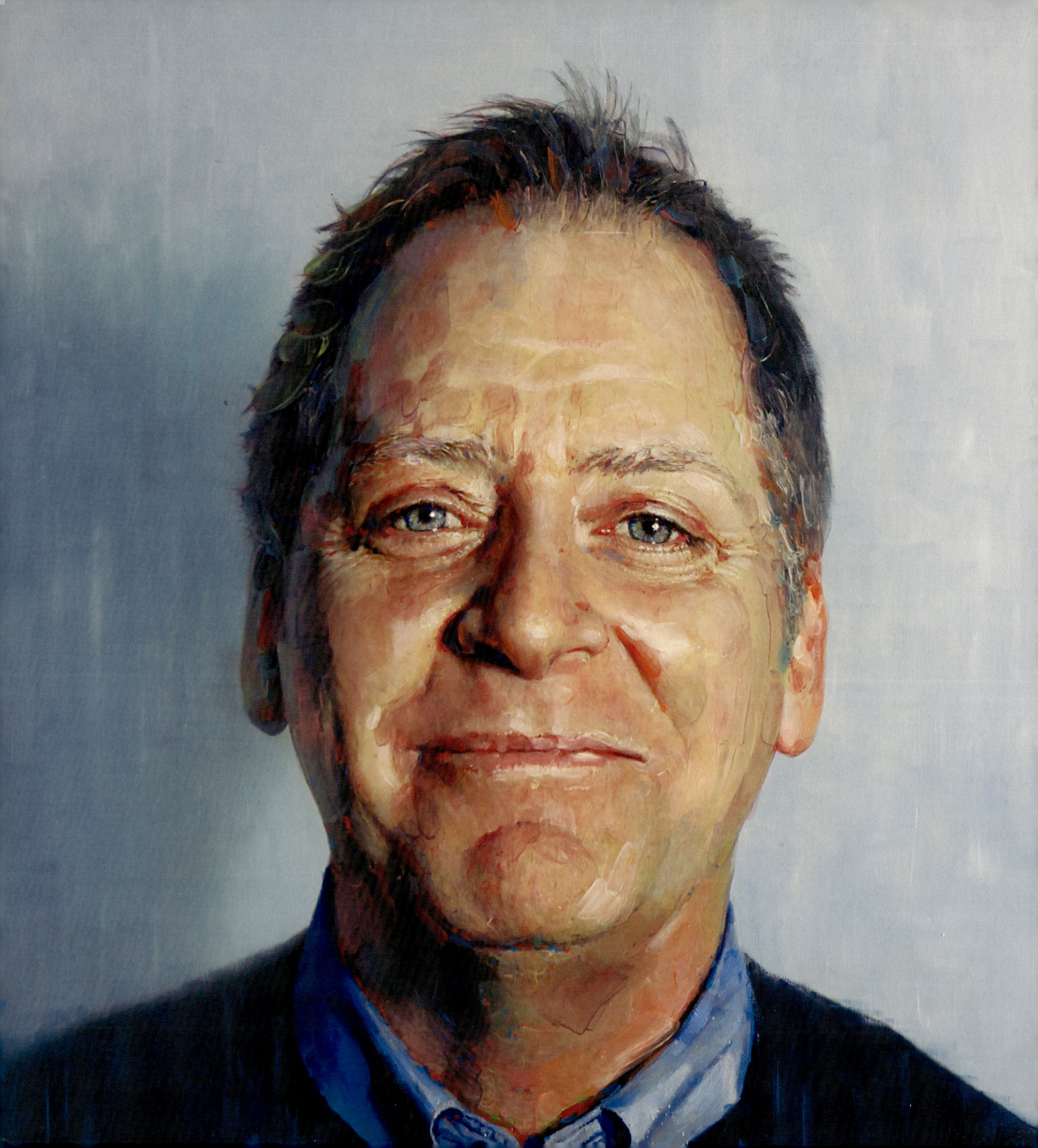

JOHNNY MEIER, 2013
Oil on canvas, 28 × 26 in.

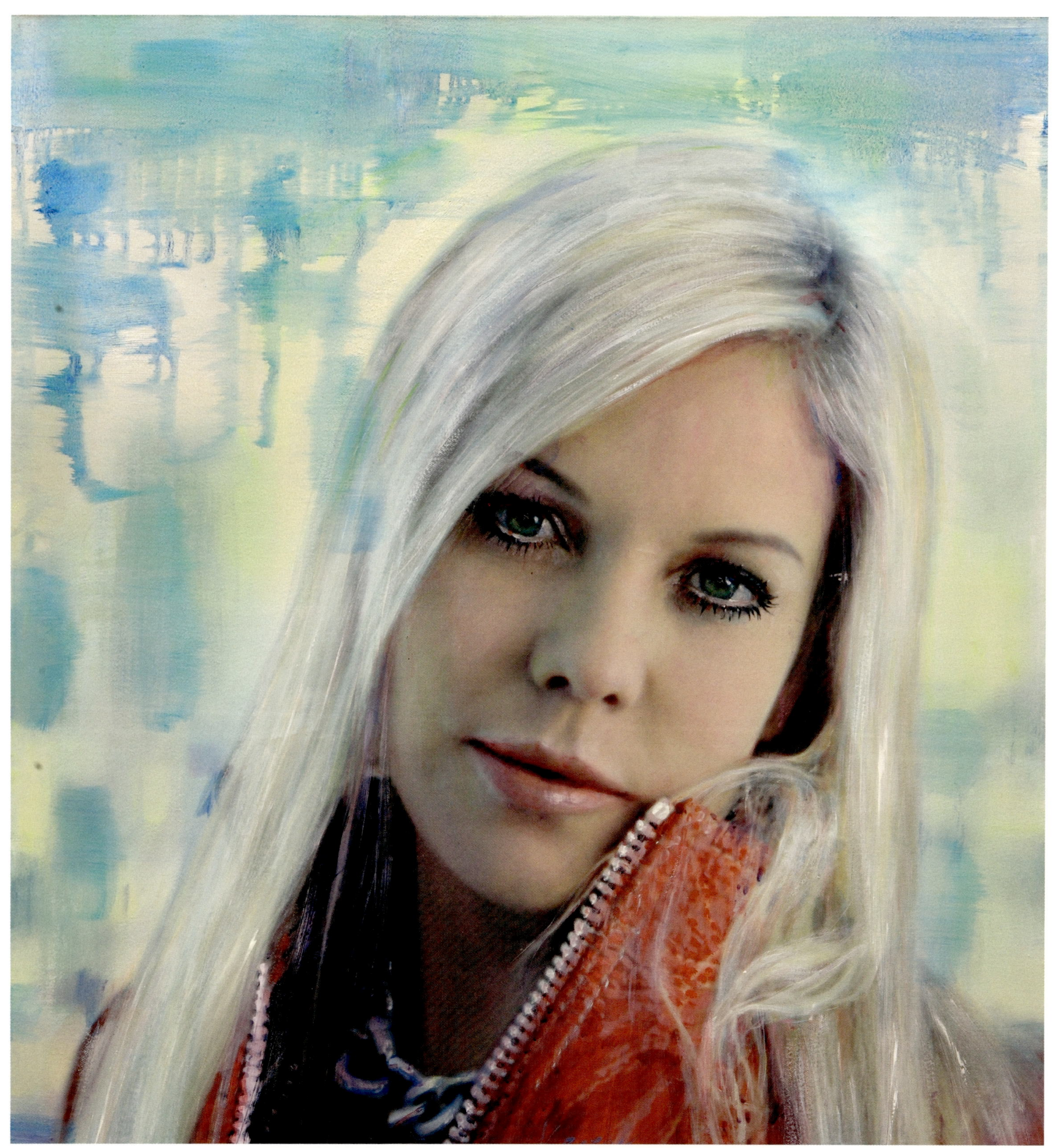

following, left: **HOPE MARIE GOULD**, 2015. Oil on canvas, 28 × 26 in.

right: **GRACE MARIE GOULD**, 2015. Oil on canvas, 28 × 26 in.

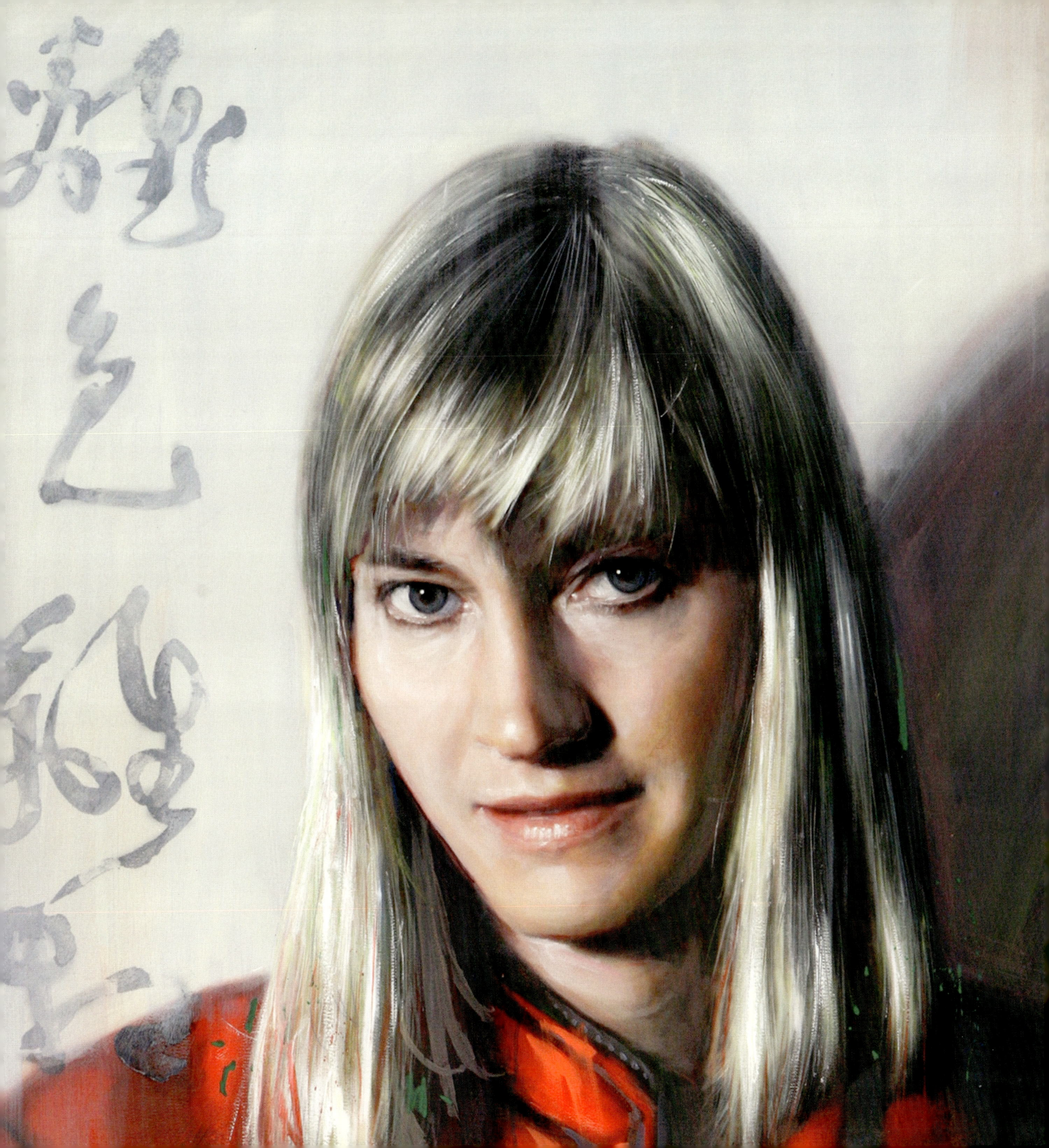

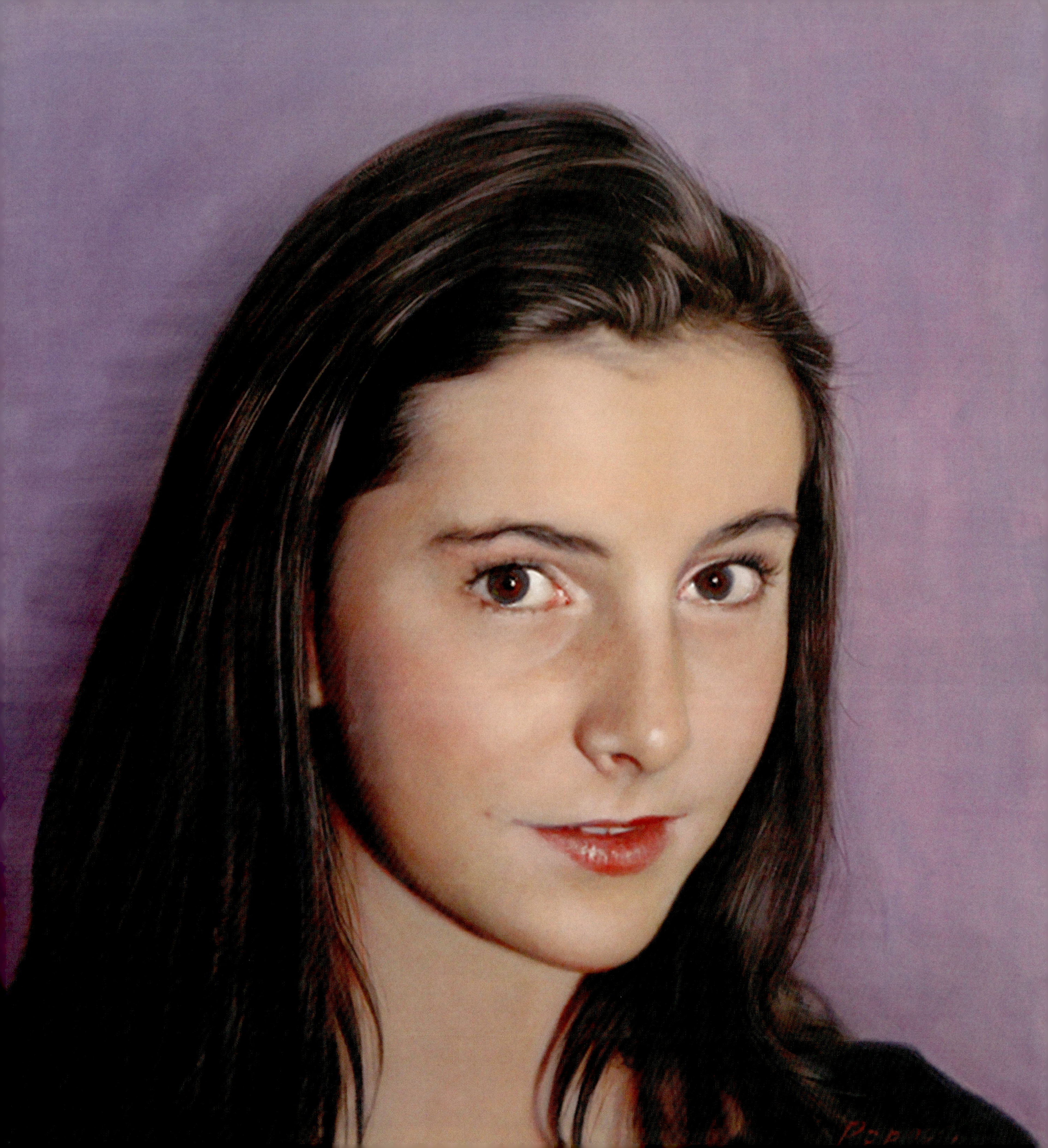

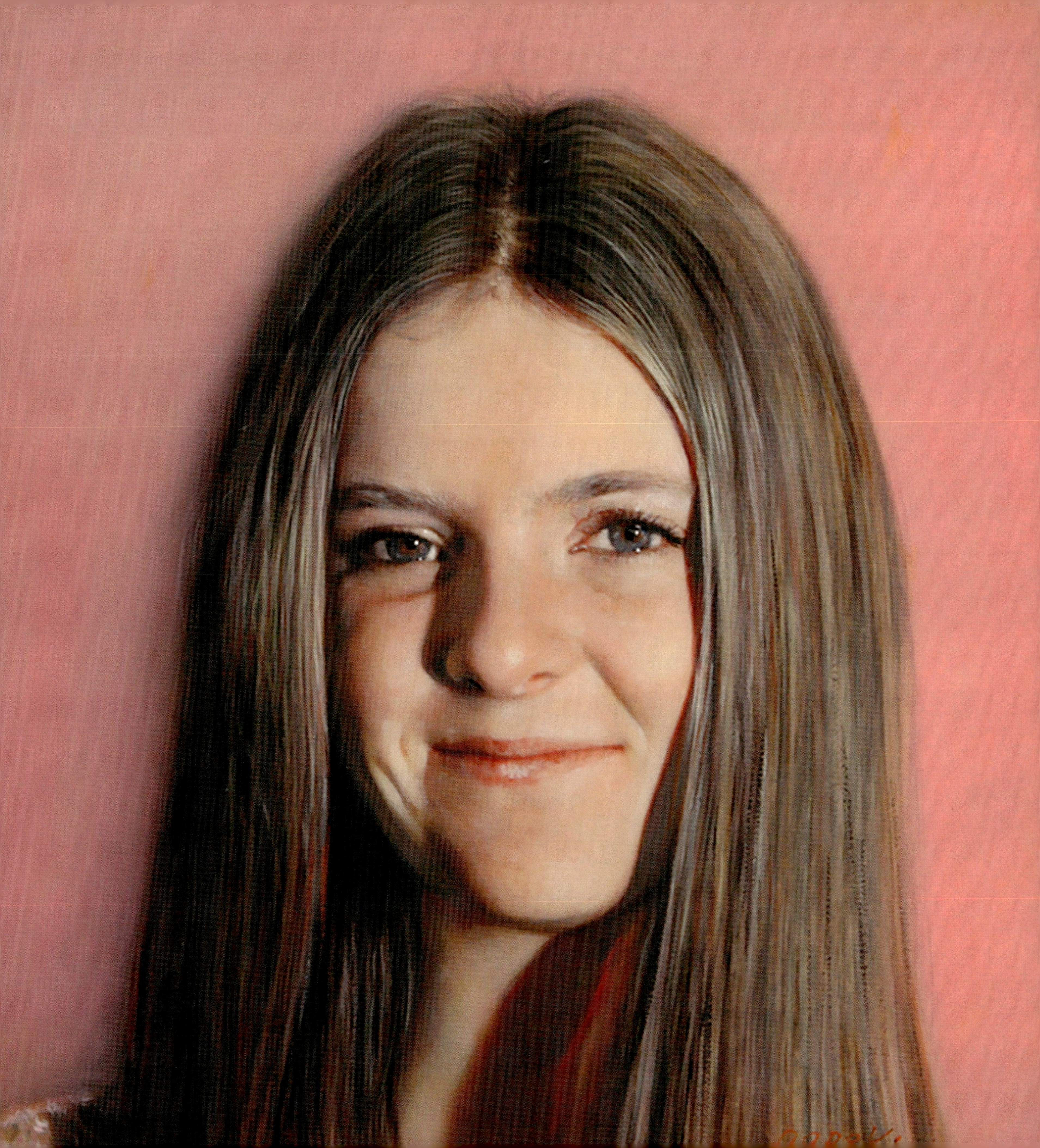

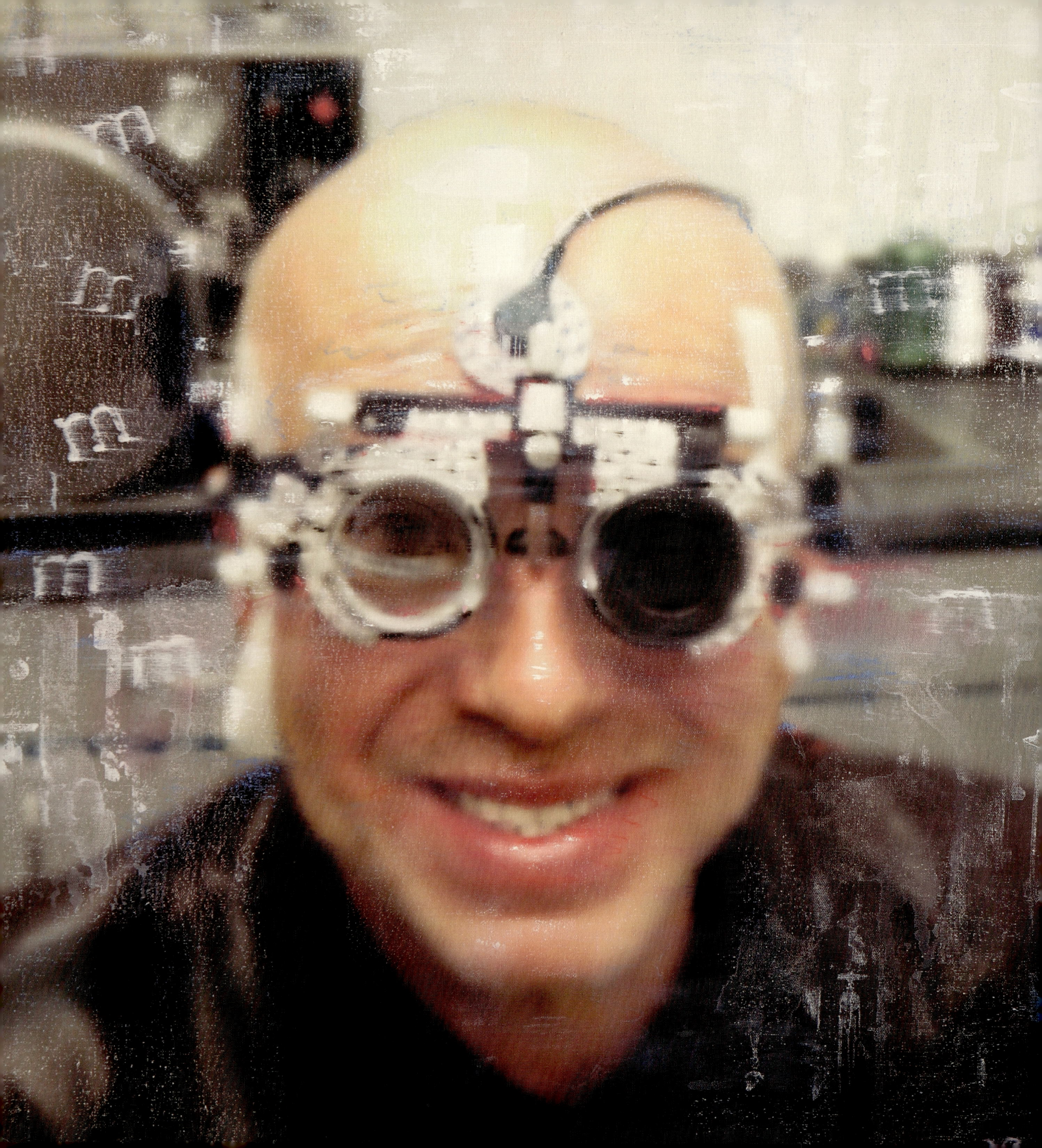

Valentin Popov

CIRCULAR JOURNEY THE LONG WAY ROUND
OR
CHRONICLE OF AN UNPLANNED ESCAPE

Where to begin?

I was a youth of many talents, and the biggest fascination of my early childhood was horseback riding, which is still my passion. At the age of five, I first conceived a precocious predilection for the piano, which has persisted to the present day. At seven, the initial signs of a lifelong devotion to art began to manifest, and, eventually, this newfound preoccupation took the place of all others. My family encouraged my artistic development and hurled me into a swirl of private lessons imparted by the finest tutors. When I reached maturity, my father insisted I attend a business school, so as to learn how to support myself and any future family, and I dutifully complied. . . .

It was a blissful childhood overall, interspersed with travel and summers spent in Mexico, where my family owned a small estate. Winters were spent skiing in Saint Moritz. This was the era in which I first visited Venice and fell in love with that most ethereal of cities. Nature, music, art, and philosophy interblended to form the magical pageant of my childhood.

This isn't quite what happened.

I remember, at age three, attending the funeral of my favorite grandfather, Ivan. It was raining that day, and I huddled under the circle of umbrellas clutched by a shadowy cluster of adults whose dark shoes dotted the moistly glistening sod. According to my mother's account, I had memorized the poems of Pushkin at the age of four and recited them while perched on a little stool. My glamorous musical career started at the age of seven, when I won the First Quadrennial International Tchaikovsky Piano Competition in Moscow.

Whoops! I must have blundered, once again, into the wrong opera. . . .

I hated piano lessons, and very often, before class, my piano teacher had to dig me out of the snow outside my apartment building. I was unable to practice for at least twenty minutes because of terrible pain in my frozen fingers. It took seven years of begging before my parents let me discontinue that.

From age six, I studied in an English-Ukrainian school. When I was eleven, I refused to take an entrance examination for the best boarding art school in the country. I felt tortured when my father used me as a model for his drawings (which I later realized was incredibly beautiful work) and was hopelessly bored while watching him spend hours and hours bending over a wooden drawing board and sheet of paper with a pencil in his hand. I was afraid to go through the living room, which my father used as his studio, because of the inevitable requests that I freeze on the spot and serve as an impromptu model for the hand, neck, or other anatomical component needed for a particular picture. I felt trapped. . . . The apartment building where we used to live belonged to the Association of Fine Arts, and most of my friends and neighbors were enrolled in art school. As we hung around, we talked about art, and I slowly started developing an interest in the subject, making small sketches from nature and paintings of trees. Through my father's connections I was accepted to art school at fourteen, and it took me only one year to achieve a level of skill commensurate with that of most of my classmates—and some of them were really good!

At age eighteen, I applied for admission to the Ukrainian Academy of Fine Art and was accepted as a printmaking student. Later I decided to study in the illustration department. The main reason I made this choice was to avoid painting tractors and people hoeing potato fields in the spirit of state-sponsored Communism. These works were oversaturated with red. . . . I got away, instead, with doing illustrations of contemporary Japanese poetry and the stories of Mikhail Bulgakov, Gogol, Tolstoy, and Dostoevsky. Officially, I was a "bad" student. Bad because I got married at twenty and my wife was studying ceramics in Lvov, a Ukrainian city near the Polish border. Naturally, I divided my time between Lvov and Kiev and ended up skipping lectures. My father was my lithography teacher at the time and chief of the print department, and we had many arguments over my absences from school. There was one lecture,

in particular, which I never bothered to attend: it was titled "Scientific Theory of Communism." My attitude was: I'll live my life and nobody's going to tell me what to do. Nice!

As time passed, I began more and more to enjoy etching and studying the history of art and literature. My graduation series was a sheaf of historical drawings based on the history of Kiev, and it was ranked by the faculty as some of the best work to come out of the school. After graduation I quickly found myself facing the real-life worries of finding a job and caring for a family—worries doubly daunting, perhaps, for someone intending to make a living as an artist, teacher, and printmaker.

What took place next were the two best things that can happen to a graduate student. The first was the grant of a three-year pension from the USSR Academy of Fine Art. This meant one's own studio, money, and free art supplies. The second stroke of supreme good fortune was the award of a two-year grant from the Association of Fine Arts of the USSR, which meant work in an artist-in-residence program in Senej, near Moscow, and, to top it all off, major attention from art critics. Two or three artists from each republic were chosen every second year. I got both of these career-shaping honors, one after the other. It was one of the most fascinating periods in my life. I was the youngest among the artists, and my work was shown in huge all–Soviet Union exhibitions. I had done an enormous quantity of work, which brought me deep satisfaction as well as pragmatic results. But I nursed a secret pain.

I was traveling and working like crazy and felt almost like a god. Everything was going my way. Fortified by a combination of youth, early success, and obvious talent, the sky seemed my limit. But it was precisely at this time that my marriage fell apart. Traveling and focusing on my own work made me neglectful of many things. My marriage was on

autopilot for a long time. Divorce came out of the
blue and caused me a huge shock and put many
things in my life in sharp perspective. A bigger shock
came two years later, when my ex-wife was killed
in a car crash in Kazakhstan while I was working in
a beautiful one-person print shop in Pécs, a city in
western Hungary. As they say, "What doesn't kill
you makes you stronger."

I am fifty-one now. I've been living full-time
in California for the past fifteen years. More and
more, lately, I find my memories running back to
my beginnings, to the Ukrainian years—the cold
winters, the long months working in various residency
programs (I didn't have a studio then), drinking vodka
with artists from all over the place and seriously
talking about changing art and the world around us.
Some of those people are already dead. With others,
I am still in constant touch. Some of them have
become important bureaucrats in the Association of
Fine Arts; some are still producing wonderful art and
exchanging ideas about philosophy, poetry, and life—
not having a life of one's own, that is—but struggling.
Some of them are still making pretty pictures to be
sold to assorted levels of tourists. Oh, well. . . .

Now that you have tagged along for this much of
my journey, Dear Reader, I will try to share certain
moments which had a big impact on my life, along
with the observations and insights, acquired easily or
hard, which accompanied them. Sometimes it was a
matter of pure luck.

Having had the luck to be born with a talent
undoubtedly inherited from a father who was an
important person in the Ukrainian art world, I enjoyed
making art and was able to push the boundaries a
little further—an action which would have caused
another artist to be put on a "blacklist" for much less
liberalfreedomism. But, most of my life I'd dared to
challenge the status quo and got plenty of attention.

Of all the pieces of art I've made over the years,

a set of etchings based on *Torrents of Spring*, by
Turgenev, holds a special place. It was a labor of love
from the beginning. I started doing the etchings in
1983 as a bid for a stipend from the USSR, and it
took me three years to complete them. I had always
wanted to illustrate some classical Russian literature,
and, after reading some Dostoevsky and Chekov, I
stumbled onto a little story which touched me a lot.
The story resonated with my emotional state at that
time. I threw myself into a serious study of mid-
nineteenth-century fashions, home decoration, and
cityscapes in Germany and Russia. I can still tell you
the difference between men's formal dress in 1830
and 1850. I rented nineteenth-century costumes from
the Kiev Opera, organized a dinner party, had my
friends wear costumes, invited a photographer, and
became for one evening a stage director. I staged my
illustrations . . . and photographed them. The ones
that came out best were based on totally improvised
scenes. The staged ones were hardly any good at all.
It somehow always works this way (insight #1). I used
to draw for days and days—creating interiors, clouds
in the sky, people. . . .

Sometime during the winter of 1983, in the late
evening, I was trudging through the snow near a
church in the little village of Sedvin, near Tchernigov.
I was starting two months of art residency there. Night
was beginning to settle over the town, silent except
for one dog barking and a few workers tinkering on
the roof of the church. They were recovering the roof
with new copper (in midwinter, for God's sake!) and
flinging the leftover strips down onto the snow. Those
strips became my Turgenev etchings (insight #2:
sometimes good things come from religion). I snipped
the copper leftovers to size and chucked them into a
hot fire in the boiler room. When they turned white
from the heat, I annealed them in the snow. The
cooling process makes copper, unlike steel, more
malleable and easier for acid to etch. My impromptu

experiments that winter in the sleepy village of Sedvin not only taught me a lot about preparing plates, it also gave me a great lesson in physics.

I worked on the Turgenev project for almost three years, but the Academy of Fine Art did not accept it as a valid submission for the stipend. Reason: there was "not enough of Russian flavor in it." They probably forgot that the story was set in Germany and the main character was Italian. Artworks the Academy considered the most important were awarded medals every other year. Two years later, I won a government prize for the same work—a silver medal. The gold one was awarded to a famous sculptor for one of those giant monuments of *The Russian Soldier*. My etchings were considered the best prints in the USSR. I think there have been only five people in the history of the Soviet Ukraine who have received this medal—but never for romantic etchings based on a nineteenth-century novel.

Yes, it changed things in my life: it created lots of jealousy and animosity in the Association of Fine Art. And, as never before, I got a markedly unwelcome vibe being a Russian in the Ukraine.

Then perestroika began.

Overall, thinking back on those years, the late eighties and early nineties, I had a wonderful time. I got a lot of work done, and I traveled a good deal, mostly working in different art residency programs. (I didn't have a studio then.) I spent almost ten years making etchings. It was my passion, and, if I say so my-self, I was one of the best. Slowly my small black-and-white etchings became bigger and bigger. I started to add more and more color, and, one day . . . boom! . . . I started painting. And I'm painting to this day.

At this point it might be appropriate to take a breather from the formal time line and mention my relationship with my father. As a young artist with a strong personality, I felt he and I were completely different people, and, at that time, it was very important for me not to become like him. Many years later, now, I understand him better and realize how much I learned from him. He is really an incredible, special man. I admire him for choices he made in his life, as well as for his profound talent and the high position he achieved in art. At the age of eighty, he still teaches twice a week and spends more time in his studio than I do. Successful in his career, pursuing his goals, he never became corrupt or sleazy, as had so many other men of his difficult-to-survive generation. We used to fight a lot. If you ask him now what he thinks about his son, he says, "I am proud of him, but I still don't understand him." I don't think I ever got "I love you" from him. It was a very different generation. Lots of things were kept inside. One day, following a long conversation about principles and beliefs, I unloaded on him that I would never become a member of the Communist Party, as he was, despite not believing in it. I declined after I was "invited." That almost killed my career. My father pointed out that if he had not become a member of the "Party," our family would never have been able to move to Kiev from the little village of Boyarka (a one-hour drive from the capital), we would never have gotten an apartment there, and he would never have become a professor. Only a few years ago I found out from my mother that part of our family had moved to Paris during the first part of the twentieth century. My father's two uncles were high-ranking officers in the White Army. My parents kept this fact a secret, because it could create big problems for our family under Communist rule. Also, just recently, I found out that the official celebration of my father's eightieth birthday would be postponed for one year. To avoid being drafted into the army in 1942, he lied about his age, making himself one year younger. He never got drafted, but spent two years under German occupation and ran from the train which was taking young men to Germany. He was nearly shot.

I am glad I do not have to face such choices in my life. Even so, I, too, ran and happily made my way to the Oakland hills, and if I continue running, I may eventually reach the land of my birth from the opposite side of the planet (insight #3: run).

Unlike some of my friends who still live in Kiev, I never had fantasies about emigrating to the United States. One day, I got a telephone call from Valentin Suslov, an older friend, a doctor. He was entertaining visitors from Stanford University, a couple, professors of anesthesia. "Can we throw a party for my friends at your place?" he asked me. My answer was yes, and two days later, I met a charming couple: Richard Mazze and Sheila Cohen. I have to say, quite a bit of vodka was consumed that night. The party ended in a euphoric, alcohol-induced haze punctuated by merry hugs and kisses of fast friendship. I was invited to visit Stanford. Recently, Richard teased, "If there had been no vodka that night, you would probably still be living in Kiev!" After the Cohen-Mazzes returned to California, I received a postcard from Stanford, saying that my new friends were looking forward to my visit. To expedite that end, we got creative. Knowing that a personal invitation would get me nowhere at the US consulate in Kiev, they sent me an invitation on Stanford stationery to come with a show of my work. After using some of my connections in Moscow, I was shortly sitting on a United Airlines jet heading towards San Francisco as a "one-person official delegation of the Association of Fine Art of the USSR" to open my show at Stanford. I vividly remember that first arrival in the United States. It was in the summer of 1988, and I was so excited that, when I disembarked, I left my portfolio of etchings behind on the plane. Fortunately, the portfolio was found the next day.

Something special happened on that trip, which eventually changed my life. It was afternoon, and I was lying face up on the sand near Santa Cruz, gazing at the sky. I remember feeling a boundless happiness and freedom, a sense of fulfillment and total contentment, in which I didn't have to prove anything to anybody. It was a sense of the sheer biological pleasure of existence, of being young, free, at the perfect place at the perfect time. No concerns about the past. No worries for the future. I think it was that afternoon that made me emigrate to the United States.

Once in California, I found myself driving around San Francisco with Richard. As we passed a gallery, I asked him to stop so that I could show my art, in hopes of finding representation.

It did not work out. So I came up with a better idea: I decided to go directly to the San Francisco Museum of Modern Art and show my work there. "May as well start at the top," I said to myself. SFMOMA curator John Caldwell would be out of town for the next two days, and I was scheduled to return to Kiev in four days. I left a single set of Kodak slides with Caldwell's secretary. Two days later, I got a call. A deep male voice introduced itself: "This is John Caldwell . . . I like your work. . . . Would you like to meet with me?"

Just like that.

At five the following afternoon, I met him at the museum. A very tall man, Mr. Caldwell greeted me and handed me a little note asking me to call Richard immediately. Excusing myself, I quickly called "home." "Don't make any plans for tomorrow," Richard insisted. "We've made an appointment for you to interview for the Djerassi Program."

Caldwell suggested showing my work in two galleries and arranged to give me a solo show in half a year. Next afternoon, I met Sally Stillman, the director of the Djerassi Program. I still can remember that beautiful ride through the "middle of nowhere" in Woodside. I started showing my prints. Breaking a heavy silence, she asked, "Can I buy this one?" I got a residency. I thought: *Man, I am one lucky s.o.b.!*

I traveled a second time to the United States for the opening of my solo show. Once again, I constituted an official one-person delegation of the Association of Fine Art of the USSR. My first art dealer, Ardis Allport, introduced me to Magnolia Editions in Oakland, and for two months I worked there as a master printer. I did some work there with Joseph Goldyne and John Register. It was during this period that I met Barnaby Conrad III and Martin Muller. It would be another thirteen years before I'd start working with Muller's Modernism gallery, the best institution I could ever have dreamed of working with. As they say, "Better late than never." At Magnolia Editions, I discovered handmade paper and thus began a persistent passion for making collages. By this time, I knew for certain there was no going back to Kiev. I don't remember how many collages I've made. Quite a few. There is something special about the collage-making process. As a postmodern artist, which is how I regard myself, I'm constantly comparing, contrasting, and combining different things. There's an intriguing process of creating new quantities by juxtaposing signs and symbols, patterns and textures. Copying Rembrandt for some of the collages was fascinating. Even though I make my living by making art, I didn't make the collages for money. I enjoyed every minute of that work. Every piece was special. I know some artists who fashion their output with easy sales in mind. I never wanted to go that way. My art is my life. Nevertheless, the demand for my collages became so great that everybody was interested in buying or selling them. That was when I started my work with Mimi Ferzt Gallery in New York. Christine Sperber, one of the owners, fell in love with my work, and for a few years the collages became a subject of interest to many collectors.

But, after a while, other techniques and media attracted my attention. Painting on aluminum panels, I invented *Romantic Cynicism* and spent three years working on the *Saint Batman* project. During my show in Palo Alto, California, in 1991, I met Paula Kirkeby, owner of Smith Andersen Editions, and she spoiled me rotten by introducing me to monotype. We did a few projects together. I was working with three great printers, using the finest paper imaginable. . . . Caramba! It was a heady experience!

But before all that happened, before my success with collages, there was a time (the early nineties) when the market was terrible and it was nearly impossible to sell art. I was lucky to have a couple of dealers who supported me during those times. One of them was Pasquale Iannetti, my great friend and patron.

During the slump, you'd have a show and sell one and a half pieces! You'd have another show and sell a single piece! *Great*, I thought. *Now what?* At the same time, I was quickly coming to the realization that I wanted to stay in the United States for good. I didn't have a permanent residence yet, I had no green card, and I was subletting studios from different artists in Emeryville. I was lodging one month here, one month there. At one point, I was staying in a place in Emeryville where my girlfriend from the Ukraine had just left after visiting me. I felt so lost. I had abandoned a pretty good career in the Ukraine, along with a girlfriend, a studio, an apartment full of books and personal effects, not to mention my sister, my parents. . . . I'd never felt so lonely in my life as I felt that morning, but all of it was my own doing. I felt as if I were lying in a coffin which I'd built for myself.

The telephone rang. It was an artist from New York, a very funny guy whom I'd met in London two years before. "I showed your work to some people in New York," he said. "Kentler International Drawing Space—and they want to give you a one-man show!"

A snap of the fingers. And suddenly everything in my life changed again. It was a very funky show in a funky place. Few people came. One of them, however—my future dealer Christine—liked the show very much. Two months later, she opened her own gallery in Soho. Another twist of fate . . .

Now for the first time in my American history, indeed, for the first time in my life, I started selling my art. Shows sold out. I attribute these successes to the efforts of my first serious promoter, Christine Sperber. She loved my art and made things happen. After some time, we started showing my monotypes, paintings on woodblock, and *Romantic Cynicism* pieces. No sales eventuated from the *Batman* project, because the Mimi Ferzt Gallery was afraid of a copyright infringement lawsuit by DC Comics. I spent three years doing that project. Most of the associated artworks have ended up in museums. Thanks to Christine and her marketing of my collages, I had enough money to invest 80 percent of my creative time doing high-concept and experimental work which, at the time, nobody wanted to show or buy. My collage phase was the first I didn't terminate at the peak of its popularity. Most others come to an abrupt close the moment I hear the phrase "I l…o…o…o…v…e your work!" Or the classic, "Your previous pieces were so different and beautiful. I don't understand the new ones." Three years later, the same people fall in love with the new work, but I've already changed again. They look at the latest stuff, and again comes, "I don't understand. . . ." You know how I like my viewer to feel? A little scared and slightly confused.

I decided to develop the collage medium as deeply as possible until it had run its course. Eventually, the immediacy of my interest petered out. C'est la vie. . . .

About twelve years ago, my parents and I spent a month together in California. They were staying with me in the first Emeryville studio I was directly renting, not subletting. It was so nice to hear from my father how he was impressed with what I had achieved, but, at the same time, he said that if he were ever faced with the choice of dropping his established career and everything he owned and moving to the United States, he wouldn't do it. He told me he admired my courage, and it was one of the few compliments I ever got from him.

One day, during my parents' visit, we were on our way to rendezvous with my friend Dale Djerassi to have lunch together at Alice's Restaurant in La Honda. To pass the time, I asked my father if he knew anything about hippies. "Long hair and negative connotation" was his confused reply. For the rest of the trip I "filled him in." Dale was fashionably late, so I had enough time to tell my folks the Djerassi story— about his father being the creator of the birth control pill, the Resident Artists Program, the hundreds of acres of beautiful land. . . . Dale showed up wearing sweatpants, flip-flops, and loose, long hair, which had forsaken the comb long ago. My father's eyes slowly swiveled in my direction as he whispered, "And this man is rich?" He probably expected Dale to show up in a tuxedo with a cigar in a holder. Later the same day, while hiking through the Djerassi Foundation sculpture park, we stopped to look at the wonderful Mauro Staccioli concrete blocks penetrating the branches of the trees. Under his breath, stunned and incredulous, my father quietly asked me, "You call that ART?" He almost lost his voice! It was a difficult day for my father. I still laugh inside when I think about that day. The same year, after my parents' visit, my father and I had a tandem show at the Mimi Ferzt Gallery—*Papa Popov + Valentin Popov*—consisting of my collages and Father's academic drawings from the fifties.

Parallel to my mainline endeavors is another body of art-related projects. One of them involved the extraordinary man and famous collector of

Russian/Soviet art, Norton Dodge. On behalf of Mr. Dodge, I went twice to Kiev for a one-month stay. On these trips, I filmed a documentary about Ukrainian artists working in the period preceding perestroika. Based on material from my film, Dodge selected a number of paintings, prints, and sculptures that interested him. Two months later, I went to Kiev again and spent thousands of dollars buying art for the Dodge collection. Most important of all, I was able to bring the work to the United States. I remember paying a $3,000 surcharge (in 1997!) for seven pieces of excess baggage! The Dodge purchases constituted a major injection of cash into the Ukrainian art market. Mr. Dodge picked me up at Kennedy Airport in his truck with rusted mirrors attached by silver duct tape, and we drove to Maryland, where I spent three days at the Cremona Foundation helping them catalog the freshly arrived art. We talked a lot about Dodge's trips to the USSR in the sixties, when his obsession for collecting art by noncomformist artists had begun. In a number of his anecdotes, the name of Garig Basmadjian kept cropping up. Basmadjian was a Paris-based art dealer. I was already familiar with this name—legendary in Moscow, Basmadjian was buying tons of art and shifting it to the West. One day he left his hotel in Moscow in the mid-eighties and was never seen again. I remember a couple of KGB guys coming to my studio and asking me if I knew the guy or had ever met him. I wasn't aware at the time that Garig had been doing exactly the same job for Norton in Moscow as I had been doing in Kiev. I never knew sweat could run so cold. I'm happy to report that my mission was successfully accomplished!

Meanwhile, things were going well in New York, and I was very happy with my life. I was making lots of art and lots of money. But I realized how much I liked to live with my art and not sell it immediately. I've learned, and I'm still learning, a lot about myself through my art. I've always enjoyed answering frequently asked questions at my receptions in New York. When queried as to my address in Manhattan, my answer is, "Oh, no. I live in California." When, on the other hand, someone on the West Coast asks what gallery represents me in San Francisco, I say, "I'm working with a gallery in New York." How cool is that?

At one point, people pushed me more and more to move to New York. There are some artists who want to be famous, and there are those who just want to be artists. I consider myself as belonging to the second category. I had a disturbing feeling I was missing some kind of connection with myself. I voluntarily stopped working with my New York galleries.

I deliberately bought a house in the middle of nowhere, far away from everybody I knew. It took me a year and a half to change everything inside of the house and build a painting studio. Finally, everything was set up exactly the way I wanted it. My house and studio were a dream come true. And still are. They form the habitat where I want to spend the rest of my life.

After some time, I got back to my art, refreshed and hungry for action. It dawned on me that it might be tricky getting back in the art market. I didn't have a gallery. I was trying to show here and there, but nothing special was happening. It seemed as if everyone had forgotten about me. Then I learned another thing about myself: I like attention.

So I continue to work hard. I've done more monotypes. I've done more paintings on aluminum panels: paintings of sky and water with incorporated text. And I've done some new paintings on canvas. I've gotten back to canvas, which, at the beginning of my career, I had eliminated from my repertoire as being too traditional. The newest works are simultaneously photorealistic and slightly out of focus. They're like memories of my journeys. No text.

Cityscapes. Fantasy journeys simulating reality. They have a fuzziness that allows you to read in things.

We've almost reached the end of the story. I have a few words to say about special people and special projects in my life. One of my favorite shows was *Romantic Cynicism*, which convened in 1994 at the de Saisset Museum in Santa Clara, and the main hero of the show was *Saint Batman*. It really set off some fireworks. ("Pray that the blasphemous art work be removed from the museum on the Santa Clara University campus . . ." reads one sample from a pile of letters to the university president.) Another very interesting show was held at the National Museum in Kiev, Ukraine, in 2000. It was an emotional experience for me, but afforded me no peace. Then there was the 2002 *VAL POP* show at the Huntington Beach Art Center, another venue where I showed many styles of art placed together.

I also participated in the *San Francisco Hearts* project, and I made a sculpture for the Swatch company for the recent Olympic Games in Greece. I painted a portrait of Dalai Lama XIV. We met. He blessed me and the portrait, and then he looked at me through his old-fashioned glasses and said, "You made me look old." He left me speechless with a Mona Lisa smile on my confused face.

The first and last conventional "job" in my life was a two-month stint as a printer at Magnolia Editions, in Oakland. A fantastic learning experience! At age twelve I had decided to be an artist and have never, ever looked back (not even while muttering to myself while pacing the floor in the middle of the night). I have been blessed with the great good fortune to have met special people who have given me special attention and have changed my life: Sheila Cohen and Richard Mazze, who invited me to the United States for the very first time; Paula Kirkeby, who sponsored a number of my monotype projects at her Smith Andersen Press in Palo Alto; Pasquale Iannetti, who gave me shows when nobody could sell a thing; Christine Sperber, my New York dealer, who liked my art so much that she was able to project her wild energy directly into her clients' heads; my friend Dale Djerassi, who was always making sure I was OK; and, of course, Martin Muller, who was not afraid to offer me a "committed relationship," and with whom I am proudly affiliated to this day. I was, and I still am, lucky to have wonderful friends.

Here I am in California, thousands of miles away from "home." I am American and I feel American. I achieved a golden dream of going as far west as possible. But sometimes, to fully understand myself, I have to pause amidst the wonder of it all and humbly reflect on my roots. Then, and only then, can I see THE BIG PICTURE.

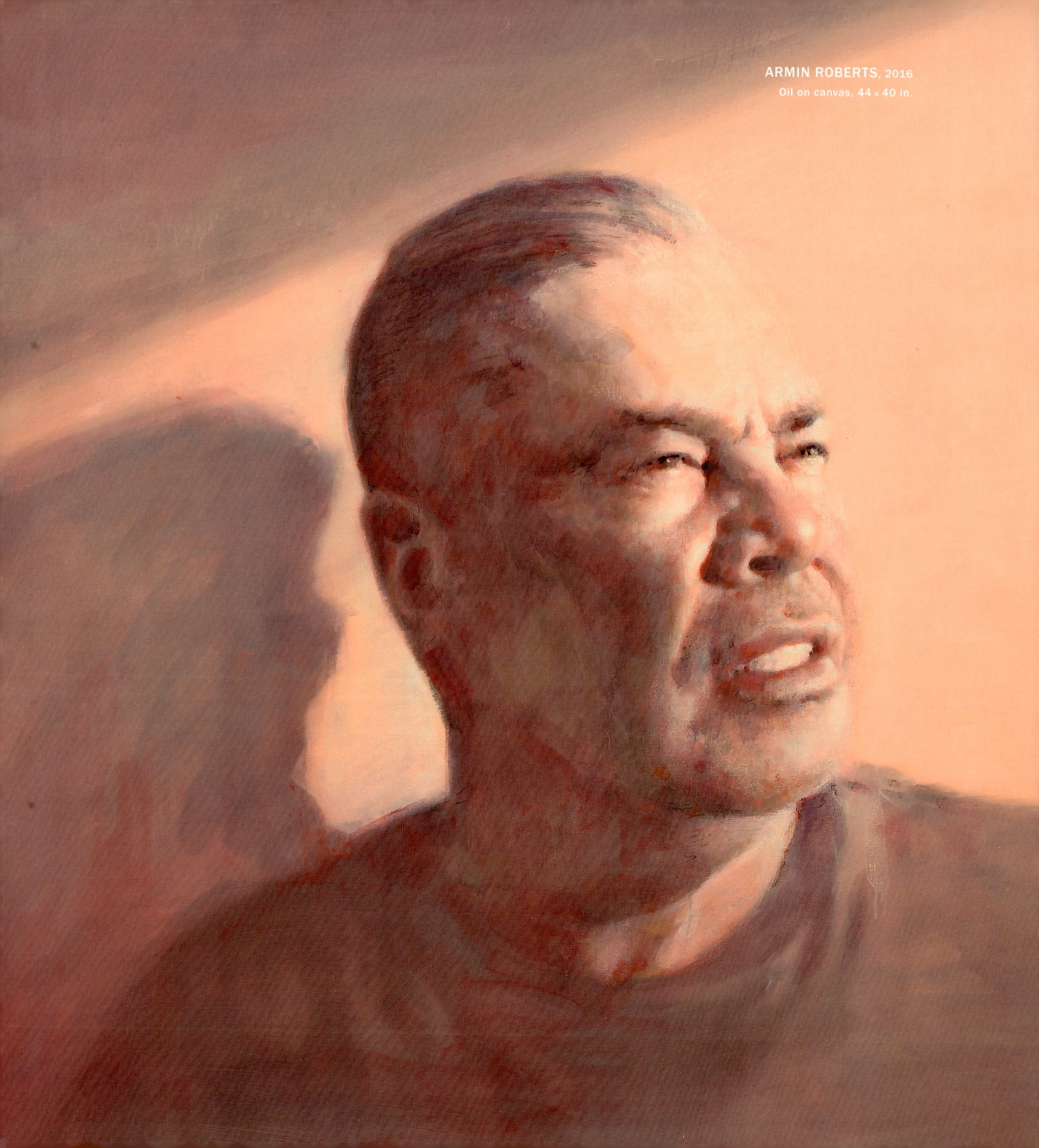

ARMIN ROBERTS, 2016
Oil on canvas, 44 × 40 in.

FACE VS. FACADE

Much has been made of the capacity of the portrait, like the face itself, to act as a mask to conceal certain aspects of character or camouflage facets of personal dynamics. While this hypothesis may be valid, it is equally true that portraiture can unmask, expose, and reveal.

One of the great Impressionists once described his technique as not a matter of painting a speeding train, but expressing what it feels like to be riding on the train. Belle Époque French sculptor Auguste Rodin noted that "One has only to look at a human face to find a soul. No feature deceives; hypocrisy is as transparent as sincerity. The inclining of the brow, the least furrowing of a look may reveal the secrets of the heart." Rodin also once famously advised his secretary, the fledgling German poet Rainer Maria Rilke, to observe the panther in its cage at the Paris Zoological Gardens until he could truly "see" it. The poet dutifully complied, every day spending hours intently watching the restless creature monotonously pacing back and forth within its iron enclosure. After maintaining this routine for a month or so, the poet breathlessly reported to his master that he had had a "lo and behold" moment of realization, having become one with the imprisoned feline. Rodin referred to this phenomenon as "inseeing." In Valentin Popov's prescient portrait of Russian-born artist, economist, art collector, and erstwhile captain of industry Armin Roberts, the portrayer, having exhaustively scrutinized his subject, has attained an "inseeing" state of synthesis with it, and rendered the sitter an analog for the artist himself who, in turn, is captured at a moment of awakening and transformative insight.

Irrespective of the catalyst triggering this metaphysical principle, its product is a point at which contraries are reconciled and flux is superseded by fusion. At this instant, suffused with rhapsodic awe as the inner man emerges from the confines of the physical chrysalis, the apertures of perception are paradoxically blurred by a suspension of differentiation between subject and object and projection and reflection.

A man of both ideas and action, noted for his keen mathematical mind, intellectual precision, and intuitive powers, Roberts is depicted on the oblique with his smoldering gaze upturned towards some off-frame source of instreaming luminosity. His face bathed in light, his steely gaze fixed on the veils of the unknown, Roberts' inner qualities and psychic constitution stand in relief as clearly as if chiseled in stone. In the lineaments of Roberts' face, portraitist Popov has expertly evoked every nuance of his sitter's powerful personality: psychic strength, authenticity, wonder, curiosity, audacity and defiance. Roberts' expression belies a cocktail of emotions and a sense of urgent life force consonant with his distinctive temperament. It's as if Roberts is struggling to decrypt a mathematical riddle, or is poised to re-enact his seminal, trailblazing role as an early discoverer and champion of Russian Sots artists, and promoter of their careers.

Popov has expertly crafted, without resorting to props or symbolic devices, both a pitch-perfect physical likeness of Roberts as well as a dead-on evocation of his bold spirit of adventure and penchant for chasing new horizons and tackling intricate challenges. Ultimately, Roberts is presented in the raw fullness of his prowess and vitality in a portrait embodying the drama of life itself in all its power and mystery.

B. R. Gilbert

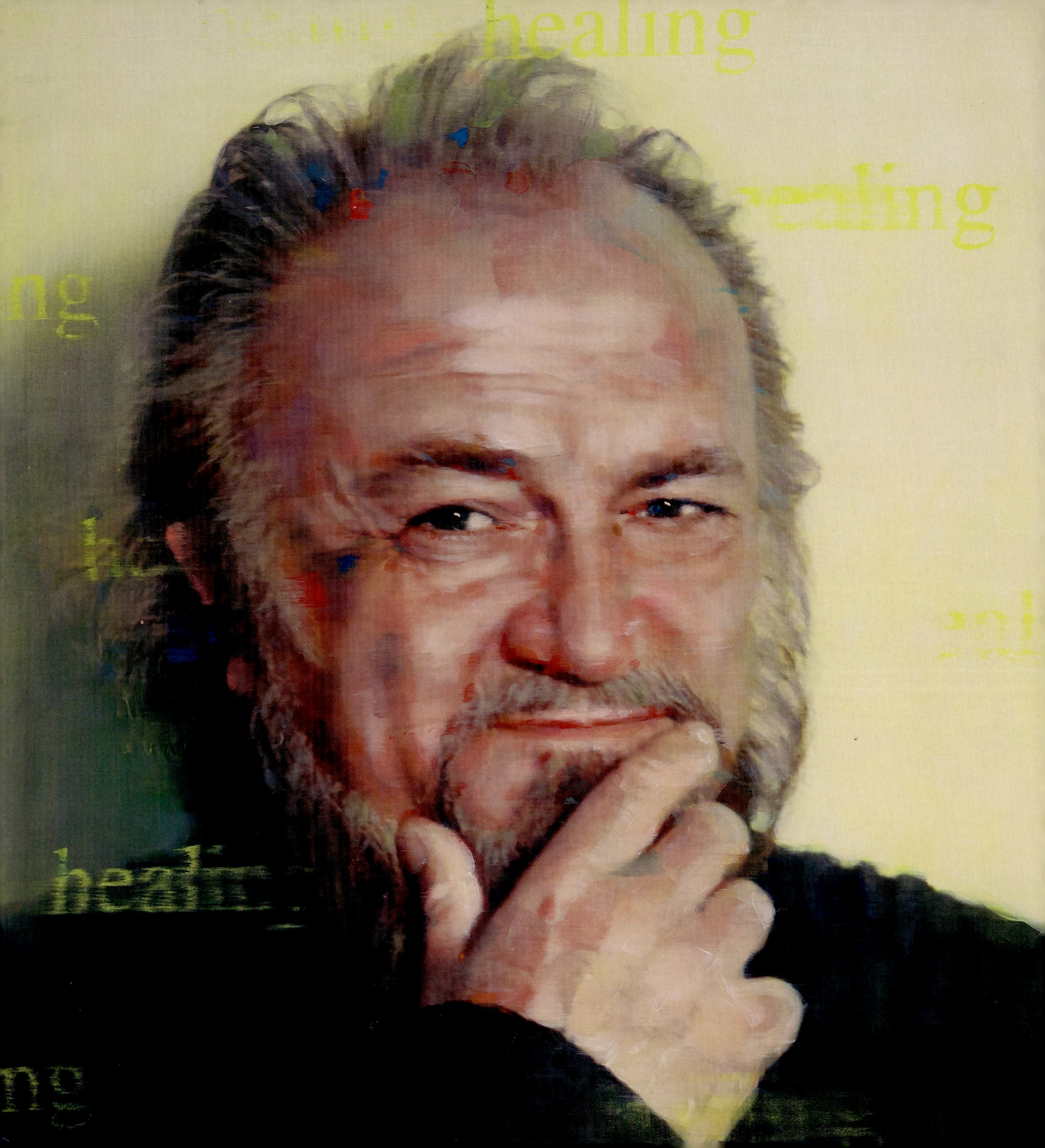
healing
healing
healing

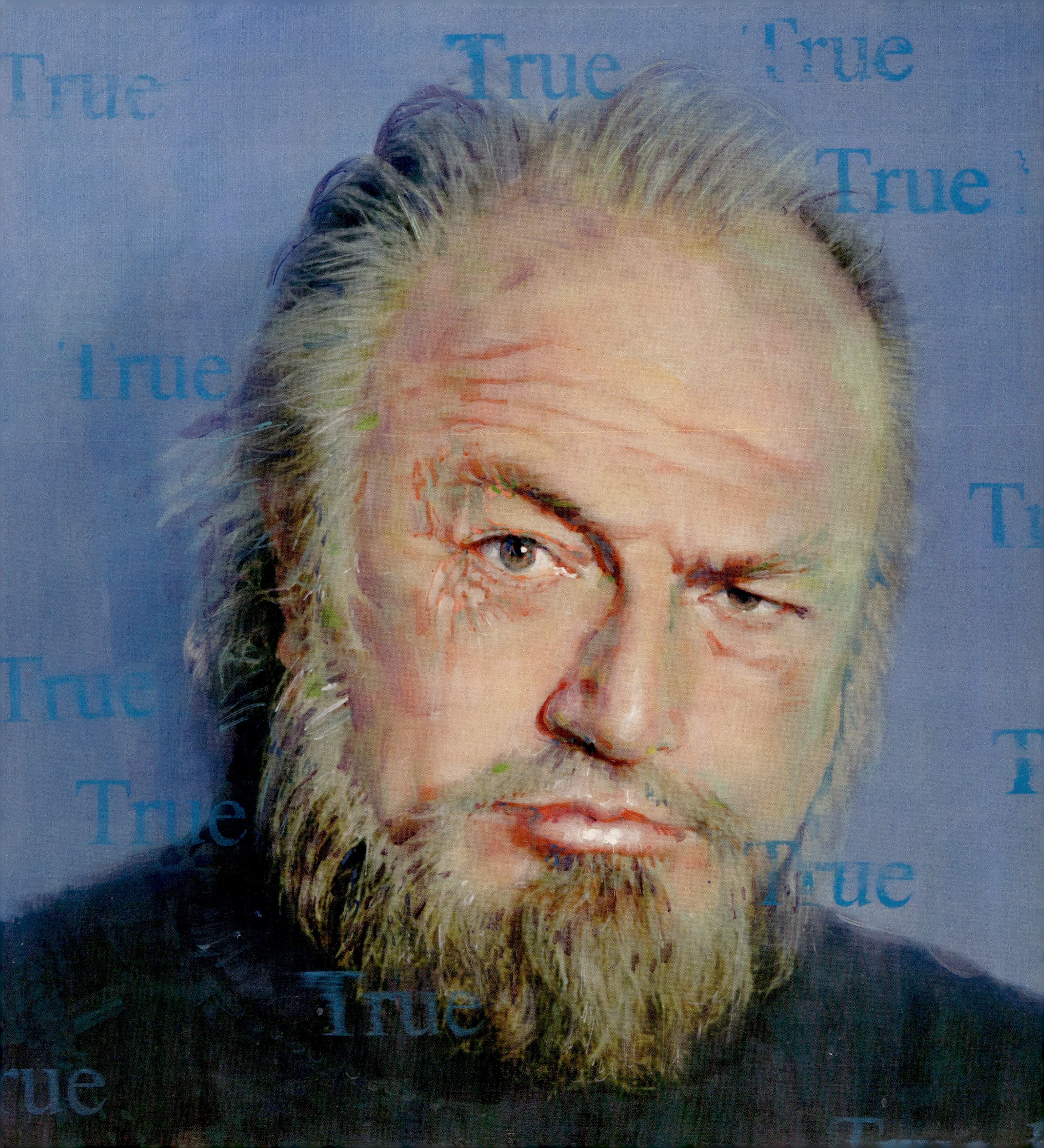

True
True
True
True
True
True
True
True

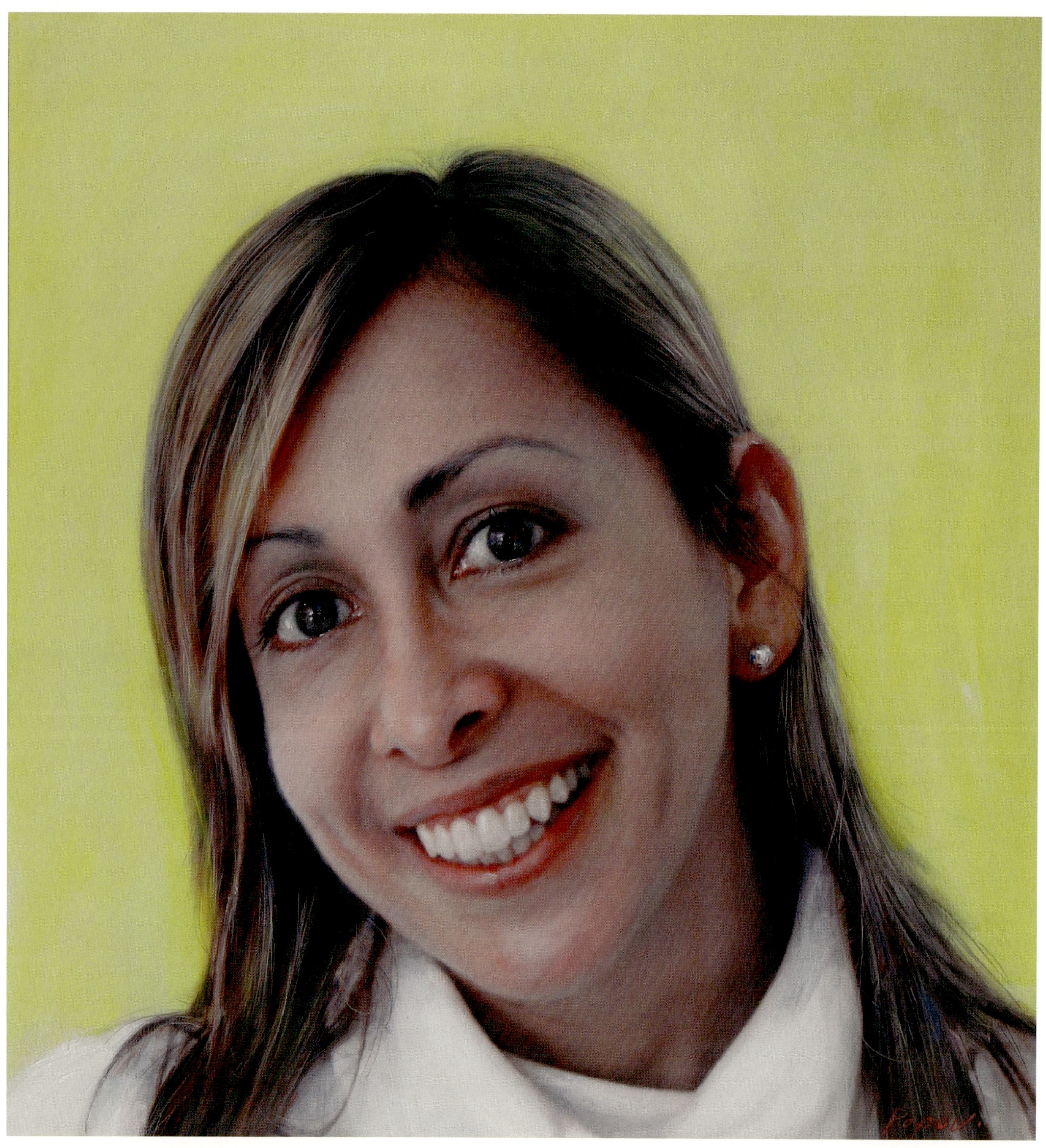

previous, left: **CELIK KAYALAR 1**, 2012. Oil on canvas, 28 × 26 in.

right: **CELIK KAYALAR 2**, 2012. Oil on canvas, 28 × 26 in.

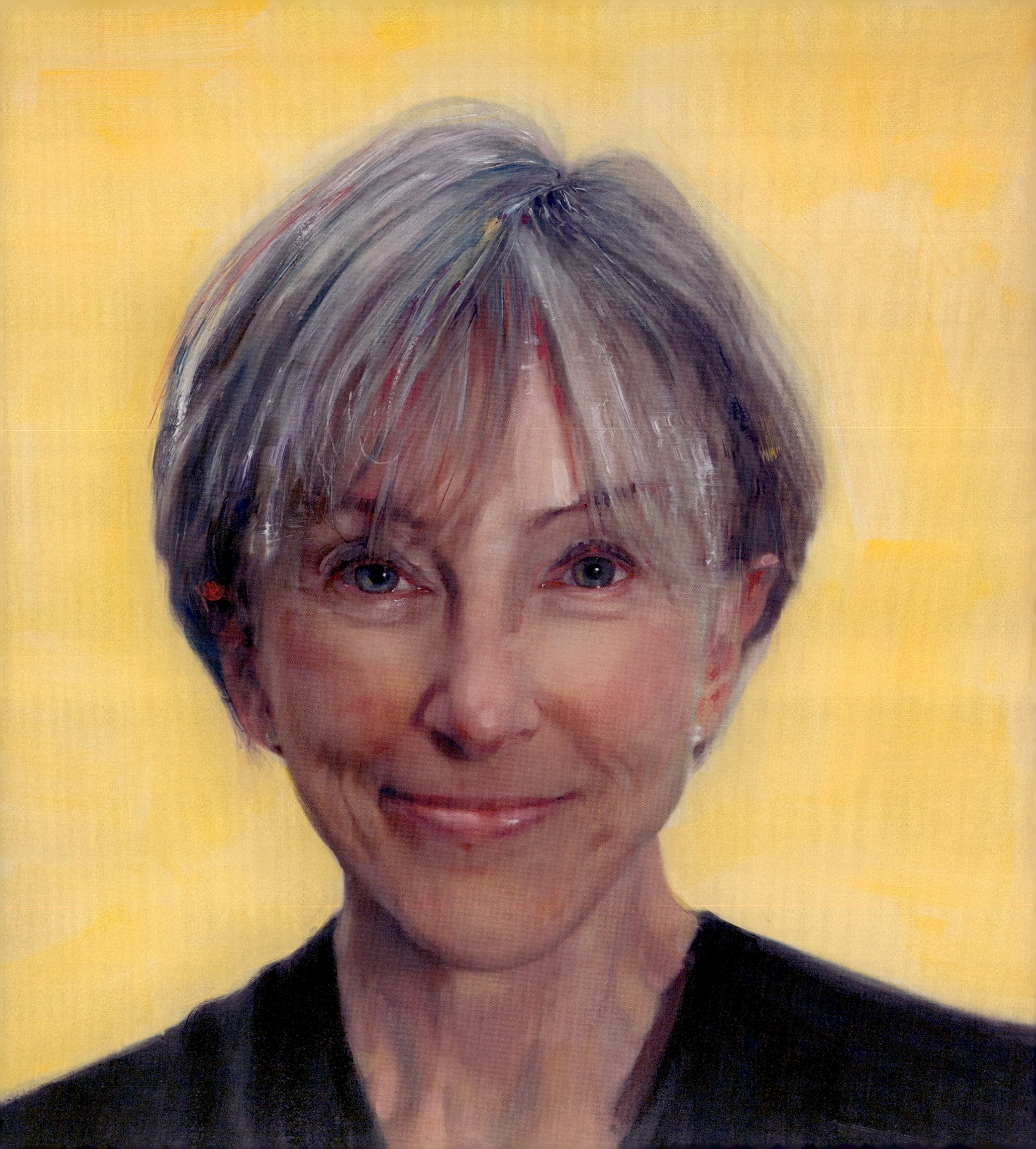

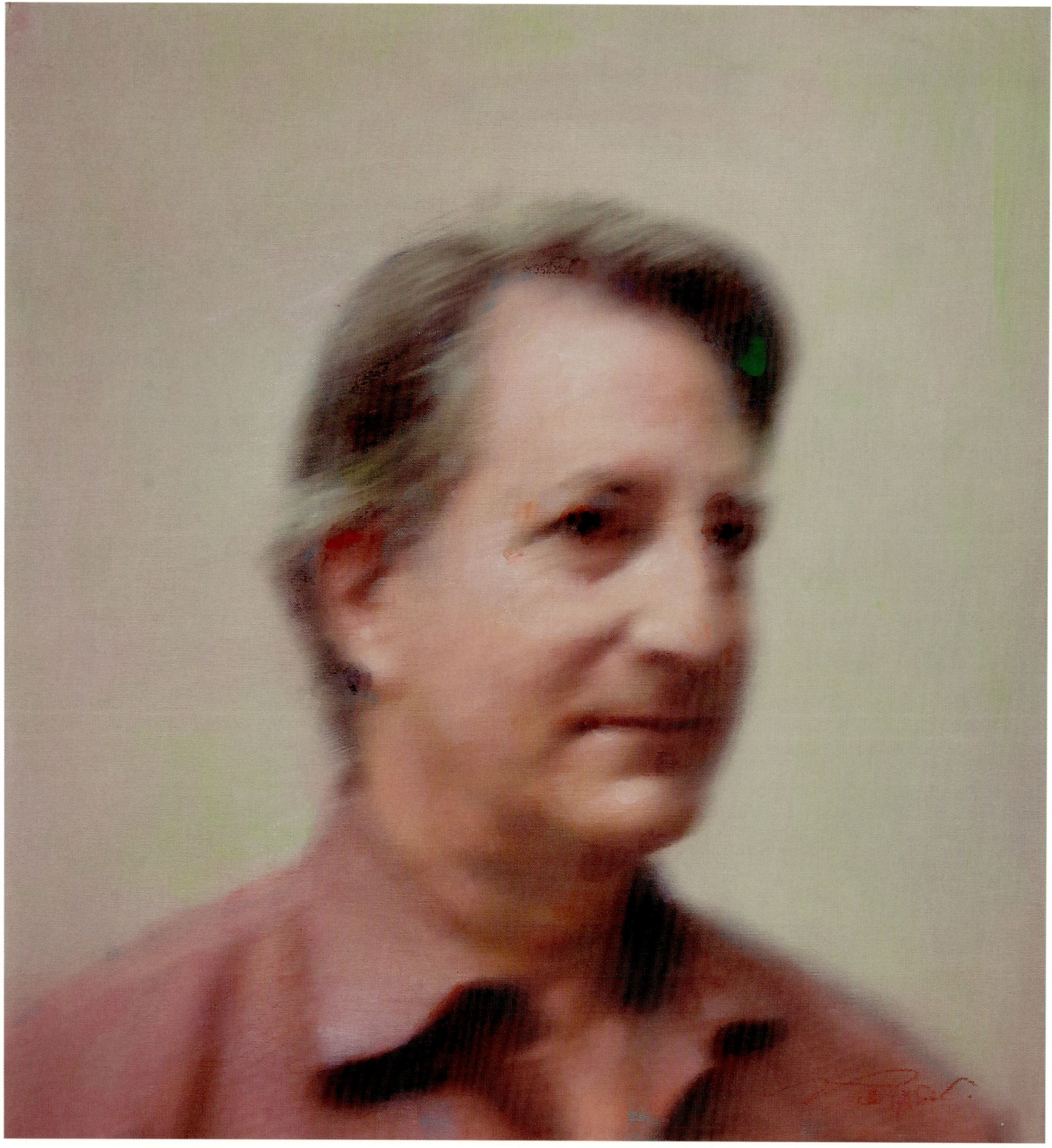

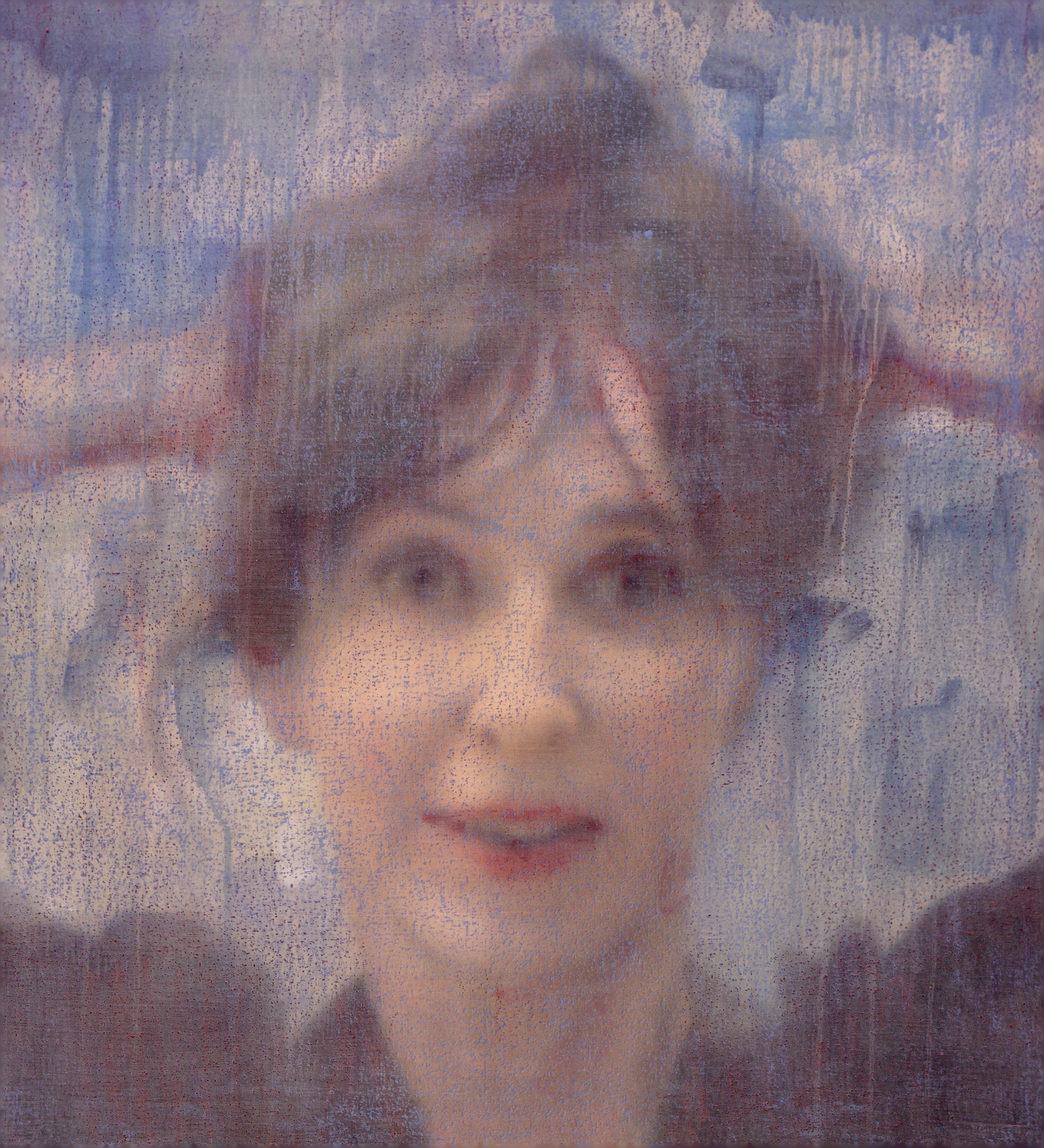

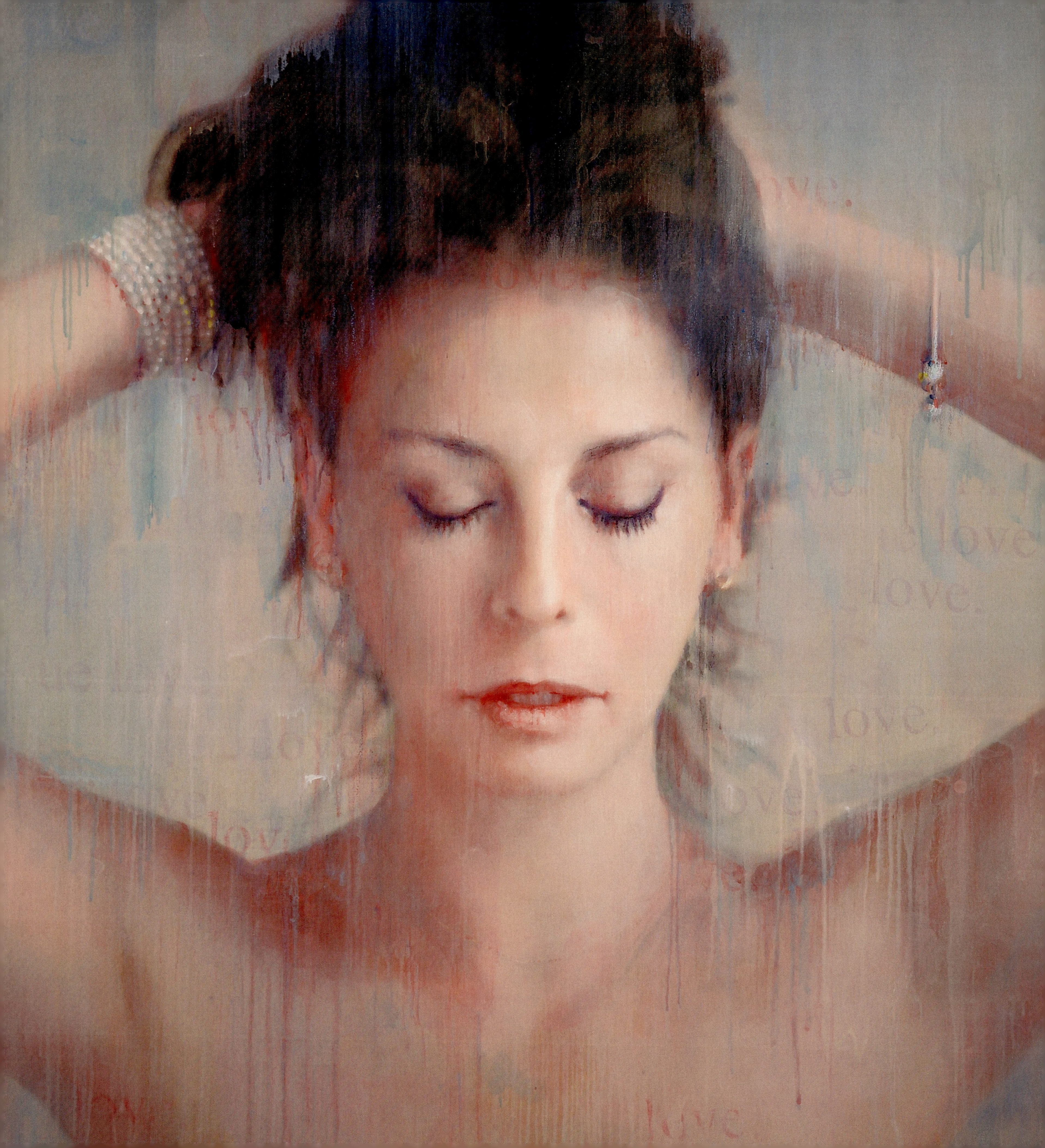

OSNAT, 2016
Oil on canvas, 44 × 40 in.

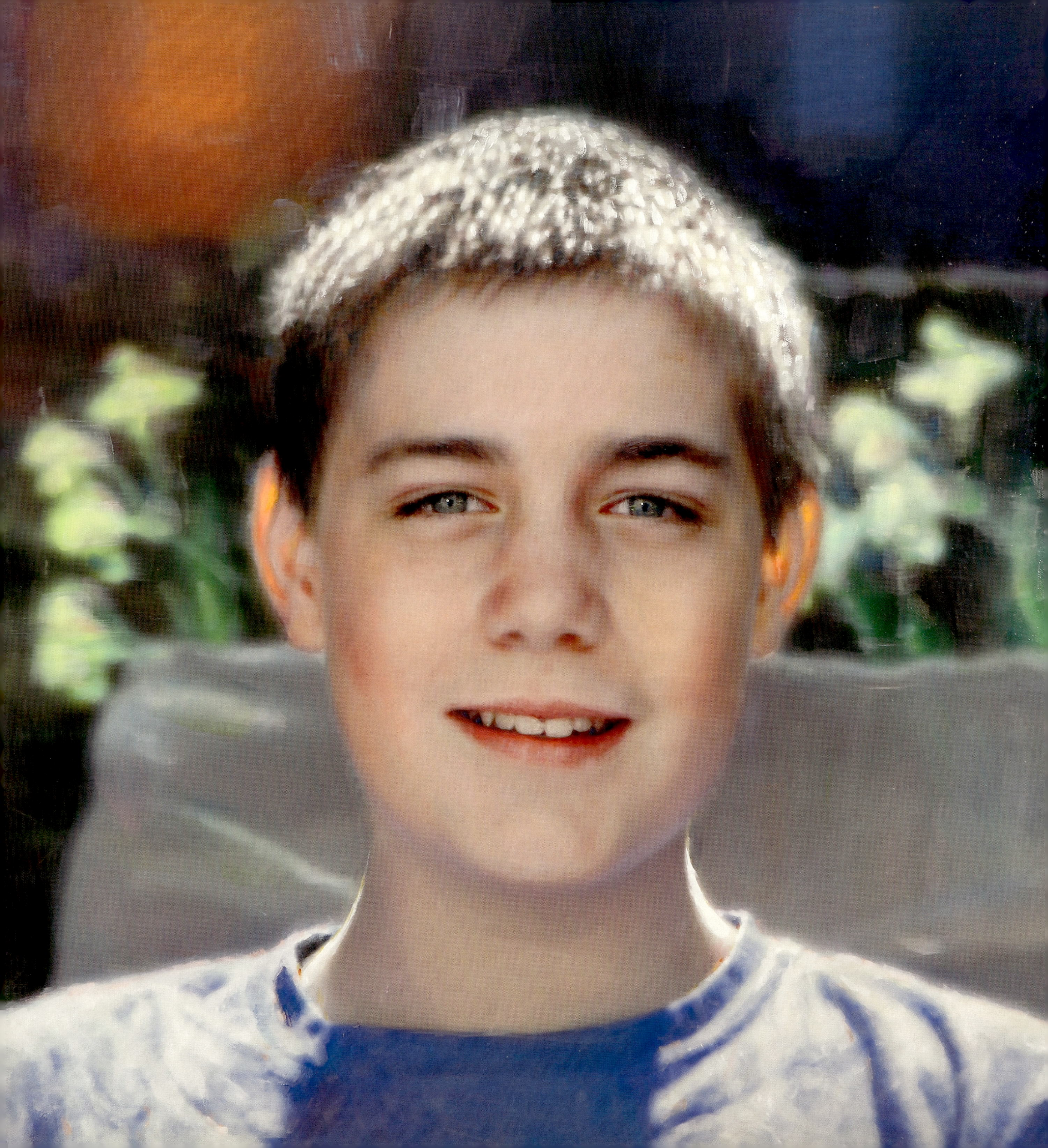

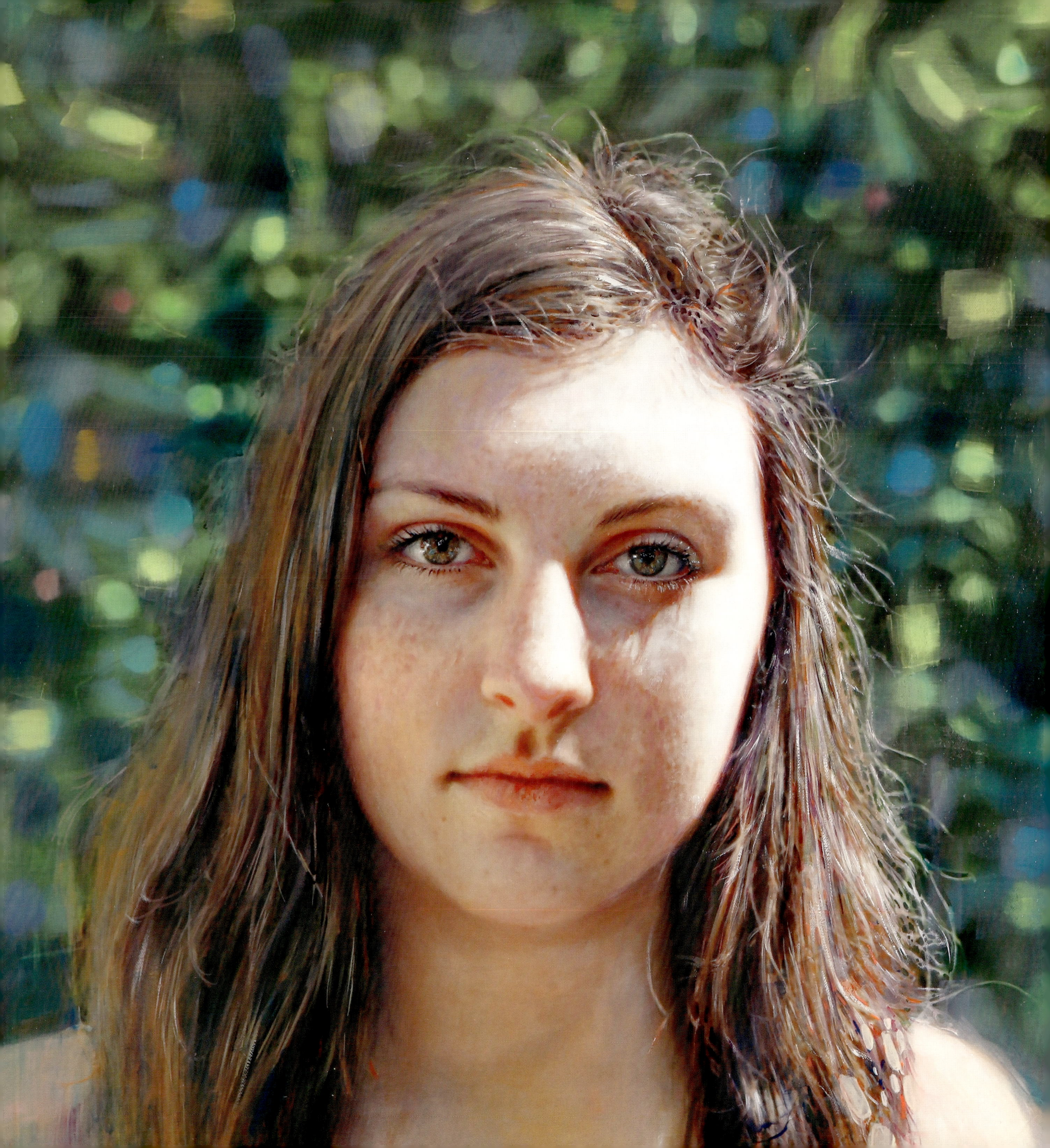

SELECTED EXHIBITIONS AND COLLECTIONS

Iris & B. Gerald Cantor Center for Visual Arts at Stanford University, Stanford, California

de Saisset Museum, Santa Clara University, Santa Clara, California

Fine Arts Museums of San Francisco, Achenbach Foundation for Graphic Arts

Fine Arts Museums of San Francisco, Rena and David Logan Collection of Illustrated Books

Flint Institute of Arts, Flint, Michigan

Harvey S. Firestone Memorial Library, Princeton University, New Jersey

Haggerty Museum of Art, Marquette University, Milwaukee, Wisconsin

Metropolitan Museum of Art, New York

Minneapolis Institute of Arts, Minneapolis, Minnesota

Museum of Russian-American History of Alaska, Sitka, Alaska

Nasher Museum of Art at Duke University, Durham, North Carolina

National Museum of Ukrainian Art, Kiev, Ukraine

New York Public Library, New York

Philadelphia Museum of Art, Philadelphia, Pennsylvania

Schow Foundation, San Marino, California

Spencer Museum of Art, The University of Kansas, Lawrence

Stanford University Libraries, Department of Special Collections, Stanford, California

University of California, Berkeley Art Museum, Berkeley, California

University of Michigan Museum of Art, Ann Arbor

Yale University Art Gallery, New Haven, Connecticut

Jane Voorhees Zimmerli Art Museum—Rutgers, The State University of New Jersey

2017　Long Beach Museum of Art, Long Beach, California. *Ironic Icons.*

2016　Long-Sharp Gallery, Indianapolis, Indiana. *Reflections.*

2013　de Saisset Museum, Santa Clara University, Santa Clara, California. *FACE.*

2011　New Gallery / Thom Andriola, Houston, Texas. *61.8%.*

2010　Modernism Inc., San Francisco. *In the Water.*

2009　New Gallery / Thom Andriola, Houston, Texas. *Vision and Light.*

2008　Modernism Inc., San Francisco. *Then and Now.*

2006　Modernism Inc., San Francisco. *Venice at Night.*

Alysia Duckler Gallery, Portland, Oregon.

Modernism West, San Francisco. *Valentin Popov: 25 Years.*

2005　Alysia Duckler Gallery, Portland, Oregon.

2004　Modernism Inc., San Francisco.

Lora D. Art Gallery, Chicago.

2003　Lora D. Art Gallery, Chicago.

Elizabeth Rice Fine Art, Sarasota, Florida.

2002　Huntington Beach Art Center, Huntington Beach, California. *VAL POP.*

De Pree Art Center, Holland, Michigan. *Going Dutch.*

2001　Robert Berman Gallery, Santa Monica, California.

2000　National Museum of Ukrainian Art, Kiev, Ukraine.

Pasquale Iannetti Art Galleries, San Francisco. *Collage & Sculpture.*

1998–99　Pasquale Iannetti Art Galleries, San Francisco. *Rembrandt—Not Rembrandt.*

1998　Diane Nelson Fine Art, Laguna Beach, California. *Rembrandt—Not Rembrandt.*

1997　Kismet Gallery, San Jose, California. *Crucifixion of St. Batman.*

1996　Mimi Ferzt Gallery, New York. *Romantic Cynicism.*

Kismet Gallery, San Jose, California. *Romantic Cynicism.*

1995　Mimi Ferzt Gallery, New York. *Torrents of Spring.*

1994　de Saisset Museum, Santa Clara University, Santa Clara, California. *Romantic Cynicism.*

Mimi Ferzt Gallery, New York. *Rembrandt Collage.*

1993　Mimi Ferzt Gallery, New York. *Popov + Popov.*

Pasquale Iannetti Art Galleries, San Francisco. *Weird Monotypes.*

1992   Kentler International Drawing Space, New York.

1991   Warner Roberts Gallery, Palo Alto, California.

Arts Council of San Mateo, Belmont, California.

Central Exhibition Space of the Association of Fine Arts, Ukraine.

1990   University of California, Berkeley, California.

Allport Gallery, San Francisco.

1988   Kisgaleria, Pecs, Hungary.

2016   National Academy of Arts of Ukraine, Kiev, Ukraine. *Super Hero.*

2015–16   Long-Sharp Gallery, Indianapolis, Indiana.

2014   Imago Galleries, Palm Desert, California.

2013   Imago Galleries, Palm Desert, California.

2012   New Gallery / Thom Andriola, Houston, Texas.

Modernism Inc., San Francisco. *Summer selection.*

2011   Imago Galleries, Palm Desert, California.

2008   Peninsula Museum of Art, Belmont, California. *Beaux & Eros.*

2005   Sandy Carson Gallery, Denver, Colorado.

2004   Modernism Inc., San Francisco. *25th Anniversary Show.*

2003   Modernism Inc., San Francisco.

2002   Robert Berman Gallery, Santa Monica, California.

1998   Mimi Ferzt Gallery, New York. *Group Show.*

Diane Nelson Fine Art, Laguna Beach, California. *Contingent Reality.*

1997   Kismet Gallery, San Jose, California. *Group Show.*

Mimi Ferzt Gallery, New York. *Group Show.*

1996   Mimi Ferzt Gallery, New York. *Group Show.*

1995   Mimi Ferzt Gallery, New York. *Group Show.*

1994   Mimi Ferzt Gallery, New York. *Ascending Angels.*

de Saisset Museum, Santa Clara University, Santa Clara, California. *Ideal Landscapes.*

Kala Art Institute, Berkeley, California. *Fellowship Award.*

Aurobora Press, San Francisco. *The Figure.*

1993   California Crafts Museum, San Francisco. *Icons in Contemporary Art.*

J. Claramunt Gallery, New York. *Sacrifice.*

Olga Dollar Gallery, San Francisco. *Miniatures.*

Ruth Benjamin Fine Art, Napa Valley, California. *The Spirit Within.*

Davidson Galleries, Seattle, Washington. *Group Show.*

Smith Andersen Gallery, Palo Alto, California. *The Black & White Show.*

1992   Emeryville 6th Annual Exhibition, Emeryville, California.

Pasquale Iannetti Art Galleries, San Francisco. *12 Contemporary Artists.*

One Market Plaza, San Francisco. *Russian Art at Home & Abroad.*

1991   West Cal Bank, San Mateo, California. *Coming to America— World View Point.*

Ayzenberg Gallery, Los Angeles.

1990   International Gallery, Minneapolis, Minnesota.

Warner Roberts Gallery, Palo Alto, California.

Olga Dollar Gallery, San Francisco. *Summer Selection.*

Gabriel Gallery, Vienna, Austria.

Cultural Center, Belgrade, Yugoslavia. *Summer 90.*

Premio Internazionale per l'Incisione, Biella, Italy.

1989   Kyoto Gallery, Kyoto, Japan.

Kisgaleria Pecs, Pecs, Hungary.

1988   Ukraine Institute of America, New York. *Contemporary Art of the Ukraine.*

New Jersey Institute of Technology, Newark. *Modern Art of the Ukraine.*

Crane Club Gallery, New York.

Bologna, Italy. *New Direction in the USSR.*

Sapporo, Japan. *Graphic Biennial.*

Vilnius, Lithuania. *Five Artists Prints.*

1987   Brunswiker Pavillon, Kiel, Germany. *Young Artists.*

Rostock, Germany. *Twelfth Biennial of Norway, Scandinavia, and the Baltic States.*

Moscow, Russia. *Sixth International Youth Festival.*

Manezh, Moscow, Russia. *70 Years of the Great October.*

1986   Manezh, Moscow, Russia. *We Are Building Communism.*

Manezh, Moscow, Russia. *Benefactors of Culture in the Fight for Peace.*

1985   Moscow, Russia. *Ukraine Art Exhibition in Manezh.*

1984   Academy of Arts of the USSR, Leningrad, Russia. *All-Union Young Artists.*

1983   Dortmund, Germany. *Young Soviet Artists Exhibition.*

Kabul, Afghanistan. *Young Soviet Artists Exhibition.*

Academy of Arts of the USSR (now the Russian Academy of Arts), Moscow, Russia. *All-Union Young Artists.*

1982   Bologna, Italy. *Bologna Children's Book Fair Exhibition.*

1992   Kala Art Institute, Berkeley, California.

1991   Smith-Andersen Editions, Palo Alto, California.

1990   Djerassi Foundation, Woodside, California.

1980, 1983–89   Senezh Artists' Residence, Moscow, Russia.

1980–82, 1984–86   Republic Sednev Artists' Residence, Chernigov, Ukraine.

2016   National Academy of Arts of Ukraine, Foreign Member.

1988   Silver Medal, Academy of Arts of the USSR.

1984–86   Grant from the Association of Fine Arts of the USSR.

1981–84   Grant from the Academy of Arts of the USSR.

INDEX OF DETAILS

Details of the following paintings appear on pages i–xxix, xxxv, and 221–240.

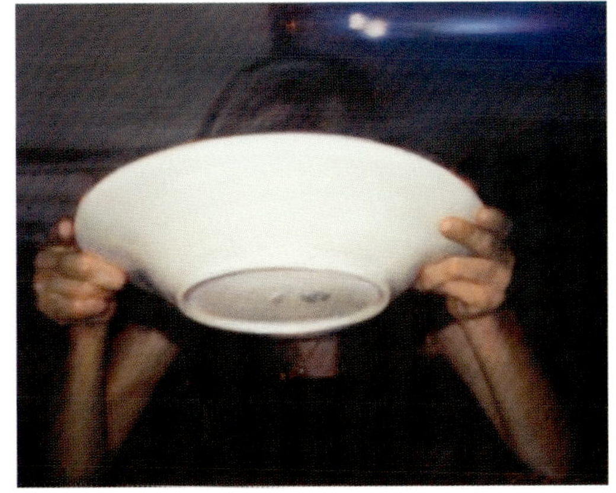

RAN, 2014   *p. i*

OIL ON CANVAS, 32 × 40 IN.

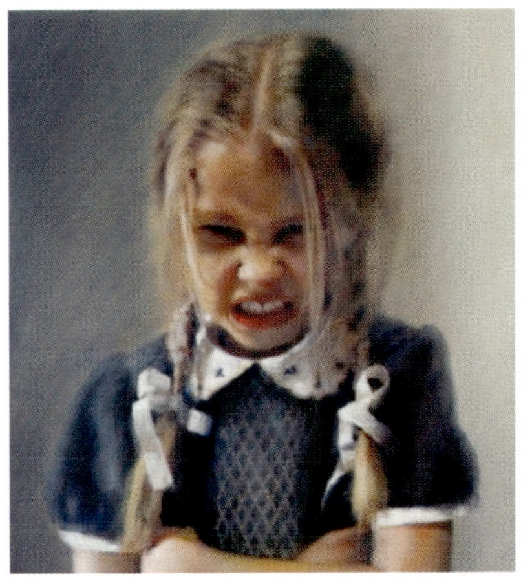

GROUCHY GIRL, 2006   *p. ii*

OIL ON CANVAS, 38 × 35 IN.

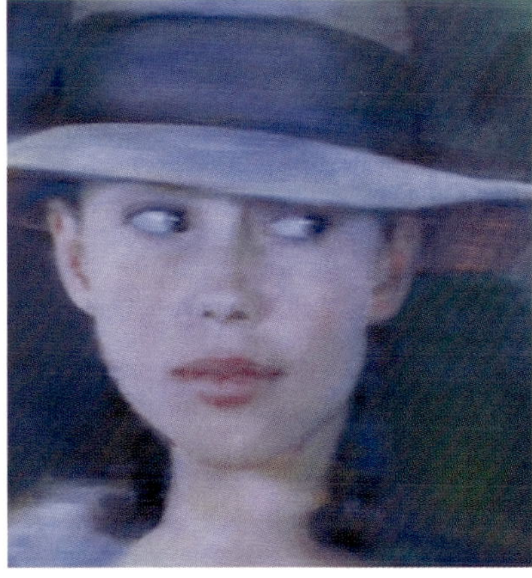

LOVER, 2010   *p. iii*

OIL ON CANVAS, 20 × 20 IN.

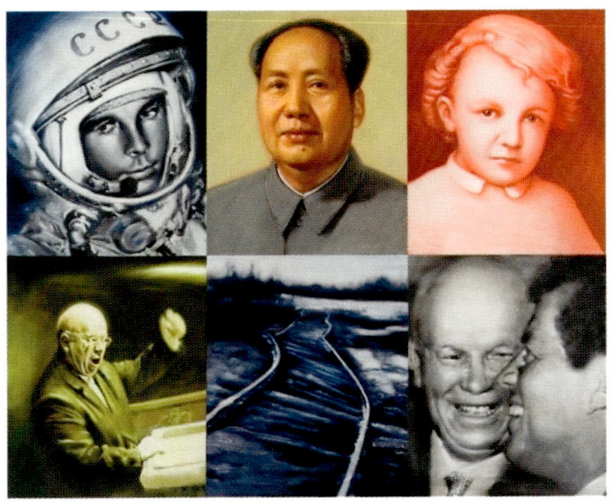

TIME, 2009   *pp. iv, xii, xix, 228*

OIL ON CANVAS, 48 × 60 IN.

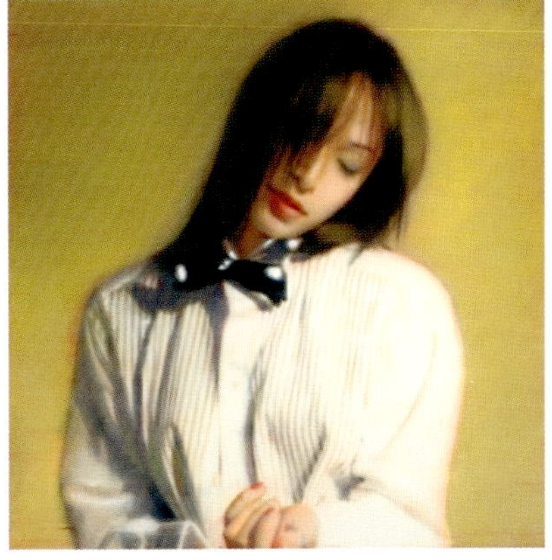

BOW TIE, 2010   *p. v*

OIL ON CANVAS, 40 × 40 IN.

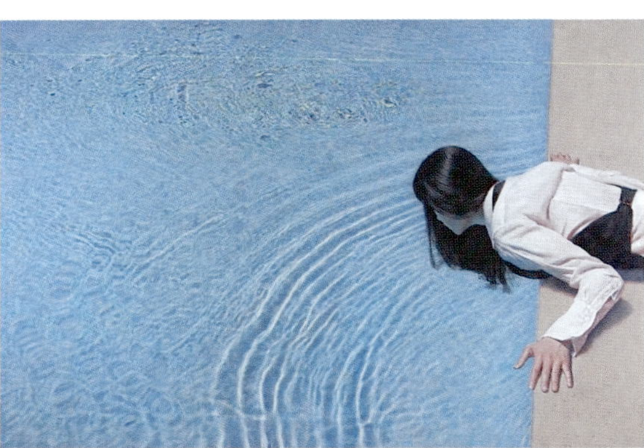

LOOKING INTO, 2009   *pp. vi–vii*

OIL ON CANVAS, 48 × 72 IN.

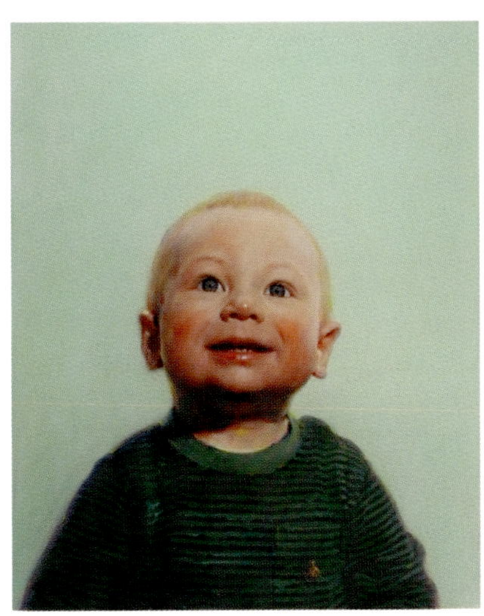

IAN, 2014   *p. viii*

OIL ON CANVAS, 30 × 24 IN.

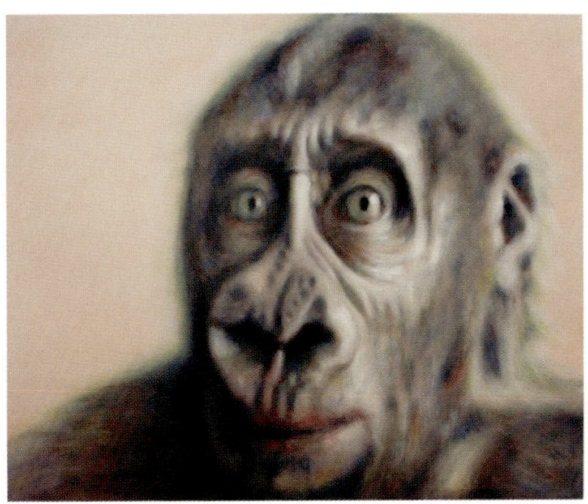

APE ON ORANGE, 2015   *p. ix*

OIL ON CANVAS, 40 × 50 IN.

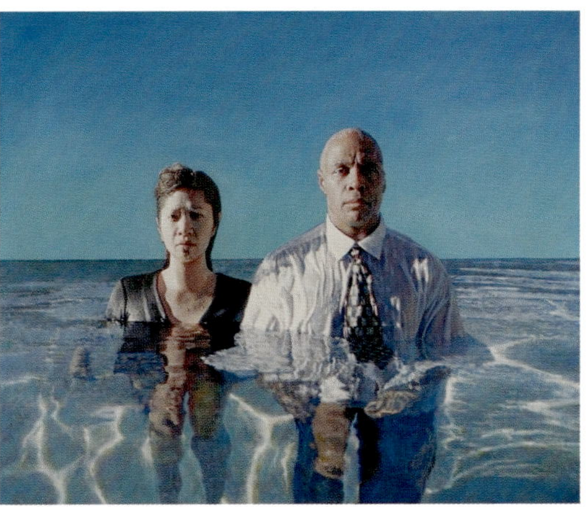

EMPTY SKY, 2009   *pp. x–xi*

OIL ON CANVAS, 37 × 45 IN.

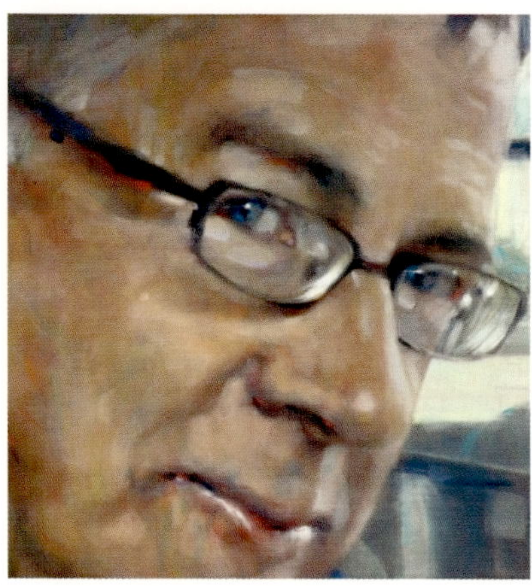

PORTRAIT OF ROGER EVANS, 2007 *p. xiii*
OIL ON CANVAS, 22 × 22 IN.

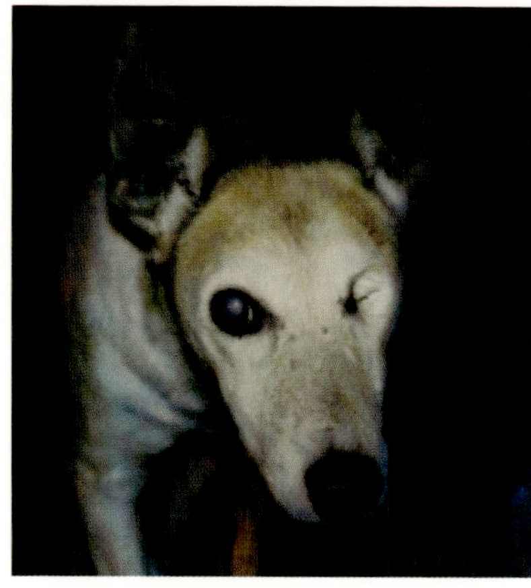

BLIND AND DEAF, 2014 *p. xiv*
OIL ON CANVAS, 30 × 28 IN.

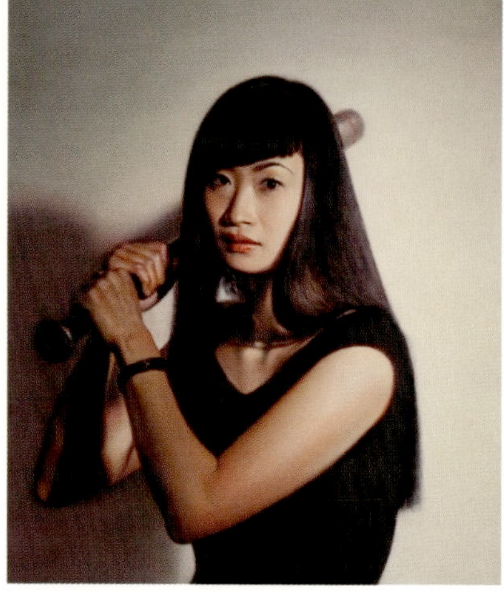

FRIDAY NIGHT, 2011 *p. xv*
OIL ON CANVAS, 45 × 37 IN.

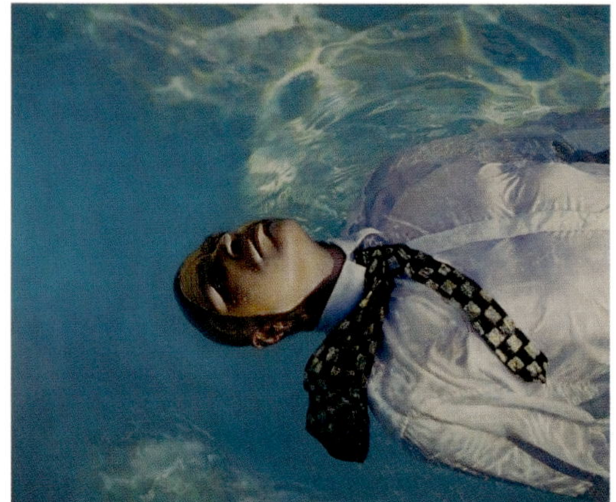

MARE, 2009 *p. xvi*
OIL ON CANVAS, 37 × 45 IN.

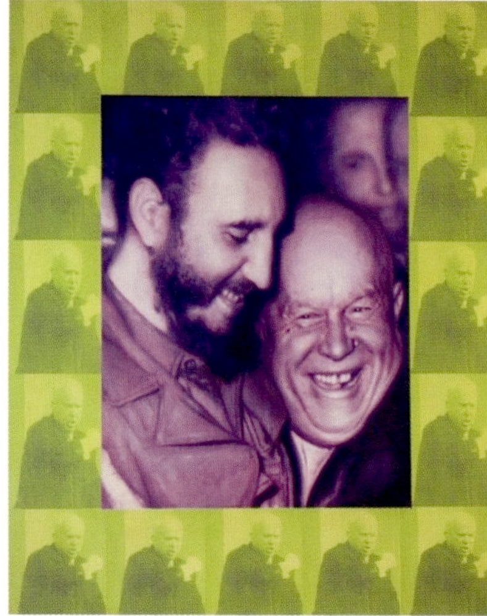

CASTRO-KHRUSHCHEV, 2008 *p. xvii*
OIL ON CANVAS, 45 × 37 IN.

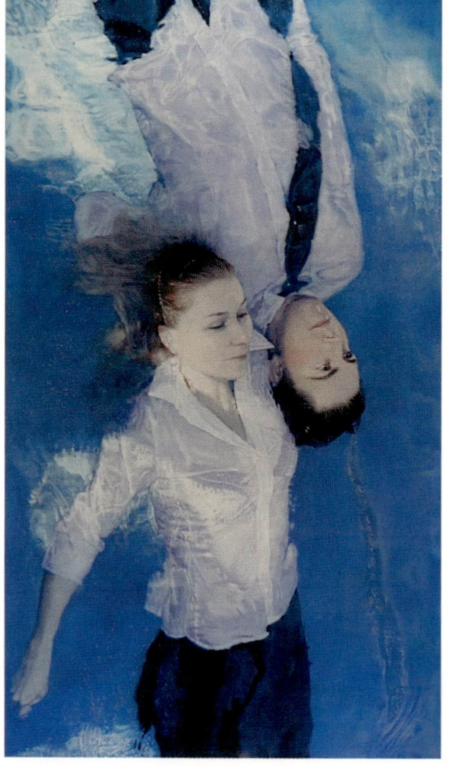

PINK, 2010 *p. xxi*
OIL ON CANVAS, 75 × 43 IN.

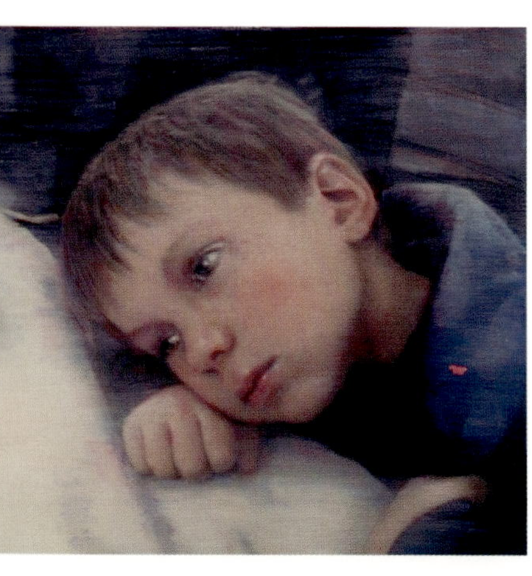

IVKO, 2017 *p. xviii*
OIL ON CANVAS, 40 × 44 IN.

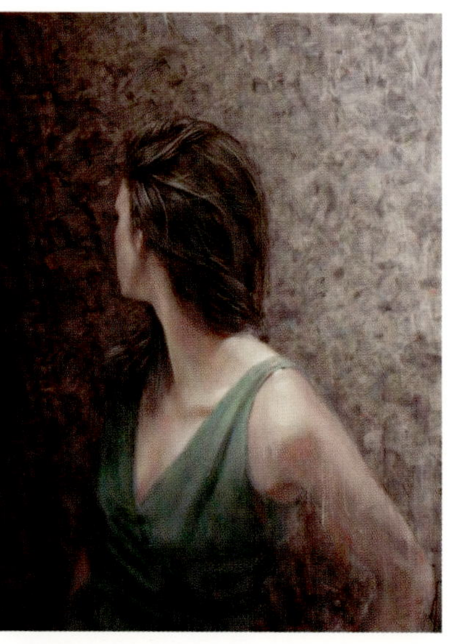

JESSIQUA, 2017 *p. xx*
OIL ON CANVAS, 70 × 52 IN.

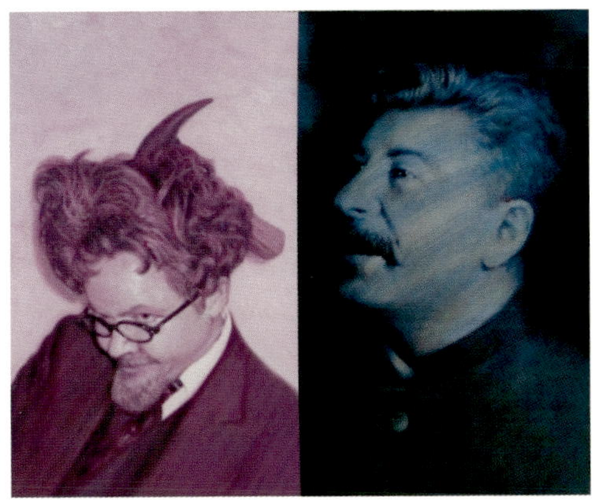
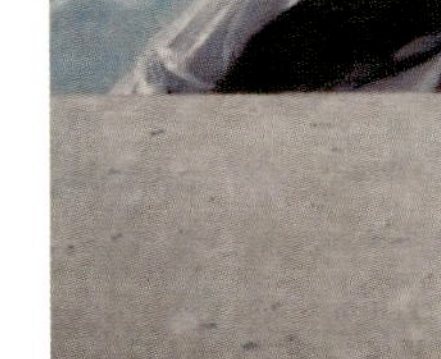
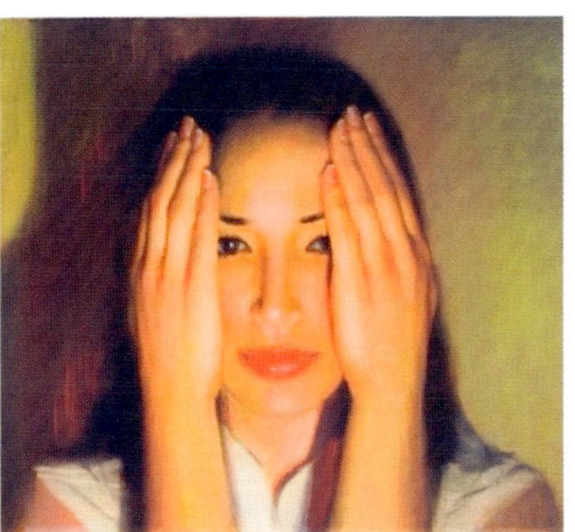
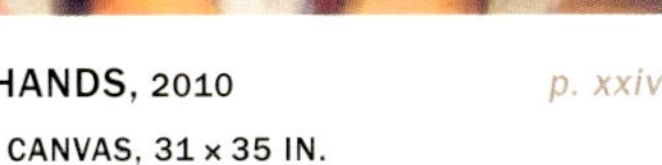

BEGINNING, 2010   *pp. xxii, xxvi*
OIL ON CANVAS, 37 × 45 IN.

SUN, 2012   *p. xxiii*
OIL ON CANVAS, 40 × 50 IN.

TWO HANDS, 2010   *p. xxiv*
OIL ON CANVAS, 31 × 35 IN.

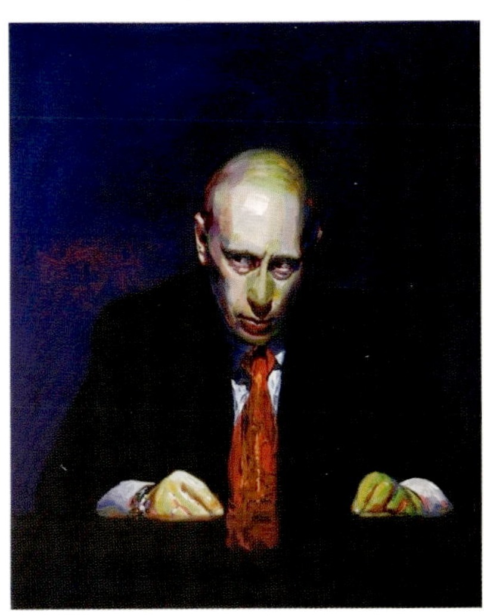
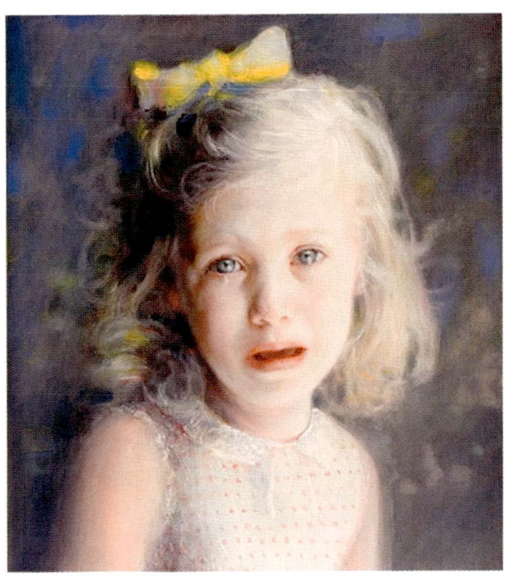
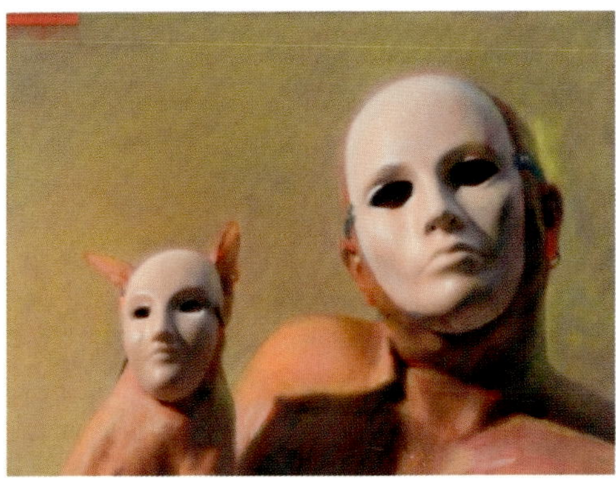

PUTIN, 2008   *p. xxv*
OIL ON CANVAS, 45 × 37 IN.

NATALIA, 2012   *p. xxvii*
OIL ON CANVAS, 38 × 35 IN.

VENICE, 2009   *p. xxviii*
OIL ON CANVAS, 37 × 45 IN.

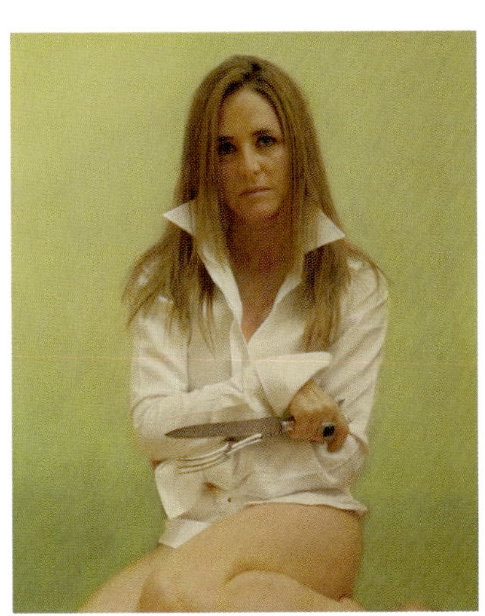
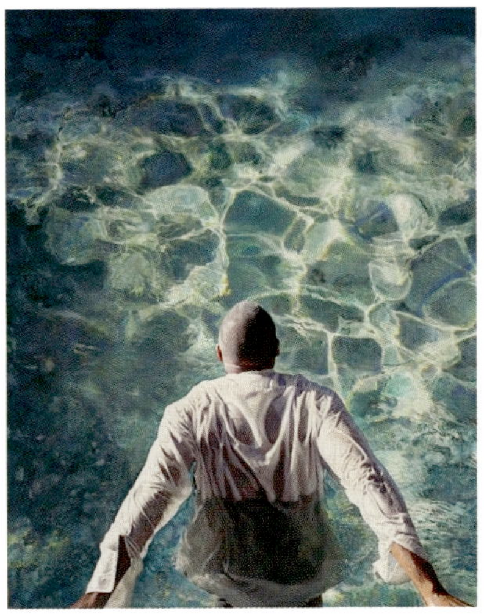
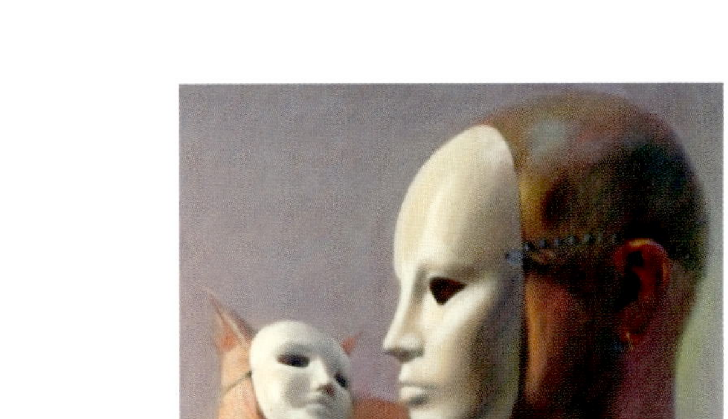

JILL RITCHIE, 2008   *p. xxix*
OIL ON CANVAS, 45 × 37 IN.

FROM . . . TO . . . , 2009   *p. xxxv*
OIL ON CANVAS, 45 × 37 IN.

THE PHANTOM OF THE OPERA, 2009   *p. 221*
OIL ON CANVAS, 36 × 42 IN.

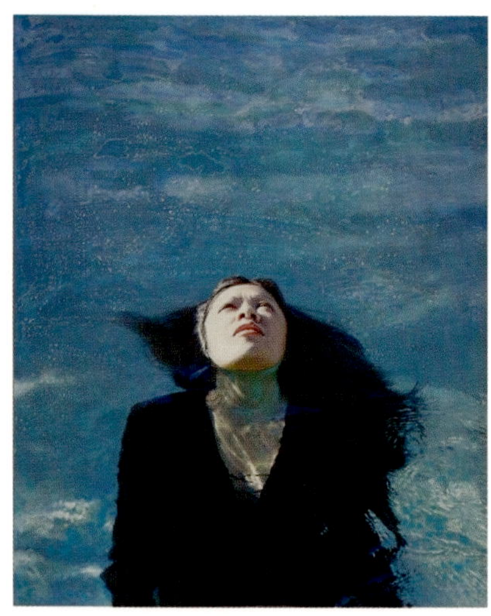

SUZY, 2010 *p. 222*
OIL ON CANVAS, 45 × 37 IN.

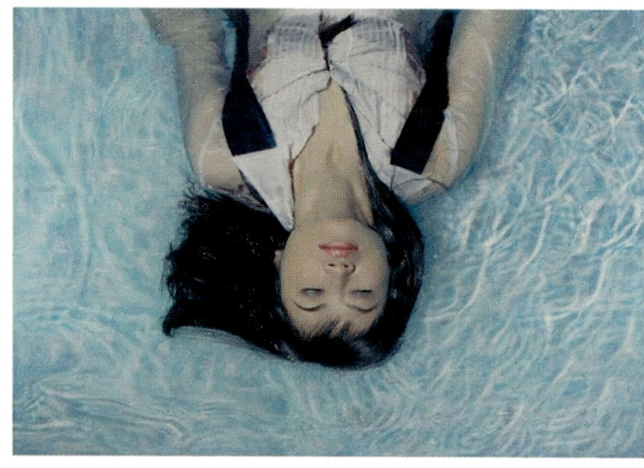

UPSIDE DOWN, 2009 *p. 223*
OIL ON CANVAS, 50 × 67 IN.

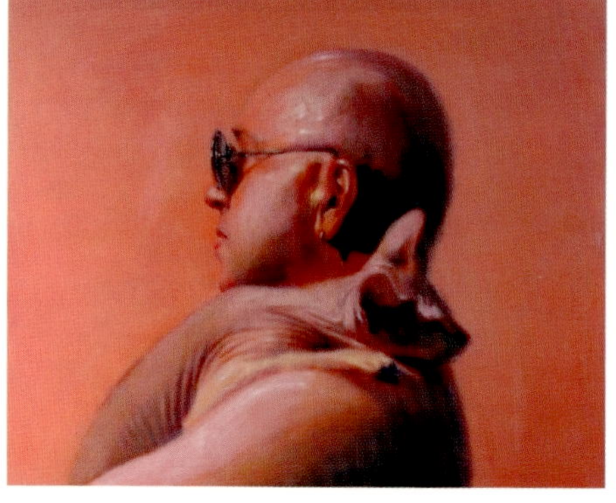

ME AND CAT, 2008 *p. 224*
OIL ON CANVAS, 49 × 40 IN.

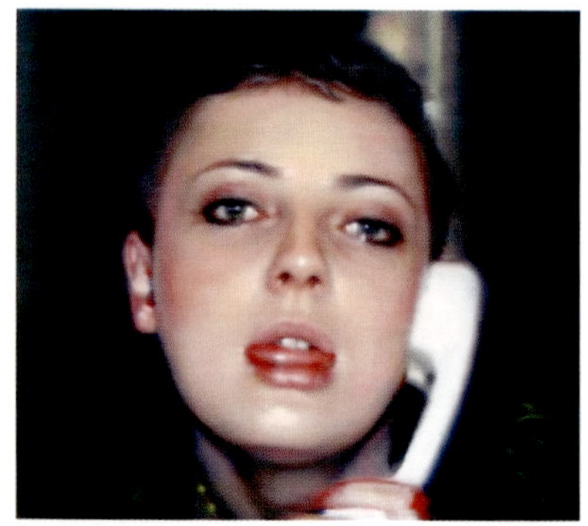

TELEPHONE CALL, 2010 *p. 225*
OIL ON CANVAS, 37 × 42 IN.

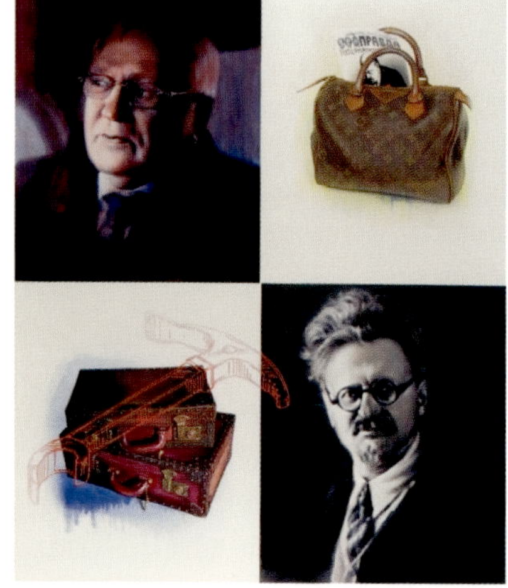

FIRST CLASS TRAVELING, 2008 *p. 226*
OIL ON CANVAS, 50 × 42 IN.

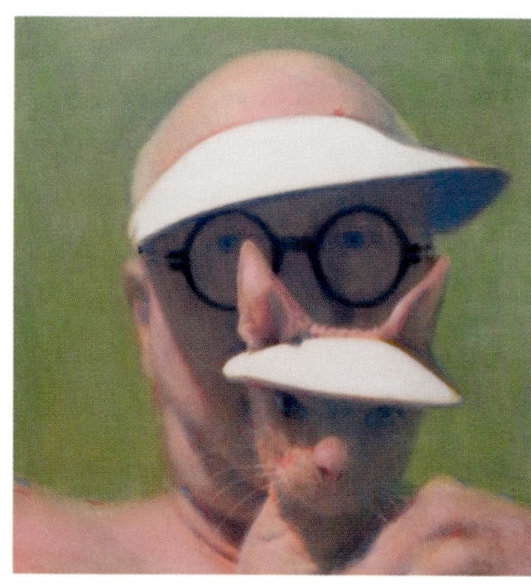

TWO FACE, 2007 *p. 227*
OIL ON CANVAS, 38 × 36 IN.

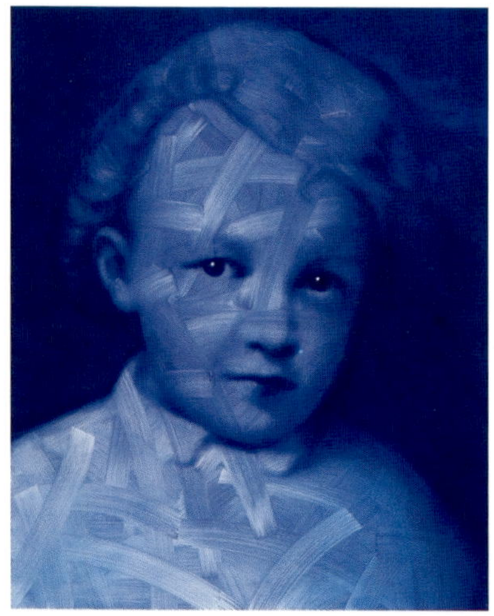

BABY LENIN IN BLUE, 2009 *p. 229*
OIL ON CANVAS, 35 × 29 IN.

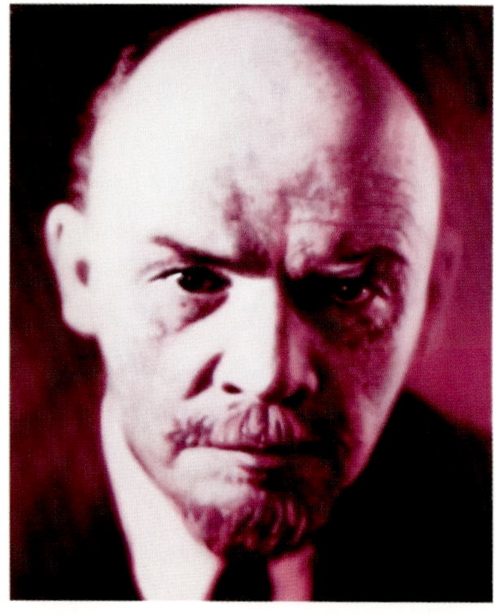

LENIN, 2009 *p. 230*
OIL ON CANVAS, 35 × 29 IN.

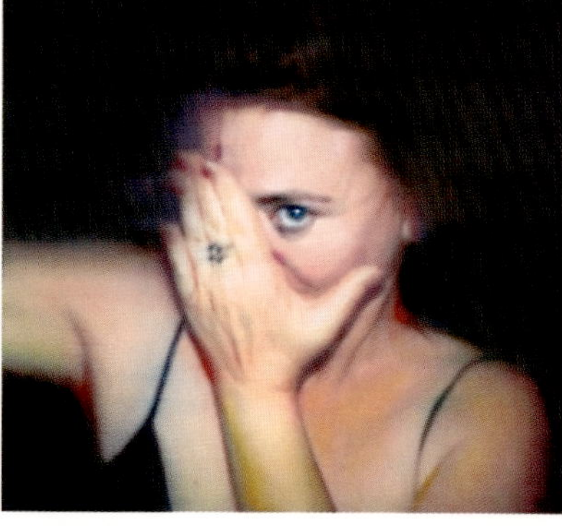

WOMAN COVERING AN EYE, 2005 *p. 231*
OIL ON CANVAS, 32 × 33½ IN.

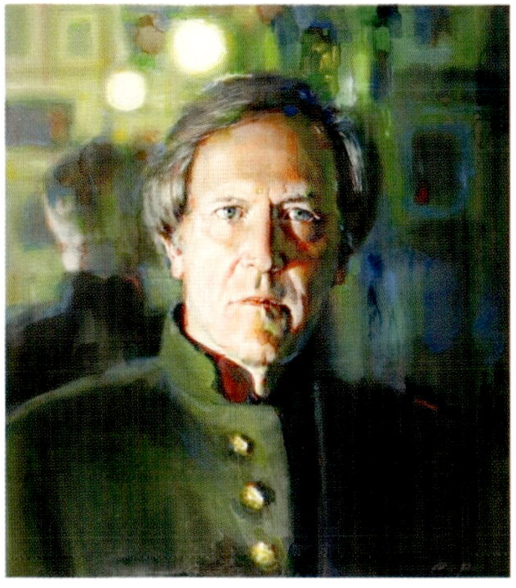

ROBERT JOHNSON, 2010 *p. 232*
OIL ON CANVAS, 40 × 36 IN.

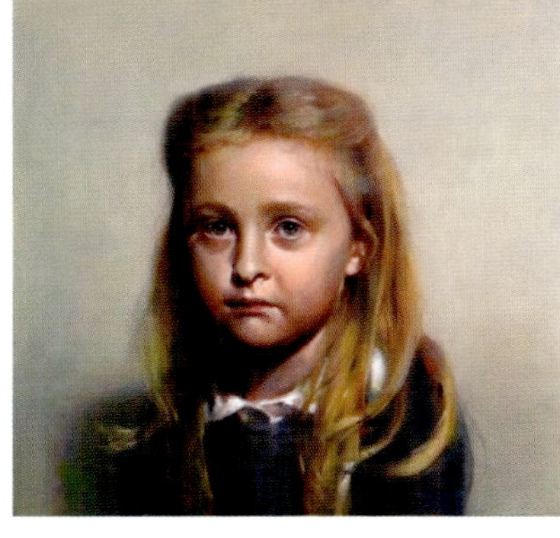

LILLIAN, 2007 *p. 233*
OIL ON CANVAS, 35 × 37 IN.

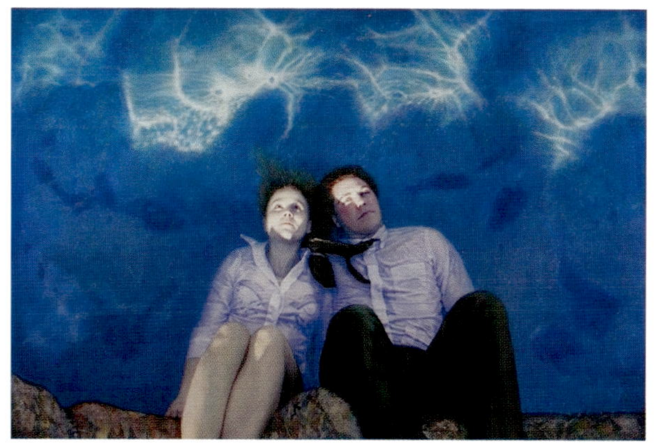

MUTUAL DREAMS, 2009 *p. 234*
OIL ON CANVAS, 48 × 72 IN.

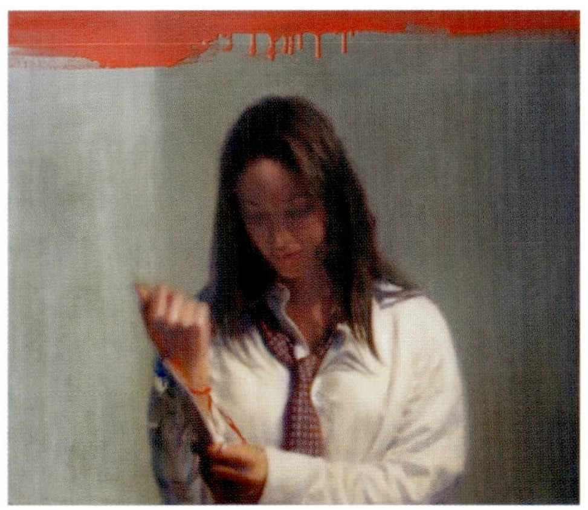

KABBALAH, 2008 *p. 235*
OIL ON CANVAS, 32 × 39 IN.

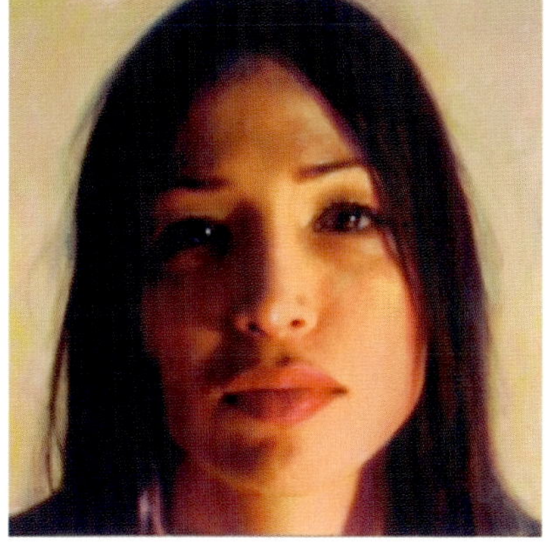

LIPS, 2010 *p. 236*
OIL ON CANVAS, 32 × 30 IN.

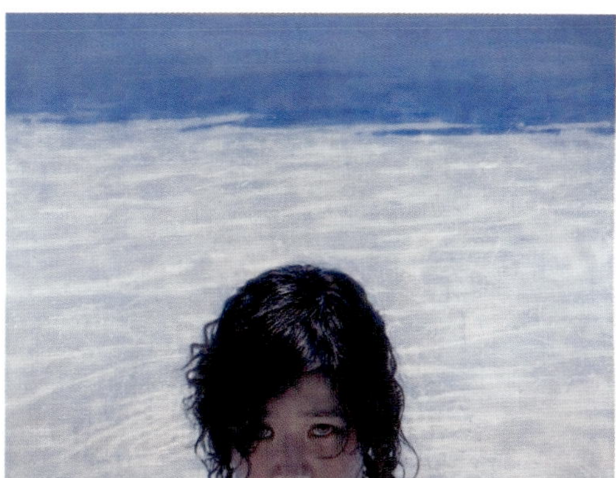

ICE, 2008 *p. 237*
OIL ON CANVAS, 30 × 40 IN.

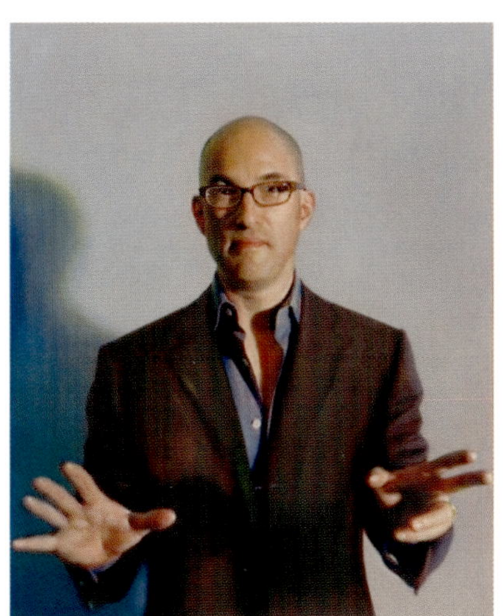
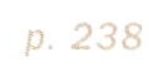

ERIC MCDOUGAL, 2008 *p. 238*
OIL ON CANVAS, 45 × 37 IN.

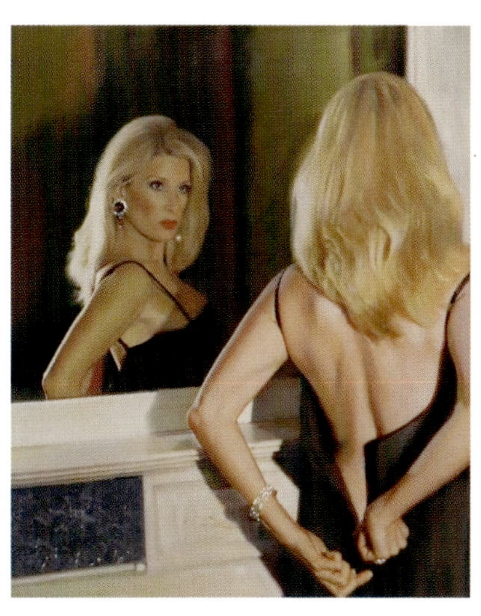

KIMBERLY BAKKER, 2008 *p. 239*
OIL ON CANVAS, 45 × 37 IN.

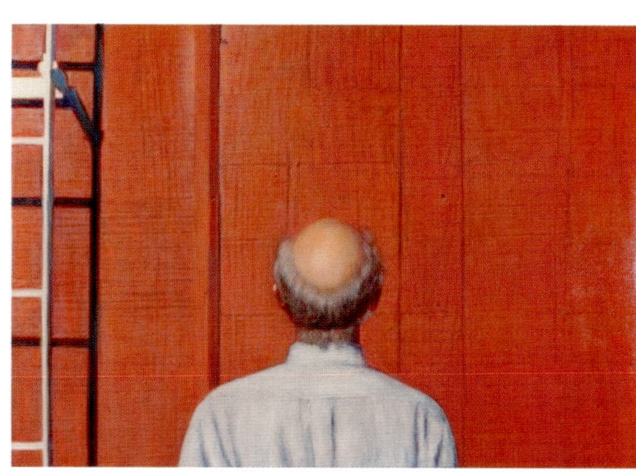

MOSCOW, 2008 *p. 240*
OIL ON CANVAS, 34 × 50 IN.

I thought documenting Valentin's work on video would be a difficult undertaking. First, I assumed all painters were solitary artists, and therefore Valentin might not be willing to give access to my camera and its inevitably intrusive ways. Second, he is a very close friend, and therefore I might fail in my objectivity with him and his art (after all, I wasn't going to make an advertisement). Third, I'm a narrative filmmaker who tries to tell my own fictional stories, so a documentary film would be a new challenge for me. As interesting as Valentin is as a person, friend, and artist, what would be the STORY that I would be telling?

"Stop speculating, stop worrying, and start rolling the camera!" I said one day to my inner documentarian.

After two years shooting at many different locations including three gallery openings, filming numerous on-camera interviews with collectors, curators, art critics, friends, fans, and associates, and, yes, spending many, many hours at Valentin's studio while he put paint on canvas in total solitude (except for me with my camera), we ended up creating tons of footage.

And the most pleasantly surprising part of it all was that Valentin turned out to be a delight to collaborate with: no demands, no temper tantrums, no interference with what I needed to do. I attribute this to his vast knowledge, wisdom, and unwavering discipline to respect another art form different from the one he is a master of. What a joy it was to find that out about him during this journey.

CELIK KAYALAR

DIRECTOR, *VALENTIN POPOV, FACE*

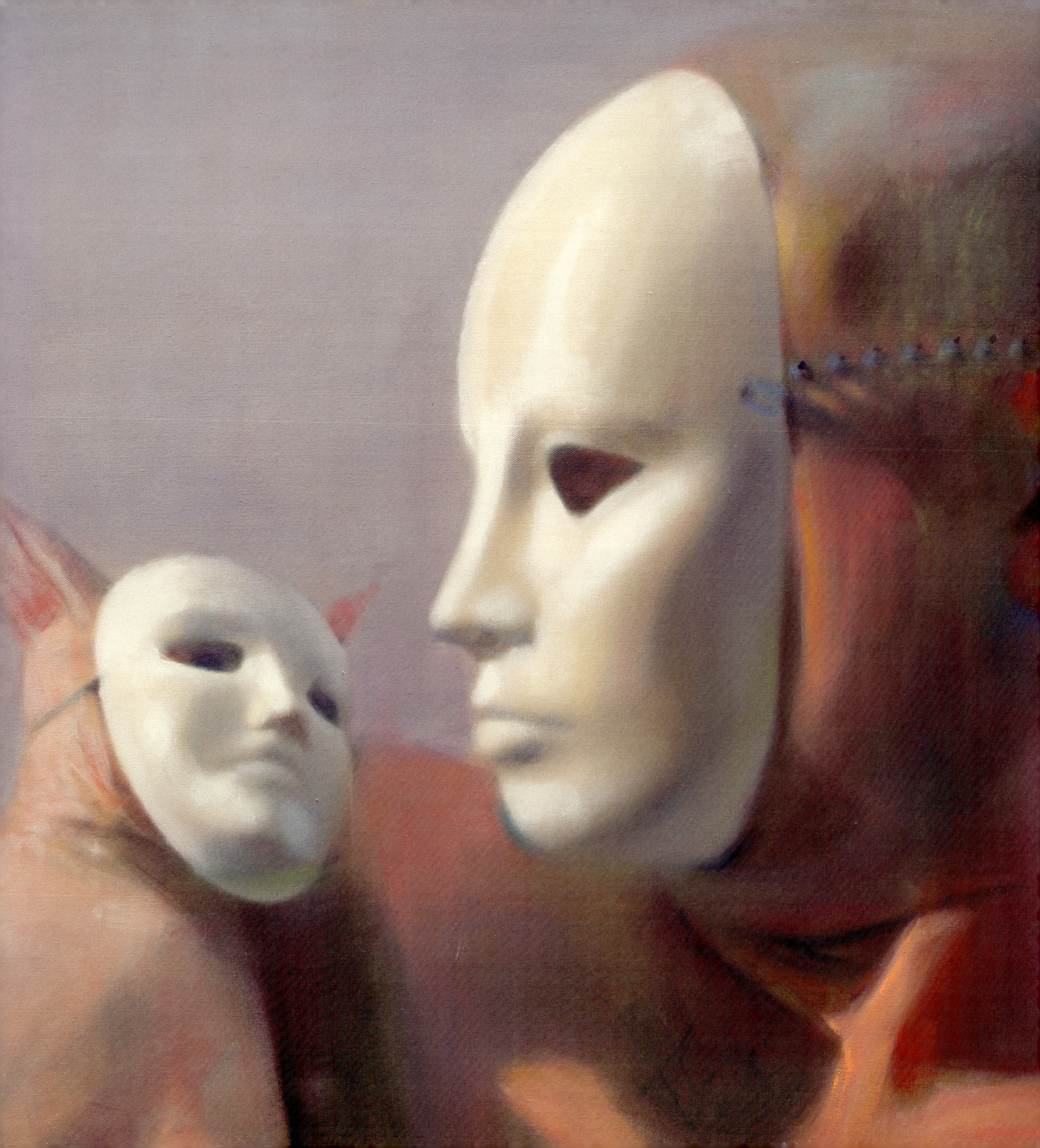

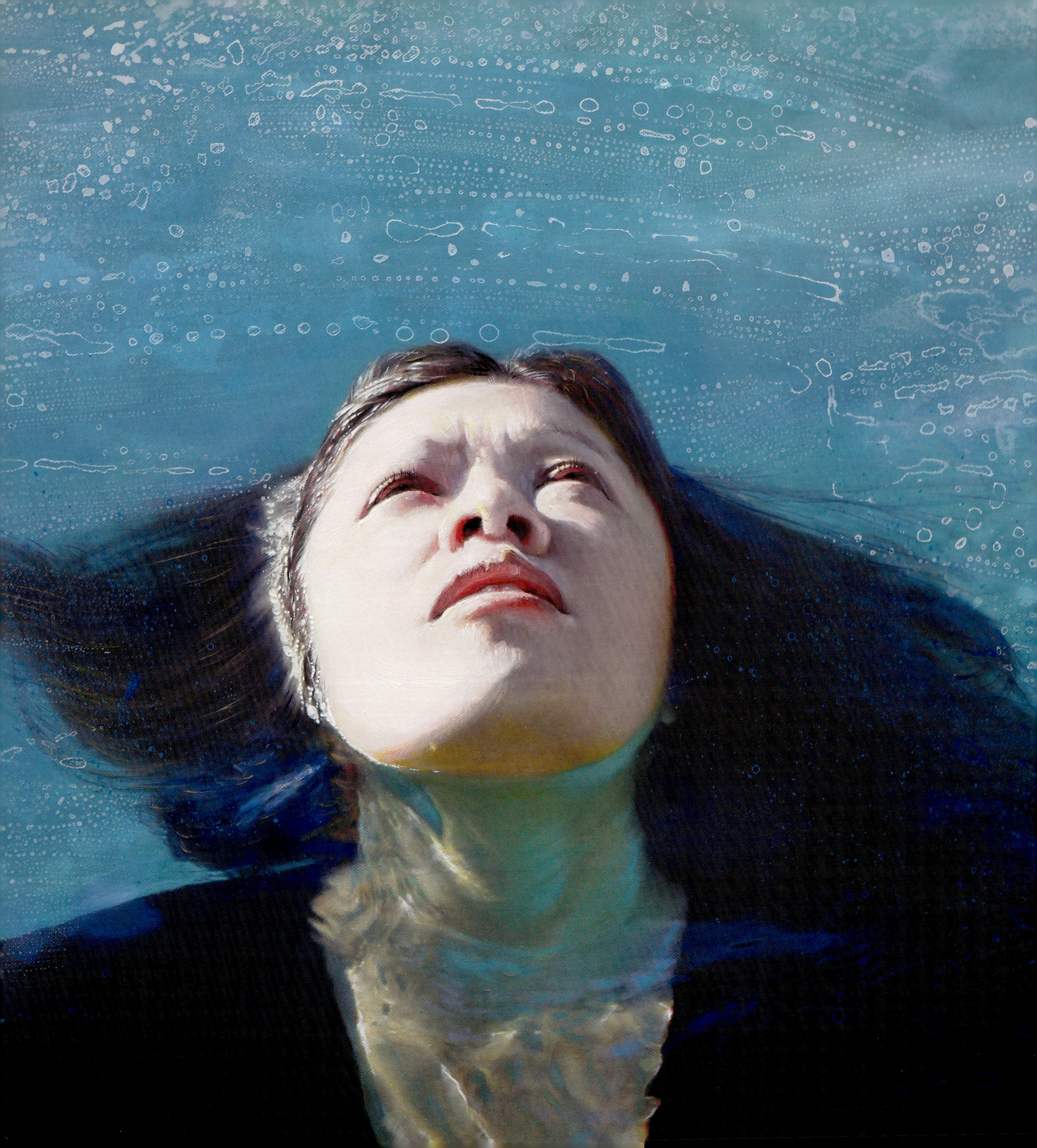

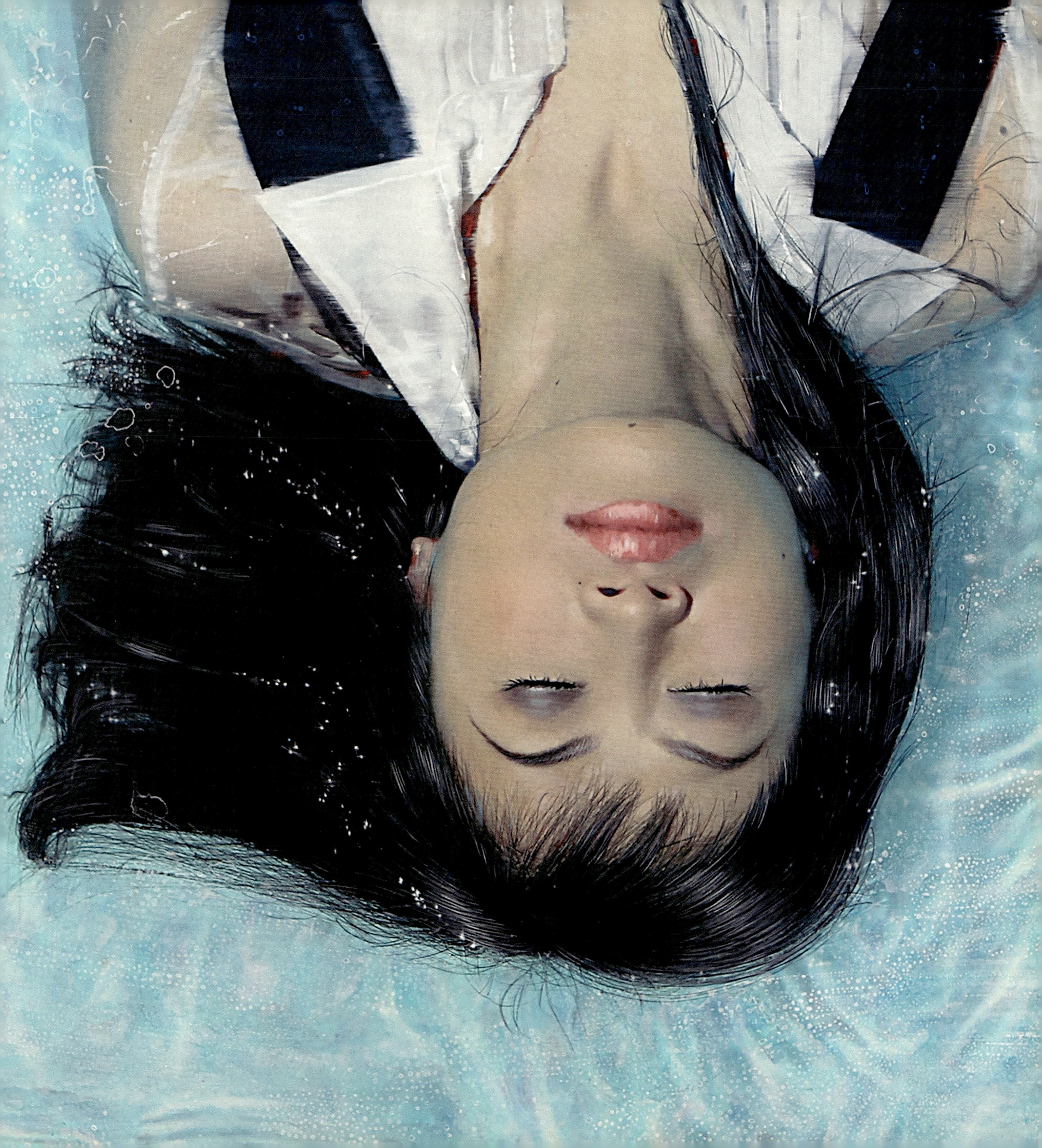

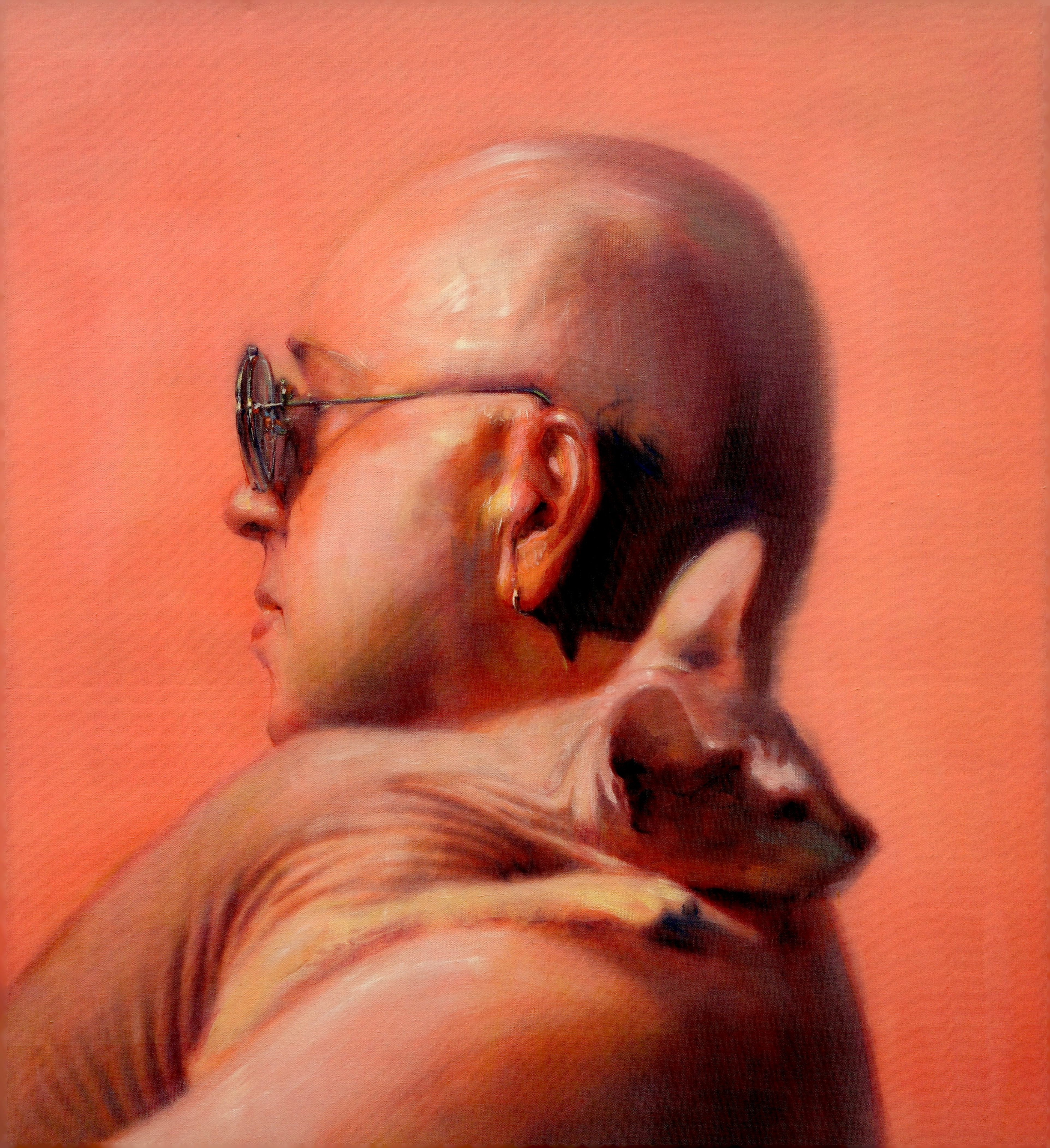

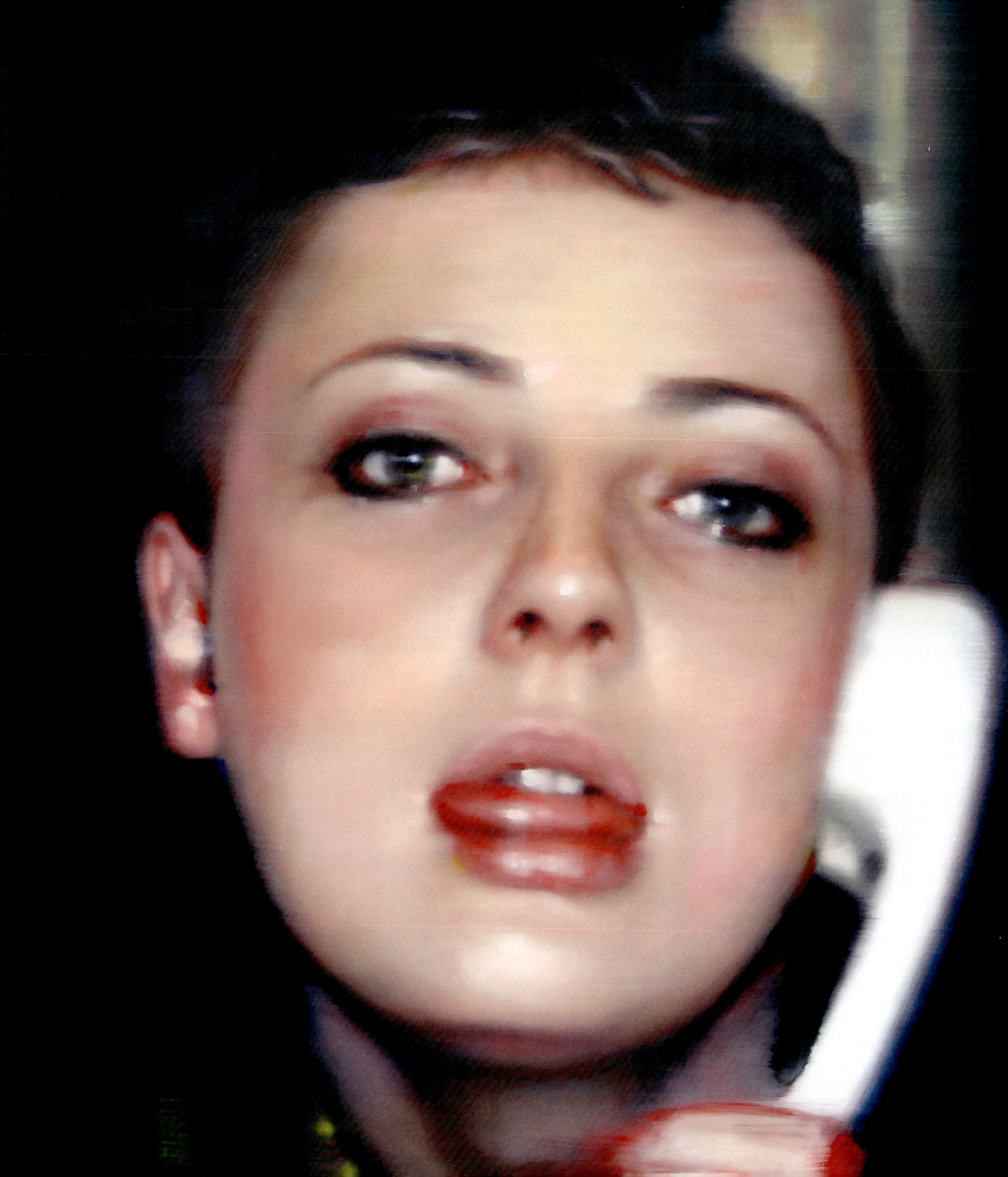

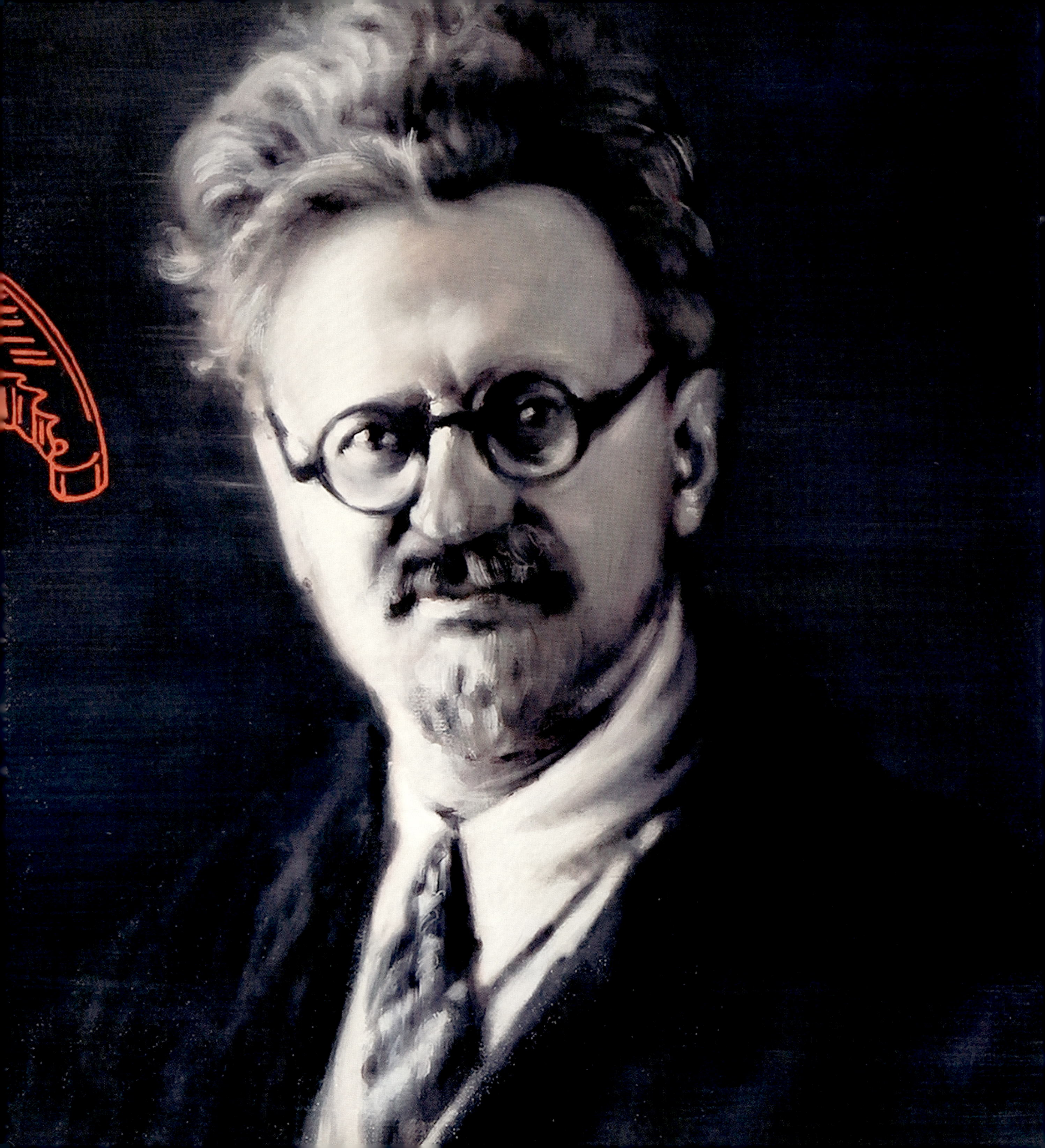

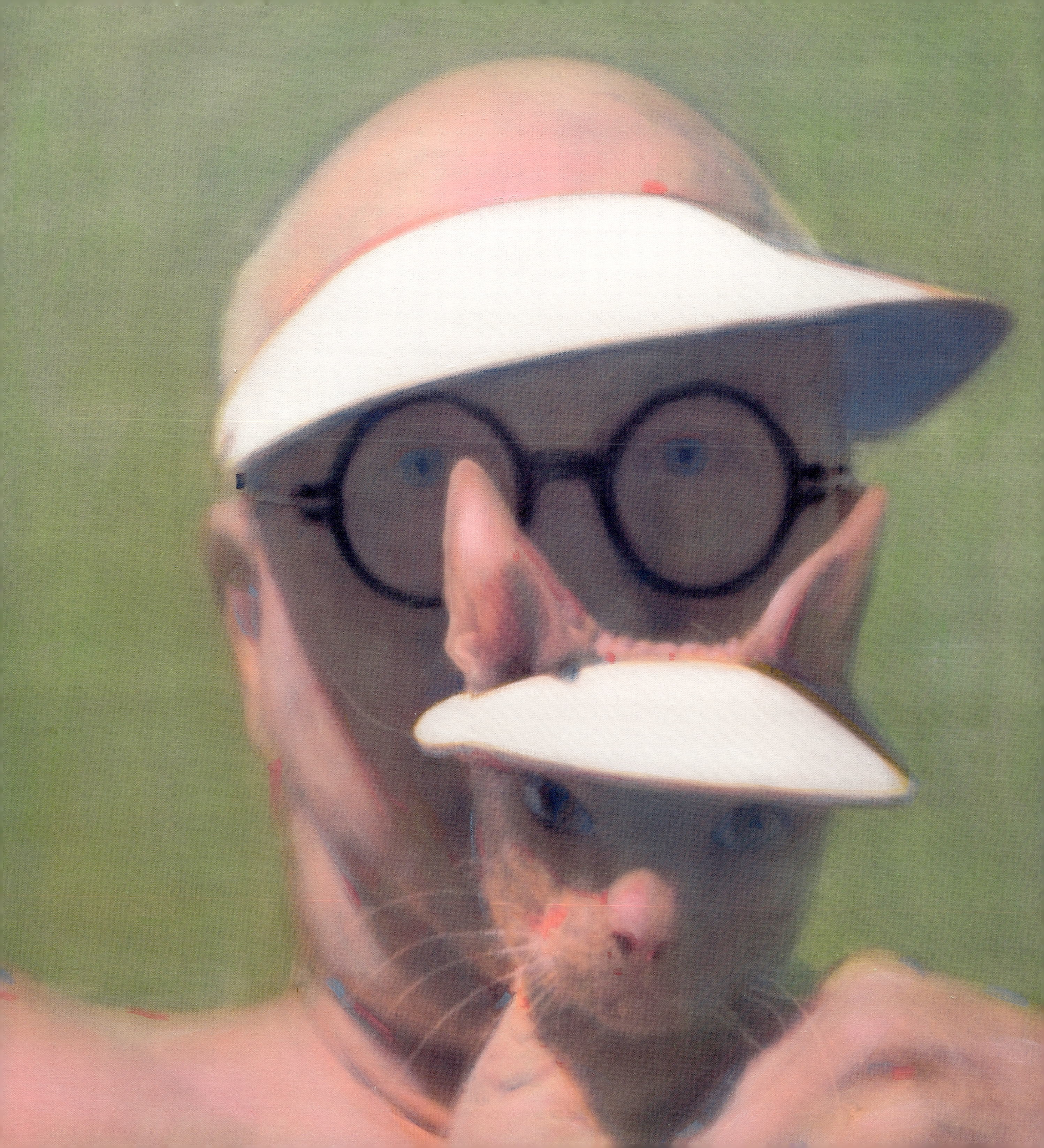

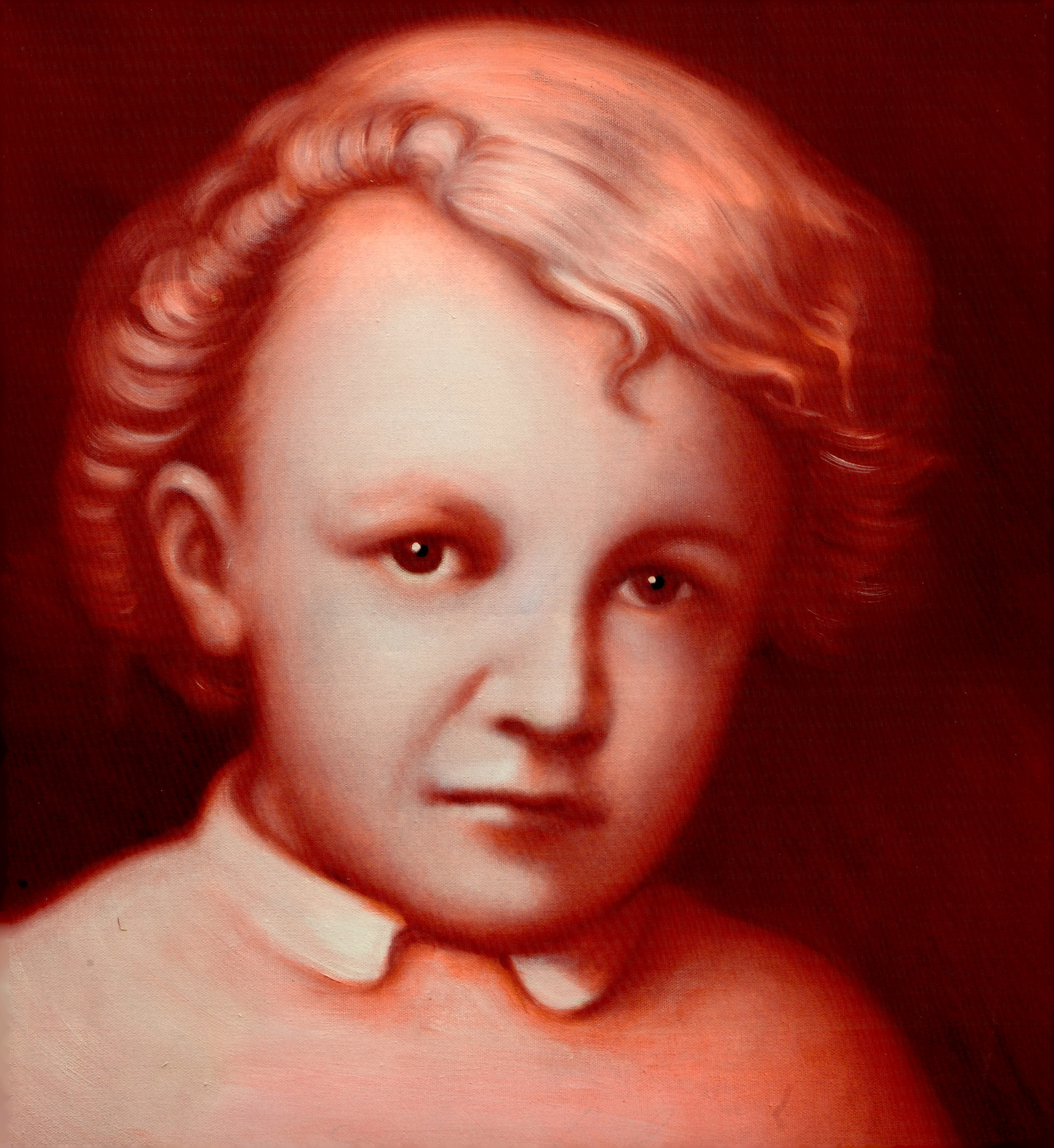

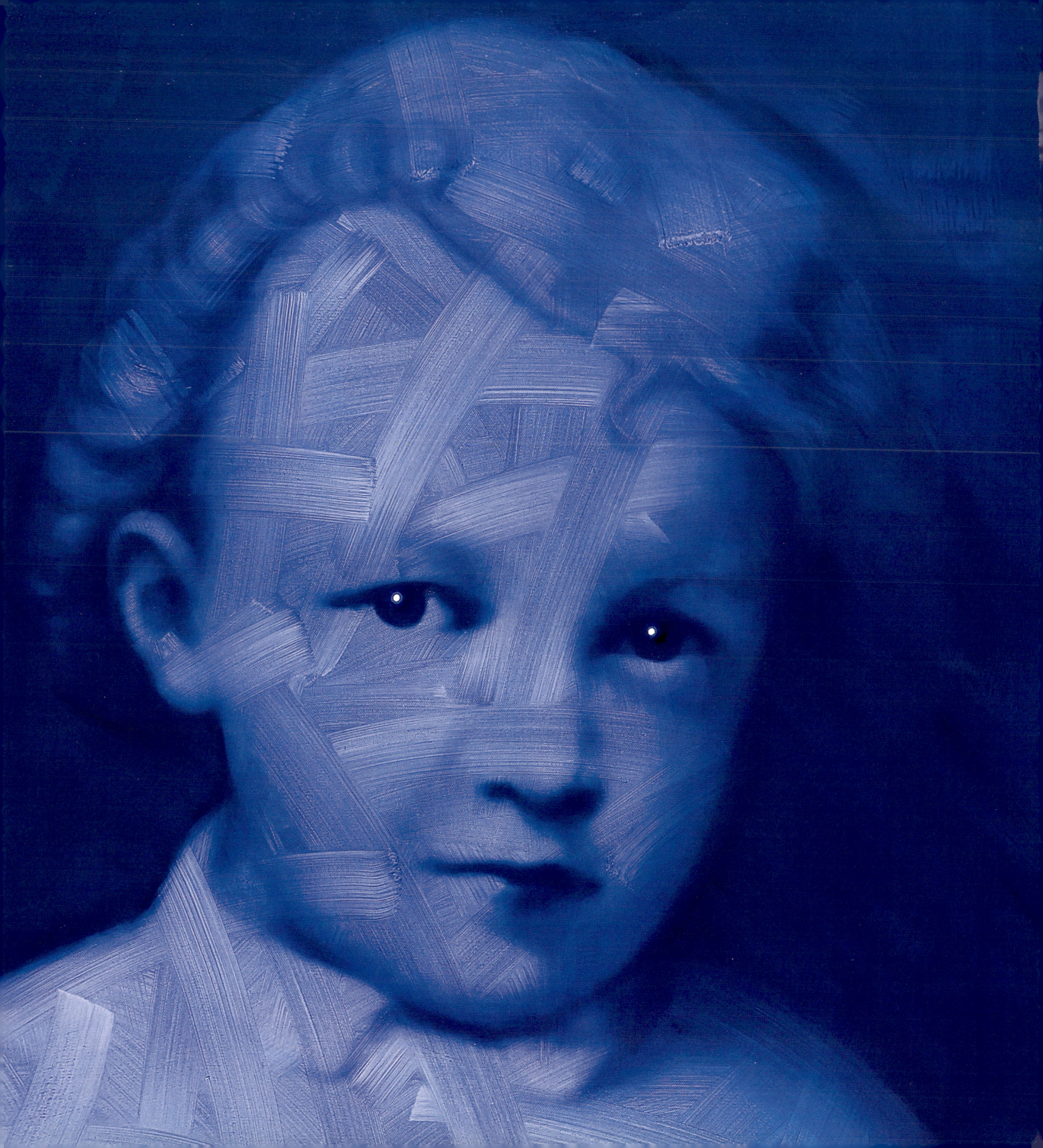

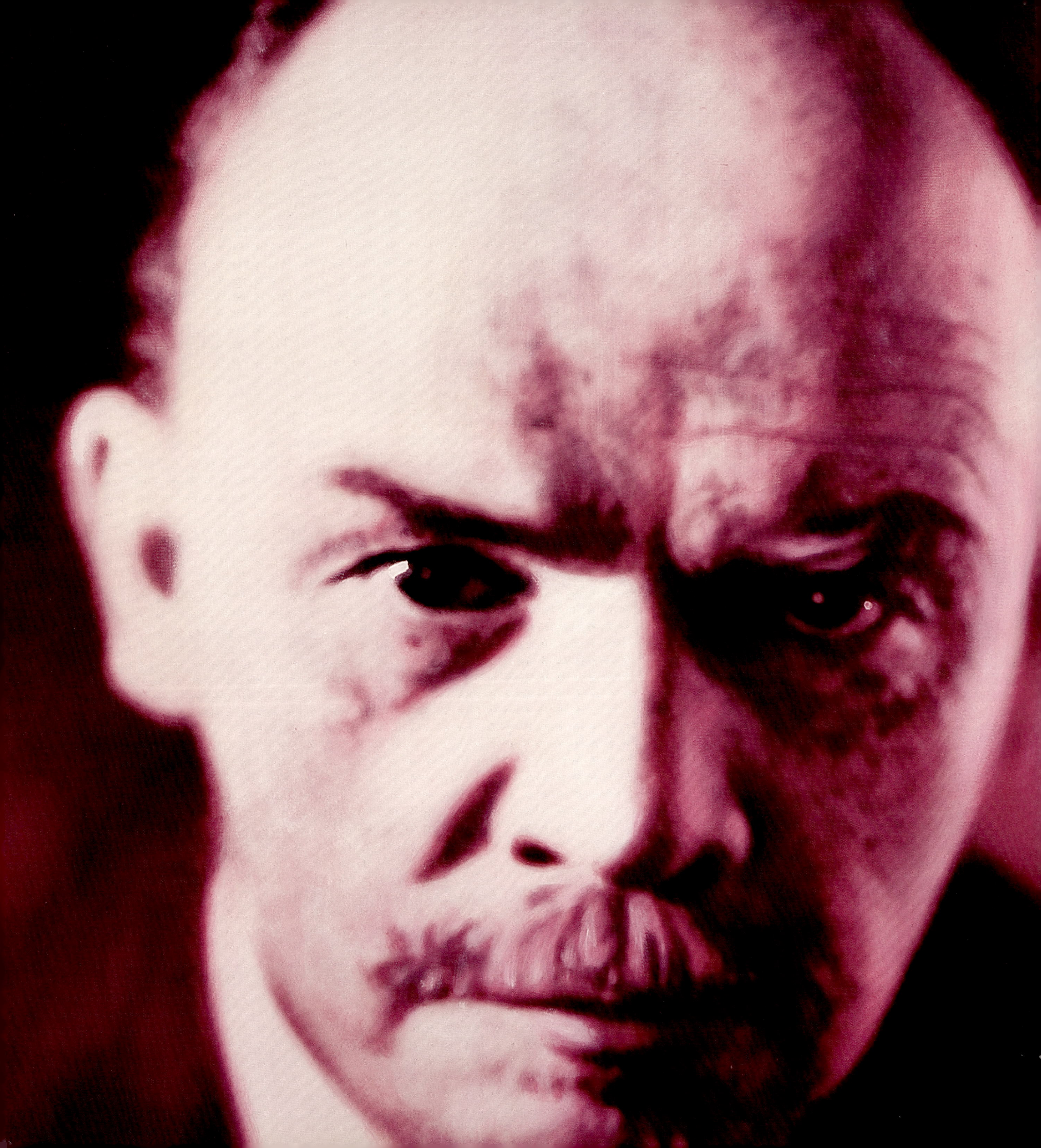

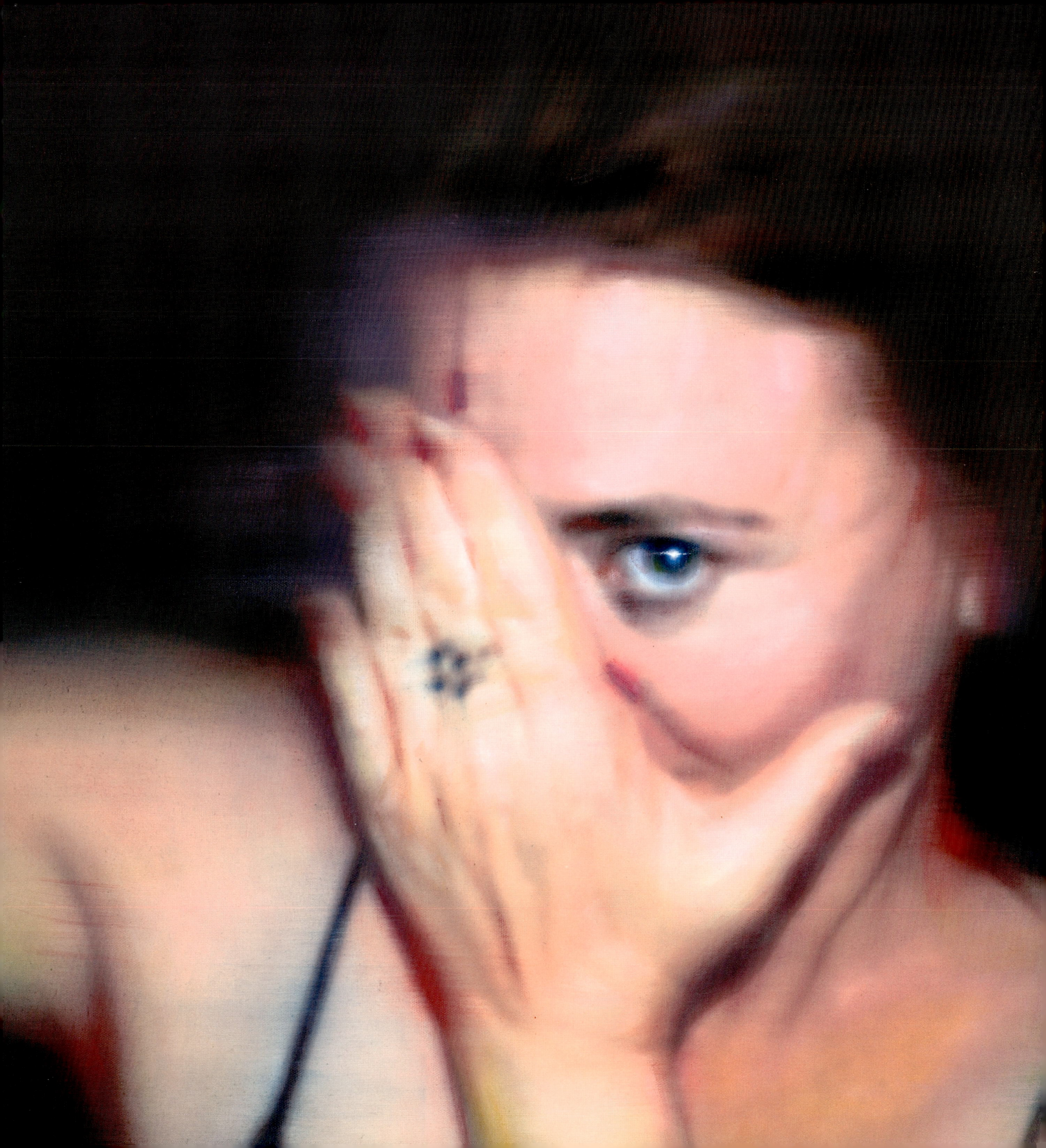

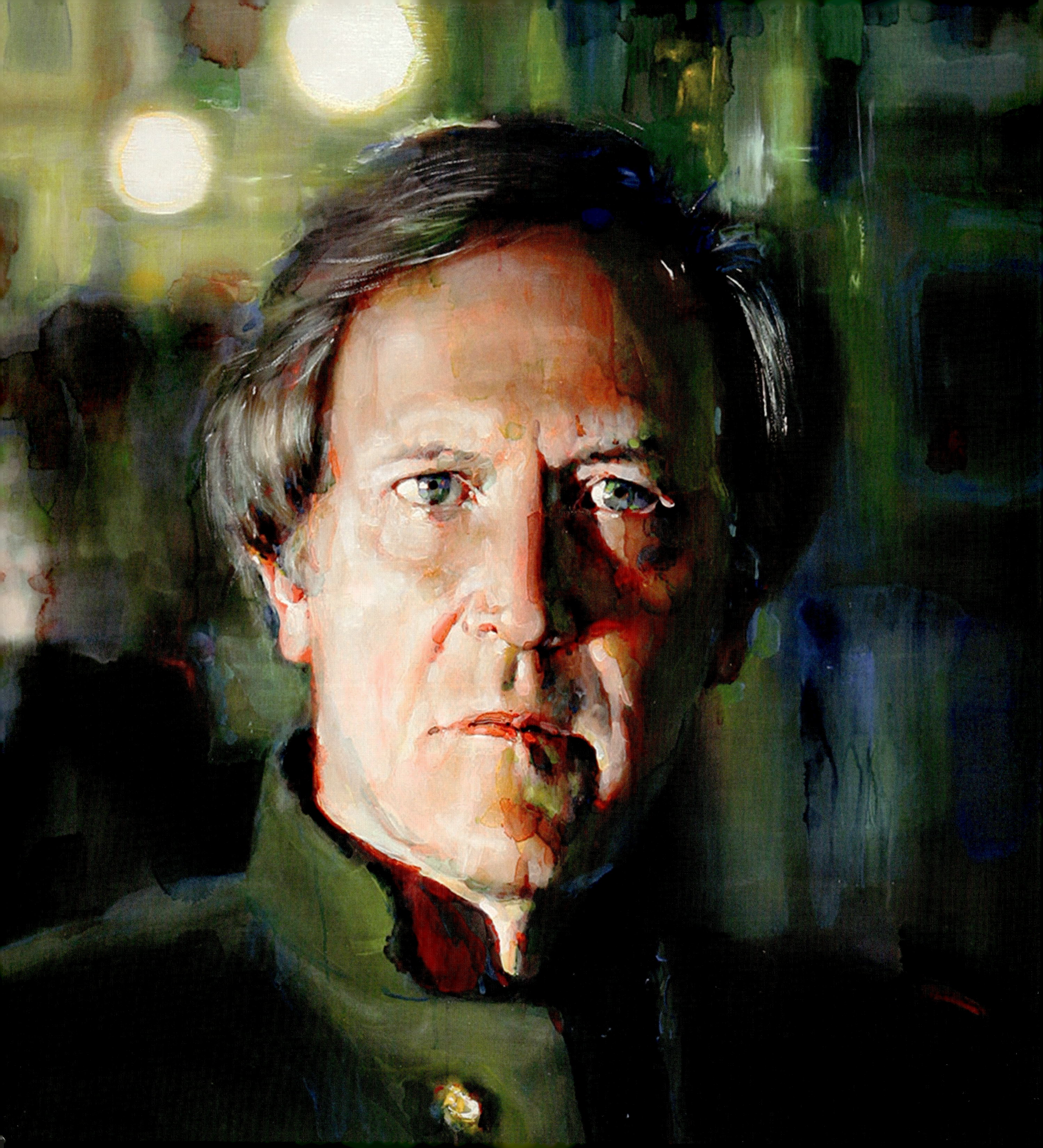

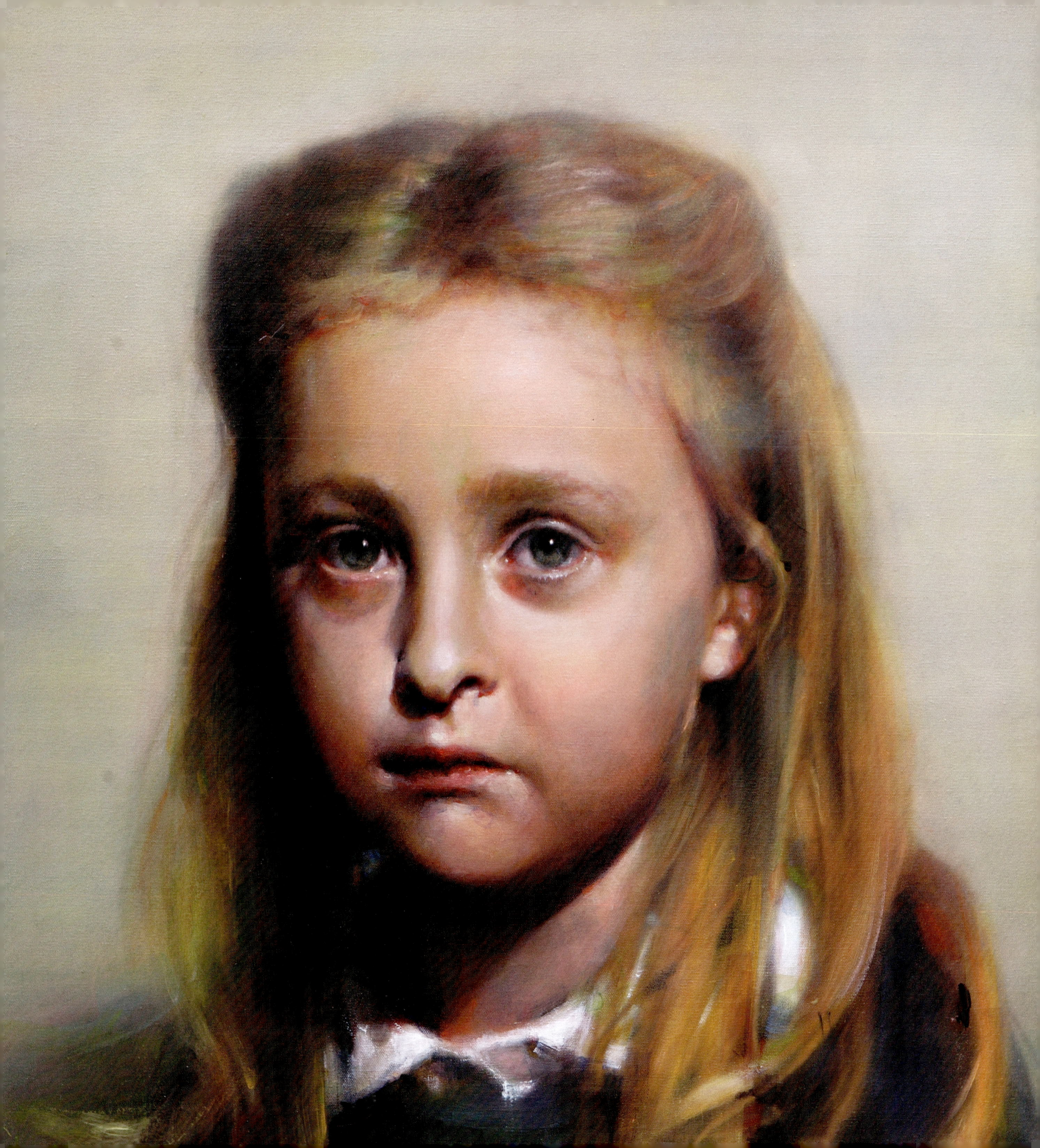

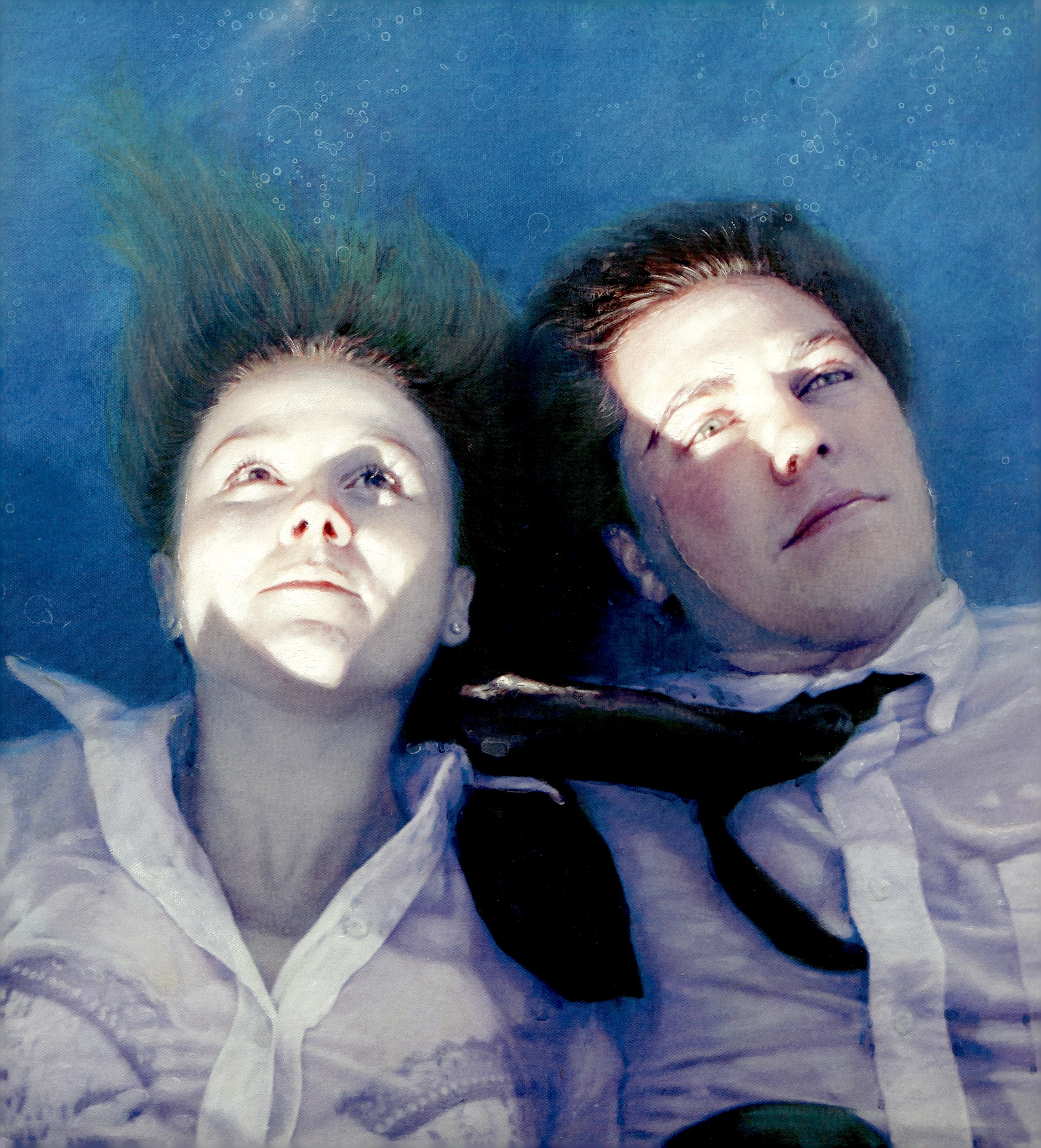

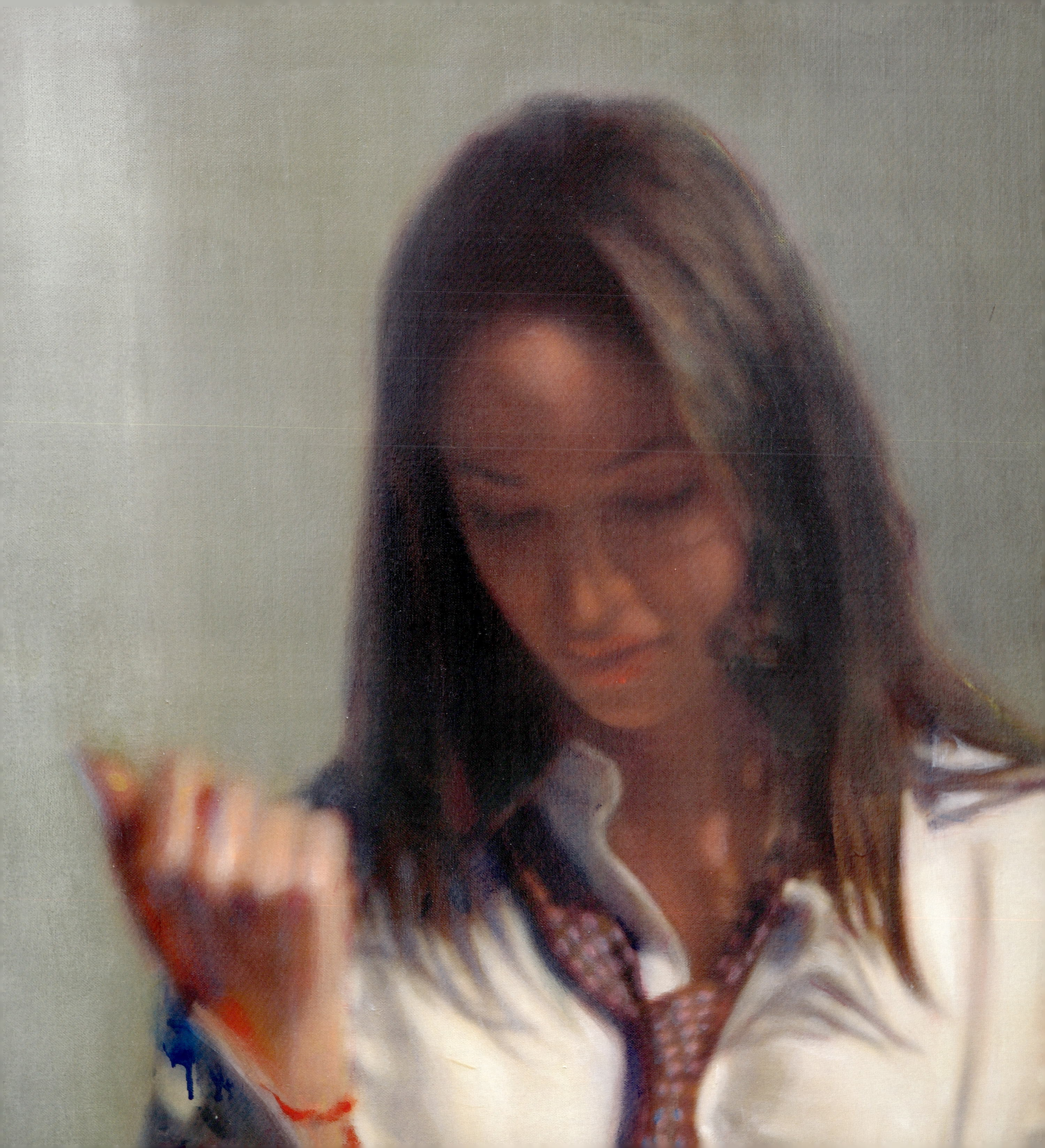

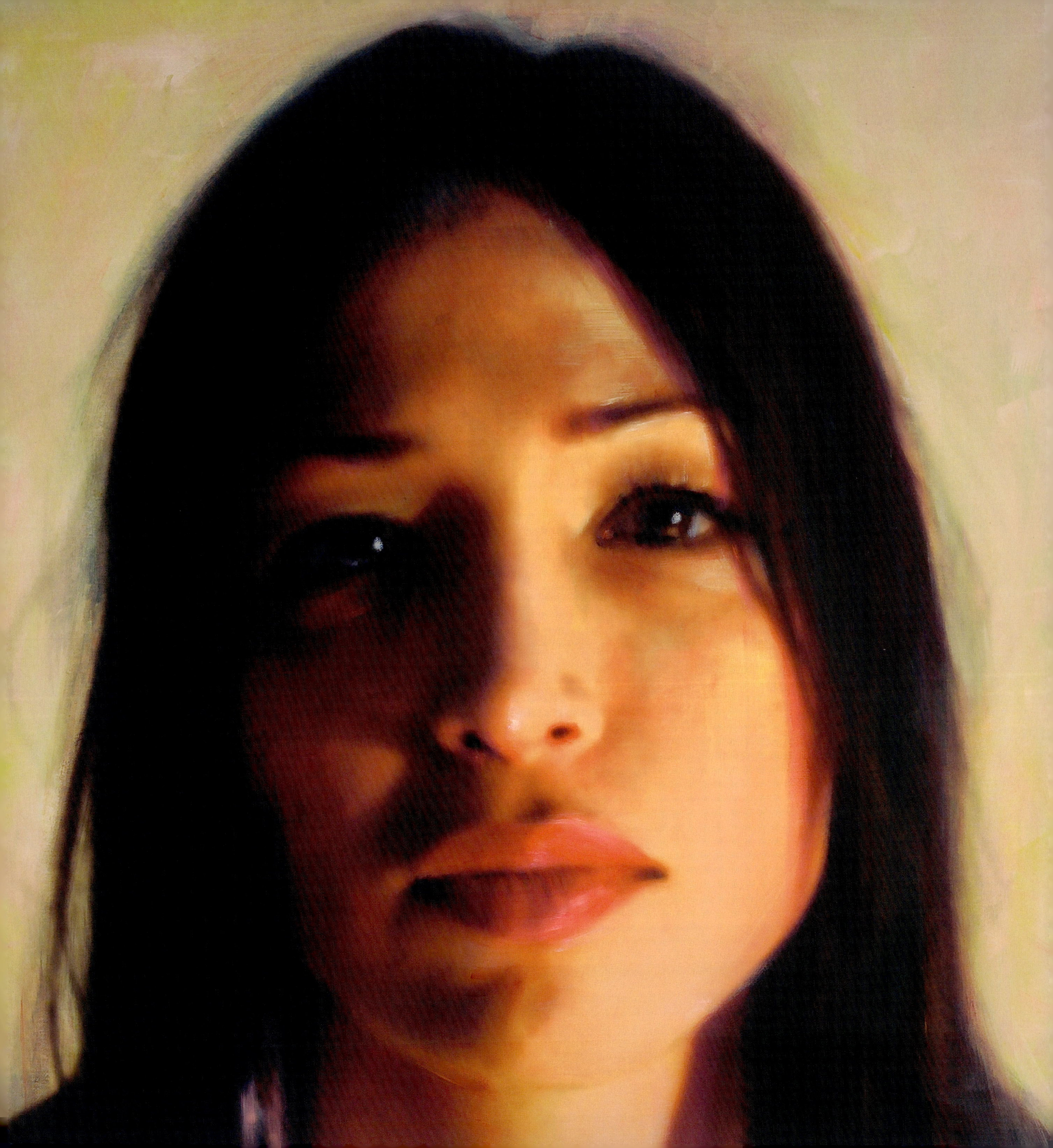

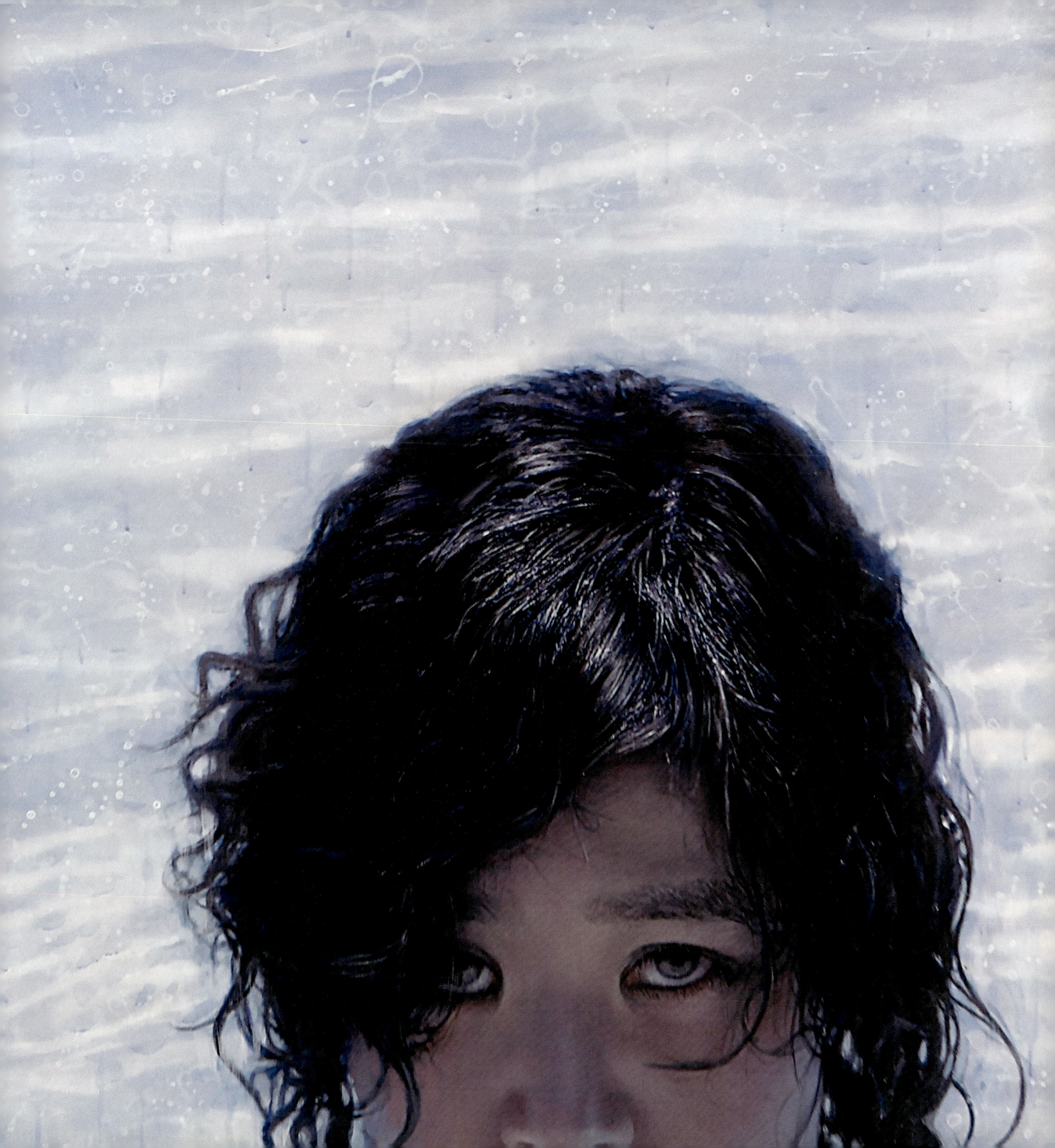

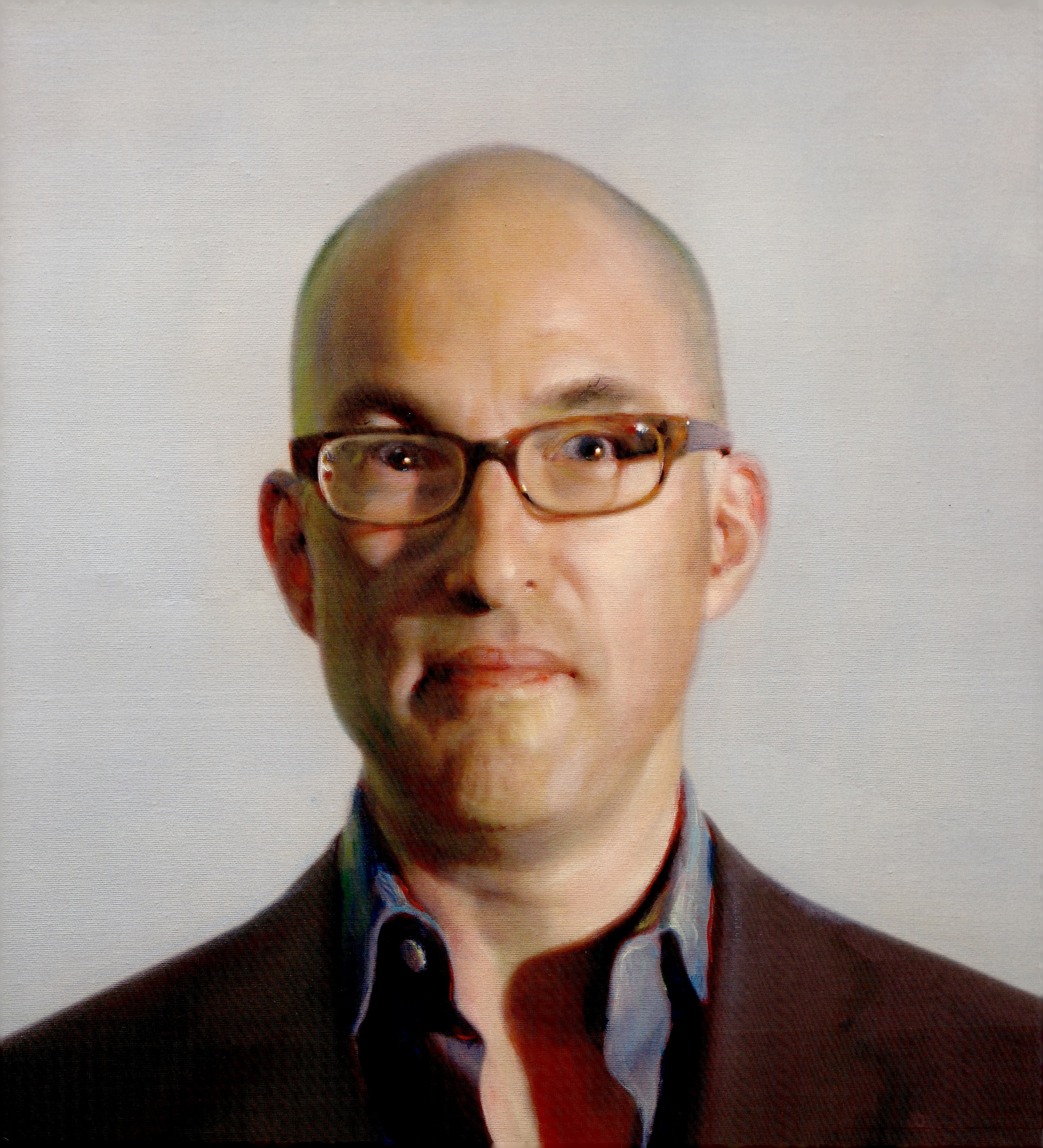

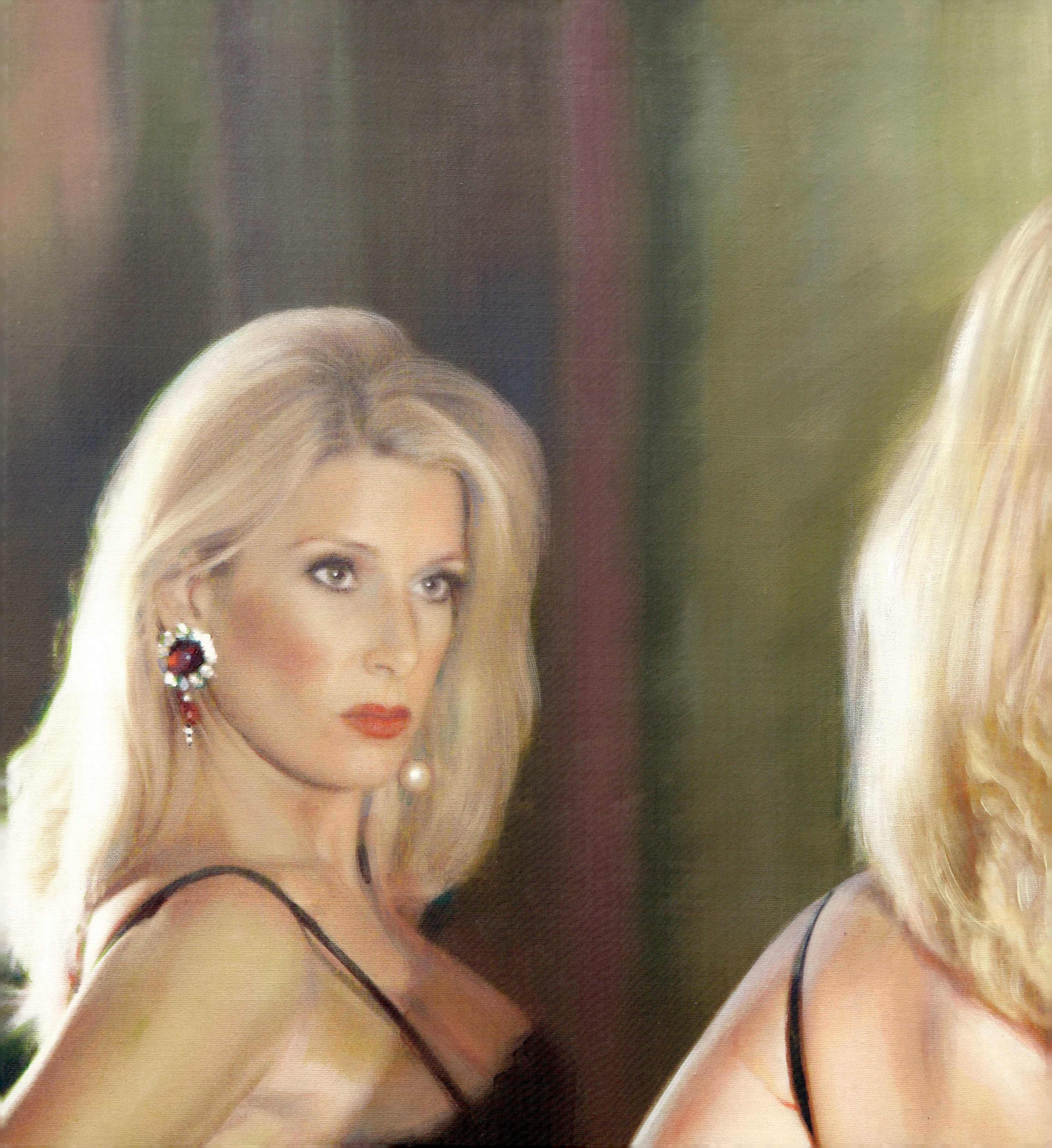

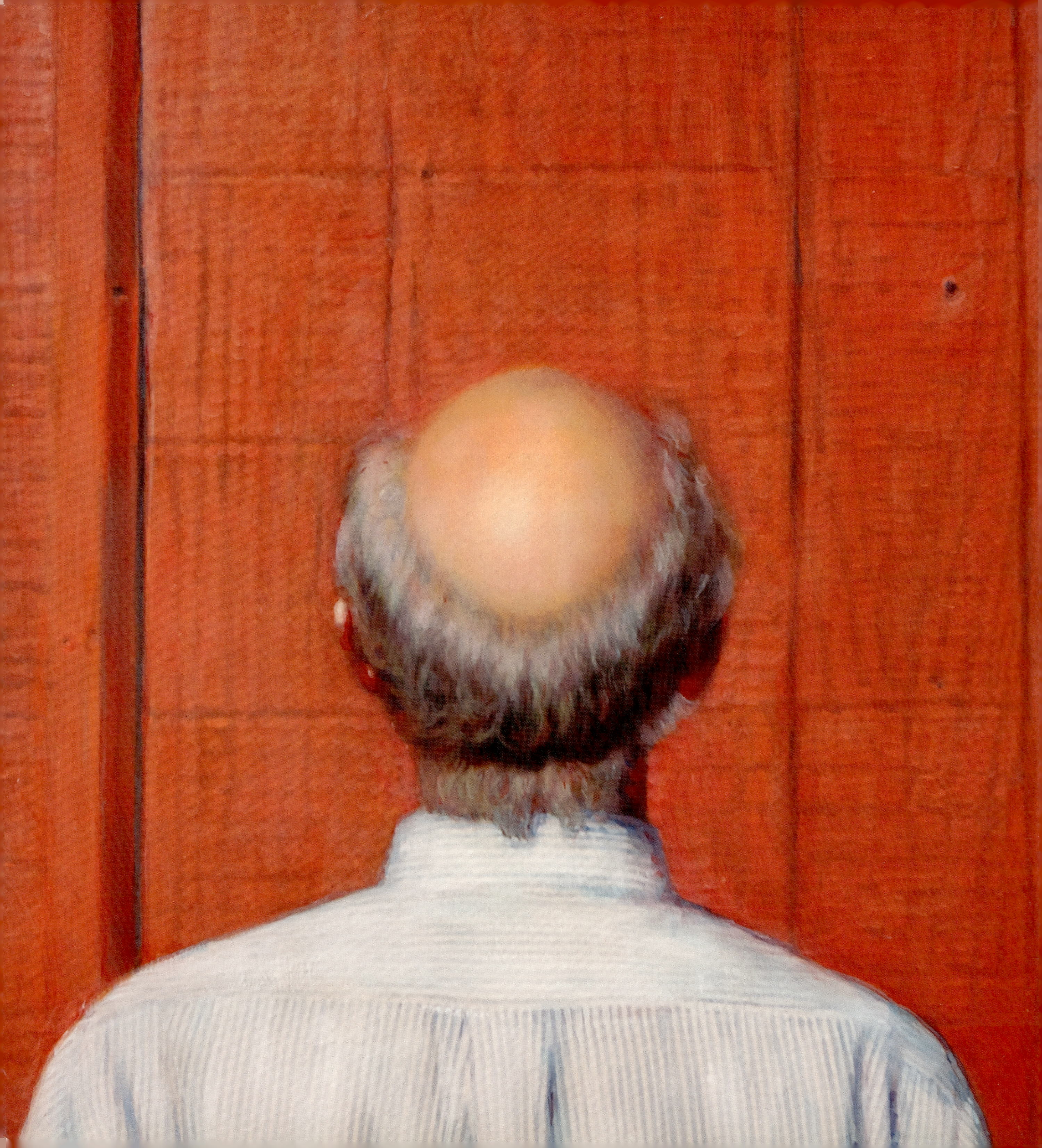

CONTRIBUTORS

Barnaby Conrad III is the author of *Absinthe: History in a Bottle*, *Ghost Hunting in Montana: A Search for Roots in the Old West*, *The Martini: An Illustrated History of an American Classic*, and *Pan Am: An Aviation Legend*. He also has written books on the artists John Register and Mark Stock, and his biographical essay on Valentin Popov appeared in the artist's 2008 monograph. A former editor at *Art World*, senior editor at *Horizon*, and editor-at-large for *Forbes Life*, Conrad is currently a consultant to the crowdfunding publisher Inkshares, and he is completing a biography of the French artist Jacques Villeglé.

B. R. Gilbert is a visual arts commentator across a broad bandwidth of inquiry.

Paul J. Karlstrom, former West Coast Regional Director of the Smithsonian's Archives of American Art (1973–2003), wrote the authorized biography of Peter Selz and is the author of *Raimonds Staprans: Art of Tranquility and Turbulence*. He is editor of *On the Edge of America: California Modernist Art, 1900–1950* and a coeditor of *Asian American Art: A History, 1860–1970*. Karlstrom's current work continues a career-long fascination with the psychological relationship between artists and their art as a creative collaboration as uncovered through oral history.

Lindsey Kouvaris is an independent curator and writer and a former Assistant Director of the de Saisset Museum, Santa Clara University. She was curator of the 2013 exhibition *FACE: Portraits by Valentin Popov*, at the de Saisset Museum.

Peter Selz is Professor Emeritus of the History of Art at the University of California, Berkeley. He was curator of painting and sculpture at the Museum of Modern Art in New York and the founding director of the UC Berkeley Art Museum, where he served as director from 1965–1973. Among his many books are *Nathan Oliveira*, *Barbara Chase-Riboud: Sculptor*, *Beyond the Mainstream: Essays on Modern and Contemporary Art*, and *Art in Our Times: A Pictorial History, 1890–1980*.

Andrei Ustinov is a recognized scholar of twentieth-century Russian literature, art, and culture. Among his many essays and several books is a comprehensive history of the Russian avant-garde in Paris coauthored with Leonid Livak. He has also written about the World of Art circle of painters, Futurism, and Soviet underground poetry. He is currently completing a history of Russian contributions to the Dada movement, *Dossier Dada Russe*.

MOSCOW, 2008 (detail, page 219)
Oil on canvas, 34 × 50 in.

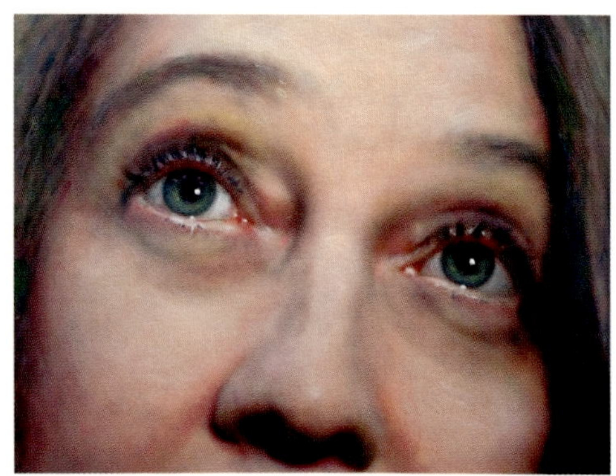

PRODUCED BY WILSTED & TAYLOR PUBLISHING SERVICES

Project manager Christine Taylor
Production assistant LeRoy Wilsted
Copy editor Lynn Meinhardt
Designers Jody Hanson and Nancy Koerner
Proofreader Nancy Evans
Printer's devil Lillian Marie Wilsted

FACE was composed in Avenir and Franklin Gothic with Univers and
Helvetica display. The book was printed and bound by R. R. Donnelley Asia.